We Do Know How

We Do Know How
A Buyer-Led Approach
to Creating Jobs for the Poor

JAMES T. RIORDAN

NEW ACADEMIA
PUBLISHING

VELLUM

Washington, DC

New Academia Publishing, 2011

Printed in the United States of America

Library of Congress Control Number: 2011921075
ISBN 978-0-9832451-1-7 paperback (alk. paper)

VELLUM   An imprint of New Academia Publishing
         P.O. Box 27420 - Washington, DC 20008

NAP NEW ACADEMIA
     PUBLISHING   info@newacademia.com - www.newacademia.com

Contents

Foreword

If someone had asked me at the beginning of my career whether I could see myself writing a book like *We Do Know How*, I would have said no. For two reasons.

First, international development seized my attention in the 1960s, an era of government activism and distrust of business. Uncritically, I bought into that mindset. Like many of my peers, I looked to government to lead and saw business as almost a necessary evil. In writing *We Do Know How*, I have come practically full circle. Yes, government policy is a critical determinant of economic growth, job creation, and poverty reduction. The negative effects of poor government policies on economic performance—the sad state of failed states is the extreme case in point—are witness to that truism. But the mixed track record of governments in conceiving and implementing good policy also has to make one skeptical about government as the answer. Even when governments do get it right, where do economic transactions actually take place, where do jobs get created, and where do poor people earn the wherewithal to better their standard of living? In businesses! In the final analysis, the growth of businesses is not something just to tolerate; it is something to encourage, not only with government policy—whose impact on businesses is often far from automatic—but, sometimes as or even more importantly, directly with businesses themselves.

Second, when I started in development, the halo effect of the Marshall Plan was still strong. As a young development economist, I was joining an optimistic profession. My job, as I conceived it then, was not to rock the boat but to take received wisdom, tweak it at the edges perhaps, and put it into practice. During the early years of my career, I was content to do just that. As time went by, though,

I could not fail to notice that much of conventional development wisdom failed to deliver the results it promised. So my skepticism grew. Luckily, about 15 years ago in Peru I had the opportunity to shape an approach I thought had the potential to work. The approach did not work perfectly—what ever does?—but it did work demonstrably better than competing approaches. In recent years, I have been privileged to take lessons learned in Peru and, with appropriate adjustments, apply them in programs in more than a dozen other countries around the world. Again, the approach has not always worked perfectly, but it definitely has shown its adaptability to very different working environments. The result is what I now call the "buyer-led approach to creating jobs for the poor," and that approach is the subject of this book.

> "What was the nature of the answers, the solutions, that Jonah caused us to develop? They all had one thing in common. They all made common sense, and at the same time, they flew directly in the face of everything I'd ever learned."
>
> Eliyahu M. Goldratt and Jeff Cox, *The Goal*, 3rd rev. ed. (Great Barrington, Massachusetts: North River Press, 2004), p. 267.

The buyer-led approach differs in a number of significant respects from much development practice. Among other things, the approach urges development practitioners to take market demand as their starting point, to set results targets and hold themselves accountable for them, to manage with discipline, to let clients' binding problems dictate development solutions, to take numbers seriously. In practice, I have found that most development practitioners think the programs they manage already are demand-driven, results-oriented, accountable, and so on. I have also found that when you peel away the layers of the onion, that is very often far from the case. In writing *We Do Know How*, therefore, I have felt obliged not only to describe the buyer-led approach, but to draw contrasts with the flaws I see in other approaches. I have not done so willingly, but I see no other realistic alternative to convince readers that the buyer-led approach is not just old wine in a new bottle. In my experience, it is only when I draw out the differences explicitly that others can really appreciate just how different—some of my colleagues would say revolutionary—the buyer-led approach really is, and just how much development practitioners need to shift gears from what they are currently doing to put the approach into practice effectively. In going through *We Do Know How*, therefore, please bear with the occasional negative commentary on other development practice. If the tone comes across as iconoclastic, it is not intentional. Iconoclast I may be, but a reluctant one.

In the end, *We Do Know How* appeals to development practitioners to step back from the day-to-day, keep an open mind, and let that mind learn from experience. Speaking of the 1960s, I quote from Lyndon Johnson in a broader context:

> Most of all we need an education which will create the educated mind. This is a mind—not simply a repository of information and skills, but a source of creative skepticism—characterized by a willingness to challenge old assumptions and to be challenged, a spaciousness of outlook, and convictions deeply held; but it is a mind which new facts can modify. For we are a society which has staked its survival on the rejection of dogma, on the refusal to bend experience to belief, and in the determination to shape actions to reality as reality reveals itself to us.[1]

We Do Know How directs itself primarily to practitioners of development, broadly defined. Examples of development practitioners include employees of donor organizations (the United States Agency for International Development (USAID) and the development programs of other individual countries, the World Bank and other multilateral banks, the United Nations and affiliated agencies, etc.), developing country governments (Ministries of Economy, Agriculture, etc.), private voluntary organizations (CARE, Catholic Relief Services, Save the Children, World Vision, etc.), corporate social responsibility programs of large businesses, international development consulting companies, individual development practitioners, and university faculty and students. Since this audience is more heterogeneous than one would think at first blush, I have tried to write *We Do Know How* in plain, largely jargon-free English. The reader will judge whether I have succeeded.

If there is one group of readers to whom I direct this book preferentially, it is the young people crying for coherent development approaches that work. Almost every time I give a presentation to university students, they tell me how refreshing it is to hear from someone who has worked "in the trenches." The students do not always agree with me—no one does—but they do jump at opportunities to hear from real, live practitioners. As much as they appreciate the importance of theory and policy, they are anxious to move from development writ large to how actually to conceive, design, and operate a micro development program. *We Do Know How* fills that niche and, ideally, can serve as a useful reference, even as a classroom text, for that purpose.

I am indebted to many parties for their assistance in transforming *We Do Know How* from the germ of an idea into a fully fledged product. Institutionally, I owe special thanks to two organizations. The first is USAID. I have had the enviable good fortune to work on USAID programs throughout the world, and that experience has shaped much of this book. The second organization is Chemonics International Inc., the international development consulting company where I have worked for most of the last two decades. Within Chemonics, my special thanks go to Ashraf Rizk, who urged me to write *We Do Know How* in the first place, to Richard Dreiman, Susanna Mudge, John Nittler, and James Butcher, who made it possible for me to break out substantial chunks of time to think and write, and to Douglas Tinsler for his unflagging enthusiasm from beginning to end. For assistance day to day, I am most indebted to Joseph Jordan, who served basically as my factotum through the writing process, helping me with equal adeptness both on content and on organization and presentation. Getting *We Do Know How* to this stage owes much to his support.

Much of the book derives from my experience managing USAID's Poverty Reduction and Alleviation program in Peru. During that time so many Peruvian colleagues lent me support and helped shape my thinking that it would be foolhardy for me to try to name them all here. They know who they are, and to each one of them I give my sincere thanks. At the risk of slighting others, I owe special thanks to Juan Robles of USAID and José Iturríos of Chemonics. Each in his own way is a role model of what it means to manage for results. I have learned immensely from — and admire — their commitment to making a real difference in Peru and the discipline and hard work they bring to that task every day.

I am indebted to several colleagues past and present for contributing content to the book. They include Ana María Andrade, Marco Aspilcueta, James Butcher, Allison Coppel de Guerrero, Danilo Cruz-DePaula, Ginger Elsea, Matthew Felice, Emily Friedberg, Jerome Gutzwiller, Eric Howell, José Iturríos, Joseph Jordan, Pol Klein, James Krigbaum, Gregory Kruse, Efraín Laureano, Christopher Maness, Charles Patterson, Juan Robles, Suzanne Savage, Gerald Schmaedick, and Tracy Shanks.

A number of colleagues inside and outside Chemonics reviewed drafts, including Mercedes Barrera, Annette Brown, Donald Brown, Sally Cameron, Luis Chávez, Allison Coppel de Guerrero, Danilo Cruz-DePaula, Thomas Donnelly, Richard Dreiman, Ginger Elsea, Eric Howell, José Iturríos, Joseph Jordan, Aneel Karnani, Pol Klein, Mauricio Moscoso, Robert Myers, Charles Patterson, Reinaldo Penner, Kevin Riordan, Suzanne Savage, Gerald Schmaedick, and Roberta van Haeften. Almost without exception, reviewers offered comments incisive and probing. In many cases, their observations sent me back to the drawing board and definitely made the book better.

Interestingly, much of the feedback from the reviewers turned out to be contradictory. Some urged me to write in one tone. Others suggested exactly the opposite. Some advised me to put more flesh on some issues. Others suggested I downplay them and give more attention to others. As I was struggling to reconcile the different recommendations, Pol Klein gave me perhaps the best advice of all. He put it simply and directly, "Jim, it's your book!" and urged me to saw off and move on. In the end, that is what I have done. As much as I appreciate the variety and richness of insights of others, *We Do Know How* is my book, with all its virtues and all its warts.

A number of people lent me valuable assistance with the nuts and bolts of bringing the manuscript to this stage. They include Jane Gotiangco, who helped me organize disparate material, Erica Martin, who expedited external reviews, and Martha Moses and Deborah Aker, who put in the editorial touches to my final draft. My thanks also go to Carole Sargent, the Director of the Office of

Scholarly and Literary Publications at Georgetown University, for believing in the book and helping me see it through to completion.

Finally, and most importantly, my heartfelt thanks to my wife, Blanche. Her support has been a constant. She, more than anybody else, knows what went in to getting to this point.

PART I

Introduction

"I know the majority thinks you're right, Torvald, and plenty of books agree with you, too. But I can't go on believing what the majority says, or what's written in books. I have to think over these things myself and try to understand them."

Nora, "A Doll House"

Henrik Ibsen, *Four Major Plays: A Doll House, The Wild Duck, Hedda Gabler, The Master Builder,* translated by Rolf Fjelde (New York: Signet, 1965), p.111.

1

Attacking Poverty: Do We Know How?

More than thirty five years have passed now since William and Elizabeth Paddock published a book with the provocative title, *We Don't Know How: An Independent Audit of What They Call Success in Foreign Assistance.*[2] In it the authors reported on fieldwork they had conducted in Mexico and Central America, and concluded with the following indictment:

> In my research I learned two things:
> First, development professionals do not know how to carry out an effective economic development program, either a big one or a small one. *No one knows how*—not the U.S. government, not the Rockefeller Foundation, not the international banks and agencies, not the missionaries. I don't know how. You don't know how. No one knows how.
> Second, we don't know that we don't know how. Those who give the money are thousands of miles removed from where it is spent. No channel is provided whereby they can get unbiased opinions about their projects in the field in place of the usual fulsome reports of "great success." One barrier to this is that those who exercise their profession in the field...soon acquire a Messiah complex. To wit: a corn breeder in Iowa does not talk about his program SAVING Iowa. But a corn breeder who goes to Guatemala does talk of his program as saving not only Guatemala but all Central America and maybe even all the tropics... Add to this the fact that our aid programs maintain no memory banks. Both the files and the personnel are ignorant of previous

programs, ignorant as to the reasons why they were started, ignorant as to what the prevailing conditions were then, ignorant as to why they failed and were abandoned.

The result: We do not know that we do not know how. We have no knowledge of our own ignorance.[3]

The Paddock book is only one link in a chain of indictments of foreign development assistance over the years.[4] Foreign aid has been, is, and most likely will continue to be a target of criticism. The disconcerting feature of today's debate, however, is that it does not look like very much has changed. If one believed current critics, the only difference between 1973 and now is not that development practitioners now know how, but that they now know that they do not.

The leader of today's charge is William Easterly. An ex-World Bank research economist, Easterly has written two books currently much in vogue, *The Elusive Quest for Growth: Economists' Adventures and Misadventures in the Tropics* and *The White Man's Burden: Why the West's Efforts to Aid the Rest Have Done So Much Ill and So Little Good.*[5] Easterly writes and speaks articulately and, as an ex-insider, argues his case with authority. But whereas Easterly has succeeded in dismantling a lot of development castles—that is, in showing what does not work—he has not succeeded as well in constructing a solid edifice in their place—that is, in showing what does. His distinction between Searchers and Planners—to which this book returns below—is a very useful contribution to development thinking, but most readers come away from the two books somewhat frustrated, asking, "Is that all there is?" As one reviewer of his second book put it, "Easterly is doing something harder here: not merely cataloging past failures but trying to suggest a more promising approach. Unfortunately, his alternative is still underdeveloped, devolving at time into slogans."[6]

"It is astonishing that we still know so little about what sort of aid works. Donors—and their critics—are too quick to embrace the latest fashion and too slow to ask the hard questions about what really works in development. Perhaps they feel they already know the answer, or perhaps they are afraid of what might be revealed."

Editorial comment, "Poverty: what counts," *Financial Times*, FT.com, August 15, 2006.

This book, consciously entitled, *We Do Know How*, makes no pretense to have all the answers, but it does go well beyond slogans. It presents a proven, practical approach for creating jobs for poor people—normally a necessary first step for them to escape from poverty.

Money Matters, but So Does the Approach

At the United Nations Millennium Summit in September 2000, 189 nations of the world established eight Millennium Development Goals for achievement by 2015. The goals are:

Goal 1: Eradicate extreme poverty and hunger
Goal 2: Achieve universal primary education
Goal 3: Promote gender equality and empower women
Goal 4: Reduce child mortality
Goal 5: Improve maternal health
Goal 6: Combat HIV/AIDS, malaria and other diseases
Goal 7: Ensure environmental sustainability
Goal 8: Develop a Global Partnership for Development

In contrast to declarations in the past, each goal has time-bound and measurable targets. For the first goal, that of most interest here, the targets are:

Target 1: Reduce by half the proportion of people living on less than a dollar a day
Target 2: Reduce by half the proportion of people who suffer from hunger

At first glance, setting poverty and hunger reduction targets would appear a laudable proposition: quantitative goals presumably signal that the parties committing themselves are prepared to hold themselves accountable for results. Results, however, fail to bear that presumption out. If one looks at progress to date—and especially if one excludes China as a special case, only the most sanguine of observers would wager that the world community will come close to meeting its poverty and hunger reduction targets by 2015.

Most discussion of the Millennium Development Goals in recent years has focused, not on how to meet targets, but on whether governments are backing up their moral commitment with financial ones. Little has touched upon why in fact there has been so little progress. There is no development paradigm at work that says if you do x, you will get y, but simply the hypothesis that if you spend more, you will get more. In the end, the bulk of the underlying thinking comes down to perpetuating the status quo: do what you have always done, but spend more on it.

Jeffrey Sachs has perhaps been the most vocal of the proponents of massive increases in financial support. In contrast to those preoccupied only with funding, Sachs can be extremely eloquent in advocating a comprehensive package of support to address an

> "So the case for extra aid is solid. It matters a lot, however, how the money is spent."
>
> Editorial, "Fighting Global Poverty," *Washington Post*, January 20, 2005, p. A24.

expansive array of poor people's needs. In his best-selling book, *The End of Poverty: Economic Possibilities for Our Time*, in fact, he argues forcefully that nothing short of a "Big Push," primarily in health and education, will pull the developing world out of poverty.[7]

As one might expect, Easterly has challenged Sachs, arguing that spending more money will not necessarily bring about the reductions in poverty desired.[8] Easterly also made much the same case in an open letter of advice to Bill and Melinda Gates and Warren Buffett on how the Gates Foundation should spend $60 billion on development in coming years:

> **It's not about the money.** The misguided media reaction to the Gates-Buffett union was, quite predictably, all about numbers: Warren's $31 billion gift, which roughly doubles the size of Bill's foundation to about $60 billion. Welcome to foreign aid wonderland, where it's always about the spending, never about the impact…
>
> Alas, aid flow reflects the cost of providing services for the poor, not the value of those services. Would Microsoft Corp. promote an executive who bragged about setting a

record for costs? Would Berkshire Hathaway invest in a business that headlined its remarkably high spending on office supplies?[9]

It would be incredibly naïve, of course, to claim that outside moneys cannot help reduce the numbers of the world's poor. On that score, Sachs's focus on financial support is certainly on target. But Easterly is also right. How one spends that support can make all the difference.

Managing effectively for results means making yourself accountable for what you accomplish. It also means measuring the progress you are making, not only to report your triumphs but to learn from and correct your failures.[10]

Like the international community with its Millennium Development Goals, development programs like to hold themselves accountable for what they do, not for what they achieve, making the result of their work a matter of faith. Raising the bar to measure results not only makes much more sense development-wise, but is also wise management practice. If development programs say they shall accomplish something, they need to hold themselves accountable for it.

"'This is indeed a mystery,' I remarked. 'What do you imagine that it means?'

'I have no data yet. It is a capital mistake to theorise before one has data. Insensibly one begins to twist facts to suit theories, instead of theories to suit facts.'"

Sherlock Holmes and Dr. Watson, "Power and Influence."

James Ruddick, *Death at the Priory: Love, Sex and Murder in Victorian England* (New York: Grove Press, 2001), p. 85.

More than that, if things are not working, they need to have the empirical base to understand why not, and to make required mid-course corrections.

In the parts that follow, this book describes one proven way development practitioners can create jobs for poor people, usually a precondition for reducing poverty. Unlike the Millennium Development Goals, the modest approach presented here comes with a paradigm of development that lends itself to operational accountability. It demonstrates how development programs can set realistic targets, build in incentives for managers to meet those targets, and hold them accountable. In short, this book presents an approach that delivers results—see Part II for evidence on that score—and does so cost-effectively.

Get Your Hands Dirty

In the popular mind, globalization is arguably the biggest challenge to combating poverty, and just the word can be a lightning rod for heated debate. Although the arguments for the gains to trade are compelling, none of those arguments hold much credence for those cornered by increased competition or bereft of the jobs they had held for years. As Thomas Friedman put it in *The Lexus and the Olive Tree*, his generally upbeat book on globalization:

> [G]lobalization also presents an unprecedented challenge: While it is the engine of greater long-term prosperity for every country that plugs into the globalization system, it is also the engine of greater dislocations in the short run. And it is not enough to tell a factory worker who has suddenly lost his job to a lower-wage factory abroad that, while unfortunate, our society as a whole is better off because it can now purchase the steel or tennis shoes he once made at a cheaper price. It is not enough to tell the office worker whose job has been phased out because of the installation of a new computer system that, while unfortunate, our society as a whole is better off because it will be much more productive with that new network system installed. The benefits of globalization tend to be measured in the long run, and for society as a whole, but the dislocations come immediately and for specific individuals who know they have been hurt.[11]

If resistance to globalization is strong in the developed world, then all the more understandable is the skepticism in poor countries that face formidable obstacles to plugging effectively into the world economy, whose productive apparatus is ill equipped to transition from protection to open competition, and whose safety nets to protect the poor are embryonic in comparison with those in richer countries. Former Peruvian President Alan García made the point in a speech to the Institute for International Economics:

I'm for Free Trade. But something has always bothered me about it: Free Trade has never been very successful at helping poor people. It's as if there were two parallel lines: Free Trade on this side; and over here, are the poor—and never the two shall meet. Yes, we live in an increasingly globalized world; yes, international trade is very good at generating wealth. But the trouble with Globalization—so far— is that it's not working for most of the globe: It is leaving out four billion of the world's people, eighty percent (80%) of the planet. As a President who has promised to deliver economic benefits to all Peruvians, that disconnect between trade and poverty bothers me.[12]

Academic economists would be quick to jump in here, arguing that through the linkages it forges between global buyers and local producers, trade can indeed be an effective channel to reach and benefit the poor. Problematically, most of the evidence supporting that claim depicts aggregate changes that take place over a period of time. The short run—the world in which both politicians and the poor spend most of their time—is very often another story. For a dramatic case in point, one need look no farther than India's parliamentary elections in 2004. By virtually all macro-economic measures, the country was booming, which one would have expected to give an edge to the government in power. But the government lost. Poor people, frustrated at failing to see the benefits of growth, cast their votes elsewhere.

Three years later, the tide of electoral change showed a similar pattern in Latin America, as voters, fed up with promises that markets would solve their problems, opted for candidates more amenable to delivering goods and services directly to the electorate. For many of the world's poor, the time has come to shift from "trickle-down economics" to governments that promise to do something for them now.

"Sant Raj, 29, switched his vote because the governing party had changed nothing in four years: 'I labored to eat then, and I labor to eat now.'"

"Those Left Behind Turned Indian Vote: Poor Say Economic Boom Was Just Rhetoric," *Washington Post*, May 15, 2004, p. A12.

The development community does not appear especially well armed to operate effectively in a short-run environment. For example, in its 2002 book, *Globalization, Growth, and Poverty: Building an Inclusive World Economy*, the World Bank proposes an "agenda for action" to help make globalization work better for poor countries and poor people.[13] The agenda consists of seven items:

A "development round" of trade negotiations
Improving the investment climate in developing countries
Good delivery of education and health services
Provision of social protection tailored to the more dynamic labor market in an open economy
A greater volume of foreign aid, better managed
Debt relief
Tackling greenhouse gases and global warming

Although there is nothing objectionable about any of these items, their very wording raises disturbing questions. First, put yourself in the shoes of the poor people whom these actions presume to affect. For them, the connection of the action agenda with the problems they face day to day is indirect, to say the least. That would not be so bad if one-size-fits-all solutions addressed their problems effectively, but as any on-the-ground practitioner can attest, the problems in question evidence substantially more heterogeneity than uniformity. The solution to one of the poor's problems—lack of access to finance, say—may bear no relation whatsoever to the most binding constraint of many others—no buyers, for example. The actions proposed by the World Bank are fine as far as they go, but they do not go far enough. Second, and in a related vein, the agenda places an almost exclusive premium on policy and institutional reform. Policy and institutional reform is essential, but, arguably, simply not enough—by itself—to make a dent in the problems of substantial numbers of poor people. On reading the World Bank's agenda, one cannot help but be struck by the almost complete absence of guidance on how actually to go about interacting with the poor. Yes, the agenda does acknowledge, almost in passing, that action programs are important, but it shows little appreciation that the kinds of action programs one chooses, and how one implements them, make any difference. On how to link poor people with markets in a practical way, the document is almost entirely silent. Third, to the extent that the document does talk about action programs, it focuses primarily on the delivery of social services like health and education and the compensation of the "losers" from globalization. Those challenges are important, obviously, but it would have been nice if the Bank had offered some practical guidance on how to help the poor connect with markets themselves and emerge as winners from that process. Put another way, the agenda emphasizes the need to generate employment, but it says precious little about what measures to take—aside from broad policy and institutional reform—to make that happen.

USAID's most recent strategy for economic growth reveals a similar bias toward systemic, one-size-fits-all, above-the-fray approaches:

> **Programs should seek large and systemic impacts.** The success of a few firms, farms, or communities is not enough. The goal is growth that affects thousands of firms and millions of people. This typically requires improvements in policies affecting all businesses within a sector or across the entire economy. This means that USAID will generally not finance development directly, but will seek instead the systemic reforms that can mobilize much larger savings and investment by others.
>
> **Where systemic reform is not achieved, catalytic impact is essential.** Demonstration projects can be valuable, but they should either demonstrate approaches that cause a far larger number of people or firms to follow suit without subsidies, or should have the clear potential to catalyze policy or institutional changes with a much wider, systemic impact.[14]

Although USAID does in fact finance hands-on programs around the world, it is somewhat disconcerting that official policy views them more as back-up—a Plan B, if you like—than as an integral part of the Agency's strategy for stimulating growth and attacking poverty. Not only does an approach that gives almost exclusive priority to systemic reforms fail to account for the tremendous differences among firms, farms, and communities in the binding constraints that thwart their growth. It also fails to recognize that generating successes directly with firms, farms, and communities can actually be pivotal strategically to leverage copycatting on a broad scale. More than that, working at the micro level can also elicit bottom-up intelligence on the relative importance of different policy and institutional issues so that those who work on systemic reforms can focus on those that will in fact make a difference.

None of this criticism is to deny the key role of policy and institutional reform. For example, opening developed countries' markets to more developing country products holds immense potential. So too do reforms that improve developing countries' investment climates. In both instances, though, it could take years to shape the reforms in question, put them into effect, and see measurable declines in poverty. And if experience is any guide, many of the reform initiatives in question could abort along the way. Most policy and institutional reform called for today—what economists call "second-generation reforms"—is no easy task. As Friedman notes:

> These so-called "second generation" reforms needed to produce an emerging society take a lot more patience and hard work. "In the old days," a World Bank official once said to me, "you came into a developing country and you went to the governor of the Central Bank and you had one simple piece of advice: 'stop printing so much money.' Then you went over to the Minister of Finance and said, 'stop running such a big budget deficit so your Central Bank can stop printing so much money.' In other words, all you had to do was talk to two people and give two simple messages. But now we know that a lot more is required." And in order to get these second-generation software reforms in place, which really transform a country from an emerging market to an emerging society, you need to involve many, many more actors and it requires a much, much wider political consensus.[15]

On balance, the recipes proffered by much of the development community for making globalization work for the poor—and the action agenda proposed by the World Bank is just an example—offer no panaceas, certainly not in the time frame in which today's electorates want results. For those on the front lines of development, the World Bank's agenda is too macro and, at times, almost platitudinous. To make a dent in poverty, development practitioners cannot afford to stay above the fray, but must come down to micro earth. The devil is in the details, as they say, and in this case, at least, practitioners must do the devil's work.

This book presents a micro approach to generating the jobs required to reduce poverty. First, it shows how to link the poor effectively with markets, both domestic and international. Second, it shows how individual business transactions are the vehicle for forging those linkages. Third, it shows how to support—and how not to support—such business transactions. Fourth, it shows how working with individual businesses to solve their problems can trigger development that is transformational in scope and serve as a ground-truthing mechanism for setting policy and institutional reform priorities. The book spells out an approach that comes not as a solution looking for a problem, but as a flexible, disciplined way to tailor solutions—both transactional and systemic—to the business problems that act most as a brake on boosting sales and expanding jobs for poor people.

2

What Is the Buyer-Led Approach?

We Do Know How presents the "buyer-led approach" to creating jobs and boosting the incomes of poor people. Its essence is taking market demand as the starting point for all program activity and working backward to solve the problems that stand in the way of satisfying that demand. The rationale for proceeding in that way is straightforward. As a colleague of the author put it:

> [E]xperience has shown that increasing the supply of products and services without corresponding demand offers little promise of sales and long-term economic benefit... Economic programming is more effective when capacity building is directly linked to qualified demand. When demand is qualified—who buys, in what packaging and grades, at what price, etc.—one can target capacity building and other assistance specifically to fulfill that demand. In that way activities are directly linked to results. Demand-driven programming is results-oriented programming and ensures that investments of assistance provide economic benefits in return.[16]

Although the phrase, "demand-driven," has become a mantra in international development, few practitioners have internalized what it really means and traced out its operational consequences. Originally the author had thought of calling the approach described here the demand-driven approach to creating jobs for the poor, but since most practitioners claim they are demand-driven—but very often are not—he opted for terminology that not only is unambiguously faithful to the basic concept but conveys a sense of what the approach means operationally.

Empirically, the buyer-led approach grows out of the experience of the author, many of his colleagues, and different development organizations in a variety of anti-poverty and business development programs throughout the world. The first program to apply the buyer-led approach as a complete package was USAID's Poverty Reduction and Alleviation (PRA) program in Peru, which began in late 1998 and terminated in late 2008. From 2003 on, the author has worked with colleagues in Afghanistan, Albania, Antigua and Barbuda, Armenia, Azerbaijan, Bangladesh, Bolivia, Dominica, Kosovo, Madagascar, Moldova, Mongolia, Nigeria, Paraguay, and Saint Lucia to apply the approach either in its entirety or in significant elements. This book draws heavily from that experience and gives examples from most of those countries. A goodly number of the examples come from Peru, where the author had the good fortune to direct PRA in its early years and to live the approach day to day. The book also gives examples from programs using alternative approaches to highlight the various ways in which the buyer-led approach differs from much conventional development practice.

Because supply-push thinking is so ingrained in conventional development practice, much of *We Do Know How* harps on the need for development practitioners to practice the demand-driven gospel they preach. It also brings the concept of demand down to earth, showing how, as a practical matter, demand means buyers with first names and last names. For now, let it suffice to present two examples to illustrate why it is important to know your market before providing support (see Exhibit 1.1). In the Vietnam case, the ice maker knew the requirements of his buyers and what he had to do to meet those requirements. In the Mali case, the Government of Mali substantially overestimated effective demand for Malian arts and crafts—a miscalculation with potentially disastrous consequences. As things turned out, The Washington Post's publication of their plight may

> "**Is my idea practical?** All ideas seem award-winning at 3 a.m. But to press ahead profitably, you need to seriously assess the market, the competition, your budget, your resources and your qualifications. The biggie: Will anyone pay for what I'm selling?"
>
> "Five questions to ask before you…Start a business," *Money*, May, 2004, p. 55.

have saved the day for the parties involved, but not all programs that fail to get a handle on demand can count on such a *deus ex machina*.

Exhibit 1.1 Why Knowing Your Market is Important
What Can Happen...

If You Understand Your Market Well Beforehand...	If You Do Not...
"Mr.Nguyen runs a small ice distribution business in Vietnam's Can Tho region. With the region's tropical climate and lack of refrigeration, ice is crucial to the people of Can Tho. It is used to preserve food and for special ceremonies.	"About a month ago Vanessa Adams was sitting in a restaurant in Bamako, the capital of the West African nation of Mali, when a man called over from the next table and asked a question: 'What's new with the products?'
"Nguyen's business is located in the village of Nhon Ai at the edge of a wide river. In a region where bicycles are the primary means of transportation, this location is crucial because it allows him to distribute the heavy blocks to the villagers by boat.	"Ah. The products. That was a bit of a sore subject. "Adams is a Peace Corps volunteer detailed to Mali's ministry of handcrafts and tourism, helping to develop a foreign market for Malian goods. She spent two weeks in Washington last summer, working in the MarketPlace tent at the Smithsonian's Folklife Festival, where Mali was a featured culture.
"Nguyen's equipment was primitive and could not produce the large ice blocks the local people favored. Through a program operated by Seed Capital Development Fund's affiliate in Vietnam, Nguyen received a loan to purchase new equipment and was soon able to produce larger blocks of ice.	"In a fit of extreme optimism, the Malian government had borrowed $400,000 from the Banque de Malienne Solidarité to purchase and ship 37,000 arts and crafts items, including goatskin drums and leather change purses.
"By meeting local demand, Nguyen's business tripled its capacity and created eight new jobs within the plant." *Source*: DEVCAP Shared Return Fund, "DEVCAP Success Stories," advertisement, n.d.	"While the Malian exhibits and performances were popular—a dozen masons were flown to Washington to construct an adobe house from scratch on the Mall— fewer than 7,000 of the items were sold. "The man who approached Adams in the restaurant? "'It was the banker,' she said this week." *Source*: "Djembe Drums, Going for a Song: Sale Offers Mali Goods Left Over From Folklife Festival," *Washington Post*, October 11, 2003, p. B1.

What Is it All About?

The buyer-led approach is not rocket science. In many ways, it goes back to basics. For most business people, most of this book is common sense. For many development people, it is foreign territory—which, this book argues, is precisely the problem.

If there is anything unique about the approach, it is that its elements—no one of which is unique by itself—form a coherent, mutually reinforcing package that delivers results. The approach is not a smorgasbord from which a practitioner chooses what dishes are to his or her liking. Rather, it comes as a whole and has its impact as a whole. For example, a program that takes the market as its point of entry but fails to set targets and assess progress toward them may wind up doing some good things, but since the program does not hold itself accountable for results, there is no way of knowing whether those good things are cost-effective things. Similarly, a program may set targets, but limit those targets to the activities it undertakes. In the end, the program may be able to report how many men and women it has trained, for example, but, by itself, that tells us nothing about whether there is any cause-effect relationship between the training in question and outcomes like increases in jobs.

Even though the buyer-led approach is a package, it is far from a straightjacket. As the rest of this book illustrates, figuring out how to solve seemingly intractable business problems cost-effectively often requires considerable ingenuity and creativity. The buyer-led approach has tools, but it is not a mechanistic tool kit. To use its tools effectively, practitioners must "get it," where getting it means internalizing what it means to let market demands drive what you do, to manage with discipline, and to hold yourself accountable for results. In the development world, unfortunately, those kinds of people do not come along every day.

In the final analysis, the characteristic that most distinguishes the buyer-led approach from others is the demand-driven, disciplined thinking underlying it. Those who have been most successful in putting it into practice will be the first to say amen to that contention. Many of them have commented, "The battle we wage is not one of money; it is one of ideas." Although some development professionals might prefer it otherwise, the approach challenges thought and demands thought.

"One perceptive historian, viewing a classic case of a science's reorientation by paradigm change, recently described it as 'picking up the other end of the stick,' a process that involves 'handling the same bundle of data as before, but placing them in a new system of relations with one another by giving them a different framework."

Thomas S. Kuhn, *The Structure of Scientific Revolutions*, 3rd ed. (Chicago: The University of Chicago Press, 1996), p. 85.

For those who have internalized the rationale of the approach, the operational procedures suggested in this book fall out almost as a natural corollary. The application of those procedures requires judgment, which in turn requires understanding. For that reason, Part II, the paradigmatic part of *We Do Know How*, is key.

The author remembers meeting an old development hand once who commented, "As development professionals, we spend 90 percent of our careers running around trying to answer the wrong questions." For better or for worse, this book tries to ask at least some of the right ones.

"Often would the deaf man know the answers had he but the faculty of hearing the questions. Likewise would the unimaginative man guess wisely at the answers had he but the wit of posing to himself the appropriate questions."

Viscount Mumbles, from *Essays on the Imagination*.

Colin Dexter, *The Remorseful Day* (New York: Fawcett Books, 1999), p. 116.

At the risk of reducing the approach to sound-bites, it is useful to preview here the core elements of the buyer-led approach as a point of reference for the reader. In schematic form, the core elements appear in Exhibit 1.2.

Exhibit 1.2 Core Elements of the Buyer-Led Approach
(page 1 of 2)

Principles	Operational Strategies	Operational Tactics
Make "Demand-Driven" Real	Let demand drive what you do	Support only those business opportunities for which there is market demand—abide by the maxim, "produce what you can sell," not "sell what you produce"
	Make demand operational	Define demand as buyers with first names and last names, not statistical trends or market studies
Focus on Specific Problems	Solve the specific problems that stand most in the way of meeting specific buyers' requirements	Focus on each transaction's *problema*, not its *problemática**
	Let the problem dictate the solution	Do not become a pre-packaged solution looking for your problem
	Solve the problems with transactional business solutions	As a rule, rely on systemic—that is, policy—solutions only when necessary and the probability of success is high
	Search for micro solutions	As a rule, resist the urge to plan macro solutions
	Get your hands dirty in the details	Resist above-the-fray solutions
	Build capacity in a learning-by-doing mode	Do not do generic, one-size-fits-all training

*In Spanish, *el problema* means the specific problem of a specific situation; *la problemática*, the gamut of all interrelated problems.

Exhibit 1.2 Core Elements of the Buyer-Led Approach
(page 2 of 2)

Principles	Operational Strategies	Operational Tactics
Manage for Results	Manage for final results like sales and jobs, not lower-level results like business plans and training courses	Set targets and hold yourself accountable for meeting them
	Manage with discipline	Apply at least some quantitative rule of thumb to sift out cost-effective program actions from just good ones
	Take monitoring and evaluation seriously	Focus attention on performance–use monitoring and evaluation as a management tool, not just to report results
Facilitate Buyer-Seller Relationships	Promote commercial relationships between buyers and small producers	Look to out-grower and similar contracting arrangements
	Nurture trust between buyers and sellers	Establish physical presence for that purpose–honest brokering will normally be the most important service you provide
	Focus on the sustainability of buyer-seller relationships	Do not focus on sustainability of your program and its participating organizations
Organize Geographically	Organize work by economic corridors	Do not organize by product or sector– do not pre-pick the sectors or clusters that will be the winners

In short, the buyer-led approach takes specific market demands as its point of departure. It facilitates transactions, manages resources with discipline, and holds itself accountable for results.

3

If We Do Know How, Why Do We Not Act Accordingly?

As the rest of this book shows in some detail, the buyer-led approach is one proven way to manage development programs in a cost-effective way to generate jobs for poor people. The buyer-led approach does not offer magic bullets, but, with hard work, it can deliver verifiable results. Moreover, if one looks at the core elements of the approach outlined above, there is not much terribly controversial there, certainly nothing that deviates dramatically from good management practice. Why, then, do development practitioners not apply approaches like the buyer-led approach as a matter of course?

There is no one simple answer, of course, but it is possible to offer a number of explanations, many of them overlapping:

Development practitioners say they are demand-driven but gravitate toward programming supply-push solutions. Part II goes into some depth on this point, so suffice it here to illustrate how insidious supply-push thinking can be. Take the following examples:

In development it is common to talk about farm-to-market roads. If one really thought from the market backward, would not the correct terminology be, "market-to-farm roads"?

When professional agricultural associations hold conferences for their members, they often use catch-phrases like "From Farm to Table" or "From Farm to Fork." If the associations had really internalized what demand-driven means, would not they say, "From Table to Farm" and "From Fork to Farm"?

Along the same lines, Elsevier's prestigious *Handbook of Agricultural Economics, Volume 1*, comes in two parts, *Volume 1A:*

Agricultural Production, and *Volume 1B: Marketing, Distribution, and Consumers.*[17] Again, if demand-driven thinking were operative here, would not it be appropriate for Volume 1B to precede Volume 1A?

Finally, Aid to Artisans, a development organization that understands very well what demand-driven means, uses the saying, "From Maker to Market," to describe its work.[18] How ironic, in that its whole *modus operandi* is in fact first to transmit the requirements of the market to artisans and then—and only then—to help them meet those requirements.

The reader may object that these examples amount to semantic nitpicking and argue that the author cannot be all that serious in his critique. At one level, the reader is right. Throughout, this book talks about connecting the poor with markets, and that terminology suffers from the same failing. That said, the examples are only half tongue in cheek. The bottom-line point is indeed a very serious one—that the very language of development betrays its users, that they do not even realize it, and, thus, that they rarely take the time to examine the thinking implicit in that language. Development practitioners may say they are demand-driven, but how they speak often drives them in directions at odds with that contention.

Aside from the question of language, much development practice takes the form of "projects," that is, undertakings for which development practitioners receive budget and under which they program monies to achieve certain ends. Projects may be fine for vaccination campaigns, but oftentimes they are not flexible enough to enable businesspeople to react effectively to market demands. The allocation of a project's budget typically revolves around activities—training courses, market studies, extension visits, etc.—that are means to accomplish some higher-order objective like increasing sales and jobs. All too often, managers program those activities during the design phase, well before they know what buyers really want, creating personnel and budget rigidities that later stand in the way of their responding flexibly and rapidly to promising market opportunities. None of this is to say that managers of development programs can exempt themselves from the discipline of allocating the monies assigned them wisely. It is simply to point out that conventional development practice obligates them to make those allocation decisions much too early. The result is that the managers' day-to-day attention gets so monopolized by supplying training courses, extension visits, etc., that they miss the forest for the trees. In contrast to the market incentives that drive businesspeople to be opportunistic in responding to what buyers want, the project incentives that drive development professionals focus them on churning out activities and "spending the money" with little concern for what the activities add up to in the end. As argued below, yes, allocate monies to help businesses produce more, but only—repeat, only—after market demand is tied down.

For the reader uninitiated in development, much of this discussion must seem like common sense. For many development professionals, though, it is not. A few years ago, Kathryn Sell, a work colleague of the author at the time, made the following revealing comment on the graduate economic development course she was taking at night, "For years I had heard in the office about the Poverty Reduction and Alleviation Project in Peru and found its approach quite logical. It was only when I heard my professor going through a whole slew of supply-side interventions in class that I realized just how revolutionary PRA really is."

"All we need is a market."

Herman Choque, llama and alpaca herder, Bolivia

Jimmy Langman, "The Sweet Spot: Latin America's poorest farmers find rich niches in the United States and Europe," *Latin Trade*, January 2003.

Development practitioners tire of the old and get impatient for something new and "innovative." In the early 2000s, the author had the good fortune to assist in the business development component of USAID's Micro Enterprise Development Initiative (MEDI) in Armenia. Although funded modestly and lasting only 15 months, the component adopted the buyer-led approach and succeeded in expanding client sales and increasing jobs to levels much higher than expected. When it ended, an interviewer asked the author what innovations had made this little component so successful. From the way the interviewer asked the question, it was clear she wanted him to say that MEDI had done something novel and different from other projects. As he pondered his response, it hit the author that MEDI had indeed been very innovative, but not at all in the way she expected. The program had not done anything "sexy," but stuck rigorously to the approach it had adopted. Day in and day out, it ground out results, not allowing itself to get distracted by temptations to deviate from the straight and narrow. In the end, the real innovation was management discipline, not pizzazz.

Development practitioners want to have massive, not piece-meal impact. Many development professionals are concerned that the buyer-led approach is too micro, and, as such, will not have the transformational impact that other, more macro approaches presumably can have. The obsession with big impact probably goes back to the Marshall Plan, when Europe grew with a burst with large-scale United States assistance. Since then, expectations of success have continued apace, but countries like Afghanistan, Egypt, and Iraq aside, budget allocations have not kept up in real terms.[19] The upshot is indeed a bit of the Messiah complex alluded to by the Paddocks back in 1973. Even with modest resources, the development professional is expected somehow to deliver mammoth results.

> "What our two governments want is something big, that really helps people right away."
>
> William J. Lederer and Eugene Burdick, *The Ugly American* (New York: W.W. Norton & Company, 1958), p. 137.

No one, of course, wants development assistance to result just in "patches of green," a phrase popularized by Ambassador James Michel, USAID's Assistant Administrator for Latin America and the Caribbean in the early 1990s. Encouragingly, a body of evidence is emerging that the buyer-led approach, starting with individual businesses and working from the bottom up, can, under certain conditions—buoyant market demand, especially—have widespread, transformational effects. In contrast, more aggregate approaches—structural policy reform and sectoral and cluster development initiatives, for example—may aim higher, but the evidence is far from clear that they do any better in inducing sizeable increases in economic activity and jobs. At least under certain conditions—and somewhat ironically, therefore, the think-small tortoise often beats the think-big hare.

Development practitioners view fighting poverty more as charity than as a business proposition. Counterbalancing the urge to save the entire world at once is the tendency to go to the other extreme of attending to the basic human needs of the poor one by one. That approach makes eminent sense in humanitarian crises, obviously, but by definition, is not a self-sustaining solution to their plight.

TechnoServe is a development organization that applies most elements of the buyer-led approach. A letter it sent to potential contributors soliciting funds is very telling:

> Our mission is not relief. It is economic growth. And in the world of international development, we're the boat rockers—the heretics—the folks who do what many believe cannot be done.
>
> What is it we do?
>
> TechnoServe goes into villages in remote rural areas and helps local people turn dreams and opportunities into profitable businesses.
>
> We are not talking about one or two tailor shops or shoe repair stands. These are substantial, wealth-creating enterprises that *generate income, create jobs* and *spark the entrepreneurial spirit* that lies untapped in so many men and women.[20]

The language of funding solicitations has to be punchy to capture the attention of potential contributors. But even if one discounts the context whence this quote derives, TechnoServe's self-description as "boat rockers" and "heretics" comes off as strange. At the end of the day, what is heretical about attacking poverty by generating permanent, wealth-creating jobs? Is that not what development is all about?

Development practitioners tend to distrust business. Most development professionals see their calling—and a goodly number of them do see it as a calling—as a noble enterprise. In contrast, business appears to be the most ignoble of professions, making it difficult for them to embrace it as the vehicle they should look to for job creation. As Clive Crook has put it,

> Seen a movie lately? Watched television or read a newspaper? The culture that speaks to Americans, and hence to the Western world, radiates suspicion of free

enterprise—cordial and restrained, as a rule, but dubious nonetheless. Yes, the system does work, says this culture, and there appears to be no alternative. But what a shame this is, it continues, because capitalism rewards our worst and most selfish instincts. "Greed is good" may stock the shelves, but is somewhat less than inspiring.

Popular culture understands that the market economy creates material prosperity, albeit for some more than others. It seeks out and worships business celebrities. But at the same time it sees the system as spiritually—and politically—corrupting. As viewed from Hollywood, workers are usually downtrodden, bosses are usually grasping, consumers are usually gulled, and shadowy global finance is *always* calling the geopolitical shots. We manage to prosper, most of us, but this system of ours is not very noble...

The point is not that such movies, or the culture more generally, argue that capitalism is evil. Just the opposite: it is that they so often merely *assume*, innocently and expecting to arouse no skepticism, that capitalism is evil.[21]

"Money! Nothing worse

In our lives, so current, rampant, so corrupting.

Money—you demolish cities, root men from their homes,

you train and twist good minds and set them on

to the most atrocious schemes. No limit,

you make them adept at every kind of outrage,

every godless crime—money!"

Creon, "Antigone"

Sophocles, *The Three Theban Plays: Antigone, Oedipus the King, Oedipus at Colonus*, translated by Robert Fagles (New York: Penguin Books, 1984), p. 73.

Interestingly, the very same assumption underlies many corporate social responsibility (CSR) programs. As *The Economist*, which takes issue with the basic premise, puts it,

Simply put, advocates of CSR work from the premise that unadorned capitalism fails to serve the public interest. The search for profit, they argue, may be a regrettable necessity in the modern world, a sad fact of life if there is to be any private enterprise…

This is wrong. The goal of a well-run company may be to make profits for its shareholders, but merely in doing that—provided it faces competition in its markets, behaves honestly and obeys the law—the company, without even trying, is doing good works. [22]

Regardless of whether one agrees with *The Economist*, it is indeed ironic that the corporate social responsibility programs of most corporations—entities that know very well how to make money in the market—do not look to market forces to benefit populations of interest to them. Rather, most such programs are essentially charity.

How does the presumption that capitalism is evil play out in the development world? A quote from the popular press is instructive:

For six years straight, Aaron Mihaly spent his summer vacations toiling for nonprofits in Latin America. So when he told friends and family what he would be doing last summer—an intensive program at an Ivy League business school—they thought he had given up on changing the world. "The common reaction I got was 'You're selling your soul to the devil,'" says Mihaly, 23, with a laugh.

Far from it. This fall Mihaly moved to Mozambique and dedicated himself to fighting poverty. But he carried a new weapon in his battle against social ills: aggressive business skills.[23]

Development practitioners use the pretext of the complexity of development to shirk accountability. If the literature on development has one common thread, it is how complex it is. Unfortunately, that very complexity can tie practitioners up in knots. No matter what practitioners do, third parties can be quick to second-guess them, asking, "Ah, but what about x?"—where, interestingly, the x in question often is those third parties' own professional specialization! As one might expect, the combination of the abundance of angles from which one can approach development and the politically charged and socially unstable environments in which development practitioners work deters them from committing themselves to meeting quantifiable performance targets. Although that reaction is understandable, the failure to spell out where one is going and how to get there is tantamount to throwing accountability out the window. As well intentioned as they may be, practitioners cannot do development effectively if there is no clear yardstick to measure progress against and in essence, everybody can try out whatever they please without anybody holding them to account for it.

> "Why did the Lord give us agility
> If not to evade responsibility?"
>
> Ogden Nash
>
> "Common Sense" in *Comic Poems*, ed. by Peter Washington (New York: Alfred A. Knopf, 2001), p. 26.

Development practitioners are creatures of habit. Finally, most development practitioners learn development by doing it, and gradually absorb ways of thinking about development problems that may or may not be conducive to bringing about results. As a case in point, the author had the occasion to revisit a report he had written in Nicaragua over ten years ago. In light of his thinking today, much of that report is embarrassing. Instead of hewing to the management principles laid out here, the author devoted the bulk of the report to picking winning products to support, extrapolating almost entirely from existing patterns of small and medium farmer production. Although the report pays lip service to applying a market-driven, problem-solving, hands-on transactional approach, it is silent on actual market demand.[24] As of that writing, the author had obviously accepted the paradigms he had inherited uncritically, failing to examine whether they were appropriate to the case at hand.

> "We do what we do because we don't know any other way to be."
>
> Martha Grimes, *The Lamorna Wink* (New York: New American Library, 1999), p. 228.

Taken together, the factors discussed in this chapter, both singly and in combination, militate against disciplined application of demand-driven thinking to generate jobs for poor people, diminishing, in the process, real accountability for results.

4

Planning, Searching, and the Rest of the Book

As noted in Chapter 1, Easterly draws a useful distinction between Searchers and Planners. That distinction turns out to be extremely relevant to the buyer-led approach and, in fact, pulls together many of the strands above.

Easterly defines "Planners" and "Searchers" as follows:

> In foreign aid, Planners announce good intentions but don't motivate anyone to carry them out; Searchers find things that work and get some reward. Planners raise expectations but take no responsibility for meeting them; Searchers accept responsibility for their actions. Planners determine what to supply; Searchers find out what is in demand. Planners apply global blueprints; Searchers adapt to local conditions. Planners at the top lack knowledge of the bottom; Searchers find out what the reality is at the bottom. Planners never hear whether the planned got what it needed; Searchers find out whether the customer is satisfied.[25]

"[I]t is more important…to release the creative energy of individuals than to devise further machinery for 'guiding' and 'directing' them—to create conditions favorable to progress than to 'plan progress.'"

F.A. Hayek, *The Road to Serfdom*, Fiftieth Anniversary Edition (Chicago: The University of Chicago Press, 1994), p. 261.

Although not entirely coincident, the demand-driven approach described in this book corresponds closely to the mindset and activities of the Searcher: the point of entry of the buyer-led approach is specific and transactional, the incentive driving clients is demand in the market, support activities do not bring preconceived answers but focus on solving specific problems, and, more than that, outside agents set targets for the impact of their assistance and hold themselves accountable for results. In contrast, more aggregate approaches to development often fit the stereotype of the Planner: picking beforehand the sectors or clusters that are likely to be the winners, defining technocratically the needs of the sector or cluster and programming support activities accordingly, applying a limited number of solutions to the heterogeneity of individual business problems, and failing to establish clear targets against which to assess progress.

The remainder of *We Do Know How* presents numerous real-world examples that drive home even more the fundamental differences between the approach of the Planner and the approach of the Searcher.

"[T]raveler, there is no road; You make your path as you walk."

Antonio Machado, "Caminante no hay camino," in *Poesias completas de Antonio Machado* (Madrid, Spain: Espasa Calpe, 2006).

An analogous distinction that helps explain why development programs have had limited success in helping poor people take advantage of economic opportunities is the divide between the cultures that typically drive development organizations and those that drive their clients. As Gregory Robison argues in an incisive 1994 article in the journal of the Inter-American Foundation,[26] most development organizations are budget-based, not market-based, and their clients just the opposite—and it is the chasm between those two cultures, more than anything else, that accounts for much of the ineffectiveness of development organizations in generating jobs and growing incomes. One may quibble with some details of the argument, but the basic thesis is intriguing, and Robison traces out the operational ramifications of that clash of cultures convincingly. Accordingly, the appendix to this part of the book presents extensive excerpts from Robison's article verbatim. From those excerpts, the reader can appreciate a bit more just why *We Do Know How* is in fact so countercultural and why it makes a point of challenging conventional development wisdom as much as it does.

The Rest of the Book

We Do Know How is a book for practitioners, not a theoretical treatise or a handyman's reference guide. It suggests procedures to follow, but the most important change it calls for is mental. Even though not one of its elements may be that different from other approaches', the overall package is.

Part II goes into some depth on the paradigm shifts embodied in the buyer-led approach, explaining why it is the way it is and setting the stage for what the practitioner is actually to do. Part III offers specific suggestions on how to make the paradigm operational. And, finally, Part IV presents examples of materials that have proven useful in the application of the approach around the world.

In short, *We Do Know How* shows how to shed the bad habits of the Planner and structure the work of the Searcher. Part II presents the why of the buyer-led approach; Part III, the what; and Part IV, the how.

Appendix to Part I

Excerpts From "The Cultural Challenge of Supporting Enterprise"[27]

Many languages have a saying about adversity being a school. Participants in failed ventures, however, too often pay for such lessons at the exorbitantly high cost of their jobs and savings. For this reason, economic projects imply a heightened level of responsibility on the part of donors...

The nature of the financing of donor agencies and their NGO [non-governmental organization] partners produces a radically different culture than that of the economic ventures of the poor they propose to assist. It is this cultural disjunction, more than a lack of technical skills, which accounts for much of the ineffectiveness by development organizations in supporting economic enterprise projects. Donor failure to recognize the divergence and compensate for it compounds the risk of their doing harm...

If income derives primarily from consumers who are free to accept or reject an organization's output, the venture is 'market based'...If financing comes principally from nonconsumers, the organization or venture may be said to be 'budget based'...

Each of these two kinds of organization faces a different challenge in raising the resources needed to accomplish its goals and remain viable. A budget-based institution lives primarily by *words*—by convincing its nonconsumer supporters that financing is merited. Since the funders of such an organization do not consume its output, survival depends upon generating consistent, coherent, reassuring language *about* the output...

A venture whose survival depends upon the market, on the other hand, lives by *deeds*—by delivering an acceptable product or service to its clients or consumers. The market-based enterprise's main source of income—its consumers—neither requires nor values 'coherent explanations' of methodology or intentions. The only thing that really matters to consumers is the value that they themselves perceive in the product or service... The producer must live within the limits set by the consumer's willingness and ability to buy...

Peter F. Drucker (1973), one of the most influential, contemporary conceptualizers of management issues, emphasizes this idea of constraint by making the consumer the starting point for any analysis of economic enterprise:

> A business is not defined by the company's name, statutes, or articles of incorporation. It is defined by the want the consumer satisfies when he buys a product or service. To satisfy the customer is the mission and purpose of every business. The question 'What is our business?' can, therefore, be answered only by looking at the business from the outside, from the point of view of the customer and the market...The consumer defines the business...

The determination of whether or not an enterprise is market based ought...to be the first step in analyzing a request for grant assistance. If the answer is yes, the grant conditions ought to draw the beneficiary's attention to the need to focus on the market and respond to it, reinforcing the necessary entrepreneurial disciplines. In other words, success must be understood to require much more than compliance with procedural or administrative terms of the grant agreement if its primary purpose is to promote a sustainable business. Donor intervention must be based on the conviction that there can be no dependable creation of jobs or improvement in income without respecting the continuous, definitive, and irrevocable judgment of consumers. In a certain sense, these consumers—external to the project, unmanageable, and largely unpredictable—are the only 'project monitors' who really matter in the long run.

Unfortunately, the budget-based culture of donors and most development NGOs makes it notoriously difficult for them to give the economic initiatives of the poor this kind of attention. The need to sell its metaproduct to nonconsumers forces a budget-based organization to value predictability, order, planning, hierarchy, and standard procedures—'bureaucratic virtues.' This characteristic, in itself, is not a defect. Budget-based organizations are excellently adapted to delivering standard products or universal services whose value has been predetermined... It is also true, however, that the culture of budget-based, bureaucratic organizations is far from that of market-based, entrepreneurial ones. The two scarcely speak the same language.

Nothing more clearly illustrates the chasm between the two organizational cultures than their differing understanding of the idea of profit. Concern for profit—the positive difference between what consumers pay for something and what it costs to produce it—underpins all aspects of the culture of the market-based enterprise; it is a meaningless concept for the budget-based one.

In the culture of the market, profits are not a luxury; they are a necessity...

However they are labeled, profits are vital because the present is risky and the future uncertain...

Equally important, profits are the first and most reliable indicator that an enterprise is actually satisfying a need and doing so sustainably...

A good working definition of poverty is the absence of markets within a particular community. There is ample evidence of the frightfully high cost of being poor when economic choices are limited or nonexistent...

It is at precisely this juncture, when development organizations intervene to assist the poor's economic initiatives, that donors are often distinctly unhelpful. Tone-deaf to the keynote sounded by profit, they risk replicating their own bureaucratic values in their beneficiaries and counterparts and fatally drawing their attention away from the market.

Sometimes this tendency takes the form of attempting to establish the economic worth of a product or service without reference to the role of the producer as an economic agent operating within the constraints of the market. It is easy to see how this well-intentioned concern for producers on the part of many NGOs and donors flows directly from a budget mentality. Competition that results in better prices for the consumer makes life more precarious for the producer. Since grants aim to improve the latter's well-being, a sufficient justification to support many ventures becomes the securing of 'economic justice' for producers. In practice, this often comes to mean a bureaucratically determined 'fair return,' irrespective of what the consumer may think of the resulting product or service...

This phenomenon is especially pernicious in the case of support for craftspeople—long favored as beneficiaries of choice at many development organizations—because it encourages the natural tendency of the grantee to reason in the same way. For the artisan, the idea of 'quality' is something that inheres in the thing produced. It is objectively observable; it speaks for itself. The hand that can generate such excellence is that of a skilled producer, one who 'deserves' a good, or at least decent, return. Such a person 'ought' to survive and prosper.

In market terms, however, quality is not a feature of the thing produced; it means desirability in the eyes of the buyer or user. Quality in this commercial sense—its only relevant economic meaning—is clearly a matter of perception, residing entirely in the mind of the consumer...

Donors whose objective is to help create jobs and income perform no useful service to their beneficiaries by encouraging the idea that there is a single 'fair price' unrelated to consumer demand and productive efficiency. Such a mentality leads grantees to view their problems as entirely the fault of the 'grasping middleman' who blocks their direct access to the sympathetic final consumer...

Innovative lending and savings programs in many parts of Latin America are now demonstrating that the poor can in fact be business clients rather than passive beneficiaries. This new market-based approach offers potential for far greater expansion of services than donors ever could have achieved, and establishes a relationship of dignity with the poor that is absent when they are viewed as recipients of largesse...

The cultural predisposition of budget-based organizations is to view human resources as interchangeable, highly manageable inputs. In budget-based organizations, individuals assume positions of leadership and responsibility only under strict and well-understood rules. The lines of authority are clear. There are career paths in which credentials or performance appraisals, and sometimes both, usually weigh heavily. In short, the world of words in which budget-based organizations live is as evident in their internal treatment of human resources as it is in their approach to financing.

In the market there is no such orderly procedure, no institutional sanction for human creativity or assumption of authority. The general rule in the market is that individuals *propose themselves* for positions of leadership. The leader is not the one invested with authority by some higher power, but the one who—when he or she says 'follow me'—is in fact followed. It is a process utterly illogical from the bureaucratic point of view, and one that, predictably, produces a high failure rate. Venture capitalist Louis Allen (1968), reflecting on a professional lifetime connected with business creation, noted that 85 percent of entrepreneurs think they can make something better, 15 percent think they can sell something better, and both groups are nearly always wrong...

It is taken as axiomatic that if profit is an organizational necessity and a residual indicator of responsiveness to people's real needs, it is also—and primarily—a motivator at the personal level, and such motivations are held in very low regard. The idea of profit is therefore not only the great stumbling block to donors' and NGOs' understanding of how the market constrains enterprise, but also an obstacle to their comprehending the indispensable personal dimension of private-venture creation.

Failure to allow for such legitimate personal motivations often leads to a dearth of entrepreneurial talent in many market-based initiatives supported by donors. Rather than reexamine the cultural bias against profit that contributes to this condition, many budget-based donors are much more comfortable with attempting to train a beneficiary's existing employees or members to fill the void. Training in fact harmonizes well with budget-based culture. It lends itself to precisely quantifiable levels of participation. It has tidy starting and ending points. It can evoke fashionable concepts that resonate with the donor's own funders and thereby enhance its metaproduct.

Perhaps most important from the donor's standpoint, however, freshly minted managers up from the ranks are perceived to be free of the ambition and greed that are thought to possess entrepreneurs. In other words, they look like technically proficient, bureaucratic administrators.

This widely held belief at budget-based institutions that training supplies an adequate answer for the personal dimension of enterprise reveals another deep-seated value that is at odds with the culture of the market. Training presupposes that what the poor lack to make their ventures succeed, at least from the human-resources point of view, is knowledge. Knowledge is power, after all; so to empower disadvantaged populations must mean to bring them the knowledge—boiled down, translated, and appropriately packaged—that has allowed others to succeed.

Unfortunately, no one really knows what combination of skill and experience is necessary or sufficient to make a business succeed, and how much of it can be imparted formally...

Concern with redistribution, social progress, and environmental impact will be fruitless . . . unless it is in harmony with the essential cultural values of business enterprise itself—with the limiting discipline of the market, with individual initiative, and with the central role of profits in each.

It is clear that budget-based donors and their NGO partners can achieve this harmony only if they graft onto their own language of order, coherence, and procedural correctness a new and culturally foreign vocabulary of market quality, productivity, and profitability. It is by no means obvious how they can do so. Many of their deepest instincts are against it.

On the other hand, the mere recognition that the organizational culture of budget-based development agencies prevents them from speaking—or understanding—the entrepreneurial language of market-based initiatives would be a major step in the right direction. How that recognition finds expression in concrete steps taken by donors and development NGOs will vary according to the circumstances. At a minimum it should involve, first, financial benchmarks and performance milestones as integral parts of market-based project objectives. In this way it will be clear to both donor and beneficiary whether or not an economic initiative is actually creating value and is solvent.

PART II

The Overall Approach— Paradigms and Principles

5

Where to Start—Poverty, Jobs, Sales, and Market Demand

Strategic decisions at the start of a program can have far-reaching consequences. Getting off on the right foot can pave the way to making a demonstrable difference. Getting off on the wrong foot can lead to disappointing results down the road.

This first chapter of Part II traces out the basic logic of the buyer-led approach. It shows: first, how creating jobs is key to reducing poverty; second, how increasing sales is key to increasing jobs; and, third, how starting with market demand is key to increasing sales. The chapter consists of four sections, which illustrate:

The multidisciplinary nature of poverty and the need for strategic thinking to reduce it;
How creating jobs is a necessary condition for reducing poverty;
How increasing sales drives job creation; and
How market demand drives increases in sales.

For readers relatively new to international development, much of the discussion that follows may seem like common sense. Not all development programs start with this kind of thinking, however, and many that do founder on failing to think through how to translate the thinking into practice. The appendix to this part of the book presents examples of mistakes practitioners commonly make at the outset of development programs.

The Nature of Poverty and the Need for Strategic Thinking to Reduce it

Poverty is arguably the world's most significant and intractable problem. Governments, international donors, think-tanks, and private voluntary organizations all spend significant time, energy, and resources assessing the dimensions of poverty and attacking them in different ways. To signal their concern, the member states of the United Nations have declared their intention to halve extreme poverty and hunger by 2015. Even though results have not measured up to expectations so far, it is certainly not because poverty is off the world's radar screen.

Since 9/11, fighting poverty has become even more topical. "Numerous studies show that poverty fuels conflict. Britain's Department of International Development found that countries with per capita gross domestic product of less than $250 face a 15 percent chance of conflict within the next five years. When per capita income reaches $1,000, the risk drops dramatically, and at $5,000 it is less than 1 percent."[28]

Not surprisingly, the literature on poverty is voluminous.[29] Generically, it has two non-mutually exclusive threads. One is definitional, the other normative. The definitional thread of the literature concerns itself with trying to understand the nature of poverty — what it is and what dimensions it encompasses. As one might expect, it concludes that poverty is a multidimensional phenomenon: no one discipline can clutch it within its grasp, and, *a fortiori*, coming to grips with it is a task multidisciplinary in nature. For its part, the normative thread of the poverty literature proposes responses to the poverty problem. Again, as one might expect, the proposed responses are legion, running the gamut of the various dimensions of poverty. The typical normative document tends to be encyclopedically taxonomic in recommending what to do, but rarely prescribes what not to do.

For development practitioners concerned about what actions to take to attack poverty, the bulk of this literature is very frustrating. In practice, resources to attack poverty are scarce, and one must make choices in their use. Yet little of the literature provides guidance in that regard. Most treatments of poverty are diagnostic, but what decision makers need is strategic.

A couple of examples of the all-encompassing nature of the discussion of poverty make the point.

First is the definition of poverty used by the United Nations:

> Fundamentally, poverty is a denial of choices and opportunities, a violation of human dignity. It means lack of basic capacity to participate effectively in society. It means not having enough to feed and cloth [sic] a family, not having a school or clinic to go to, not having the land on which to grow one's food or a job to earn one's living, not having access to credit. It means insecurity, powerlessness and exclusion of individuals, households and communities. It means susceptibility to violence, and it often implies living on marginal or fragile environments, without access to clean water or sanitation.[30]

This definition amply describes the various manifestations of poverty, but provides little clue as to where to enter the fray to have an impact. If anything, it sends the implicit message that you need to attack everything to accomplish anything. But once again, the typical development program does not have the resources to attack all dimensions at once.

The second example is an advertisement for a book about poverty:[31]

> Understanding poverty and what to do about it, is perhaps the central concern of all of economics...This volume brings together twenty-eight essays by some of the world leaders in the field, who were invited to tell the lay reader about the most important things they have learnt from their research that relate to poverty. The essays cover a wide array of topics: the first essay is about how poverty gets measured. The next section is about the causes of poverty and its persistence, and the ideas range from the impact of colonialism and globalization to the problems of "excessive" population growth, corruption and ethnic conflict. The next section is about policy: how should we fight poverty? The essays discuss how to get drug companies to produce more

vaccines for the diseases of the poor, what we should and should not expect from micro-credit, what we should do about child labor, how to design welfare policies that work better and a host of other topics. The final section is about where the puzzles lie: what are the most important anomalies, the big gaps in the way economists think about poverty? The essays talk about the puzzling reluctance of Kenyan farmers to fertilizers, the enduring power of social relationships in economic transactions in developing countries and the need to understand where aspirations come from, and much else.[32]

Again, just the array of topics in this book is enough to boggle the mind. Although it gives a sense of the diverse ramifications of poverty, it offers little guidance on how to make operational choices—that is, what dimension(s) to concentrate on first in order to bring about effects in other dimensions later.

Exhibit 2.1 presents a conceptual framework that has proven a useful first step in choosing among competing policy and programmatic alternatives for fighting poverty. Its primary virtue is the clear distinction it draws between reducing poverty and alleviating poverty, concepts that practitioners tend to blur in theory and in practice. It is also straightforward and pragmatic, highlighting the essentials.

Exhibit 2.1 Conceptual Framework for Attacking Poverty

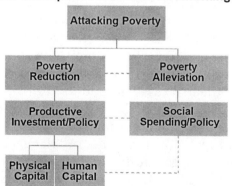

Source: Attacking Poverty: A Market Approach (Lima, Peru: Universidad del Pacifico, 2003).

In general, one can fight poverty in two ways. The first way is to institute those policies and take those programmatic actions that reduce poverty, that is, that lower permanently the number of people who are poor. The second way is to institute those policies and take those programmatic actions that alleviate poverty, that is, that ease the burden of poor people but do not have a lasting impact. In the first instance, the incomes of poor people rise, and the likelihood is high that their income stream will continue, through either self- or other-generated gainful employment. In the second instance, the well-being of poor people rises in the short run, but its maintenance at that level typically requires recurrent expenditure. The first effect normally is identified with and results from "productive investment." The second effect normally is identified with and results from "social safety net expenditures."

Actions to reduce poverty generally affect relatively few people in the short term, but can trigger broader medium- and long-term effects. In contrast, actions to alleviate poverty can affect many people, but are limited in their impact to the short run. There is a tradeoff between focusing on poverty reduction and focusing on poverty alleviation: one cannot limit oneself to either one or the other. A key challenge for public policy is to find the appropriate balance between the two, which is more art than science. Exhibit 2.1 reflects the tradeoff and the need for balance both through the dotted line connecting the poverty reduction and alleviation boxes and through the dotted line connecting the productive investment/policy and social expenditure/policy boxes.

"By treating economic growth and the alleviation of poverty as distinct aims of development…, and by observing that 'aid is rarely concentrated on the services that benefit the poorest', your article appears (probably unintentionally) to endorse the view that rapid growth has little to do with reducing poverty. Yet economic growth is the only mechanism through which the welfare of the poor can be improved in a sustainable way."

Michael Roemer, Letter, *Economist*, June 4, 1994, p. 6.

As a rule, the more capital people have at their disposal, the more productive they will be—and, all other things being equal, the higher the incomes they will earn. The capital in question can take two forms. The first form is physical—plant and equipment, for example—which results from what one commonly thinks of as productive investment. The second form is human, which results, among other things, from education. Although it may not be common to think of education in investment terms, it as an investment no less "productive" than investment in physical capital, especially for the poor.[33] For that reason, the exhibit breaks out investment in human capital explicitly, to highlight its significance.

"We won't eradicate poverty by eradicating capital or alienating investors but by joining forces with them."

José Daniel Ortega

Tim Padgett and Elaine Shannon, "How anti-U.S. cold warrior Daniel Ortega made his way back to power in Nicaragua," *Time*, November 20, 2006, p. 51.

The dotted line between the human capital and social spending/policy boxes serves two purposes: first, to point up the close connection between education and other "social" sectors; and, second, to blur somewhat the distinction between what is "productive" and what is "social." As a practical matter, expenditures on health, nutrition, and education represent significant investment in people and, potentially, at least, can yield high returns in lifetime income.[34]

We Do Know How focuses primarily on the left branch of Exhibit 2.1, that is, on how to reduce poverty through the generation of jobs for and by poor people. The rest of this book shows how jobs can emerge by building on incentives inherent in market forces. In contrast to much of the literature on poverty, the discussion points out at least one proven path to venture down as well as a number of paths not to.

Reducing Poverty Hinges on Creating Jobs

On arrival at their destination, most international travelers are quick to engage local people—taxi drivers, especially—in conversations about the state of affairs in their country. Nine times out of ten—not a scientifically derived probability, but probably not far off the mark—people talk about the lack of jobs. Comments like,

"There is not enough work to go around," or "We desperately need more jobs," are so common as to be almost truisms. In most people's minds, poverty is not an abstract concept, but the often very wearying challenge of securing employment.

It is one thing to recognize that poverty is multidimensional, and that those dimensions cross a broad spectrum of disciplines. It is quite another thing to argue that development practitioners give equal programmatic weight to all those dimensions. Given scarce resources, one has to ask, "What dimension do I attack first to trigger a chain reaction of salutary effects elsewhere?" Or to put it another way, "How do I distinguish underlying causes from the symptoms of poverty, so that I can use the scarce development resources at my disposal wisely?"

> "Life is so hard in this world Happiness ends if you have no work."
>
> Freddie Aguilar, "Trabaho," translated by Brian-James T. Matibag, Pinoyvision Records, 2004.

Taxi drivers in developing countries would not hesitate long before answering. For them, the answer is simple: increase jobs. Taxi drivers know fully well that poverty often entails living in inadequate housing, in physical and financial insecurity, with limited access to health and education services, etc., etc. But they also know that the most effective way to do away with those manifestations of poverty is by earning more money, which generally means obtaining gainful employment.

> "[F]undamentally and unequivocally poverty is about a lack of cash. Virtually everyone, including the very poor in Africa, lives in a cash economy. With cash, you can access food, clothing, shelter, healthcare and education. And cash comes, for most of us including poor people, from having a job."
>
> Kurt Hoffman, "Aid industry reform and the role of enterprise," Shell Foundation, London, 2005, p. 2.

To fulfill the requirements of a course at the Stanford Graduate School of Business, M.B.A. students interviewed representatives of eight mining or oil and gas companies on the lessons they learned from engaging with the communities where they work. The responses square with what taxi drivers say. The most typical responses to questions on "major community needs/demands" were:

> Livelihood is always the most important for communities—this is manifested in requests for *jobs* at the mine. [emphasis added]
>
> When we do surveys, we find that *jobs* and education come to the top of the list. [emphasis added][35]

As one might expect, the economics literature on poverty echoes the opinions of taxi drivers and mining and oil and gas communities. Illustrative statements on the connection between poverty and employment include:

> Labor is the most abundant asset of the poor, and in low-income countries what distinguishes the poor from the non-poor is, for the most part, access to productive employment. Thus the quality and quantity of employment opportunities are increasingly recognized as one of the main transmission channels between growth and poverty reduction.[36]

> The key to poverty reduction in the medium term is growth that is sufficiently rapid to absorb additions to the labor force and to make inroads on unemployment and under-employment.[37]

> The key finding is that growth reduced poverty…, largely via increased labor demand in firms in more productive sectors that induced a change in the composition of employment away from agriculture (where income growth opportunities are most limited) and increased real earnings. In its analysis (and correctly in my view), the chapter goes back to the core lesson of The World Bank's 1990 *World Development Report*, with its focus on the need to make fuller use of the poor's most abundant asset: their labor.[38]

> Creating opportunities for steady employment at reasonable wages is the best way to take people out of poverty.

"Nothing is more fundamental to poverty reduction than employment," states the ILO [International Labour Organization].[39]

In formal terms, generating employment may not be a sufficient condition, but it is a necessary condition for reducing poverty. For that reason, it is the principal aim of the buyer-led approach.

How can one go about increasing jobs? One way to look at that task is to drill down on the conceptual framework in the left branch of Exhibit 2.1. Exhibit 2.2, which practitioners applied first in Peru and have extended to other countries, presents one useful way to do so.

Exhibit 2.2 Programmatic Strategy for Reducing Poverty

Source: Adaptation of Exhibit 3.1, USAID/Peru Poverty Reduction and Alleviation Framework.

Exhibit 2.2 posits that poverty reduction results from generating employment and income in the private sector, which in turn depends on expansion of productive activities, which in turns depends on investment, which in turn depends on four factors: a policy environment conducive to private sector investment; access to functioning output and input markets in the broadest sense—that is, the wherewithal to trade both domestically and internationally; adequate physical capital; and adequate human capital.[40] With its lateral arrows along the bottom row, it also illustrates the key role that business development can play in helping set priorities on the policy, infrastructure, and education fronts.

On the policy front, development programs generally have little difficulty in identifying norms, regulations, etc., they can work on: secure property rights, reliable contract enforcement, an open trade and investment regime, and fiscal prudence, for example. As a practical matter, though, no development program can do "policy" across the board. Development programs need focus, for which they need a priority-setting mechanism. Intelligence surfacing from business development activities can provide just such a mechanism, that is, a way to pinpoint those policy deficiencies that are actually the most significant constraints to business growth—or, to put it another way, to identify those policy issues whose resolution is likely to have the highest economic rate of return.

In a similar vein, most developing countries have shortfalls in physical infrastructure far in excess of available resources. One way to set infrastructure investment priorities is from the top down. The other, suggested here, is from the bottom up, relying heavily on intelligence from businesses themselves on what investments will likely yield the highest return.

Finally, business and vocational training generally lacks focus unless it is tied to business transactions. As a rule, businesses themselves are the best judge of what skills will make the most difference.

Sales Drive Jobs

Every development program needs a management North Star. Although most programs have a multiplicity of objectives, all do not carry equal weight. Some program objectives are ends, others are means, and managers who fail to distinguish clearly between the two do so at their peril. Experience in programs with demonstrated results strongly suggests the wisdom, first, of program managers focusing on very few well defined ends and, second, of funding agencies allowing them to adjust the means at their disposal to achieve those ends. In such programs, program managers

track both final and intermediate results, but funding agencies hold them **accountable** only for the **former**.

Increasing sales and jobs is the logical North Star in business promotion and market-driven poverty reduction programs. **Just as jobs are a necessary condition for reducing poverty, sales are a necessary condition for increasing jobs. Without sales, growth in jobs simply will not occur.**

Not all development professionals are comfortable with zooming in on sales as the driver of employment growth and reductions in poverty. Academic economists, especially, argue that development is all about growth in productivity. As a recent issue of *The Economist* puts it, "Productivity growth is perhaps the single most important gauge of an economy's health. Nothing matters more for long-term living standards than improvements in the efficiency with which an economy combines capital and labour."[41]

Although making productivity growth one's North Star is attractive intellectually, it suffers from two big drawbacks operationally. The first is measurement. The productivity at issue here is not labor productivity or return on capital, but "total factor productivity," that is the portion of output not explained by the amount of inputs used in production. Its level is determined by the efficiency of input use.[42] The problem is that calculating total factor productivity is no easy task, and it normally requires resources well beyond what development programs can assign to it.

Second, and much more importantly, is the question of what drives productivity. Productivity does not drive itself. Interestingly, increasing sales is appealing, not just because it normally drives increases in jobs, but also because it normally drives competitiveness as well.[43] Increased sales, after all, do more than increase revenue. Not only do they normally induce more input use, but, more often than not, they also stimulate increased coordination with (and among) suppliers, boosting efficiency and generating economies of scale. In response to rising world demand, for example, timber suppliers in Bolivia have begun forming Japanese-style "just in time" central distribution hubs to reduce the number of point-to-point shipment channels and to avoid shortages and deal-busting delays for buyers who cannot afford to stockpile on site—making the supply chains in question more sophisticated and efficient—and more competitive.[44]

Operationally, focusing on sales expansion also has a very practical advantage. As the PRA final report put it,

> PRA set itself only three objectives: new sales, new jobs, and investment. That design decision not only gave the entire program focus; it also resonated with PRA's clients. Increasing sales is an objective that processors, traders, and their suppliers not only identify with but embrace. Having all its personnel focused on increasing sales put PRA on the same wavelength with those whom it set out to serve.[45]

The link between sales and jobs is not mechanistic or automatic. Jobs depend on sales, but sales do not always create jobs. The only way some businesses can sell more is if they become more cost-competitive, which occasionally—and occasionally definitely means as an exception to the rule—means that they have to lay off people. Should development programs shy away from such cases? Certainly not if doing so winds up saving jobs that would have disappeared otherwise—which is frequently the case. An example from the Dominican Republic, written by the author, illustrates how what happens in an accounting sense can differ substantially from what happens in an economic sense:

> Paredes Dominicanas is a shoe factory founded in 1983. In 1990 the company received a Section 108 sub-loan for RD$2 million from Banco del Progreso. According to [Jesús] Gonzáles [the General Manager], the sub-loan saved the company by allowing it to purchase new Italian machinery and other equipment, thus making Paredes Dominicanas more competitive. Transactions costs are high in the shoe industry. Power is out eight to ten hours a day, clearing inputs through customs is a tedious and costly process (much of the raw input for the factory consists of semi-finished products from China and Thailand), and there is considerable competition from illegally imported shoes...In 1990 the factory had 200 workers; it now has 115, half of whom are women. On the one hand, the decline in employment can be attributed to the more efficient machinery purchased with

the sub-loan. On the other hand, Gonzáles stressed, without the machinery, all 200 workers would have been out on the street. In effect, therefore, the sub-loan *saved* 115 jobs.[46]

Even in the outlier cases when capital deepening leads to dead-weight losses of jobs, it is important not to become overly myopic, to look beyond the individual firm, and to distinguish between effects in the short term and effects in the medium term. In the years after World War II, development economists spent a lot of time agonizing over the "elasticity of substitution between capital and labor," that is, the degree to which investments in physical capital would substitute for labor and generate job losses. In retrospect, that concern appears to have been overblown. Yes, individual firms do let people go, but, as a rule, economies at wide have proven much more resilient in creating jobs than a firm-by-firm view would lead one to conclude.

Despite the appeal of sales as the principal operational objective of business-oriented programs, some observers object to that focus on the grounds that it can degenerate into chasing one-shot deals. As Vicki Moore, a USAID Mission Director, once expressed it, "[i]t is important that the parties involved not confuse the goal of increasing Competitiveness with increasing short-term earnings and profits by the private sector, as these are not one and the same."[47] That is true, of course, and a temptation to resist. But one-shot sales are not what the buyer-led approach is about. As explained at some length below, the buyer-led approach looks beyond the individual deal to the sustainability of commercial relationships between buyers and sellers over time. But in contrast to approaches that tend to agonize over long-term strategy, the buyer-led approach recognizes explicitly that individual transactions are the necessary stepping stones to growth. In short, the vision is long-term, but programmatically the approach moves forward one step—that is, one transaction—at a time.[48]

For that reason, this book disagrees with Moore's comment that "Competitiveness . . . requires a significant degree of analysis, before work commences."[49] As a practical

> "The key was to think big but focus relentlessly on near-term deadlines."
>
> Reuben E. Slone, "Leading a Supply Chain Turnaround," *Harvard Business Review*, Reprint R0410G, October, 2004, p. 5.

matter, a "significant degree of analysis" can devolve into waiting for Godot. In the end, sustainable relationships will take place between buyers and sellers only if deals actually take place between buyers and sellers. Evidence from a cross-section of buyer-led programs suggests that the earlier a program becomes operational, the higher the results. When in doubt, do not do a study! Jump in the water and swim!

An organization in Russell, New Zealand, presumably oriented more toward action than toward studies. *Photo:* Courtesy of J. Peter Bittner.

None of this is to say that the buyer-led approach is not analytical, or that it is wise to rush headlong into things without forethought for the big picture. Any program that holds itself accountable for results must do its due diligence. But it is one thing to be analytical; it is another to undertake mammoth studies and develop big program "strategies" before venturing to get one's feet wet.

In principle, there are so many things one can do to increase sales and jobs that opportunity-cost thinking is essential. Experience suggests a useful analytical criterion to bring discipline to the due diligence process: only provide a service if it is reasonable to expect an increase in a client's sales five times the cost of the service in question.

Adopting a decision criterion like this so called 5:1 rule is a key strategic element of the buyer-led approach, and much depends on the degree to which program managers make it a priority. There is nothing magical about that particular ratio, but some such rule of thumb is essential to put a brake on good ideas that are not cost-effective ideas. For programs that take return on investment seriously, hewing to a quantitative criterion is critical. Programs that have maintained such discipline have exhibited relatively high returns to program resources. Many other programs have not.

"I just believe that if you buy the cheapest stocks in the market, you will be pretty well rewarded no matter what the market does. ...It's your philosophy that really protects you from yourself, because left to your own devices you will go out and buy whatever."

James P. Barrow

"Figuring Big Oil Isn't Losing Energy: Fund Manager Expects More Gains," *Washington Post*, July 17, 2005, p. F4.

In a closely related vein, many development programs look to monitoring and evaluation systems simply to report results to funding agencies, and essentially nothing more. For a program that sets sales and employment targets and holds itself accountable for meeting them, monitoring and evaluation cannot be an afterthought. Rather, program managers must embed monitoring and evaluation into operations as an ongoing, hands-on management tool.

Demand Drives Sales

The Shipibo-Conibo tribe in the jungle of Peru has always produced beautiful ceramics.[50] Traditionally, its women molded each piece by hand, fired it, and then painted on intricate designs with their own hair. Although beautiful, the pieces did not sell well locally, and the community was poor. The tribe had never produced large volumes of uniform quality, and traders, who could sell into broader markets, were reluctant to source from them.

Shipibo-Conibo ceramic pottery.
Photo: USAID/Peru Poverty Reduction and Alleviation program.

American Trading, an export company based in Lima, Peru's capital city, was an exception. In 2001, it badgered Pier 1 Imports to give it an order for Shipibo-Conibo ceramics. Pier 1 Imports finally agreed, but wanted 25,000 pieces! There was no way the Shipibo-Conibo could produce that many high-quality pieces on schedule using their traditional practices. American Trading had capital to invest, but feared it would lose heavily if it had to provide the community with intensive training in mass-production techniques and monitor operations 300 miles away from its own offices. After all the work it had put in, American Trading was actually considering turning the Pier 1 Imports order down.

Worried and unsure what to do, American Trading approached PRA to see if it could help. Seeing the opportunity to bring money and jobs to a region that desperately needed them and recognizing that the opportunity would not materialize without external support, PRA committed itself to help American Trading solve the main business problems jeopardizing the deal. PRA helped pay for a skilled technician to train the artisans in mass-production technology, monitor production day to day, and exercise quality control. After many twists and turns, the company and the artisans succeeded. About 200 community members—mostly women—worked directly in the operation, and 200 others benefited indirectly from ancillary employment. In addition, four micro-enterprises learned how to organize, monitor, and quality-control production, thus creating capacity within the community itself to respond expeditiously—and without subsidy—to future orders.

The experience of linking Pier 1 Imports with the Shipibo-Conibo points up several lessons, including how international development programs, with surgically targeted interventions tied to market transactions, can have a tangible impact on the lives of poor people. **The biggest lesson, though, is the power of specific market demands—that is, orders—to make seemingly unsolvable supply problems suddenly solvable.** With the order from Pier 1

Imports in hand, everyone had an incentive to succeed. Why? Because everyone stood to make money.

Only a few hours drive away, in the jungle near Aguaytía, lies a banana growing area. To sell more easily, the growers had organized themselves in associations—five in all. Buyers of bananas came to the area only irregularly, so when they did, the five associations were quick to pounce, each pressuring the buyers to purchase from them. With effective demand so small, much banana production went unsold, and the rivalry among the five associations actually came to take on violent proportions.

In 2004, PRA facilitated the visit of a buyer from Santa Isabel to the area. Santa Isabel was one of the two major supermarket chains in the country. At a meeting with the five associations, the buyer announced that Santa Isabel was willing to purchase all the bananas they could sell, but that it would not deal with the five associations separately. He told them, "We are going to have just one bar code, not five. If you want us to buy from you, work it out." Almost instantly the bitterest of enemies became intimate friends!

As in the ceramics example, the reaction of the banana growers shows just how powerful market demand—be that demand foreign or domestic—can be in driving sales and job creation.

If market demand drives sales and jobs, the implication for the development practitioner is clear: build creatively on market incentives in such a way as to capitalize on job-creating sales opportunities. The chapters that follow lay out a framework of thinking to do just that.

6

What Does "Demand-Driven" Really Mean?

How can development practitioners help clients access market demand to boost their sales? This chapter traces out what taking a demand-driven approach really means and how it differs from common practice. The chapter has three sections. They discuss:

The meaning of the term, "demand-driven";
Practical implications of taking a demand-driven approach; and
How, operationally, demand means a buyer with a name and address.

The Meaning of the Term, "Demand-Driven"

In international development circles, the phrases, "market-oriented" and "demand-driven," have become the mantras of the day. Despite the rhetoric, however, most development practice remains very much "supply-push." More than that, most practitioners do not even realize it. To illustrate the point, five statements appear below that normally raise no eyebrows about whether they are demand-driven. In fact, each calls for a closer look.

---

1. Is This Approach "Demand-driven"?

"In the highlands there are a number of market 'niche' opportunities. ...Among the specific niche products are fruits and vegetables, traditional cereals (quinoa and kanihua), tubers (maca), condiments (oregano and anis), fish products, and handicrafts (ceramics and weavings). Developing markets for these products can have a big impact on the local economy."

Draft donor rural development strategy for the highlands of Peru, 2002.

A quick glance at the first box might lead one to think that the proposed rural development strategy is demand-driven: certainly use of the phraseology, "market 'niche' opportunities," makes it sound like there is a market already in place, just waiting for supply. But a closer look reveals just the opposite, that farmers in Peru simply have a bevy of goods they can produce. But that is no reason for donors, the government, contractors, or non-governmental organizations to promote them. If the suppliers in question—typically poor small farmers—cannot sell what they produce, who bears the cost? Not the donors, the government, contractors, or non-governmental organizations, but the intended beneficiaries themselves, the small farmers who can least afford the risk.

> **2. Is This Approach "Demand-driven"?**
>
> "A few private companies in Madagascar offer a range of business services but they appear expensive, and as such are rarely used by small and medium sized agribusinesses. In identifying commercial solutions..., the contractor will develop private-sector suppliers. ...This can be done in building local capacity for commercial service provision to ensure sustainable impacts."
>
> Draft donor scope of work for program in Madagascar, 2003.

The statement in the second box is similarly self-contradictory. Few companies in Madagascar are willing to buy business development services. Yet the strategy proposed is to build even more capacity on the supply side of the equation, attempting to resolve with more supply what, in essence, remains a problem of insufficient demand.

In the end, the market for business development services is a derived-demand market, and will not grow unless demand for those services grows. Operationally, the trick to expanding the business development services market is to concentrate on expanding the volume of sales of its client businesses. It is that growth that will provide the inducement for service providers either to expand or to start up in the first place (see the discussion of sustainability in Chapter 8).

3. Is This Approach "Demand-driven"?

"Many food processors are only working three to six months out of the year [to process fruit]. ...There is a need for cold storage to store more product to process longer."

Consultant report for program in Azerbaijan, 2005.

The statement in the third box fails to distinguish between demand and need. Technocratically, there is need for cold storage, but that does not mean that anyone is able and willing to pay for it—or for the additional processed fruit production it would presumably facilitate. In the final analysis, cold storage is only a way of increasing supply, which, by itself, says nothing about effective demand.

In practice, economists and non-economists alike often use the terms, "demand," "need," and "interest," almost interchangeably. But the need for or the interest in something is quite different from the demand for something, which implies ability and willingness to pay. Most elementary economics texts highlight this distinction, but it seems to get lost in practice.

The failure to distinguish clearly between need and demand is not just an academic concern. It can have serious consequences. Many development programs commence operations by canvassing their target populations, asking them what they need. When the programs respond to those needs—with grants of machinery and equipment, for example—they often justify their actions as demand-driven. The grants may help the people in question produce more, but by themselves, the grants offer no assurance of effective demand—buyers—for the additional goods and services. White elephant factories throughout the world bear ample witness to the possibility that if they build it, they may very well not come.

The PRA final report gives the following example to make the point:

> Under the Alternative Development Program, a number of pineapple-producing communities in Aguaytía signed agreements to eradicate their coca. In negotiating the agreements, the producers "demanded" that the program plant

an additional 80 hectares of smooth cayenne pineapple, presumably to satisfy the market.

In fact, the market for smooth cayenne pineapple is very much a niche market—and, at the time, was limited largely to supermarkets in Lima. As PRA talked to those supermarkets, it became clear that they were ready and willing to buy smooth cayenne pineapple only in much smaller quantities than what 80 additional hectares would yield. If the communities added more than 11.5 hectares, in fact, there was a real danger that the market would be flooded and sales prices pushed substantially downward, thereby jeopardizing the very people the expansion of hectares was meant to benefit.

The farmers in the coca-eradicating communities undoubtedly thought that adding 80 hectares of smooth cayenne pineapple made good economic sense, but their "demand" did not meet the market test. From this case and many others, PRA has learned to distinguish clearly between *demand* and *need* or *interest*. A potential client's request for some kind of support from a development program is not demand. A buyer disposed to purchase a good or service in a certain quantity, of a certain quality, at a certain time, is. Even though reacting to the perceived needs or interests of potential clients may be a good thing to do in some circumstances, it is not demand-driven development.[51]

The need for something can be so compelling technocratically that it can be very difficult for a demand-driven program to stay the course and say no. A few years ago, furniture makers in La Paz, Bolivia, lobbied hard for someone, anyone, to invest in a drying facility, arguing that the unavailability of dried wood was the biggest obstacle to producing and selling high-value furniture— and that solving that problem would benefit both the sector and the country enormously. They may very well have been right, but if they were, why were they unwilling to invest in a drying facility themselves? If they could add so much value to their product, would not the market pay them more for its higher quality? Interestingly, none of the furniture makers stepped to the plate and took the lead, suggesting that maybe the venture was not quite so profitable as they professed. In the final analysis, the furniture makers were acting essentially as free riders, waiting to board someone else's train for free: yes, there was a need for something, but not a solid enough business proposition for people to put their money on the line. Needless to say, it is hard for a development program to nudge a promising business proposition along if the businesspeople in question look to the program to pay the freight.

---

4. Is This Approach "Demand-driven"?

"The Green Revolution for Africa has a clear logic model behind it. If AGRA [the Alliance for a Green Revolution in Africa] can provide farmers with more resilient seed varieties and if it can then supplement them with strategies to enhance soil fertility, greater and more stable crop yields will result. And if AGRA can do all that where more equitable and efficient agricultural markets prevail..., then those increased yields should lead to increased profits for the farmers. In turn the combinations of higher yields and profits will lead to greater food security and economic growth for the farmers and their countries."

Jon Gertner, "For Good Measure," The Money Issue, New York Times, nytimes.com, March 9, 2008.

The fourth statement appears here not because the approach outlined therein claims to be demand-driven, but because it basically assumes demand away. Bringing the Green Revolution to Africa has its obvious merits, but to assume that equitable and efficient markets will absorb the resultant increases in production is a risky proposition. There are too many instances worldwide in which initiatives to expand production dramatically have not had the positive consequences intended and, in certain instances, in fact, have actually harmed the very people they purported to benefit—through steep drops in prices, for example. Even in a cause as noble as the Green Revolution, therefore, it behooves the development practitioner to tie down demand beforehand.

A fifth example is also of interest, not because it comes from development circles but because it gets at how development practitioners often think. The example comes from the dictionary, and is the definition of "marketing."

> ### 5. Is This Approach "Demand-driven"?
>
> "mar•ket•ing
> Function: noun
> 1 a: the act or process of selling or purchasing in a market b: the process or technique of promoting, selling, and distributing a product or service
> 2: an aggregate of functions involved in moving goods from producer to consumer."
>
> Merriam-Webster Online Dictionary, 2006.

Many people assume that marketing is a demand-driven approach to business. When practiced correctly, it is. When practiced incorrectly, however, much marketing is actually supply-push.

A widely used textbook on marketing defines the term as follows:

> The marketing concept means that an organization aims all of its efforts at satisfying its customers—at a profit...The marketing concept is not a new idea—it's been around for a long time. But some managers show little interest in customers' needs. These managers still have a production orientation—making whatever products are easy to produce and *then* trying to sell them...Well-managed firms have replaced this production orientation with a marketing orientation. A marketing orientation means trying to carry out the marketing concept. Instead of just trying to get customers to buy what the firm has produced, a market-oriented firm tries to offer the customer what they need.[52]

In common development parlance, unfortunately, marketing frequently means taking a product already in hand and finding somebody to buy it— that is, starting with supply and finding demand. Most development practitioners are not students of marketing.

> "Gaining a foothold in the marketplace is the artisans' first step toward creating lasting, sustainable enterprises."
>
> "Aiding African Artisans," *aid to artisans: From Maker to Market*, Winter, 2005, p. 5.

Rather, having learned what they think marketing means through operational osmosis, they wind up willy-nilly applying the dictionary approach: instead of helping businesses ascertain what buyers really want and produce to those specifications, they take what businesses already produce as a given, help them produce more or better, and only then worry about who will actually buy the product in question.

Examining how development practitioners commonly practice marketing points up how people bring to the development arena thought patterns they have inherited uncritically. For example, economists are schooled in the micro-economic proposition that supply equals demand when markets clear, thus suggesting to the practitioner with economics training that neither enjoys operational primacy over the other.[53] But the paradigm shifts practitioners need to make are not confined to the micro-economic sphere. Friedman cites the following example:

> "The day after...I happened to go to Israel and meet with Jacob Frenkel, governor of Israel's Central Bank and a University of Chicago-trained economist. Frenkel remarked that he too was going through a perspective change: "Before, when we talked about macroeconomics, we started by looking at the local markets, local financial systems and the interrelationship between them, and then, as an afterthought, we looked at the international economy. There was a feeling that what we do is primarily our own business and then there are some outlets where we will sell abroad. Now we reverse the perspective. Let's not ask what markets we should export to, after having decided what to produce; rather let's first study the global framework within which we operate and then decide what to produce. It changes your whole perspective."[54]

Interestingly, many development practitioners are willing to accept the argument that lack of demand constitutes developing economies' principal constraint and argue, accordingly, that trade is essential for broadly based economic growth. Relatively few, though, apply the same logic to micro-economic phenomena. Even with "market-oriented" and "demand-driven" approaches in vogue, few put the demand horse squarely in front of the supply cart. It is one thing to argue for connections with markets; it is quite another to look to—and accept—demand as the engine of the process. Development experience is replete with agricultural technology transfer programs that have foundered in the absence of demand. But development experience also points up the opposite side of the coin: small farmers can and will adopt modern practices, but when they know beforehand that someone will buy their product at an acceptable price. In short, when demand is present, it furnishes incentives to address supply constraints; when it is absent, attacking supply constraints is tantamount to pushing on a string.

The literature that has burgeoned in recent years on the importance of non-farm income to poor farm households is a further illustration of the need to rethink inherited development paradigms. Although the literature in question acknowledges the potentially significant role that linkages with intermediate cities can play in reducing poverty, the underlying paradigm arguably has it backwards: instead of starting at the market and looking back to the farm, it starts at the farm and looks out to the market. In the final analysis, the thinking is the conventional production-based farm management model with demand simply grafted on to it. Again, despite claims to be demand-driven, the model is really supply-push: do what you normally do on-farm and then figure out how to connect to the market afterwards—as opposed to taking the market as the starting point and adjusting productive activity to it.

> "When it comes to finding a better job for this poor farmer, the question is: Is there someone out there who wants or might want to buy something that this poor farmer is or could be producing?"
>
> Charles Patterson, Strategies for International Development, personal communication with the author, 2008.

Save the Children in Bolivia uses Exhibit 2.3 as a didactic device to shock its personnel into internalizing the point. If consumers want square watermelons, sell them square watermelons. Do not go blithely on producing regular watermelons if that is not what they want to buy.

Exhibit 2.3 Save the Children Pedagogical Tool in Bolivia

MARKET FOCUS

PRODUCE WHAT
YOU CAN SELL

AND DO NOT

SELL WHAT YOU
PRODUCE

Save the Children.

To sum up, development practitioners' thinking frequently is *"sell what you produce,"* when what is called for is *"produce what you can sell."* A market-driven approach is not one that figures out how to sell one's given product. It is one that heeds what the market is demanding—quantity-, quality-, and timing-wise—in the first place.

Practical Implications of a Demand-Driven Approach

In the marketplace of supply and demand, poor people are generally suppliers. Under a demand-driven approach to development, however, the first task is not to help the poor produce more. Rather, it is first and foremost to help them identify sources of demand and, then and only then, to help them respond to that demand.

"I'm still amazed that the notion of taking a sourcing approach to developing production remains such an erudite concept. We recently met a fellow who returned from 30 years in the Boston area to start a farm in the Dominican Republic. He was growing beautiful tomatoes with an excellent mini irrigation system he'd installed with help from an IDB [Inter-American Development Bank] technology transfer project...but not only had he not chosen his production based on the market, but one month after planting he was still not sure where he was going to sell! Mind boggling."

John Horton, Inter-American Development Bank, email to the author, December 15, 2006.

Giving primacy to the demand side of the equation is not to ignore the supply side. Of course it makes sense to focus on solving production-related problems, but only—repeat, only—after—repeat, after—the development practitioner has seen to it that the demand side is tied down. **PRA spent roughly two thirds of its budget on supply-side problems, but only after identifying who in fact was going to buy that additional supply in the first place.**

Experience under USAID's Competitiveness Enhancement and Enterprise Development (CEED) program in Moldova squares with that pattern. CEED saw the potential for local apparel companies to sell to sophisticated Western European buyers, but only if they made significant productivity improvements. The program helped one to improve production flow, which allowed it to sell to a fashion giant in Milan and invest in an industrial-size enterprise that now employs 40 people. It helped another improve productivity by 26 percent, enabling it to sell to the Dutch fashion retailer M&S.[55]

Exhibit 2.4 makes the point diagrammatically. Although product moves physically from producer to consumer, programmatically the starting point must be the market, not the supplier. Adopting a market-driven approach does not mean producing what you normally do and then figuring out how to connect to the market afterwards. It is connecting to the market first and then figuring out how to satisfy what that market really wants.

In the late 1980s, Peru's government took very much the opposite approach, and suffered the consequences. Since farmers in

Exhibit 2.4 Demand as the Driver

Demand Pulls Supply

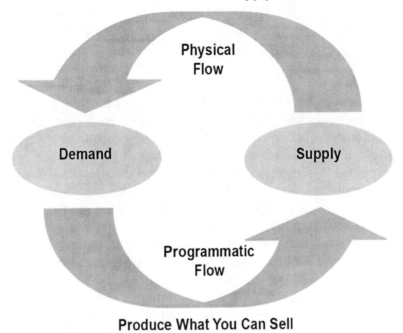

Produce What You Can Sell

Source: USAID/Peru Poverty Reduction and Alleviation program.

the south of the country were among the country's poorest people, it decided to help them improve their lot. Unfortunately, it fell into a common logical trap, concluding that because the south produced lots of potatoes, it made good sense to promote even more potato production there. After the government subsidized farmers' production inputs through a variety of means, potato production boomed. With inelastic demand, however, prices plummeted. Even with the subsidies, the farmers had difficulty covering their costs, and a well intentioned policy wound up hurting the very people it was supposed to help. It also had serious political consequences as many of the farmers took to the streets in ugly street demonstrations in front of the Ministry of Agriculture.

"Goods have value only
if consumers want them.
Otherwise sheer production does
little to raise standards of living."

William W. Lewis, "The power of
productivity: Poor countries should put
their consumers first," *McKinsey Quarterly*,
No. 2, 2004, http://www.mckinseyquarterly.
com/Public_Sector/Economic_Policy/
The_power_of_productivity_1423.

This example illustrates dramatically how things can go wrong when development practitioners fail to take the demand-driven principle seriously. It also suggests the desirability of spelling out in explicit detail two corollaries of that principle that strike at the heart of much conventional development wisdom:

The demand for the products of the countryside is typically found in cities. The starting point for fostering rural development, therefore, is the city. Most developing countries spend considerable energy debating the advisability of giving preference to the city or to the countryside. Much of that debate is a straw man. Operationally, the issue is not whether to favor one over the other, but to bring the two together in firm commercial relationships. In short, the well bandied distinction between city and countryside does not make much programmatic sense—nor, analogously, does the proclivity of funding agencies to set up programs separately for agriculture and for non-agriculture.[56]

"I am not preaching Tolstoyan austerity and the return to the land. ...Our economy is too mixed. What we produce ourselves—potatoes and vegetables—is only a small part of what we need; the rest comes from other sources."

Doctor Zhivago

Boris Pasternak, *Doctor Zhivago* (New York: Pantheon Books, Inc., 1958), p. 232.

The demand for the goods and services produced by micro- and small enterprises is typically found in medium and large enterprises. The starting point for fostering the growth of micro- and small enterprises, therefore, is medium and large enterprises. Only market demand will furnish adequate incentive for micro- and small enterprises to increase (in size) and multiply (in numbers). In other words, improving the lot of micro- and small entrepreneurs means looking elsewhere—to the sources of demand for their goods and services. Doing so is not "trickle-down" economics, but a simple recognition of the demand-driven nature of the development process as well as the employment-generating potential of outsourcing mechanisms, a point explored in some depth below.

In short, all points of entry for generating sales and jobs are not created equal. Demand is the driver and that is where one must start.

Operationally, Demand Means a Buyer with a Name and Address

When PRA began operating in Peru, it went about identifying demand in fairly conventional fashion. It commissioned 11 traditional market studies, but, very tellingly, none of them bore fruit. The typical market study collects detailed information on supply—for example, the kinds of pineapples growing in the jungles of Peru, farming practices there, and potential production volume. It also provides statistical information from international sources, pointing out, for example, that "demand for pineapples has been increasing three percent per year in Brazil." Strangely, though, most market studies offer relatively few specifics on the market itself—for example, which companies actually buy pineapple and in what quantities.[57]

Somewhat paradoxically, at the very time PRA was conducting its market studies it scored its first success—one that entailed identifying a real buyer and linking it with a real supplier. The program had just opened an office in La Merced, a market town on the eastern slope of the Andes, and was canvassing it for business prospects. It made contact with Teresa Romero, a small-scale entrepreneur. Romero owned several trucks, which she used to buy pineapples from growers in the area, truck them westward over the Andes, and resell them—at rock-bottom prices—in the wholesale market in Lima.

Meanwhile, back at PRA's office in Lima, a staffer was talking with the president of Nutreina, a large pineapple company based in the coastal city of Pisco, south of Lima. Nutreina imported its pineapples from Ecuador, hundreds of expensive miles to the north.

PRA introduced Nutreina to Romero, and the two formed a mutually beneficial business alliance. Romero was able not only to sell her pineapples at a higher price in a secure market, but to pass along some of the windfall to the pineapple growers. Nutreina, in turn, paid less for pineapples than it did when it bought them from Ecuador.

The experience with Nutreina and Romero called into serious question the advisability of investing substantially more time and resources in studies, statistics, and reports. Matchmaking the two parties taught program managers a valuable lesson that they adopted thereafter: not only to tie demand down before everything else, but to tie it down in very personal terms.[58]

Interestingly, the only PRA-supported market study that turned into anything was one for artichokes. In contrast to the generic studies at the beginning of the program, the artichoke study addressed **specific questions that already identified and committed investors said they needed answers to before putting their money on the table**—essentially where to sell and in what form. The marked expansion in artichoke production in the Peruvian Sierra has its roots in that study.

Operationally, studies, statistics, and reports mean very little unless they lead you to someone with a first name, a last name, a telephone number, and an address—in today's world, an email address—able and willing to buy your product. As a practical matter, demand means orders.

7

Market Chains, Building Trust, and Job Creation

By definition, linking demand with supply entails forging relationships between buyers and sellers. In practice, the smooth functioning of those relationships hinges heavily on trust. Interestingly, experience suggests that the nurturing of trust between buyers and sellers is the most important service a development program can provide them. More than that, it suggests that building trust can have a big payoff in job creation. This chapter touches on these themes. It shows:

How demand and supply meet in "market chains";
How nurturing trust typically is the most important service a development program can provide market chains; and
How trust building, especially between connector firms and their suppliers, can generate jobs.

Demand and Supply Meet in Market Chains

Individual businesses—not products, sectors, industries, clusters, or projects—make productive investments. Although businesses have shared problems—and sometimes collective action is necessary to resolve them—the individual business is the place for a development program to start to have an impact. That said, businesses do not operate in isolation. Often the problems that most constrain their growth lie beyond their direct control—for example, in the markets they sell to or the suppliers they source from.

The concept of a market chain is useful both for understanding the context in which a business works and for guiding the activities of development practitioners in bringing about increases in sales and jobs. Exhibit 2.5 illustrates the concept and serves as a point of reference for much of the discussion that follows.

Exhibit 2.5 The Market Chain

| Program Activities | | Vertically Coordinated Market Chain Driven by Demand |
Conventional Business Development Services	Facilitation	
• Identify and engage buyer		Final Demand ◄
	• Facilitate commercial relationship between buyer and connector firm, including delivery of assistance to connector firm and of product to buyer	*Orders* ↓ *Delivery*
• Identify and engage connector firm • Identify and solve problems related to: • Marketing • Technology • Management • Access to finance		Connector Firm (large or medium processor/trader) ◄
	• Facilitate commercial relationship between connector firm and suppliers, including delivery of assistance to suppliers and of product to connector firm	*Orders* ↓ *Delivery*
• Identify and engage suppliers • Identify and solve problems related to: • Marketing • Technology • Management • Access to finance		Suppliers (micro, small, and medium enterprises)

Source: Adaptation of USAID/Nigeria Maximizing Agricultural Revenue and Key Enterprises in Targeted Sites (MARKETS) Work Plan FY 2006.

The first thing to note about the concept of a market chain is its name. This book chooses to introduce new terminology instead of using other terms—"supply chain" and "value chain," for instance—commonly in use. Why? The guiding concept here differs from the concept of a supply chain because, once again, where one starts and ends programmatically runs counter to where one starts and ends physically. In a similar vein, value chains commonly span entire sectors or industries, whereas the commercial relationships of interest here are much more circumscribed, revolving around one—and only one—connector firm.

Most businesspeople use the expression, "supply chain," to describe the process of creating goods and delivering them to market. Although the term indicates the direction goods and services actually move, the starting point for transactions is not suppliers, but the buyers that communicate their requirements to suppliers. In the right panel of the exhibit, therefore, the arrow points downward, not upward. The direction of the arrow is not an academic nicety. It transmits a vital lesson for development practitioners: it makes no sense to work on problems with suppliers until you are first sure that there are specific, known buyers. For example, it makes no sense to help the Shipibo-Conibo produce more pottery until the connector firm, American Trading, knows what Pier 1 Imports actually wants.

Interestingly, Whirlpool has become famous in international business circles precisely for deviating from the conventional supply chain approach:

> Looking to the future, what would it mean to be world-class in supply chain performance?
>
> The decision we made at this very early point in the process was, I think, a pivotal one. We decided that we could answer that question only by focusing on customer requirements first. Our approach to developing our supply chain strategy would be to start with the last link—the consumer—and proceed backward.
>
> It's an obvious thought, isn't it? Except that it wasn't. The overwhelming tendency in a manufacturing organization is to think about the supply chain as something that originates

with the supply base and moves forward. It's understandable: This is the part of the chain over which the company
has control. But the unfortunate effect is that supply chain
initiatives typically run out of steam before they get to their
end point—and real point.[59]

In recent years international donors—USAID, especially—have
been promoting "value chains" as a framework for enhancing the
competitiveness of industries and contributing to the reduction of
poverty. According to USAID,

> A value chain is a supply chain made up of a series of
> actors—from input suppliers to producers and processors
> to exporters and buyers—engaged in the full range of ac-
> tivities required to bring a product from its conception to
> its end use.[60]

Although the proponents of the value chain approach acknowledge that the consolidation of linkages between buyers and sellers
must come before the building of cooperative relationships among
buyers or sellers, most value chain analysis gravitates toward bringing as many actors as possible under the tent, making value chain
analysis almost indistinguishable from the supposedly broader
analysis of clusters discussed below. Again, as USAID puts it,

> The Value Chain Approach assesses the constraints to
> and opportunities for enhancing an industry's competitive-
> ness through a diagnostic framework that includes five [sic]
> elements:

> End Market Opportunities
> Enabling Environment (international and national)
> Inter-firm Cooperation: Vertical Linkages
> Inter-firm Cooperation: Horizontal Linkages
> Supporting markets (sector-specific and non-sector specific
> services, including financial services)
> Firm-level Upgrading (product and process upgrading)[61]

Exhibit 2.6, taken from the same reference, portrays the potentially all-encompassing reach of value chain analysis diagrammatically.[62] Although elegant intellectually, the framework falls into the same trap as many strategic frameworks commonly in use (for examples, see the appendix to this part of the book). In its urge not to leave anything out, the value chain framework induces practitioners to study everything before doing anything and, in the process, keeps them a step removed from the transaction-specific constraints that often stand most in the way of facilitating sales and generating jobs. Again, the Shipibo-Conibo ceramics example is pertinent: yes, it would have been nice if the overall environment had been more conducive to artisanry production, but the problems jeopardizing the Pier 1 Imports deal were very much cut and dried. It was obviously imperative to understand the constraints facing American Trading, the connector firm in question, but a sweeping industry-wide value-chain analysis would have been of little use.

Exhibit 2.6 The Value Chain

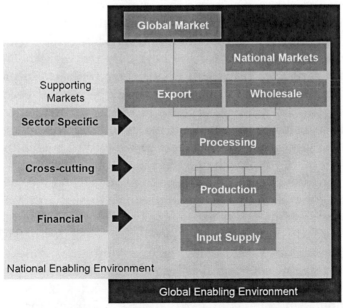

Source: USAID Accelerated Microenterprise Advancement Project–Business Development Services.

None of this discussion is to downplay the potential significance of the overall enabling environment in boosting sales. The discussion that follows argues for a pragmatic problem-solving approach to facilitating the growth of market chains. If the key constraint goes beyond the capacity of the market chain to solve itself—the allocation of public monies for road construction and rehabilitation, for example—then broaden your focus and attack it, by all means. But do not walk in thinking that solving the big picture is the answer. If you can solve a problem with a backhoe, there is no reason to bring in a bulldozer.

To sum up, the market chain is a useful construct for looking at relationships between buyers and sellers. Operationally, it underlies much of the buyer-led approach. It also underlies much of the discussion in this book.

Fostering Trust

Most economic theory assumes that the parties to a business transaction trust each other.[63] Consumers trust the beef they buy from the grocery store is uncontaminated. Connector firms trust the grocery store will pay them for the beef they deliver. And ranchers trust that connector firms will honor their contracts to pay them for the beef they have raised. In the developed world people usually take trust for granted, because most buyers and sellers know and act according to the social norms governing business relationships. And when they do not, there are laws and law enforcement to make sure they honor their agreements and contracts.

In many developing countries, social norms and the rule of law are not strong enough to engender mutual trust, and many economic transactions taken for granted in developed countries are much more difficult to carry out. Large buyers and small sellers—processing factories and isolated farm communities, for example—often hold deeply set prejudices against one another.

Take, for example, Piscifactoría de los Andes, a trout processing company in Huancayo, Peru, and SAIS Tupac Amaru, a large farm that lies almost next door. For years Piscifactoría could have sold up to three times what its own ponds could produce, but the company was hesitant to source from third parties. For its part, the SAIS, a *hacienda* that the Peruvian government had expropriated and turned over to small farmers in the 1970s, had once produced quality trout, but its ponds had deteriorated over the years.

Processing trout at Piscifactoría's plant. *Photo:* USAID/Peru Poverty Reduction and Alleviation program.

By the time PRA came along in 2001, the SAIS was bankrupt and profoundly suspicious of overtures from outsiders, and Piscifactoría had dismissed working with them as a losing proposition. In short, there was a complete lack of trust between the two parties. To put it in stereotypes common in colloquial English, the SAIS regarded Piscifactoría as a "fat cat" waiting to rip them off, while Piscifactoría saw the small farmers as "lazy slobs" whom they could not count on to deliver enough quality fish on time.

PRA recognized that an alliance between the two would not only make more money for Piscifactoría but provide jobs for poor SAIS farmers. But to wed supply to demand, PRA had to play the role of honest broker.

One of PRA's business promoters spent almost a year nurturing trust between the two parties, breaking down preconceptions and convincing them to join together in a commercial relationship. People came to refer to him as the human ping-pong ball because he bounced back and forth between the two so many times. In the end, Piscifactoría agreed to invest $70,000 in rehabilitating the SAIS's ponds and to furnish raw materials and technical assistance. The SAIS agreed to abide by Piscifactoría's technical direction and sell trout to Piscifactoría at a mutually agreed upon price.

Piscifactoría has sourced from the SAIS for a number of years now. Despite periodic hiccups, the experience with SAIS Tupac Amaru has made Piscifactoría a believer in the value of contracting production out to third parties. Applying that model, it has now expanded en masse to three other regions of Peru, expanding sales by $5.8 million and creating 550 jobs.

> "[T]he market transaction that takes place is more than a quick financial exchange: it is the culmination of a long and ongoing process of interaction between the parties."
>
> Marjolein C.J. Caniëls, Henny A. Romjin, and Marieke de Ruijter-De Wildt, "Can Business Development Services practitioners learn from theories of innovation and services marketing?" *Development in Practice*, XVI (No. 5, 2006), p. 437.

The first two panels of Exhibit 2.5 distinguish between conventional business development services and "facilitation," the type of honest brokering exemplified by PRA's experience with Piscifactoría and SAIS Tupac Amaru. In that case, facilitation, not the delivery of conventional business development services by a third party, was the deal maker. But that experience was not an isolated case. As an independent evaluation of PRA as a whole concluded,

> [W]hat is most lacking to the successful forging of the marketing link along the value chain is trust between the parties to a deal. The long history of mutual deception between buyer and seller has left an attitude of mutual distrust that is extremely difficult to overcome. In fact, the evidence of this investigation suggests that the role of the ESC [PRA's Economic Service Center] advisor as a "moral guarantor" of the performance of the parties to a deal is as important as any technical or informational input.[64]

To reach this conclusion the evaluation team met confidentially and one on one with PRA's principal clients. When they asked those clients to assess the assistance they had received from the program, one after the other used the word, *acompañamiento*, to describe the big difference PRA had made. Yes, they appreciated PRA's help in identifying new buyers, in bringing in modern technology, in improving their management. But what they most appreciated was the ESC advisors "accompanying" them in new and unfamiliar business transactions. Whether in discussing prices or delivery dates or quality standards, the ESC advisors were there to help clients interpret, understand, and gain confidence in themselves and their business partners. In short, they drew strength from the ready access to an independent third party willing to serve as a sounding board for testing ideas and as a source of objective advice and encouragement.

Since leaving Peru, the author has seen the key role accompaniment has played in other programs, and his contacts with colleagues throughout the world attest to the same conclusion. The high premium clients attach to accompaniment is not peculiar to Peru, but is a worldwide phenomenon.

Even though many practitioners see honest brokering as the linchpin of their work, many program designs still give higher priority to the provision of conventional business development services.[65] The buyer-led approach shifts the focus consciously to facilitation, which experience suggests likely has a higher return.

Outsourcing Within Market Chains Generates Jobs

Another way to look at Exhibit 2.5 is as an outsourcing scheme. In developed countries, many see "outsourcing" as the transfer of domestic jobs overseas, and thus the very word carries with it negative connotations. In fact, the use of outsourcing, domestically as well as internationally, is quite widespread. In general, connector firms can produce their raw materials themselves or they can procure them from third parties. More and more, connector firms throughout the world are choosing the second option, opening up opportunities for small farmers and micro- and small enterprises to grow—and for buoyant job expansion to take place.

In 2003, the author had the pleasure of visiting the largest bakery in Bucharest, Romania. For a number of years, its managers had tried to procure wheat for their bread from local farmers, but found they could not count on them. As a back-up, they placed orders with suppliers in Kazakhstan only to find stones mixed in with the grain. As a last resort, therefore, they decided to buy an enormous state farm and grow the wheat they needed themselves. Talk about lack of trust between parties!

Fortunately or unfortunately, the bakery in Bucharest is very much the exception to the worldwide trend of firms looking to third parties to supply their intermediate goods and services. As the author put it in a different context,

> Worldwide, outsourcing is burgeoning. More than that, it is the touchstone of a veritable revolution in industrial organization. Gone are the days of Henry Ford and the assembly line. Back are the days of Adam Smith and atomization. Observers refer to the current structure of production internationally as vertical disintegration. As a practical matter, vertical disintegration means not only a breakdown of production processes into their constituent parts, but the dispersion of production geographically. Today, automobile producers contract out production of intermediate products to those locations most adept at producing them. In the end, an automobile may have well over a dozen sources of origin. In short, the structure of production worldwide has become increasingly specialized.[66]

Reliance on outsourcing mechanisms characterizes the behavior not only of multinational corporations, which receive so much press on that account, but companies in developing countries as well. Take the examples from Peru cited above. Each conforms to the market chain paradigm, each has a connector firm sourcing from small suppliers, and each generates employment on that account (see box). The 550 jobs generated by Piscifactoría de los Andes are a particularly dramatic example of outsourcing's employment impact, but, again, are by no means an isolated case. In late 2007, PRA had 194 active clients, the majority of them connector firms, and through them was reaching an estimated 37,800 micro- and small producers. Ratio-wise, the relationship is even more remarkable in Paraguay, where a year later Paraguay Vende's support for 39 connector firms had an impact on 25,000 small producers, a dramatic multiplier effect.

Source: USAID/Peru Poverty Reduction and Alleviation program.

As one might expect, the employment generated by multinational corporations through outsourcing schemes is large as well. A 2006 study estimated that Nestlé employs 38,000 people in its factories in Latin America, and, through them, sources from 150,000 farmers throughout the region.[67]

Practitioners of the buyer-led approach do not wed themselves to outsourcing as the one and only "magic bullet" to expand jobs in the countries in which they work. As a dramatic counterpoint on a large scale, much of China's job growth in recent years has come, not through backward linkages, but on the factory floor. Interestingly, though, even that phenomenon points up the power of outsourcing: it is just that in this instance Chinese firms are not the outsourcers, but the outsourcees. Regardless, promoting outsourcing through market chains normally does not constitute a radical departure from conventional business practice in the developing world.[68] On the contrary, in country after country outsourcing is a surprisingly well established business model that development practitioners can capitalize on to expand sales and generate new employment. The examples from ten other countries in the boxes below demonstrate just how widespread the use of outsourcing indeed is. Some of the cases also give a preview of how the buyer-led approach plays out in practice, to which Part III turns in detail.[69]

Market Chain Example from Bolivia

Wilma Rocha is a leader in Nueva Esperanza (New Hope), a mothers' club in El Alto, one of Bolivia's most conflict-ridden and poorest cities. For some time, members of the club had known how to sew, but until recently, most were unemployed.

USAID's Bolivia Trade and Business Competitiveness (BTBC) program was looking for ways to generate jobs for people like the members of Nueva Esperanza and introduced the club to Ametex, the largest textile exporter in Bolivia. Ametex indicated its willingness to source from Nueva Esperanza and BTBC agreed to provide the club targeted assistance to help the women increase productivity and control quality. As a result, 75 women moved from unemployment to embroidering high-end clothing for consumers abroad.

Nueva Esperanza now produces 15,000 garments for Ametex every month. It has also received orders from two other buyers, which will increase their sales by 30 percent.

With market opportunities, Nueva Esperanza has become a launching pad for its members to earn income for themselves and their households. "Now, we have our own business and we thank God for this opportunity," says Rocha.

Final Demand
Textile importers in the United States

Connector Firm
Ametex

Suppliers
Nueva Esperanza Mothers' Club

Source: USAID/Bolivia, "Success Story: Partnerships Make the Difference," La Paz, n.d., Bolivia Trade and Business Competitiveness program.

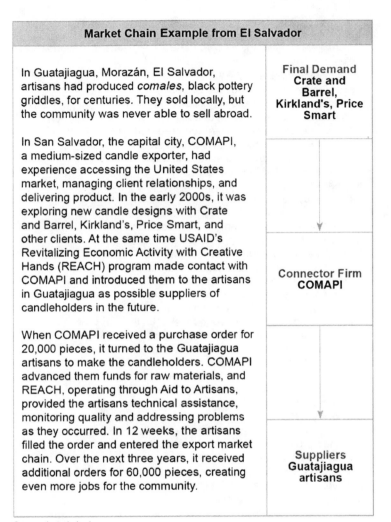

Market Chain Example from El Salvador

In Guatajiagua, Morazán, El Salvador, artisans had produced *comales*, black pottery griddles, for centuries. They sold locally, but the community was never able to sell abroad.

In San Salvador, the capital city, COMAPI, a medium-sized candle exporter, had experience accessing the United States market, managing client relationships, and delivering product. In the early 2000s, it was exploring new candle designs with Crate and Barrel, Kirkland's, Price Smart, and other clients. At the same time USAID's Revitalizing Economic Activity with Creative Hands (REACH) program made contact with COMAPI and introduced them to the artisans in Guatajiagua as possible suppliers of candleholders in the future.

When COMAPI received a purchase order for 20,000 pieces, it turned to the Guatajiagua artisans to make the candleholders. COMAPI advanced them funds for raw materials, and REACH, operating through Aid to Artisans, provided the artisans technical assistance, monitoring quality and addressing problems as they occurred. In 12 weeks, the artisans filled the order and entered the export market chain. Over the next three years, it received additional orders for 60,000 pieces, creating even more jobs for the community.

Final Demand
Crate and Barrel, Kirkland's, Price Smart

Connector Firm
COMAPI

Suppliers
Guatajiagua artisans

Source: Joseph Jordan.

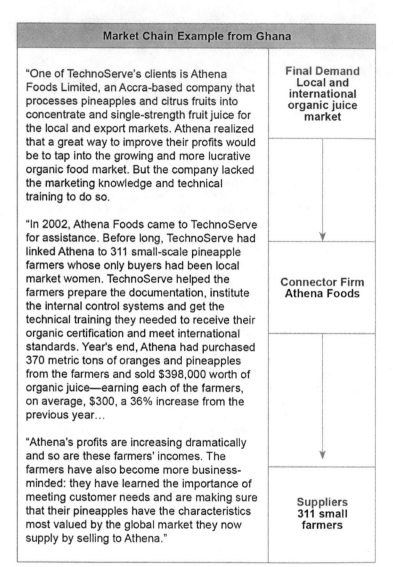

Market Chain Example from Ghana

"One of TechnoServe's clients is Athena Foods Limited, an Accra-based company that processes pineapples and citrus fruits into concentrate and single-strength fruit juice for the local and export markets. Athena realized that a great way to improve their profits would be to tap into the growing and more lucrative organic food market. But the company lacked the marketing knowledge and technical training to do so.

"In 2002, Athena Foods came to TechnoServe for assistance. Before long, TechnoServe had linked Athena to 311 small-scale pineapple farmers whose only buyers had been local market women. TechnoServe helped the farmers prepare the documentation, institute the internal control systems and get the technical training they needed to receive their organic certification and meet international standards. Year's end, Athena had purchased 370 metric tons of oranges and pineapples from the farmers and sold $398,000 worth of organic juice—earning each of the farmers, on average, $300, a 36% increase from the previous year...

"Athena's profits are increasing dramatically and so are these farmers' incomes. The farmers have also become more business-minded: they have learned the importance of meeting customer needs and are making sure that their pineapples have the characteristics most valued by the global market they now supply by selling to Athena."

Final Demand
Local and international organic juice market

Connector Firm
Athena Foods

Suppliers
311 small farmers

Source: TechnoServe, "Organic Market Proves Sweet for Ghana Pineapple Farmers," *World: A Newsletter for Friends of TechnoServe*, Winter 2003/2004, p. 2.

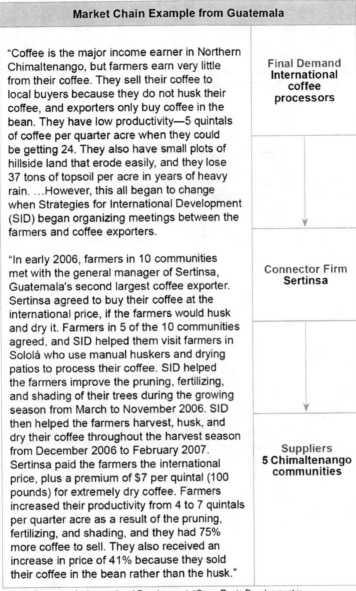

Market Chain Example from Guatemala	
"Coffee is the major income earner in Northern Chimaltenango, but farmers earn very little from their coffee. They sell their coffee to local buyers because they do not husk coffee, and exporters only buy coffee in the bean. They have low productivity—5 quintals of coffee per quarter acre when they could be getting 24. They also have small plots of hillside land that erode easily, and they lose 37 tons of topsoil per acre in years of heavy rain. ...However, this all began to change when Strategies for International Development (SID) began organizing meetings between the farmers and coffee exporters.	**Final Demand** **International coffee processors**
"In early 2006, farmers in 10 communities met with the general manager of Sertinsa, Guatemala's second largest coffee exporter. Sertinsa agreed to buy their coffee at the international price, if the farmers would husk and dry it. Farmers in 5 of the 10 communities agreed, and SID helped them visit farmers in Sololá who use manual huskers and drying patios to process their coffee. SID helped the farmers improve the pruning, fertilizing, and shading of their trees during the growing season from March to November 2006. SID then helped the farmers harvest, husk, and dry their coffee throughout the harvest season from December 2006 to February 2007. Sertinsa paid the farmers the international price, plus a premium of $7 per quintal (100 pounds) for extremely dry coffee. Farmers increased their productivity from 4 to 7 quintals per quarter acre as a result of the pruning, fertilizing, and shading, and they had 75% more coffee to sell. They also received an increase in price of 41% because they sold their coffee in the bean rather than the husk."	**Connector Firm** **Sertinsa** **Suppliers** **5 Chimaltenango communities**

Source: Strategies for International Development, "Grass Roots Development in Chimaltenango, Guatemala," Washington, D.C., n.d.

Market Chain Example from Kosovo

Until very recently, most of the high-end cheese and yogurt sold in food establishments in Kosovo came from abroad. For local companies able to meet international standards, this situation represented a nice import-substitution sales opportunity.

With technical assistance from USAID's Kosovo Cluster and Business Support (KCBS) program, four local dairy processors are now making new cheeses and yogurts for the local market. The new products are replacing imports as consumers discover locally produced cheeses and yogurts that taste great.

One processor, Abi Company, has added feta, ricotta, and mozzarella cheeses to its production line. Abi's new mozzarella has won favor in popular pizzerias. Another processor, Rona, has developed new yogurts and feta, mozzarella, ricotta, and gouda cheeses. A third processor, Shala, upgraded its cheese processing, and added feta and whey drinks to its product line. Ajka, the fourth processor, improved its yogurts and launched a whey drink product. The processors each buy about 5,000 more liters of milk from local dairy farms each day and have boosted their income from new product sales by $2,000 per day.

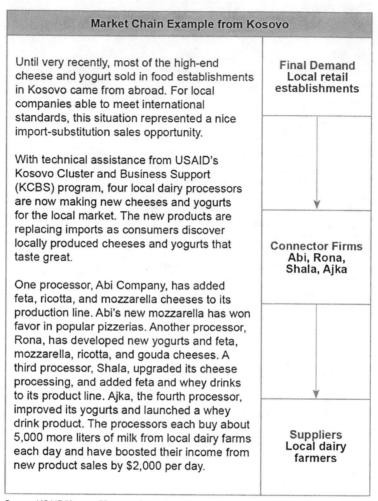

Final Demand
Local retail
establishments

Connector Firms
Abi, Rona,
Shala, Ajka

Suppliers
Local dairy
farmers

Source: USAID/Kosovo, "Success Story: New Cheeses Capture Local Market," n.d., Kosovo Cluster and Business Support program.

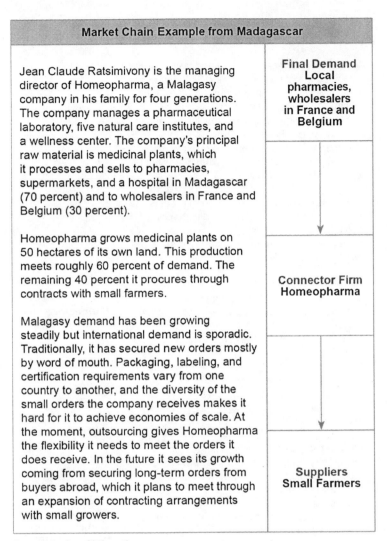

Market Chain Example from Madagascar

Jean Claude Ratsimivony is the managing director of Homeopharma, a Malagasy company in his family for four generations. The company manages a pharmaceutical laboratory, five natural care institutes, and a wellness center. The company's principal raw material is medicinal plants, which it processes and sells to pharmacies, supermarkets, and a hospital in Madagascar (70 percent) and to wholesalers in France and Belgium (30 percent).

Homeopharma grows medicinal plants on 50 hectares of its own land. This production meets roughly 60 percent of demand. The remaining 40 percent it procures through contracts with small farmers.

Malagasy demand has been growing steadily but international demand is sporadic. Traditionally, it has secured new orders mostly by word of mouth. Packaging, labeling, and certification requirements vary from one country to another, and the diversity of the small orders the company receives makes it hard for it to achieve economies of scale. At the moment, outsourcing gives Homeopharma the flexibility it needs to meet the orders it does receive. In the future it sees its growth coming from securing long-term orders from buyers abroad, which it plans to meet through an expansion of contracting arrangements with small growers.

Final Demand
Local pharmacies, wholesalers in France and Belgium

Connector Firm
Homeopharma

Suppliers
Small Farmers

Source: Interview with the author.

Market Chain Example from Mongolia

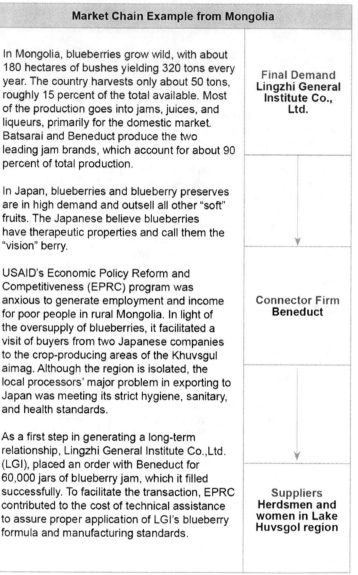

In Mongolia, blueberries grow wild, with about 180 hectares of bushes yielding 320 tons every year. The country harvests only about 50 tons, roughly 15 percent of the total available. Most of the production goes into jams, juices, and liqueurs, primarily for the domestic market. Batsarai and Beneduct produce the two leading jam brands, which account for about 90 percent of total production.

In Japan, blueberries and blueberry preserves are in high demand and outsell all other "soft" fruits. The Japanese believe blueberries have therapeutic properties and call them the "vision" berry.

USAID's Economic Policy Reform and Competitiveness (EPRC) program was anxious to generate employment and income for poor people in rural Mongolia. In light of the oversupply of blueberries, it facilitated a visit of buyers from two Japanese companies to the crop-producing areas of the Khuvsgul aimag. Although the region is isolated, the local processors' major problem in exporting to Japan was meeting its strict hygiene, sanitary, and health standards.

As a first step in generating a long-term relationship, Lingzhi General Institute Co.,Ltd. (LGI), placed an order with Beneduct for 60,000 jars of blueberry jam, which it filled successfully. To facilitate the transaction, EPRC contributed to the cost of technical assistance to assure proper application of LGI's blueberry formula and manufacturing standards.

**Final Demand
Lingzhi General
Institute Co.,
Ltd.**

**Connector Firm
Beneduct**

**Suppliers
Herdsmen and
women in Lake
Huvsgol region**

Source: Chemonics International Inc.

Market Chain Example from Pakistan

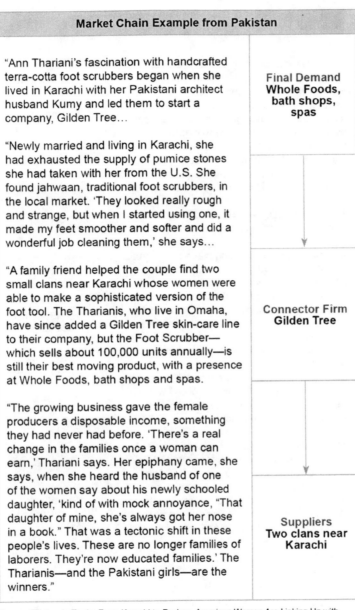

"Ann Thariani's fascination with handcrafted terra-cotta foot scrubbers began when she lived in Karachi with her Pakistani architect husband Kumy and led them to start a company, Gilden Tree...

"Newly married and living in Karachi, she had exhausted the supply of pumice stones she had taken with her from the U.S. She found jahwaan, traditional foot scrubbers, in the local market. 'They looked really rough and strange, but when I started using one, it made my feet smoother and softer and did a wonderful job cleaning them,' she says...

"A family friend helped the couple find two small clans near Karachi whose women were able to make a sophisticated version of the foot tool. The Tharianis, who live in Omaha, have since added a Gilden Tree skin-care line to their company, but the Foot Scrubber—which sells about 100,000 units annually—is still their best moving product, with a presence at Whole Foods, bath shops and spas.

"The growing business gave the female producers a disposable income, something they had never had before. 'There's a real change in the families once a woman can earn,' Thariani says. Her epiphany came, she says, when she heard the husband of one of the women say about his newly schooled daughter, 'kind of with mock annoyance, "That daughter of mine, she's always got her nose in a book." That was a tectonic shift in these people's lives. These are no longer families of laborers. They're now educated families.' The Tharianis—and the Pakistani girls—are the winners."

Final Demand
Whole Foods, bath shops, spas

Connector Firm
Gilden Tree

Suppliers
Two clans near Karachi

Source: "Sisters in Trade: From Karachi to Durban, American Women Are Linking Up with Female Artisans," *Inside Business*, *Time*, January, 2006, pp. A26-A27.

Market Chain Example from Paraguay

After three consecutive bad soybean crops, Pelagio Velázquez, a farmer in Caaguazú, Paraguay, found himself in debt and near bankruptcy. At the same time, Destisur, the main processor of sugar cane in Caaguazú, was looking for more cane to expand production of ethanol at its Guyra Hugua plant. USAID's Paraguay Vende program put Velázquez in touch with Destisur. Now Velázquez is making a new start, cultivating 30 hectares of sugar cane. After getting a loan from his brother, he contracted a tractor and employs more than ten day workers.

A small revolution is taking place in Caaguazú, fueled by demand for ethanol. To start things off, Paraguay Vende canvassed farmers in the department and put them in direct contact with Destisur to introduce them to pricing and quality issues and to nurture trust between the two parties. It hired agronomists to help them increase their yields. It also helped truck companies schedule crop pick-up and delivery times to be sure sucrose content did not drop before processing. Finally, it worked with Destisur so that small farmers could secure loans to increase production.

As of this writing, Destisur's suppliers have expanded from 100 to 500 farmers and its production has grown from 60 to 450 tons of sugar cane per day. Employment has increased by 10,000 person-days. The factory absorbs all the additional production and small producers like Pelagio Velázquez continue to expand cultivation.

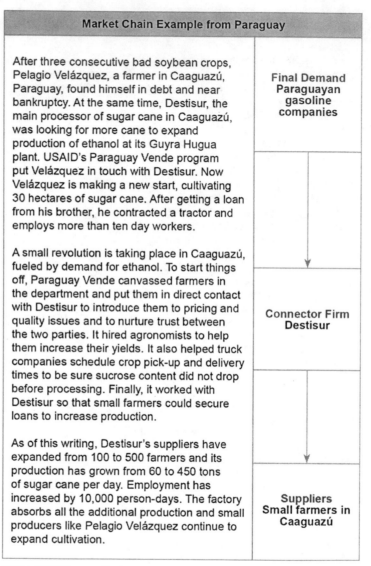

Final Demand
Paraguayan gasoline companies

Connector Firm
Destisur

Suppliers
Small farmers in Caaguazú

Source: USAID/Paraguay Vende program.

Market Chain Example from Uganda

Although sunflower is an attractive crop for small farmers in Uganda, it failed to take off until a large connector firm made a commitment to extend a high-yielding variety, pay growers attractive prices, and operate at a scale at which a broad spectrum of small growers could participate as suppliers.

Final Demand
Local market

About ten oil processors operate in Uganda. The local market is strong, as is the market for sunflower cake in Kenya. The largest processor is a company called Mukwano.

Mukwano had produced sunflower oil for some time, but had become disenchanted with the local variety. When it learned of the availability of a high-yielding hybrid seed from USAID/Uganda's Investment in Developing Export Agriculture (IDEA) program and Agricultural Productivity Enhancement Program (APEP), it decided to move ahead. IDEA and APEP also agreed to provide technical support to assure that the program involved as many small growers as feasible.

Connector Firm
Mukwano

Each production cycle, Mukwano enters into one-page contracts with growers. The contracts include the company's commitment to furnish growers improved seed at cost and to buy all they produce at a predetermined price. It also pays a premium to lead farmers for each kilogram of product it receives. In the beginning, IDEA and APEP contributed to the cost of district and site coordinators, but Mukwano has since picked up the lion's share of that cost.

Suppliers
Small growers

More than 20,000 growers participate in the program. On average, the revenue each receives has risen from $42 to $135 per hectare.

Source: Chemonics International Inc.

Of the programs applying the buyer-led approach, PRA and Paraguay Vende have had notable success in exploiting the potential of outsourcing to generate jobs. A large proportion of both programs' clients are agricultural processors or traders, which suggests that agriculture may be an especially apt place to look to create employment. Certainly the total employment effect is likely to be high if a program works with connector firms that depend heavily on agriculture locally, but, as the Bolivia textile example above illustrates, the potential is by no means limited to that sector. In the end, the issue is not so much sectoral as the degree to which connector firms have strong ties backward to the local economy.

To the degree that connector firms make a commitment to its suppliers, outsourcing can also be a powerful mechanism for technology transfer. As PRA's final report expressed it:

> Many poor producers do not have the technical knowhow to produce competitively what the market demands. In PRA's experience, the best incentive for poor people to adopt new technological practices is the existence of a specific buyer with a specific demand and the commitment of that buyer to the supply side of the equation—the transfer of technology to suppliers to produce to market requirements. Many of PRA's clients meet these criteria: for example, Piscifactoría de los Andes with a network of trout suppliers throughout the country; AGROMANTARO, with suppliers of artichokes in the Mantaro Valley; Romero Trading, with a network of organic cacao producers in San Martín; and Avena Don Lucho, with industrial oat farmers in Ayacucho. In each case, the company not only committed to buy at a minimum price; it also collaborated in the transfer of an appropriate technological package, supervised the quality of the product, assigned its best technicians to advise producers, and invested in inputs and equipment with the producers themselves. In and of itself, no development project—whether sponsored by the government, a donor, or a non-governmental organization—can replicate the incentives that the market and its economic agents bring to real transactions.

Ultimately, the key for business to increase and multiply in the *Sierra* and *Selva*—and for the effective transfer of technology to poor people there—is the presence of entrepreneurial "glue" that connects the demand of final markets and small local suppliers and brings dynamism and cohesiveness to the entire market-small producer chain. Whereas for many in Peru, development revolves around identifying "star products," for PRA, it revolves around identifying "star connector firms."

Star connector firms are critical not only in agriculture. Royal Knit specializes in the export of alpaca sweaters and accessories. To sell abroad, it participates regularly in fairs; visits potential clients; and stays abreast of trends in models, colors, and sizing. It also has invested in a product development department. Like most companies of its kind, Royal Knit always welcomes new buyers, but a key constraint over the years has been the absence of a critical mass of suppliers with the skills to knit sweaters in accordance with the requirements of exacting buyers such as Peruvian Connection. With PRA's assistance, Royal Knit has gradually solved that problem by training more workers in Puno in finishing and quality control. The company can now call on 250 people—mostly women—as needed. Some of the women have become skilled enough to train others, thereby multiplying the effect of PRA's assistance and redounding to the benefit not only of Royal Knit but of other exporters as well.[70]

Market chains dominated by what takes place "on the factory floor" can be highly labor–intensive—again, witness the boom in job creation in factories in China in recent years. Oftentimes, though, they offer very limited scope for employment generation.

In 2006, the author had the opportunity to participate in interviews of 54 firms in Antigua-Barbuda and Dominica under USAID's Caribbean Open Trade Support (COTS) program. Of the 54, only about four demonstrated any potentially significant backward linkages. Why? Because the input content of both economies is predominantly imports. Both countries depend heavily on tourism, and most hotels import practically everything, from food to furniture. One luxury hotel has the orchids for its lobby flown in from Europe even though there is a nursery no more than a half mile away. For an array of reasons, the image of local products pales against that of imports, which makes exploiting local outsourcing opportunities problematic—and generating employment more of a challenge there than elsewhere.

The same suboptimal outcome can result from pre-selecting products, sectors, or industries to support. In USAID's Competitive Enhancement and Enterprise Development (CEED) program in Moldova, for example, the design called for program managers to limit their support to three target industries, textiles and apparel, information and communication technology, and wine. Wine producers use locally grown grapes, of course, but companies in the other two industries rely heavily on imported inputs, which, all other things being equal, makes it harder to induce job creation there. As a rule, programs that limit the businesses they can work with also limit their ability to create jobs.

In sum, increasing sales normally brings about increases in jobs, but not all programs enjoy the same degree of latitude in generating employment. There is no one magic formula for how many sales will create how many jobs that will be constant all over the world. Each program must adjust its employment targets to the peculiarities of the environment in which it works. Capitalizing on outsourcing possibilities in market chains can be a very effective way to generate employment, but some program environments are more conducive than others.

8

Principles for Supporting Market Chains

In addition to the focus on building trust between buyers and sellers, there are a number of other elements that make the buyer-led approach work. This chapter discusses five key principles:

> **Focus on transactions in individual market chains.** Broaden your horizons only when doing so addresses key problems constraining growth in client sales.
> **Let the market pick the winners.** Do not pre-pick products, sectors, or clusters.
> **Tailor what you do to the specific problem you find.** Do not become a solution looking for a problem.
> **Focus on the sustainability of the market chains you support**, not of business service providers.
> **Organize what you do geographically**, not sectorally.

One Transaction at a Time

In the last decade, "competitiveness" has become a buzzword in business development circles, and many development programs around the world have incorporated it in their names. Many of those programs have supported the creation or expansion of "clusters," and a whole approach to "cluster competitiveness" has emerged. For some market chains, the cluster competitiveness approach fits the bill, but for many others, it does not.

Definitions of competitiveness are legion, but most would agree that at its core lies increasing productivity. Programmatically, therefore, developing competitiveness comes down to figuring out what program and policy actions are most cost-effective in bringing increases in productivity about.

According to Michael Porter, a nation's competitive advantage rests on four key determinants:

Factor conditions
Demand conditions
Related and supporting industries
Firm strategy, structure, and rivalry

Porter normally arrays the four determinants in a diamond to highlight the systemic interrelationships among them. He also acknowledges the significant role that government and chance can play.[71]

A nation's competitive advantage plays itself out in industries, which tend to group themselves in clusters. Formally, clusters are geographic concentrations of interconnected firms, suppliers, related industries, and specialized institutions in particular fields. When mature, clusters not only reduce transaction costs and boost efficiency, but improve incentives and create collective assets in the form of information, specialized institutions, reputation, etc. More importantly, clusters facilitate innovation, speed productivity growth, and make possible the formation of new businesses.

Porter's diamond framework is very useful for describing a cluster once it has matured. By itself, though, the framework does not tell one much about how to set priorities among competing program options to facilitate the shift from a nascent to a mature cluster, especially in a developing economy.

The concept of clusters focuses thinking both on productivity and on linkages among government entities, companies, suppliers, and local institutions. As one program put it, "[i]n today's global business, individual companies do not compete—groups of companies in a supply chain compete. These companies also depend on industry associations, government agencies, training institutions and professional associations to be effective."[72] The very breadth of competitiveness's scope makes the concept especially appealing to governments and donors. Given their desire to go beyond piecemeal successes and have as massive an impact as possible, looking at entire industries is a very attractive proposition. But proposing to have an impact on a whole industry is not the same thing as having it, as experience has borne out.

The conventional approach that has evolved to facilitate the formation of clusters in developing countries is to bring together as many parties as possible to share ideas and plot strategy, ideally around a common, actionable agenda. In practice, the approach often suffers from four major drawbacks. First, the process encourages the involvement of free riders, that is, parties willing to share in the benefits of participating, but with no real interest in investing themselves. In its best form, an "anchor firm" emerges from the process, investing heavily of its own resources and assuming a "first among equals" leadership position. In its worst form, the tendency translates into nobody investing at all and participants blaming lack of progress on third parties, especially government.[73] Second, in its well intentioned desire to contribute to the formation of clusters, donors often contribute too much—lowering the sense of ownership of the participants, and providing incentives for participants to look to others to pay the freight. Third, the plotting of strategy often fails to amount to much more than the creation of a laundry list of obstacles to the growth of the cluster, with no ordering of priorities for intervention. And fourth, rarely does the process have a clear definition of success, that is, an objective measure of how one can judge when a cluster has in fact become mature—which, in the worst case, gives cluster competitiveness practitioners the license to do "good" things without having to account in any real sense for what they add up to. Somewhat ironically, in fact, it is common for practitioners of cluster competitiveness to justify their approach by citing, not the successes of clusters in their entireties, but those of individual businesses within clusters, thereby raising

"Focusing on the firm...provides a quite different appreciation of the growth process than one gets by thinking in terms of an aggregate production function. The more disaggregated one's focus, the more Schumpeterian becomes one's vision of the growth process."

Arnold C. Harberger, "The View from the Trenches: Development Processes and Policies as Seen by a Working Professional," in *Frontiers of Development Economics: The Future in Perspective*, ed. by Gerald M. Meier and Joseph E. Stiglitz (New York: The World Bank and Oxford University Press, 2001), p. 546.

concerns, at least in some minds, about the operational usefulness of the intellectual superstructure of cluster competitiveness per se.[74]

As Porter's research itself attests, clusters grow organically from the ground up in response to the interests of its members. As noted above, it is not clusters, sectors, or industries that invest: it is individual firms that do, either individually or collectively, in response to economic incentives.[75] Looked at from that perspective, therefore, working with individual firms is not antithetical to developing clusters, but in fact is the appropriate point of entry. More than that, it squares with the way most firms grow.

As a practical matter, how do firms grow and become more competitive? Experienced businesspeople will attest that the process is not a smooth ride to riches, but one of fits and starts in which they knock off, one by one, the obstacles that stand in the way of their making money.[76] In the fictitious example in Exhibit 2.7, the business in question faces a succession of constraints to its growth. It first resolves its fundamental demand constraint, identifying a new buyer and shifting production to meet that buyer's requirements. It then deals with supply issues, raising the quality of its product. In the third instance, it handles a policy constraint, lobbying a government agency for change, most likely

> "We didn't make the choice seeing all the way; no one ever does. We do it step by step, doing our best with each one, trying to see where it will lead."
>
> Anne Perry, *We Shall Not Sleep* (New York: Ballantine Books, 2007), p. 172.

Exhibit 2.7 How Firms Grow

Problem 4 — Bigger market demands collaboration with others. Firms band together, form cluster.

Problem 3 — A regulatory agency raises objections. Companies lobby for and effect policy change.

Problem 2 — The buyer demands higher quality. The company improves its workmanship.

Problem 1 — A leather company has a limited market. It finds a new buyer, but of a new design. It adjusts its design and expands production.

Source: James T. Riordan.

in concert with other producers. And finally, it recognizes that it can go "big time" only if it agrees to collaborate with others, and participates in forming a cluster for that purpose.

Although fictitious, the example illustrates three facets of the way businesses behave. First, different businesses have different growth trajectories, and outside assistance needs to respect the peculiarities of each case, entering at the point the businesses find themselves. In sum, the nature of the problem must dictate the response. Second, most businesses would prefer to solve problems as individual business propositions, but some responses call for interaction with government on policy matters or collaboration with other parties—often both government and other businesses—to solve them. Third, the need for collaboration—or, put another way, the incentive to create clusters—normally is a function of volume. The larger the scale of the demand and the concomitant possibilities of supply, the greater the incentives will be for both copycat investors and ancillary support industries to enter the fray. The expansion of bean and corn production on the Ucayali River in Peru is a case in point (see box on next page).

The Ucayali River example illustrates a number of compelling programmatic lessons:

Once again, demand is the driver. Strategically, all the determinants of Porter's diamond are not created equal. Demand is the driver, and is what ultimately sets incentives in motion for other things to happen. Operationally, to work on the other determinants in the absence of demand does not make good programmatic sense.

All other things being equal, the best point of entry for a development program is the connector firm in a market chain. Not only is the connector firm the glue that holds the whole chain together. It is also the source of demand for suppliers—who, from an anti-poverty perspective, are normally the population of interest.

Copycatting can be a powerful force for boosting sales and jobs. Working with individual firms and addressing their problems one by one does not preclude development programs from working with other firms as well.[77] Nor does it necessarily create monopoly

Building Competitiveness from the Ground Up: The Ucayali River Basin in Peru

For almost a half a century, Peru has invested hefty sums in large irrigation schemes to water the fertile lands on its dry Pacific coast. Meanwhile, the Ucayali River, in the country's eastern jungle, recedes every year, leaving approximately 100,000 hectares of rich soil in its beds. Until recently, no one had taken on the management challenge of converting this Nile-like opportunity into a commercial venture.

In 2001, two Peruvian exporting companies asked PRA to help them grow beans on the Ucayali during the four-month dry season. Both had buyers in Colombia and needed land to grow for those markets. Although the Ucayali River was a logical choice, they had no experience in riverbeds and were reluctant to jump in alone. Given the potential for a dramatic expansion of sales and jobs, PRA decided to give them a nudge.

Three parties played catalytic roles. First, the companies supervised the entire operation and up-fronted the costs of seeds to small farmers. Second, PRA brought in a consultant in riverbed farming from Bolivia and shared the costs of the companies' technical supervision of small growers. Third, the government regularized the rights of the investors to farm what previously had been "no man's land."

In the first cycle, the companies planted 1,600 hectares, an expanse that boosted demand for labor and raised the wage rate in the region 30 percent—a dramatic, widespread effect on poverty. Later, other companies, including San Fernando, a major poultry company, grew corn for feed, and corn became even more profitable than beans. Today five companies work more than 5,000 hectares, a scale that has attracted seed, fertilizer, and machinery companies, nurturing the creation of a cluster in the area.

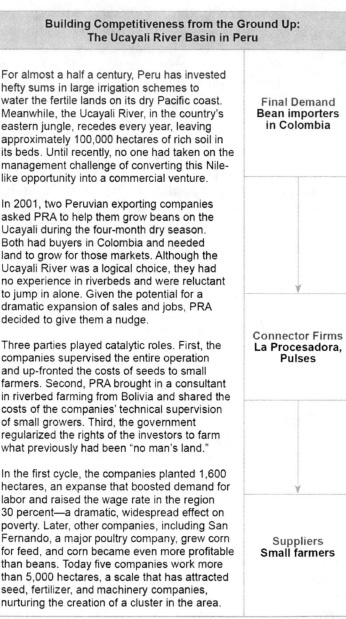

Final Demand
Bean importers in Colombia

Connector Firms
La Procesadora, Pulses

Suppliers
Small farmers

Source: USAID/Peru Poverty Reduction and Alleviation program.

positions for those it starts with. On the contrary, often the success of individual firms is precisely what piques the interest of other investors to enter the scene, saying, "If they can do it, we can do it, too." Obviously, the more firms one can work with the better, and the more firms one can entice to learn from other firms, the better.[78] The more, the merrier—but you have to start somewhere.[79]

The best technical assistance solves specific problems. Effective technical assistance is technical assistance that gets its hands dirty in the details and helps clients solve the problems—or take advantage of the opportunities—that stand in the way of their moving up their growth ladders. The underlying philosophy is **problem-solving**—not setting up and perpetuating long-term dependency relationships. Once you have helped a client solve a problem, graduate both yourself and your client. Good development programs facilitate the functioning of market chains—and, more broadly, markets; they do not insert themselves in them.

> "And if he were really to do good, he would have needed, in addition to his principles, a heart capable of violating them —a heart which knows only of particular, not of general cases, and which achieves greatness in little actions."
>
> Boris Pasternak, *Doctor Zhivago* (New York: Pantheon Books, Inc., 1958), p. 210.

The best people to provide technical assistance to suppliers are their buyers. Why? Because they have a commercial interest in the quantity, quality, and timeliness of the products in question. They also have more incentive than third parties to stay abreast of changes in broader markets and technological practices in their industries.

Government does best when it sticks to its knitting. In a market economy, government has two fundamental roles to play: first, to set clear and transparent rules for market activity and to enforce compliance with those rules; and, second, to invest in public goods—physical infrastructure, primarily—essential for the conduct of private economic activity. Although it is tempting for government to enter in a more interventionist way, it is best when it does what it is best at—in this case, the normative piece of the transaction.

"As in the atom, there is much energy...that can be and is in fact utilized in building up economic development nuclei. <u>Later on</u> these nuclei look as though they could never have been separated even for a single instant when in actual fact they might never have been assembled had not a sequential solution, i.e., an unbalanced growth sequence been found, by accident, instinct, or reasoned design. To look at unbalanced growth means, in other words, to look at the dynamics of the development process <u>in the small</u>. But perhaps it is high time we did just that."

Albert O. Hirschman, *The Strategy of Economic Development* (New Haven: Yale University Press, 1958), pp. viii-ix.

Transformational development can start small. This lesson is so fundamental that it merits relatively lengthy treatment here. In the last few years, the terminology, "transformational development," has come into vogue. Some talk about "systemic change" as well. Although hard to define and measure, the appeal of transformational development is clear. First, development ultimately goes beyond sales and jobs and inculcates changes in the way people view the world and live their lives. Such change is obviously very difficult for practitioners to set as a program target and to assess progress against, but the basic point is a valid one. Second, the yearning for transformational development is a reaction to frustration. It is indeed true that development programs often do not add up to much more than a bunch of isolated, atomistic successes—or to put it another way, they fail to transform local economies into something substantially bigger and better than they were originally. The Ucayali River example demonstrates the fallacy of the contention that transformational development cannot take place from the ground up. In fact, most clusters form that very way—the dynamic growth of the sesame industry in Paraguay in recent years is another case in point. Not every micro program will have macro effects, obviously, but under propitious circumstances—an emergent market, especially—helping individual market chains grow—and letting market incentives work their magic—can definitely snowball into a total effect much greater than the sum of its constituent snowflakes.[80] The PRA final report makes the point as follows:

Many development programs shy away from working with individual clients, believing this approach will result in only isolated successes rather than transforming local economies. Many examples of PRA's work call that reasoning into question—for example, the dramatic expansion of artichoke production in Huancayo, corn in Pucallpa, industrial potatoes in Huánuco, tara in Cajamarca, trout in Puno, to name a few. Not every instance of one-on-one support has had transformational effects. Nonetheless, under the right circumstances (particularly buoyant markets), when PRA helps individual businesses grow, the results can contribute to a total effect much larger than the sum of its parts.

PRA's experience in helping bean clients in Piura shows how working firm by firm can lead to much broader growth.

Since 2005, PRA has signed business plans with a number of bean processing or trading companies: Globe Natural, Procesadora Mejía, La Procesadora SAC, Export Import CANDRES, and ALISUR. The business plans have generated $12.4 million of new bean sales, and 4,500 additional hectares of beans have been planted—the majority by small farmers who sell their harvests to these companies.

A significant byproduct of that growth has been the entry of copycat firms such as ALISUR, which entered the bean market in Piura in 2007. Interestingly, ALISUR had previously received support from PRA's ESC in Cusco to generate bean sales from Apurímac. ALISUR's current $250,000 investment in the provinces of Morropón, Piura, Sechura, and Chulucanas is expected to raise its sales significantly in the next three years.

A second copycat is DIAGRO, which recently signed a business plan with PRA to link with and source from small bean farmers in Morropón.

In sum, the entry of more firms and the progressive incorporation of more small bean farmers is gradually consolidating a regional bean "cluster" in Piura and expanding dramatically the value of exports of beans from the region.[81]

Just because a development program wants to make poor suppliers better off does not necessarily mean that the program must commence work directly with those suppliers. In the same vein, just because a program wants to bring about the transformation of a region or country does not mean that the entire region or country is the appropriate place for that program to start. It may still make sense to start small. The same kind of thinking applies to mindset change. Just because a program wants to change the way people think and act does not necessarily mean that it must shy away from a transactional approach to things. Indeed, experience suggests that the best way for people to learn how to do something is actually to do that something. In brief, the point here is not to quibble over what one wishes to accomplish, but to distinguish clearly between means and ends, which are two very different things.

The same goes for the argument that the job of development programs is to help create smoothly functioning markets. How do markets function? Through transactions. To the extent that development programs reduce the transaction costs standing in the way of buying and selling, they contribute to the improvement of markets as a whole. As the PRA mid-term evaluation put it, "[t]he role of the PRA…is best seen as a catalyst for the structuring of complete, efficient value chains organized around efficient markets, i.e. structured and predictable channels of product flow from producers to consumers."[82] Or as the current Director of PRA makes the point, "we start from the premise that poverty derives from the absence of markets, which means the absence of opportunities for the poor."[83]

All of which hearkens back to Easterly's distinction between Planners and Searchers. Both want the same thing, but for this author, at least, the jury is definitely out on whether planning from the top delivers more bang for the buck than searching from the bottom. **Everybody wants big things to happen. This book argues that "big" schemes can lead nowhere, whereas those that start organically from the bottom up often fare much better.**

"Parturient montes, nascetur ridiculus mus."

"The mountains will be in labor and give birth to a ridiculous mouse."

Horace, "Ars Poetica."

The implication of all this discussion is not that the development and nurturing of clusters are not important—there is certainly ample evidence internationally to suggest they are. It is simply to recognize that clusters grow organically from the interests of their own members, not from the almost *dirigiste* approach that has evolved over the last decade to move them along.[84] In developing countries, many market chains are simply not at the point that cluster initiatives meet their needs. In the end, clusters are a means, not an end, and make sense only when they contribute to what ultimately drives the actors in question—making money.

Chemonics International Inc. has developed a "competitiveness continuum" to illustrate the natural evolution of industries over time (see Exhibit 2.8). The continuum is a rough guide, not a straitjacket, but it gives a sense of how one can expect industries to change as they grow and, correspondingly, what kinds of support might make sense at what stages. All other things being equal, enterprise or market chain assistance is a good fit for industries in stages one and two, while industry-level assistance is suitable for industries in stages three and four.

Most market chains in developing countries fall in stages one and two, which generally means it makes sense to focus development assistance—when appropriate—on individual market chains. Although it might be nice to accelerate the process, most of the time doing so is simply premature. USAID's Bolivia Trade and Business Competitiveness program is now taking a cluster approach to the development of the textile industry, but only after four years of working one on one with individual companies.

The data collected from the 54 firms in Antigua-Barbuda and Dominica confirm the advisability of resisting the temptation to work with aggregates, at least at the outset. The design of the Caribbean Open Trade Support program called for the program to select clusters to support. To make that selection, program personnel first interviewed a broad spectrum of local companies to identify potential lead firms. The report, to which the author contributed, concluded:

"It is...probably more accurate ...to think of development as a process of millions of small breakthroughs than as a few monumental innovations."

Lawrence E. Harrison, *Underdevelopment Is a State of Mind: The Latin American Case* (Lanham, MD: Harvard University and Madison Books, 1985), p. 3.

Exhibit 2.8 Competitiveness Continuum

Low ————————————————————————————————→ High

Stage 1	Stage 2	Stage 3	Stage 4
Enterprise Level • Production-oriented marketing • Poor understanding of quality standards • Limited use of technology • Lack of strategic vision • Poor financial management and no access to credit • No staff training or upgrading	**Enterprise Level** • Some market awareness with limited distribution • Conformity to basic local and international standards • Planning near-term • Improved financial management, but accessing credit difficult • Limited employee training	**Enterprise Level** • Customer/market-orientation • Domestic distribution with some global penetration • Emphasis on quality/service • Conformity to international grades/standards • Medium-term strategy • Cost control and financial management systems exist • Skills training at all levels	**Enterprise Level** • Global market penetration and distribution channels • Product quality, service, and innovation drive sales • Use of cutting-edge technology • Certified in global standards • Long-term strategy for growth • Strong financial management with access to credit • Skills training at all levels
Industry Level • Limited cooperation, trust between enterprises (no clusters) • Weak associations and supporting institutions • Limited number of Business Service Providers (BSPs) offering low quality services • Lack of market focus in education/training facilities • Unfavorable legal and regulatory environment	**Industry Level** • Anchor enterprises, but intra-industry cooperation limited (clusters emerging) • Vertical integration taking place on limited scale • Associations and BSPs provide basic services • Education and training system meet basic needs of private sector • Little investment by government with limited public-private dialogue	**Industry Level** • Inter-firm cooperation common with growing vertical, horizontal networks (clusters established) • Widespread membership in associations • Growing number of BSPs offer high-value services • Strong linkages with education, training centers • Key legal and regulatory constraints addressed • Government shows signs of increased commitment	**Industry Level** • Complex intra-industry networks, joint ventures (clusters robust and growing) • Anchor firms buying from SMEs • Associations and BSPs attuned to business needs and offering high-value services • Education system targeted to meet private sector needs • Public-private partnerships • Favorable business, investment climate, with strong government support

Source: Chemonics International Inc.

Although the companies fall naturally into clusters, the team strongly recommends that the criteria for providing support in the future not include whether a company falls within a predetermined cluster. As the data base created by the consultant team demonstrates, the vast majority of the proposed solutions to businesses' problems do not—at this stage, at least—require the associativity that characterizes much cluster formation. Rather, most companies require solutions that are sui generis. To have an impact on the companies in question, COTS must tailor its solutions to the problems it finds, not vice versa.[85]

In sum, the interviews revealed a finding common around the world: individual enterprises—and the market chains they belong to—typically face, not the same, but a heterogeneity of problems, which, once again, argues for adopting a market chain focus to have real impact.[86]

Independently of this discussion of clusters, attending to one firm at a time often makes sense for very practical reasons, in that frequently the most effective way to attack growth-constraining problems is one on one, not in a group format. Perhaps the best way to make the point is by analogy. Suppose five people have broken DVD players. When they go to the repair shop, they do not expect to receive group treatment. They simply want their machines fixed. In short, they have very specific problems they need solved, and, in this case, at least, the most appropriate way to solve them is individually.

None of this is to say, of course, that a group approach cannot solve business problems. For exporters to sell food products abroad, for example, their suppliers must produce to international standards. Often the best way to convey those standards and to assure their adoption is group training. In such instances, there are clearly economies to capture. Similarly, in industries like tourism, which typically has externalities to worry about, an associative approach can be the appropriate response. Again, though, what ultimately governs the specific approach to adopt is the nature of the problem. If one can attack that problem effectively en masse, great. But if one cannot, it is important not to let the urge to generate a spread effect lead one to confuse means and ends. To make a difference, one's assistance must be specific to the problem at hand, not one-size-fits-all.

For the development practitioner, the bottom line of this discussion is straightforward: tie all program assistance not only to market demand, but to transactions for which there is market demand. Transactions create sales and jobs. Working from the market backwards, focus on the specific obstacles that stand in the way of transactions taking place. Do not try to solve all of a client's or industry's problems at once. Keep your feet on micro ground and hold yourself accountable for delivering concrete, attributable, and verifiable results.

Let the Market Pick the Winners

A couple of years ago, an email circulated throughout the author's office. Its subject read, "In search of best practices for picking clusters." The author reacted in mock horror at what in essence is an oxymoron. How can there be best practices for something one should not do in the first place?

If there is one thing Michael Porter insists on, it is the need for clusters to self-select. It is not the role of outsiders to make that determination at all.

Most program designers accept the principle that it is the job of market forces to pick the "winners" and sort out the wheat from the chaff.[87] To give some focus to the programs they manage, however, they commonly restrict the programs' ambit of action to certain products, sectors, or clusters. Ironically, given Porter's emphatic position on the subject, the tendency to pre-select is especially pronounced in cluster competitiveness programs. The upshot is that designers discard *a priori* a whole range of other options, the opportunity cost of which can be high.

During its life, PRA provided support of one kind or another to over 500 clients in the interior of Peru. The 15 clients with the highest incremental sales accounted for a sizeable percentage—47 percent—of the total.[88] The clients in question produced the following products:

Client 1:   trout
Client 2:   palm oil
Client 3:   flowers
Client 4:   rice
Client 5:   rice
Client 6:   ceramic tiles
Client 7:   poultry
Client 8:   tara[89]
Client 9:   milk
Client 10: coffee
Client 11: fruits
Client 12: bixin[90]
Client 13: rice
Client 14: wooden flooring
Client 15: processed fruits

If PRA's program managers had had to select beforehand the products they would support, it is likely they would have chosen coffee, rice, and, possibly, milk, poultry, and trout. It is highly unlikely that ten years previously they would have pre-selected bixin, ceramic tiles, flowers, fruits, palm oil, processed fruits, tara, or wooden flooring—the products of eight—that is, more than half—of the program's top 15 clients. Monday morning quarterbacking is easy, of course, but there is little doubt in retrospect that the program's decision to keep its options open was indeed a wise one.

Mohammad Yunus, winner of the 2006 Nobel Peace Prize, held fast to the same principle in setting up Grameen Bank:

Yunus turned down World Bank funding many times, because bank staff wanted to tell him what to give loans for, based on their analysis of the Bangladesh economy. They were central planners at heart and wanted to fund him to do what they planned. But Yunus insisted on letting his borrowers use the money for whatever they wanted, as long as they paid it back. Yunus runs Grameen in the same opportunistic way that businesses operate, following opportunity rather than five-year plans.[91]

The first major success of USAID's Paraguay Vende program, an initiative patterned on PRA in Peru, makes the same point.

Paraguay is a country practically denuded of forests. From a vegetative map of the country, the forestry and wood products sector is the last place a technocrat would likely look for economic dynamism. But both in Brazil and across the Paraguay River in Argentina lie vast reserves of forest, much under sustainable management. Smart investors recognized that the low labor costs in Paraguay could more than make up for the costs of transporting wood in. They therefore opened up wood processing facilities in Paraguay to export to various destinations, including Home Depot in the United States.

Odila Báez was one of those smart businesspeople. But right after restructuring her company, Xtreme, in 2003, she lost her broker in the United States. She was willing to invest in new and better facilities, but desperately needed new buyers. She made contact with Paraguay Vende, which made appointments for her with possible new brokers. She traveled to the United States and established a relationship with one of them. The new broker secured her a large order for wood molding, for which she invested in new plant and more efficient equipment.

In 2004, Xtreme's export sales totaled $85,000 and, all told, generated over 10,000 additional days of labor for local workers. Xtreme has expanded its operations since then and continues to export.

Báez's story points up not only how opportunities for generating sales and jobs may lie where one least expects to find them, but the key role of entrepreneurship in the process. The lesson for development practitioners is clear: do not focus on what products to support, but be on the lookout for entrepreneurial talent, since entrepreneurship is typically the scarce resource.

> "Descompliquémoslo [Let's uncomplicate things]."
>
> Odila Báez, President of Xtreme, Ciudad del Este, Paraguay, 2003.

In the late 1980s and early 1990s, Ricardo Frohmader, a colleague of the author, worked in Central America helping businesses there learn how to grow and export non-traditional agricultural products to the United States. One of his clients was a businessman in Honduras who became a very successful melon producer and exporter.

Once the program ended, Frohmader went elsewhere to work. Ten years later, he returned to the region, taking up residence in Guatemala. On a business trip in the region, he ran into the melon grower in an airport and asked him how his melon business was going. The grower replied, "Oh, I left the melon business a number of years ago. The competition got stiffer and my profits dropped, so I figured it was time to get out. I invested in a furniture operation and have been exporting furniture to the United States ever since." Surprised, Frohmader exclaimed, "But you don't know absolutely anything about furniture!" To which the ex-grower responded, "Well, 15 years ago, I didn't know anything about melons either."

For the Honduran businessman, the goad to action was not his attachment to a product, but the opportunities the market gave him

> "In 1896 Japan's rulers deemed that their country should have a steel industry to match the best in Europe. Imperial say-so substituted for economic know-how, but met with little success. The government went to great lengths to replicate European technology, importing German engineers, machines and designs. Only after a steel mill had been built did it become apparent that German mills could not run on Japanese coke...
>
> "Neither economists nor emperors can be relied upon to pick winners. The best bet is entrepreneurial trial and error."
>
> "Finding your niche: The discovery of poor countries' industrial strengths is a matter of trial and error," *Economist*, March 1, 2003, p. 70.

to make money—and create jobs in the process. Development practitioners need to adopt the same kind of thinking.[92]

Put the Problem Horse Before the Solution Cart

A major drawback to a cluster competitiveness program is the natural tendency for those involved to become a solution looking for a problem—that is, to advertise themselves as cluster experts and then to search for fertile ground to apply their skills. The author hastens to add that this supply-push tendency is by no means unique to cluster competitiveness programs. It happens any time a program rallies its resources around a single issue, whether that issue is finance, land tenure, agricultural technology, anti-corruption, etc.

> "To a man with a hammer, everything looks like a nail."
>
> Charles Munger paraphrasing Abraham Maslow
>
> "Mind over Munger," *Money*, July, 2002, p. 39.

In 1995, USAID held a workshop in Annapolis, Maryland, for a number of its field personnel from Latin America and the Caribbean. One of the sessions had to do with micro-enterprises and microfinance. The first speaker was Donald Meade, who, with his colleague Carl Liedholm at Michigan State University, had spearheaded surveys of micro-enterprises, especially rural micro-enterprises, throughout the world, especially in Eastern and Southern Africa. The second speaker was Elizabeth Rhyne, who had worked extensively in microfinance.

In his talk, Meade reported on patterns that had emerged from the surveys they had conducted. Most micro-enterprises cited lack of a market as their number one problem. In contrast, lack of finance was of lower priority, sometimes as low as number four on

> "I believe our success in BTBC stems from the fact that we are focusing on strengthening the SMEs themselves and not the various services that they may require, including financing. Even our financial expert...agrees that financing—as important as it may be—is not among the major constraints for the success of an SME. (I think he has learned this precisely as a consequence of seeing what works in a project like ours!)"
>
> Jules Lampell, Director, Bolivia Trade and Business Competitiveness program, personal communication with the author, 2007.

the totem pole after technology and management constraints.[93]

In her talk, Rhyne reported how the field of microfinance was evolving to address micro-enterprises' finance needs. In the question-and-answer interchange afterwards, one of the participants commented, "Isn't it anomalous that a whole industry has sprung up around what normally is not the client population's major problem?" To which, Rhyne's response was, "Well, at least it's a problem we have a solution for."

The point of this story is not to downplay the virtues of

microfinance, which can play an invaluable role in stabilizing the incomes of the poor and alleviating household insecurity. But just like cluster competitiveness, microfinance is a means, not an end. Sometimes, it is the right solution, but very often it is not.[94]

The same line of argument obviously applies to fields other than cluster competitiveness and microfinance. As practitioners around the world can bear witness, yes, there are definitely market chains that can benefit from better agricultural technology, from a more agile and responsive banking system, from regularization of land titles, from the reduction of hassles in clearing inputs through customs, etc. Very often, though, bringing to bear such issue-based solutions misses the **binding** problems, that is, those that most prevent market chains from expanding operations and, directly or indirectly, hiring more people. To address those problems, it is necessary to come down to the micro level and to do one's homework.

In the end, the trick is to diagnose what a market chain's most significant problem is and then to solve it. Here is where the real creativity in international development takes place, not in devising grand new master schemes, but in using one's imagination to come up with solutions to often seemingly unsolvable business problems.

> "On the field where Ormuzd has challenged Ahriman to battle, he who chases away the dogs is wasting his time."
>
> Dag Hammarskjöld, *Markings*, translated by Lief Sjöberg and W.H. Auden (New York: Alfred A. Knopf, Inc., 1964), p. 28.

Part III offers some suggestions to aid in that process of diagnosis, but, once again, a mechanistic application of tools is not the answer. It is the ability to think ingeniously and creatively. As Matthew Stewart has put it,

> "Imagination is more important than knowledge."
>
> Albert Einstein
>
> http://thinkexist.com/quotes/albert_einstein.

The best business schools will tell you that management education is mainly about building skills—one of the most important of which is the ability to think (or what the M.B.A.s call "problem solving"). But do they manage to teach such skills?

I once sat through a presentation in which a consultant, a Harvard M.B.A., showed a client, the manager of a large financial institution in a developing country, how the client company's "competitive advantage" could be analyzed in terms of "the five forces."...Not for the first time, I was embarrassed to call myself a consultant. As it happens, the client, too, had a Harvard M.B.A. "No," he said, shaking his head with feigned chagrin. "There are only three forces in this case. And two of them are in the Finance Ministry."

What they don't seem to teach you in business school is that "the five forces" and "the seven Cs" and every other generic framework for problem solving are heuristics: they can lead you to solutions, but they cannot make you think. Case studies may provide an effective way to think business problems through, but the point is rather lost if students come away imagining that you can go home once you've put all of your eggs into a two-by-two growth-share matrix.[95]

In summary, the task is to get to the essence of market chains' most binding problems and to do what is necessary to solve them. As the market chain examples above bear witness, those problems can take many shapes and forms. In some cases, the key issue is identifying markets. In others it is organizing suppliers to meet sizeable orders. In others it is upgrading technology to meet demanding market requirements. In others it is producers getting up to speed on phytosanitary regulations in export markets. In others it is a connector firm getting its act together to convince risk-averse banks that the venture they propose is indeed a bankable proposition.[96] In others it is a local government rehabilitating a dilapidated access road to allow easy entry of inputs and exit of outputs. The list could go on and on. What the issue is not, though, is one-size-fits-all solutions. As an observer of PRA commented,

> "It doesn't matter if a cat is black or white, so long as it catches mice."
> Deng Xiaoping
> http://thinkexist.com/quotes/deng_xiaoping.

> A fundamental advantage of the program is that it does not have a "standard" type of intervention. Having only demand as the common axis that gives dynamism in all its

> "Somebody once said that right answers are easier to find than right questions."
>
> W.J. Burley, *Wycliffe in Paul's Court* (London: Orion Books Ltd., 1980), p. 138.

interventions, the program takes action as a function of the specific bottlenecks within each business. The program does not even assume that there is a common problem within each region or district but, rather, it recognizes that heterogeneity rules in rural areas.[97]

Sustainability: What to Sustain and How

It would be hard to find anyone involved in or concerned about international development who does not want development to be "sustainable."[98] In the last couple of decades, "sustainable development" has emerged as a field of its own, and, like poverty, has spawned an enormous body of literature and extended its reach in many directions:

> While many definitions of the term have been introduced over the years, the most commonly cited definition comes from the report *Our Common Future*, more commonly known as the Brundtland Report, which states that sustainable development is development that "meets the needs of the present without compromising the ability of future generations to meet their own needs".
>
> Sustainable development does not focus solely on environmental issues. More broadly, sustainable development policies encompass three general policy areas: economic, environmental and social. In support of this, several United Nations texts, most recently the 2005 World Summit Outcome Document, refer to the "interdependent and mutually reinforcing pillars" of sustainable development as economic development, social development, and environmental protection.[99]

Despite agreement on sustainability in principle, once again the devil is in the details. In programs oriented toward increasing sales and jobs, for example, sustaining those increases obviously has social and environmental dimensions. In most such programs, though, the pillar that generates the most heat is economic—or, to be more precise, financial.

Most development funding agencies do not want to make open-ended commitments to their programs. They are willing to act as a catalyst for a while, but expect the services they fund will somehow begin to pay for themselves—ideally, sooner rather than later—and become self-sustaining financially. As a case in point, most business development programs either create new or support existing organizations to provide business services to clients. As a practical matter, therefore, making those programs sustainable typically means finding ways for the organizations in question to finance themselves.

The discussion that follows calls that conclusion into question. In the end, it rests on logic that is supply-push. Once one approaches the challenge from the demand side, one reaches quite different conclusions both about what to sustain and about how to go about it.

The conventional logic underlying discussions of financial sustainability is as follows: "To make an organization

> "The U.S. Government cannot continue to provide funds for service delivery at the expense of the institutional capacity-building that will enable that service delivery to be sustained."
>
> Randall L. Tobias, Director of U.S. Foreign Assistance and USAID Administrator, "A Strategic Approach to Addressing Poverty and Global Challenges: We Are in This Together," presentation, Center for Strategic and International Studies, Washington, D.C., 2007.

we support sustainable, we need to build its 'capacity.' To build its capacity, we need to do 'institution building.' And to do institution building, we need to be sure that program personnel receive appropriate technical and management training, that they work in well equipped offices, etc." In short, the reasoning is—surprise, surprise!—very much supply-push: concentrate on supplying all the necessary inputs, and the desired outcome will almost take care of itself. Whether clients will pay for the capacity built is almost tangential to the calculus.

An alternative way to approach the issue is as follows: "What ultimately counts is increasing sales, not of business service providers, but of their clients. As those sales grow, it is likely, though not a foregone conclusion, that the clients in question will come to appreciate—and be willing to pay for—the services of business service providers. Regardless, the only way the derived–demand market of business service providers can grow is if demand for their services grows, which is most likely to happen when their clients' operations—that is, their sales—expand. Looked at that way, it does not make much sense to let concern for the financial sustainability of business service providers become high priority. To put it positively, what does make sense is to focus single-mindedly on the expansion of clients' sales—or, more accurately, on the sustainability of the commercial relationships in the market chains of which they form a part. And in the course of helping clients grow, business service providers will also increase their capacity in a learning-by-doing way—which, arguably, is the best way to build capacity in the first place." In brief, the growth of the business service provider market is a means, not an end. Treat it as such.

Exhibit 2.9 highlights the differences between the two approaches. The discussion that follows goes into more depth, explaining a number of subtleties related to the issue—of which there are many.

Exhibit 2.9 Approaches to Organizational Financial Sustainability

	Supply-Push Approach	Demand-Pull Approach
Objective	Make business service providers self-sustaining financially	Make client businesses grow
Strategy	Provide inputs to facilitate capacity building	Help clients solve problems that constrain their growth; build capacity by learning by doing
Assumption	Clients will be willing to pay for the capacity built	Clients will recognize the value of the services they have received and, in certain circumstances, will pay for more in the future

Source: James T. Riordan.

Outward-looking organizations are more sustainable than inward-looking ones. Organizations that keep their focus squarely on their clients are likely to have value in the market and recover at least a goodly portion of their costs. Conversely—and somewhat counter-intuitively, organizations that obsess over their own survival tend to lose sense of the mission for which they created themselves, wind up with less value in the market, and turn out less sustainable. As USAID's Bureau for Latin America and the Caribbean put it,

> The conventional approach to organizational development has concentrated on the provision of organizational inputs. Implicitly, the assumption has been that if an organization has office space, equipment, trained people, budget, etc., then the organization's mission will take care of itself. In practice, this focus on inputs has begged fundamental questions of definition of mission and led to a failure to develop a client base to sustain the organization financially over time.[100]

Operationally, keeping one's focus outward means helping clients solve the problems that stand in the way of their sales growth. Real estate gurus like to say the key to success is location, location, and location. In this case, the key to success is sales volume, sales volume, and sales volume. Realistically, only business service providers that help their clients grow are likely to grow themselves. As their clients increase their sales, they will likely come to recognize the worth of the business development services they have received and be willing to pay for more in the future. In addition, the growing appreciation of the worth of such services in the broader market can furnish an inducement for other business service providers to join in, either through expansion or by starting up in the first place.[101]

The "embedded services model" can obviate the need for third-party business service providers. It is important to note the use of the word, "likely," in the argument above. That is because there is nothing automatic between expanding client sales and expanding the market of business service providers. It is normally a necessary condition for that to happen, but not a sufficient condition.

> Zarmayil Mardanyan…has lived and worked in Ijivan, a remote mountainous region in the north [of Armenia], all his life. He gained his business experience running a successful grocery store that expanded into a trading company.
>
> In 2005, Mardanyan became a USAID business advisor. In this role, he helped other small business owners identify new markets, obtain financing, improve efficiency, and boost production. While working with USAID, Mardanyan helped 32 clients…increase sales by more than $44,000…
>
> After completing his USAID contract, Mardanyan started his own consulting firm, MarS Ltd. He uses many of the same methodologies he applied while working with USAID to help clients access financial services and identify market opportunities. He currently has six clients, including one potential foreign investor in a local dairy operation.
>
> "I'm grateful to USAID for providing me the opportunity to gain a better understanding of my community's market potential and allowing me to learn from my colleagues," Mardanyan said. "In the past, I was the one asking for advice. Now, people are coming to me."[102]

Although micro in scope, the story of Zarmayil Mardanyan portrays in very human terms what can happen when business advisors adopt a problem-solving approach and their clients see results. It also shows the power of learning by doing. Although the program provided training, it was hands-on and results-oriented. Mardanyan underwent baptism by fire. Finally, it is noteworthy where the story takes place. Ijivan really is remote, and was for all intents and purposes completely devoid of business development services when the program started.

In contrast, return to the case of Piscifactoría de los Andes. With support from PRA's Economic Service Centers, Piscifactoría de los Andes has succeeded in expanding its sales dramatically. PRA helped Piscifactoría de los Andes access key technical and legal information, but, once again, its principal contribution was building trust between the company and SAIS Tupac Amaru and, eventually, about 15 other suppliers. The final result is a well oiled market chain that can function very well, thank you, without additional PRA support. More than that, the conventional services a third-party business service provider might provide—identifying new buyers, accessing up-to-date technology, extending it to suppliers, accessing finance, etc.—are all ones the chain can furnish itself or knows where to find. In other words, the business development services the chain requires are "embedded" in the chain itself. Short of a significant unforeseen shock or opportunity, the chain does not require further assistance of a third-party business service provider. The same is true of the three other examples from Peru touched on in some depth above: the operation on the Ucayali River, sourcing and selling Shipibo-Conibo ceramics, and the relationship between Nutreina and Teresa Romero.[103]

Two general conclusions emerge. First, at least with the clients in question, PRA has basically put itself out of business. Second, PRA's support of those clients does not appear to have contributed to the creation of a market of independent business service providers. Is either of those results a bad thing? Of course not. On the first count, it is the job of development practitioners to put themselves out of business. For all practical purposes, PRA has done its job with those clients and it is time to give priority to others. On the second count, the business development services the market chains require they can provide themselves. Or, to look at it another way, sustainability is already there—which is precisely what one wants to happen. **All of which ratifies once again the advisability of development practitioners focusing on the sustainability of the market chains, not the organizations, they support.**

In a good number of the chains conforming to the embedded services model, connector firms upfront inputs and technical assistance to their suppliers, discounting the cost of same in the prices they pay on delivery. In principle, such a scheme can be very beneficial for the poor:

> [L]inking and organizing the very small firms of the very poor can provide a support system and access to resources that they might not otherwise have. In supply chains . . .

where buyers are willing to assume all the risks, providing suppliers with inputs, training and a market—this is a very attractive commercial arrangement for those who have few resources and/or ability to assume risks.[104, 105]

A critic will interject here, "All that is very well and good, but such schemes can contribute to the concentration of connector firms' monopsony power, which can have a deleterious effect on poor suppliers, the very ones development assistance presumably intends to help." Theoretically, the objection is a valid one. Empirically, the evidence can go both ways. The Bangladesh example (see box on next page) confirms the critic's fears, but the Indian example illustrates the other side of the coin. For many connector firms, supplier loyalty is worth paying a premium for, since developing new relationships can be even more costly. In any event, in practice one cannot assume beforehand that the impact necessarily goes one way or the other. But even when a development practitioner uncovers a propensity by buyers to abuse their asymmetric power, he or she must not let it serve as a pretext for retreating from a market-chain by market-chain approach. Again, working with one client at a time implies no exclusivity. The best way to dilute monopsony power is by aggressively facilitating the entry of new actors.[106]

Honest brokering is a public, not a private good. Most times, building trust is the most important and far-reaching of all business development services. Most economic theory assumes trust between parties already exists. Very often it does not, and the parties concerned—Piscifactoría de los Andes and SAIS Tupac Amaru, for example—will not invest in creating it. In effect, therefore, good business service providers deliver services that the market itself will not supply—that is, they correct market failures. That is why the financial sustainability of support organizations is often unattainable: it is unrealistic to expect private parties to receive payment for what in essence is a public good.

In developing countries, business service providers typically offer a mix of facilitation and conventional business development services.[107] That is certainly true of Zarmayil Mardanyan in Armenia, who, intriguingly, appears able to cross-subsidize the cost of

How Embedded Services Can Affect the Poor	
Positively	**Negatively**
"This paper explores how smallholders can benefit from the emerging opportunities from...demand-driven.changes in high-value agriculture in India. The study examines the institutional mechanisms adopted by different firms to integrate small producers of milk, broilers, and vegetables in supply chain and their effects on producers' transaction costs and farm profitability. The study finds that the innovative institutional arrangements in the form of contract farming have considerably reduced transaction costs and improved market efficiency to benefit the smallholders. The study does not find any bias against smallholders in contract farming. Also, the study does not find that the relevant firms have exploited their monopsonistic position by paying lower prices to farmers. On the contrary, contract producers were found enjoying benefits of assured procurement of their produce and higher prices."	"The poor are often locked into markets and sub-optimal contracting relationships through indebtedness. Breaking the cycle of usurious lending can expand their market options. For instance, in Bangladesh where we are currently working on a shrimp value chain analysis, the poor are locked into contracts with lenders who also buy their product (in this case shrimp fry or shrimp and prawn). The loans are usurious and contracts are enforced through violence. Were the poor...able to avoid the cycle of indebtedness that locks them into these contracts with intermediaries—they could sell in spot markets at auctions and obtain better prices."
Source: Pratap S. Birthal, P.K. Joshi, and Ashok Gulati, "Vertical Coordination in High-Value Food Commodities: Implications for Smallholders," Markets, Trade and Institutions Division Discussion Paper No. 85, International Food Policy Research Institute, Washington, D.C., 2005.	*Source:* Sarah Gammage, DTS, Inc., email, Microenterprise Learning Information and Knowledge Sharing, December 13, 2005.

the facilitation services he provides virtually gratis to new clients with the fees he collects from established ones. For one schooled in the developed world, it is tempting to interpret facilitation as simply a client development cost—that is, part of the overhead a company must cover from the receipts of its paying customers. But the distrust in question here goes much deeper than that—it is not just a matter of convincing a prospective client of the value of a business plan, for example, but one of the client entertaining the idea of expansion at all. Particularly in the absence of well established rule of law, businesses' distrust, not only of potential buyers or suppliers but of the market at large, can run very deep. Put in other terms, businesses' risk aversion can be extreme—which, once again, conventional economic theory does not take into account—and often an outside push—whose cost is generally not recoverable—is necessary to break the ice.

Distrust can extend to business service providers as well, as Aida Khachatryan, a colleague of Zarmayil Mardanyan in Armenia, found to her consternation. The first time she visited a potential client, an underwear factory, the owner of the company slammed the door in her face—literally. As she later came to learn, he had become so disillusioned by his experience with business development programs in the past that he vowed he would never work with outsiders again. Fortunately, though, that was not the end of the story. Through sheer persistence—and resolving one by one the nettlesome problems that prevented the business from expanding its sales—Khachatryan proved her mettle, and the company turned out to be her star client in the end.

In 1999, John E. Lamb and Bruce Brower conducted a metaevaluation for the World Bank of Agribusiness Development Centers throughout the developing world.[108] Their findings suggest that Mardanyan's ability to recover all his costs is very much the exception to the rule. They also raise doubt about whether he will be able to continue to do so—at least if he continues to provide facilitation in addition to conventional business development services. At least up until 1999, Lamb and Brower could not identify one instance in which an organization succeeded in achieving full cost recovery. One of the authors estimated it is probably unrealistic to expect cost recovery much above 50 percent—a conclusion entirely consistent with what one might expect after distinguishing clearly between what is a private good and what is a public good.

In short, if a business service provider is to provide facilitation in addition to conventional business development services, it is unrealistic to expect financial sustainability. Some degree of recurrent subsidy is in order.

Supporting facilitation is fine, but don't crowd out existing conventional business service providers. Subsidization of business service provision carries with it a real danger. Once a development program sets itself up to provide facilitation services to clients—or supports an existing organization to do so—it is very tempting for it to overstep the bounds of facilitation, taking advantage of the client relationships it has developed with "free" money to edge into the provision of conventional business development services as well, thereby creating unfair competition for providers already in the market and hindering the maturation of that market. For that reason, it is important to build incentives and procedures into operations to safeguard against "crowding out," a topic addressed in Part III.

That said, concern for not crowding out the rest of the market is an issue where perfection can become the enemy of the good. Take again the case of Zarmayil Mardanyan. When the program began in Armenia, the business development services market in Ijivan was so embryonic as to be almost non-existent, so contracting conventional business development services to third-party providers was not really an option. Clients had problems that called for solutions, and the program focused, appropriately, on addressing them however it could.

Fintrac Inc. found itself in much the same situation in Honduras a decade ago:

> Hurricane Mitch pummeled Central America in October 1998, hitting Honduras the hardest as compared to other countries. USAID/Honduras sought a quick fix to help bring the decimated fruit and vegetable sectors back to life. As a result, CDA [Centro de Desarrollo de Agronegocios—Agribusiness Development Center] decided early that the fruit

and vegetable sector was in need of a significant "jump-start" if it was ever to achieve a respectable level of growth.

At the same time, the country was plagued by a history of poor quality technical assistance from both government and NGO sectors. Farmers were understandably skeptical of schemes promising to boost agricultural production. This credibility problem with respect to the value of technical assistance also meant that the program needed to demonstrate effectiveness and results as soon as possible.[109]

In response to those conditions, the Agribusiness Development Center developed market linkages and provided production assistance directly to farmers, pushing for early successes as a way to leverage the copycatting instincts of others. It also put in place an exit strategy to be sure its time-conditioned assistance would indeed be time-conditioned. The first prong of the strategy was to involve buyers, exporters, brokers, seedling producers, freight forwarders, and input suppliers, both to transfer skills, methods, and technologies and to cement relationships between them and farmers. The second prong was to promote the embedded services model, securing commitments to provide technical assistance not only from buyers but also from input suppliers. In short, the program kept its eye on the prize of sales and jobs while taking a long-term view.

USAID's Azerbaijan Business Assistance and Development (ABAD) program is an instructive case study of how the tension between short- and long-term considerations can play out in practice. ABAD started with the expressed objective of promoting the financial sustainability of its business service providers and structured its sub-grants to them to be consistent with that objective. Once underway, it discovered that most program-supported transactions turned out to be simply one-shot spot sales—which contributed little to the program's higher-order objective of long-term growth in the economic corridors where it worked. As the author expressed it in a report at the time,

Guided by the good intention of making local business service providers sustainable financially, the sub-grants governing the activities of the project's Marketing Centers call for them to recover an increasing proportion of their operating costs over time. Responding rationally to the incentives given, the providers are gravitating toward simple trading deals for which they can receive a commission, giving short shrift to the kinds of facilitative activities that add value by integrating the different links in the value chain and generating sales and jobs. This tendency is particularly pronounced in the Lenkoran corridor, where the business advisors are casting themselves largely in the role of sales brokers.

It is important to note that some of the latter transactions are indeed adding value to the local economy. For example, a contract that obligates a tomato processor in Imishli to purchase tomatoes from a grower in agreed upon quantities at an agreed upon time helps to avoid a common problem in the area, namely, the losses that result at harvest from growers scurrying around looking for buyers. Such welfare gains are relatively small, however, and pale qualitatively in comparison with the backward linkages generated by the investment in the processing facility in Zagatala to produce rose oil for buyers in Europe or the interest expressed by an entrepreneur in Tovuz in investing in a facility to produce packaging material not only for his own sugar packing operation but for the corridor as a whole.[110]

ABAD is not unique in the mixed signals development programs give their operating arms. Many programs call for their business service providers to assume increasing proportions of the cost of their services over time. In its worst incarnation, the compulsion to recover costs becomes so overzealous that it straightjackets relationships with clients, focusing their attention more on what they pay today than on what they can achieve tomorrow. An example from USAID's Albania Small Business Credit and Assistance (SBCA) program portrays this worst case:

In general, participants were not highly receptive to the notion of providing services based on a tangible return on investment to clients. Most BSPs [Business Service Providers] have been spun off from international donor projects with a mandate of sustainability, and have been successful in charging clients for writing "business plans" to get loans to purchase equipment. Unfortunately, the sustainability mandate has created a conflict of interest between BSPs and clients whereby BSPs are recommending and facilitating unnecessary loans in order to generate revenue.

During the assignment, a situation surfaced in which a client had been advised by a BSP to take a loan for 150,000 Euros for new equipment that was unnecessary and not serviceable given the client's current revenue. Although SBCA is working to increase sales for this client, it may be years before new equipment will generate a rational return on investment. In the meantime, the client is financially imperiled with this loan.[111]

To their credit, the managers of ABAD recognized the error they had made in the design of that program, and eliminated the requirement to charge clients fees. Extolling ABAD's decision to remove the requirement to charge fees is not to say, of course, that clients should receive services for free. It is simply to argue against the imposition of a fee structure that militates against the provision of the very services that will have the most impact on sales and jobs. Part III discusses practical ways of striking a balance between program managers keeping their focus on final results and the appropriateness of clients contributing to the cost and taking "ownership" of the services they receive.

Learning by doing is the best capacity-building strategy. Throughout the world, meetings with businesspeople—both business development providers and their clients—commonly elicit the need on their part for information, training, and education. In response, development programs routinely finance training programs. To achieve economies of scale in the use of scarce training resources, the training programs in question are often generic in character.[112]

For those schooled in conventional approaches to capacity and institution building, the "Just do it!" approach to learning implicit in the discussion above is very much foreign territory. For them, formal training is essential first. Interestingly, though, if there is one lesson that emerges from years of experience in business development services programs, it is the low return on generalized, one-size-fits-all training.[113] That is true not only for the training business service providers give their clients but for the training they receive themselves. In the end, the way people learn best is through transactions—that is, actually by doing. By themselves, generic training courses do not do it.[114]

At the risk of anticipating the more complete discussion of management discipline in Part III, proposals for formal training courses are a perfect test case for the application of the 5:1 rule noted above. Will a proposed training course result in sales five times the cost of the training itself? If the answer is yes, then move full speed ahead. If the answer is no, go back to the drawing board.

In brief, the best way to learn to do something is not just to prepare to do it, but actually to do it. Intriguingly, such a strategy has the decided programmatic advantage of killing two birds—both developing capacity and achieving results—with one unified program approach.

Large private companies are an emerging source of financing for business development programs. Whether by historical precedent or by habit, development practitioners typically look to international donor organizations and national governments for funding for business development services programs. Since facilitation is a public good, looking to public sources would appear a natural and advisable strategy.

But another promising option is emerging. Over the last decade, large companies—multinational but also national corporations—have upped the priority they give to corporate social responsibility programs, that is, programs that contribute to the good of the communities in which they work. As a consequence, they, too, can be a source for covering the facilitation services necessary to induce substantial increases in sales and jobs in those communities.

PRA offers a nice precedent for that approach. At the beginning of the last decade, Minas Buenaventura, a Peruvian mining company listed on the New York Stock Exchange, was preparing to celebrate 50 years of operations in Huancavelica, a very poor department in the interior of Peru. Instead of constructing a monument or throwing a huge party, the company decided to finance a PRA Economic Service Center there, and signed an agreement with USAID/Peru to that effect. Every year since, it has invested $250,000 in the center to increase sales and jobs throughout the Huancavelica economic corridor.[115] PRA management treats the operation in Huancavelica just like all its other centers, applying the same system of target setting, monitoring and evaluation, and operational procedures. In principle, there is no reason that model would not make sense elsewhere as well.

In 2007, Antamina, a mining company with sizeable operations in Ancash, signed a similar agreement to finance a PRA Economic Service Center for the Huaraz economic corridor, thereby doubling the precedent.

If experience in Peru is any guide, private sector financing offers an additional advantage. USAID/Peru's budget is subject to political pressures from year to year, and some years PRA did not receive as much financing as it had counted on. In contrast, once Minas Buenaventura and Antamina committed themselves, their commitment has been firm, and program managers have not had to worry about the possibility of instability of financing over time. Ironically, therefore, the commitment of a private party may be more reliable than that of a public one—and better for assuring the continuity of services over time.

One final point related to sustainability. The entirety of the discussion above argues for focusing on the sustainability of the market chains development practitioners support, that is, just in the private sector. It does not talk at all about sustainability in the public sector. For those with a lingering predisposition to create sustainability in the public sector, please read the email below. It speaks for itself.

Why Am I Not Surprised?
(page 1 of 2)

Internal Email, Chemonics International Inc.

From: Bruce Brower
To: Latin America and Caribbean Region
Date: 10/23/96 3:30pm
Subject: Why am I not surprised?

The PROEXAG [Non-Traditional Agricultural Export Support Project]
project ended about 1½ years ago. It was a very successful project.
...[T]he businesses this Chemonics' project helped get started
are increasingly significant players in the market and are having
precisely the local economic impact that was hoped for. The project
was highly "sustainable" from the standpoint that lots of growers
and exporters who were assisted by the project are still growing
and exporting—and the business is getting bigger. Diane Bejarano
attended the Produce Marketing Association this year. A number of
project beneficiary businesses were present and hustling up more
business opportunities in products in which we were instrumental in
launching the industry. All very gratifying.

Now for the down side.

While I was in El Salvador this month, I helped host a meeting with
a number of organizations to discuss the development of the SIC
(Sistema de Información Comercial [Market Information System])
for Salvadoran agriculture. One of the people present was from
FUSADES [Salvadoran Foundation for Economic and Social
Development]. When she learned I had worked on the PROEXAG-
EXITOS [Export Industry Technology Support Project] project she
became very excited. "I need your help" she said. "I have been
trying to find out all I can about that project because we think it is
the way we want to do things here in El Salvador." She told me she
had contacted the Guatemala Regional USAID office and requested
information, in writing, on the project. All they could find in their
records to supply her was one sheet with a list of crops that are
considered nontraditional. This was very depressing to me on two
counts:

1. The Mission not only has completely forgotten about the project
and apparently purged its files in 1½ years, it is also clearly
not interested in the topic and apparently unaware of what it
accomplished through the project.

Why Am I Not Surprised?
(page 2 of 2)

2. One of the project client organizations was FUSADES. During the life of the project we sent FUSADES hundreds of pounds of documents related to the development of nontraditional exports. We helped set up their library. We did seminars and training sessions for them. We paid for them to participate in international activities related to the topic. But now, like USAID, if they have the materials, they can't find them. If they learned the lessons, they have been forgotten. This woman was unaware that FUSADES had even been a project beneficiary.

It makes one wonder if institutional memory, in these cases, should be measured in hours or minutes—certainly not years.

If there is a lesson to be learned here, and there is, it might be: if you want to have a real and lasting impact on the economy, work with private businesses or make results happen with private businesses. When it comes to making a difference in a third world economy, a pound of profit is worth more than a ton of institutional strengthening.

(Sermon is over—you can go back to work now.)

In summary, conventional approaches to financial sustainability would appear misplaced. Keep the focus on the sustainability, not of program-sponsored business service providers, but of the market chains they support.

Organize What You Do Geographically

This book argues strongly against development practitioners selecting clusters, industries, sectors, or products to work on beforehand. It is the market's job to select winners. It also urges development practitioners to keep their options open and allocate their scarce resources to those market opportunities with the highest likelihood of generating sales and jobs, regardless of the clusters, industries, sectors, or products in which those opportunities present themselves.

But resources are indeed scarce, and development practitioners cannot afford to keep their options so open that they spread themselves too thin and render themselves incapable of going into any depth on any one thing. Pre-selection of some kind often is necessary, which raises the question of how to do it.

Geography is the natural choice, not only because clusters tend to concentrate themselves geographically, not only because the burgeoning field of economic geography points up the economies obtainable through geographic agglomeration, but because, very practically, the trust required to work effectively with clients depends on personal contact, and personal contact occurs, by definition, in specific places.

As a rule, it takes time—as little as a few weeks, but sometimes months—for business facilitators to develop the trust required to build smooth working relationships with clients. They do not build trust by parachuting in and out of capital cities. Most successful facilitators spend considerable time with clients in informal settings drinking the local drink of choice, be it tea in Afghanistan, raki in Albania, yerba mate in Paraguay, or beer in Peru. Business facilitators who sit in their offices waiting for clients to come to them may never engender enough trust to be effective.[116]

Once one decides to take a spatial perspective, the question then is how to define domains appropriate to the kinds of programs under discussion here. Here is where the concept of economic corridors comes in. Economic corridors are spaces in which commerce naturally takes place, that is, spaces that link rural areas to intermediate cities, and intermediate cities, in turn, to the demands of domestic and international markets beyond. Generally economic corridors correlate closely with roads and watersheds. They do not necessarily mesh with political or agro-production boundaries. They fall naturally into hierarchies, with lower-order corridors feeding into higher-order ones. The designers of PRA defined 24 economic corridors in Peru, but had budget to establish physical presence only in ten. It selected those ten by seeing what corridors evidenced both relatively high levels of poverty and relatively high economic potential. The mechanics of selecting corridors, both for PRA and other programs, appear in Parts III and IV. Suffice it here to show PRA's original economic corridors in Exhibit 2.10.[117]

Exhibit 2.10 Original PRA Economic Corridors in Peru

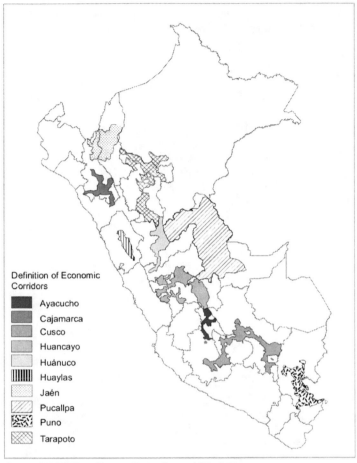

Definition of Economic
Corridors

- Ayacucho
- Cajamarca
- Cusco
- Huancayo
- Huánuco
- Huaylas
- Jaén
- Pucallpa
- Puno
- Tarapoto

Source: USAID/Peru Poverty Reduction and Alleviation program.

9

Making Accountability Real

Managing for results entails setting real targets for yourself, and holding yourself accountable for meeting those targets. Accountability requires up-to-date information on where you stand against your targets and on what problems stand in the way of meeting them.[118]

"The piecemeal engineer knows, like Socrates, how little he knows. He knows that we can learn only from our mistakes. Accordingly, he will make his way, step by step, carefully comparing the results expected with the results achieved, and always on the look-out for the unavoidable unwanted consequences of any reform; and he will avoid undertaking reforms of a complexity and scope which makes it impossible for him to disentangle causes and effects, and to know what he is really doing."

Karl Popper, *The Poverty of Historicism* (New York: Routledge Classics, 2002), p. 61 (first published 1957).

In development circles, the task of collecting, organizing, and reporting data typically falls to "monitoring and evaluation systems." Like beauty, the meaning of monitoring and evaluation often lies in the eyes of the beholder. What the phrase means in one program may not be at all what it means in another.

Given its commitment to manage for results, sound monitoring and evaluation is fundamental to the buyer-led approach. More than that, it differs in key respects from practice elsewhere. For that reason, this chapter explains the whys and wherefores of the buyer-led approach to monitoring and evaluation. Chapter 16 spells out how to do it properly.

The overriding purpose of collecting and monitoring data is to manage for greater effectiveness and impact. With data, development practitioners can learn from their mistakes, make changes, and get the biggest "bang for their buck." That truism plays out more in theory than it appears to have done in practice. Day to day, most development practitioners see monitoring and evaluation neither as a tool to help them do their jobs nor, needless to say, as a yardstick for accountability. For them, monitoring and evaluation is more often an afterthought to delegate to administrative support staff to carry out. When practitioners do focus on data, they tend to view them through the prism of comprehensive frameworks and plans, development hypotheses, and a myriad of metrics too numerous to count. It is easy to see, then, why many view monitoring and evaluation more as a necessary evil than as a management tool—and, why, as a whole, the development community appears to have learned so little.[119]

An example of how practitioners regard monitoring and evaluation as an administrative hardship occurred a few years ago in the Middle East. A year after its inception, a program there had not defined any indicators to track other than "number of training activities." When the donor representative in charge needed a monitoring and evaluation plan for the files, the program brought in a specialist on a two-week assignment. During that period, both the program director and the technical implementation team were tied up in training activities and unable to provide input to the plan. In the end, the specialist developed indicators and a 40-page plan in relative isolation. To top it all off, the donor later changed its objective tree for the entire program, rendering many of the indicators obsolete.

"Based on the analysis of 13 recently completed projects, we can say that we really do not know how successful our projects are or have been in quantitative terms because we don't really track and report on indicators in any consistent fashion...[I]ndicators and monitoring and evaluation are a matter that reliably loses attention after the initial work planning phase and that disappears along the four or five-year life of a project."

Doug Baker, "Latin America and Caribbean Monitoring and Evaluation Study," Chemonics International Inc., Washington, D.C., 2006.

In fact, most development programs begin with the best of intentions. Most have logical, results, or strategic objective frameworks that lay out hypothesized relationships between means and ends and provide the starting point for developing a monitoring and evaluation plan. Most programs break out time at their inception for a specialist to develop such a plan, which, in essence, consists of spelling out the data required to prove or disprove the framework's development hypothesis and to monitor program operations. Usually there are many parties involved in program design and start-up, so usually the plan winds up containing a multiplicity of metrics. At this stage, **everything** is important, and the more metrics the better: monitoring and evaluation specialists will receive substantially fewer kudos for parsimony than for satisfying the hopes and fears of every cook stirring the broth. In short, the incentives driving behavior at this point lean much more heavily toward covering the waterfront than toward economy. To be fair, experienced monitoring and evaluation specialists often try to swim against the comprehensiveness tide, arguing that the plans should strip away the tangential and include only what is in the managing party's direct "manageable interest." Although that principle makes sense from one perspective, in its worst form it can dumb down the whole exercise into managing just for inputs—numbers of workshops held, roundtables organized, tradeshows visited, for example—thereby vitiating any possibility of testing the relationship between implementation actions and program designers' hypothesized results.[120] To build in real accountability, one has to manage not only for higher order results, but for higher order results for which it is possible to draw a causal link between what a program does and what it accomplishes.

The key guiding principle for monitoring and evaluation under the buyer-led approach is to focus, first, on a very limited number of higher order results—sales and jobs, essentially—and, second, on the causal relationship between proposed program activities and the achievement of those results. By sticking to a few, well defined indicators, applying rigorous and carefully reasoned standards to the acceptance and rejection of data, and maintaining the discipline to make resource allocation decisions on cost-effectiveness grounds, a number of buyer-led programs have shown that it is indeed possible to learn from doing and extract a tangible return on their development investment. Interestingly, this principle, which tends to be the norm in business, has applicability in other contexts as well. The reporting of casualties in Iraq is an example:

> [T]here is significant underreporting of the violence in Iraq. The standard for recording attacks acts as a filter to keep events out of reports and databases. A murder of an Iraqi is not necessarily counted as an attack. If we cannot determine the source of a sectarian attack, that assault does not make it into the database. A roadside bomb or a rocket or mortar attack that doesn't hurt U.S. personnel doesn't count. For example, on one day in July 2006 there were 93 attacks or significant acts of violence reported. Yet a careful review of the reports for that single day brought to light 1,100 acts of violence. Good policy is difficult to make when information is systematically collected in a way that minimizes its discrepancy [sic] with policy goals.[121]

As noted in Chapter 5, the buyer-led approach uses the "5:1 rule" to decide whether to support potential clients, that is, it invests program resources only if there is a reasonable expectation that every dollar of assistance will result in at least five dollars of client sales. Monitoring and evaluation personnel play a central role in the application of the 5:1 rule. Beforehand they vet the reasonableness of projected results, proposed activities, and the presumed causal relationship between the two. Afterward, they monitor whether the 5:1 rule plays out in practice, and when it does not, flag the problem for management's attention.

Although it may appear gratuitous to say so explicitly, it is essential for monitoring and evaluation personnel to reach their conclusions independently of line personnel. Although they obviously need to work with line personnel, they must have the final word on data veracity. In essence, monitoring and evaluation personnel

"Never ask of money spent
Where the spender thinks it went
Nobody was ever meant
To remember or invent
What he did with every cent."

Robert Frost

"The Hardship of Accounting" in *Comic Poems*, ed. by Peter Washington (New York: Alfred A. Knopf, 2001), p. 24.

act as independent in-house auditors. In that capacity, they relieve line personnel of the awkward moral hazard of serving as judge and jury of results, safeguard program managers from accusations of "cooking the data," and boost the likelihood that all results reported are indeed attributable to program activities. Their ongoing review and verification of performance data also provide incentives for line personnel to report the data correctly the first time around.

Part III goes into detail on how to apply these basic principles effectively. Since the procedures laid out there depart substantially from what conventional wisdom would suggest, this chapter concludes with a number of examples of common but counterproductive practices. Without an understanding of the drawbacks of current approaches, it is hard to understand why the operational approach to monitoring and evaluation presented in this book is in fact so radical.

Programs set unrealistic targets or no targets at all. Many programs develop results frameworks, often specifying increases in sales and jobs as program objectives, but fail to quantify how much they expect the increases to amount to. Alternatively, some programs set the targets for those objectives either unreasonably high or unreasonably low, which eviscerates their worth as targets. Chapter 14 offers some guidelines for setting targets high enough to challenge program managers to meet them, but not so high as to make them pipedreams.

Programs set qualitative targets whose achievement is difficult to verify. Some programs set targets whose overall intent is clear but whose meaning is vague or subject to diverse interpretations. Examples include "increased capacity," "changing mindsets," and "behavioral change," all of which are laudable objectives, but not ones readily amenable to objective measurement—and, *a fortiori*, not ones for a program to hold itself accountable for or to hinge its credibility on.

Programs track so many results that they can wind up losing focus. A case in point is the Madagascar Market and Trade Development program (see the appendix to this part of the book).

Ironically, an assortment of targets does offer one decided advantage: it boosts a program's chances of achieving at least some of them and reporting successes. But how much those successes add up to is another question.

Programs fail to distinguish ends from means and wind up focusing inordinate attention on intermediate, not final results. Again, the Madagascar program is a pertinent example, but it is by no means the only one. Another is the Inter-American Development Bank's Río Informático program in Brazil. Río Informático starts from the premise that training in information technology is a good thing, and gauges the extent of its success essentially by its coverage, not by its impact.[122]

Programs claim results not directly attributable to their actions. Many programs set their sights very high, projecting that their actions will have an impact on regional if not national aggregates. The farther removed those aggregates are from program activities, obviously the more tenuous the causal relationship between the two. For example, business development services may indeed play a role in contributing to the overall development of a region, but sorting out their contribution from that of other factors is no easy task.

Attribution of causality can also be problematic at a more micro level. One of the business advisors in PRA's Economic Service Center in Huancayo was a motivational speaker. After giving a motivational seminar to one of his clients, he told the program's Monitoring and Evaluation Unit that the program could now take credit for increases in the client's sales in the future. The Unit ruled the advisor's case out of court—naturally—and demanded that all program results pass the test of *prima facie* cause-effect plausibility.

Economic theory says that if a household earns more income, it will spend a portion of that income on goods and services, which will generate income for other households, which will spend a portion of it on additional goods and services, etc. etc. To the extent that a development program succeeds in raising the incomes of poor households, it would appear logical for it to take credit for associated "multiplier effects" as well. In theory, the argument is impeccable. In practice, estimating those effects with a reasonable degree of assurance can be problematic.

As a rule, development programs are better off if they take a conservative approach to results measurement and reporting. If the attribution of even a penny appears dubious, the skeptic will question the whole dollar, often opening up arcane and ultimately fruitless debates on extrapolation methodology. Better to go forward with something small but sure than with something large but questionable.

Programs undertake ambitious but often unnecessary surveys. To measure change, one needs a baseline, that is, an *ex ante* snapshot of what things are like before the infusion of program support. Almost like Pavlov's dog, many monitoring and evaluation specialists hear the word, "baseline," and they jump to "surveys." But baseline surveys often are unnecessary. Under the buyer-led approach, for example, what better way to construct a baseline— sales and jobs—than to get it one by one from the clients to whom one is about to provide support?

Programs collect many too many data. From the school of hard knocks, survey statisticians have developed an illuminating rule of thumb: left to their own devices, analysts tend to let their desire for data spin out of control and, in the end, wind up looking at roughly only 15 percent of what they collect. Survey statisticians generally try to rein in analysts' voracious appetites for information, a practice that has applicability to the design not only of survey research but of monitoring and evaluation systems.

At the gestation stage, it is probably not too much of an exaggeration to say that the sky is the limit for the results those involved expect from development programs. The first drafts of monitoring and evaluation systems tend to be ambitious in scope, and, when in doubt, err on the side of including possible results rather than leaving them out. As the programs get off the ground, program managers are wont to jump on the enthusiasm bandwagon, adding other information that would be interesting to collect. For their part, funding agencies often find it hard to resist the temptation to micromanage program managers, and request considerable detail on what the programs are working on.[123] As the reader can appreciate, the cumulative effect of this cascade of mutually reinforcing accretions can be a data monster whose cost far exceeds its benefits. If ever the KISS aphorism— Keep It Sweet and Simple—has applicability in development, it is here. Once again, management parsimony trumps intellectual adventurism. A good monitoring and evaluation system—like good management generally—focuses on the essential and does not let itself get distracted by the "interesting." At a minimum, it distinguishes clearly between what results the program is holding itself accountable for and what information it is tracking for other purposes—and gives clear priority to the former, not the latter.

Programs fail to distinguish between data requirements for managing for results and data requirements for estimating impact. In recent years, the designs of some development programs have called not just for tallying up immediate results but for incorporating data collection and analysis methodologies to estimate what those results add up to in the end. The intent to get at the broader impacts induced by program support—for example, whether buyer-led program-induced sales translate into jobs, and whether those increases in jobs actually translate into reductions in poverty—is a laudable one. In trying to do so, however, program designers have tended to get carried away, creating operational problems of data overload. For example, the design of Nicaragua's Millennium Challenge Account's Rural Business Development Program called for collection of detailed business plan data on over 3,000 small and medium farm suppliers, when a sample methodology would have worked just as well. To assure comparability with control groups, the design also placed restrictions on where and when the program could work with whom, thereby tying management's hands artificially and, in essence, making the horse of program operations subservient to the cart of evaluation design. As a rule, managing for results requires periodic collection of a minimal amount of solid data on each and every program client—which, in buyer-led programs, typically means connector firms. In contrast, estimating impact normally lends itself more toward survey methodologies that collect data with much less frequency but of considerably greater depth.

Programs conceive monitoring and evaluation as a desk data-processing job. Many development practitioners see monitoring and evaluation as essentially a desk job requiring primarily information technology skills. Data processing is important, of course, but it is a tool, not the heart of the matter. In programs oriented to increasing sales and jobs, the veracity of the data coming from client businesses is key. Many personnel schooled in conventional monitoring and evaluation methodology are not particularly well suited for interacting with businesses and obtaining and analyzing data from them. Two different programs applying the buyer-led approach found that out the hard way, and had to replace monitoring and evaluation "experts" with financial analysts, whom they found much more apposite.

Programs conceive of monitoring and evaluation as an administrative support function, and budget accordingly. In the design phase, most development programs begin with big plans for monitoring and evaluation. But as budgets get squeezed and managers try to do more with less, monitoring and evaluation tends to get cut, thereby reinforcing the tendency to assign responsibility for it to administrative support staff. Regardless of the proximate cause, such a decision reveals program management's true colors: ones that fail to translate managing for results into operational terms and see monitoring and evaluation basically as nothing more than a reporting afterthought.

Programs divorce monitoring and evaluation from operations. Even programs committed to managing for results can fail to integrate monitoring and evaluation into operations.

At the risk of anticipating the expository discussion in Chapter 16, it is worthwhile to share an anecdote on the how-to of applying the buyer-led approach. In 2004, the author traveled to Armenia to assist in the start-up of the MEDI program discussed above. A young professional who had specialized in monitoring and evaluation systems accompanied him on the trip. Prior to going, the author briefed him on how monitoring and evaluation fit in the buyer-led approach, explaining that, far from an afterthought, it influenced decisions right at the beginning as to what clients to support and what ones not to. Throughout these conversations, he nodded his head in agreement, and both he and the author felt comfortable that he "got it."

A day after arrival the two traveled to the program's business promotion office in northeastern Armenia and facilitated a session with the program's new business advisors. Using the market chain framework discussed above, the director of the program asked the advisors to justify their proposals to support different clients. He insisted that they indicate who was prepared to buy each client's goods and services, what problems stood in the way of their consummating the transaction, how much the program's support would cost, by how much the client's sales would rise, and what the ratio would be between the expected sales and the cost of program support. For the advisors in question, it was the first time they had had to think through what they were doing in a rigorous, logical fashion, and the whole exercise proved extremely useful in giving focus and discipline to program activities.

In any event, during the first break the young professional accompanying the author approached him with a big smile on his face and commented, "Now I get it! Until this morning, all your talk about tying monitoring and evaluation into operations was pure theory. Now I see how **the considerations that guide monitoring and evaluation must enter at the very beginning of the process.** More than that, I now see that **unless we tie those considerations in then, we lose all discipline right from the outset.**"

In brief, the buyer-led approach asks the very same questions beforehand that any good monitoring and evaluation system must ask afterwards. At the beginning, the key questions are, "What sales do we expect to generate and at what cost?" At the end, the questions are, "Did we get the results and at what cost?"

Part III goes into detail on how to put the linkage between operations and monitoring and evaluation into practice. For now, suffice it to say that as simple, straightforward, and commonsense as the approach appears, it is a major innovation. Yes, many development programs set up monitoring and evaluation systems. But rare indeed is the program that can link step by step and in causal fashion the final results obtained with program actions undertaken.

Programs fail to capitalize on monitoring and evaluation as a communication tool. In addition to helping development practitioners manage for results, monitoring and evaluation systems can make significant contributions to the nature and content of development program communications with clients, funding agencies, and the public at large. In Peru, for example, explaining what demand-driven really means was not enough to convince skeptics of the wisdom of PRA's decision to start with the buyers of poor people's goods and services—in most cases, medium or large companies—and not with the poor themselves. Although the skeptics could appreciate the argument intellectually, fears of "fat cats" appropriating all the benefits did not die easily. But when PRA showed with numbers that the strategy of starting with buyers actually delivered more results for poor people than many traditional programs, the tide turned, and turned dramatically. In the end, results talk!

In a similar vein, the best way to convince businesspeople of the benefits of an approach is not with plans and promises, but by showing results. Again, building on people's copycat instincts is key to spreading benefits, for which, once again, monitoring and evaluation can be an invaluable tool.

> "You don't need publicity if the results of what you are doing are visible and are valuable to the people. The steam from a pot of good soup is its best advertisement."
>
> William J. Lederer and Eugene Burdick, *The Ugly American* (New York: W.W. Norton & Company, 1958), p. 127.

In summary, effective monitoring and evaluation systems perform three essential functions: they make accountability real by comparing progress against targets; they identify implementation problems in real time and set the basis for correcting them; and they provide the results grist for the communications mill to induce still more results. In contrast to much current practice, they link directly to program operations, keep focus, instill discipline, and keep it sweet and simple. Part III explains how these principles apply operationally to the buyer-led approach.

10

Solving Systemic Problems: Policy and Institutional Reform

Much of the discussion above—Chapter 8, especially—hammers home the advisability of taking business transactions as one's point of departure, of identifying the problems that stand in the way of consummating those transactions, of devising solutions to address those problems, and, if cost-effective, of implementing those solutions. Most of the time, the best way to solve a market chain problem is as an individual business problem—or to put it negatively, not to elevate the problem to a broad policy or institutional issue affecting not only the market chain in question, but, presumably, others as well. The book's insistence on this point may come across as strident, but the stridency is intentional, precisely because the temptation to leapfrog to a plane above the fray is so strong.

Why is the temptation so strong? In essence, for two reasons. First, the background, experience, and organizational imperatives of countries, donors, non-governmental organizations, and development practitioners themselves generally run counter to the approach outlined here. As discussed in Part I, much of the development community sees its mission as saving the world, not individual market chains—and, in the end, does not have faith that market incentives, working from the bottom up, can transform local, regional, and national economies. In some instances, practitioners are averse to working with individual businesses because they fear accusations of favoritism, that is, of giving unfair advantages to some businesses over others. Either way, the practical upshot is that many development programs feel compelled to enter from the top down, arguing that policy and institutional change is the best way to affect not just a limited number of poor people, but many at the same time. At the same time, they also ratchet up the realm of operations to a level where relationships between means and ends become tenuous—thereby, once again, sidestepping serious accountability for delivering results.

Second, and in a positive vein, policies and institutions do matter, and they matter keenly. For example, as far back as 1957, Peter T. Bauer and Basil S. Yamey wrote,

> [T]he functioning of the economic system is profoundly influenced by the institutional framework within which it takes place; and, in turn, the framework is necessarily affected by government action. The establishment of institutions suitable for the efficient operation of the economic system does not necessarily emerge from the operation of the system itself. For example, the market cannot be expected to bring about a suitable law of property or the institution of limited liability. Nor is the role of the state in this sphere a passive one once the minimum services have been organized and an institutional framework established. Changed conditions may render obsolete existing institutions, and the economic endeavour of individuals and firms may be frustrated unless the institutional structure is consciously and appropriately reshaped.[124]

The emergence of the field of institutional economics in the last two decades, coupled with World Bank and other research showing that countries with sound policies and institutions do a better job in reducing poverty than countries without sound economic management, has led to an emphasis in recent years on targeting development assistance to countries that have their policy and institutional acts together.[125] The jury is still out, however, on whether conventional approaches to policy and institutional reform deliver the impact desired. There are a number of reasons to believe that is not the case.

Although policy and institutional reform has many operational variants, it usually entails negotiating and implementing a policy agenda, that is, a set of policy and institutional reforms that often, though not always, become codified in a policy matrix. The policy matrix lists the reforms the government will institute and includes the actions that the parties involved will take to implement or support the reforms. In some instances, the agenda forms part of a "structural adjustment program." Under such a program, a donor agrees to transfer resources to the government once it takes the actions in question. Defenders of structural adjustment argue that such programs can be useful in helping countries bite the bullet on reforms that they want to do anyway. Critics—Easterly, among them—claim that you cannot "buy" reform in that way, and that the probability is slim that such reforms will last.[126] In any event, policy and institutional reforms can take many forms. Many policy reforms derive from the macroeconomic measures—trade liberalization, elimination of currency overvaluation, reduction of fiscal deficits, etc.—that John Williamson incorporated in what became known as the "Washington Consensus."[127] For their part, many institutional reforms have their roots in cross-country studies showing what institutions correlate closely with development. Examples include control of corruption, ease of market entry, labor market flexibility, etc.

In practice, this overall approach to policy and institutional reform suffers from a number of drawbacks, discussed in what follows.

The binding constraints faced by market chains are marked much more by their diversity than by their sameness. Although policy and institutional reforms may contribute to the resolution of market chain constraints, the choice of which ones to implement and which ones not to implement is often not informed by the specifics of the constraints in question. As a result, targeting is effectively very much hit or miss. The reforms in question may do some good, obviously, but whether they get at the most important problems is very much an open question.

About ten years ago a colleague of the author made a field trip in Honduras. During it, she met with an array of businesses. Most of them pinpointed government retention of foreign exchange as their major stumbling block to increasing exports. On her return to Tegucigalpa, the country's capital, she met with personnel of a donor-funded policy analysis and reform program. To her great surprise, the biggest concern of the businesses had not even hit the program's radar screen.

Sometimes it is better to leave policies and institutions alone. The mindset underlying the development of a policy agenda is that change is good. In some cases it may not be. Often continuity of a second-best situation is preferable to trying to zigzag your way to the first-best.

> "That is the problem with governments these days. They want to do things all the time; they are always busy thinking of what things they can do next. That is not what people want. People want to be left alone to look after their cattle."
>
> Alexander McCall Smith, *The No. 1 Ladies' Detective Agency* (New York: Anchor Books, 1998), pp. 20-21.

Twenty-five years ago, the author participated in the design of an agricultural policy program in Peru. To get a sense of perspective from outside the capital city, he traveled to Cuzco to interview interest groups there. In each case, he naïvely asked the question, "What policies do you think it would make sense for the central government to change?" To his surprise, a number of interviewees responded, "Why can't Lima just leave us alone? We know agricultural policies aren't perfect, but as long as they stay the same, we can deal with them and react accordingly. What really hurts us is when Lima changes them every six months." The author has never forgotten those interviews. Much more than he, those affected appreciated how much the credibility of a policy framework hinges on its stability.[128]

Structural adjustment or no structural adjustment, the government has to believe in reform. Unless governments "own" their reforms, implementation will be half-hearted, and the likelihood they will last very low.

> "There are allies and there are allies, Siri. There's how we see them and how they see themselves. To us, the advisers are resources we can use or ignore as we see fit. They believe they've been allocated to this or that department to steer our policies closer to their own, to make us more dependent on them.
>
> "The more advisers we allow in, the more Hanoi sees us an appendage. That's why we have a deliberate but unofficial policy of ignoring 40 percent of what they tell us."
>
> "Even if it's good advice?"
>
> "We don't throw it out completely. Rather we store it away until the chap's gone off, frustrated at our non-compliance; then we dig it out and pretend it was ours all along."
>
> Colin Cotterill, *The Coroner's Lunch* (New York: Soho Press, Inc., 2004), pp. 95-96.

As the Director of USAID's Kosovo Cluster and Business Support (KCBS) program, a seasoned development practitioner with extensive experience in the Balkans, put it,

> I was somewhat concerned...that KCBS had been identified...as the main USAID program for improving the business operating environment...[T]here are many features associated with improving the business operating environment, from many of which we are either excluded, or in which it would be patently ineffective and inefficient for us to try and get involved...
>
> I made my view known...about getting involved in the corridors of power. One can spend much time being shuffled around ministries, encountering intentional and/or unintentional delays, and accomplishing very little. Three examples of protracted resolution come to mind—a transportation agreement with Greece, licensing of quarries and construction companies, and improvements in tendering and award procedures for road contracts. Unless there is a commitment by Ministers to put a fire under their departments and correct some of the more egregious practices, our efforts are merely whistling down the wind.
>
> KCBS is a can-do, get-it-done team. Absent changes in the business environment made by the only people who can really make them, we shall press forward working around the existing constraints, trusting that in time there will be changes, but meanwhile pursuing the project objectives of increased employment, reduced imports, expanded markets and increased sales.[129]

Even when governments are committed, reform can be very slow and cumbersome. Below appears a case from Peru where the progression from inception to the passage of legislation took four years. In Guyana, the passage of a small and medium enterprises law took three years. With a visible sigh of relief, an expatriate supporting the process commented afterwards, "People have been asking us for so long what we have been accomplishing, and we finally have something to show!"

To complicate things, policymaking does not conclude with the passage of reforms. As the author and a colleague made the point years ago,

> Reforms need to be explained, implemented, evaluated, and modified; new issues arise for the policy framework to address; pressures mount to modify or subvert reforms; and, finally, decisionmakers need to avoid policy mistakes. In that sense, the policy reform opportunity, although important, is not the end point of reform, but the beginning...
>
> No matter how heady policy breakthroughs appear initially, it is during the muddling-through phase that reforms take root and become understood, accepted, and implemented—or are subverted and rendered inconsequential paper tigers. Perseverance is critical.[130]

For those in the reform trenches, textbook "best practices" often do not amount to much. Although those involved obviously need to maintain a clear vision of where they are going, "muddling through" really is the operative term. One might prefer policy and institutional reform to resemble a carefully orchestrated Beethoven symphony, but up-close observers probably would liken what they see more to the gyrations of a rock concert—messy, opportunistic, personalistic, clashing, reactive to external events, second-best, etc.

For every reform that finally takes concrete shape, there are countless others that abort along the way. The combination of low probabilities of success and inordinate time frames for them to take root makes careful selection of which reforms to work on imperative. The moral of the story is clear: if policy and institutional reform takes so long and you can not guarantee that it will happen at all, you had better be very sure that whatever reform you work on is worth the trouble. Again, the guidance for business development services applies here as well: be sure you do not just good things, but cost-effective things. Unless you know beforehand that the change in question—if and when it actually happens—is likely to have a big payoff development-wise, it may be wise to think twice about moving forward.

Ways of identifying what reforms to work on can miss the binding problems. Conventional approaches to policy and institutional reform select what reforms to work on in a variety of ways. None of them necessarily gets at market chains' binding constraints.

One alternative favored by donors is to seek the counsel of the Minister of Finance, the Minister of Economic Development, or other appropriately placed public officials. Implementation-wise, securing the backing of key government personnel can up the probability that the reform(s) under consideration will actually come to pass. But Ministers are not necessarily good pointers to what reforms are important and what ones are not. As a rule, the information they receive is filtered, often by rent seekers, and their perceptions are battered from all sides by conflicting political objectives. There are exceptions, of course, but to rely on the instincts of a Minister alone is generally not a good strategy for sorting out the important from the accidental.[131]

A second alternative is to rely on formal meetings with interest groups presumably affected by the reforms in question. One example is the councils that various countries have created under competitiveness initiatives. Another is chambers of commerce. But like government Ministers, such groups are not necessarily reliable touchstones for setting policy and institutional reform priorities. Not only are such groups not necessarily representative, but they may often be geared—consciously or unconsciously—more to the maintenance of the status quo than to what is best for the country as a whole. In addition, formal meetings often create counter-productive bandwagon effects, in which a small minority can secure majority support for narrowly based proposals. Any practitioner who has worked with businesspeople individually can attest to the disjoint between what they identify as important in one-on-one interviews and what emerges from formal gatherings.

A third alternative is essentially not to fix priorities at all but to set up a programmatic framework to accommodate whatever policy and institutional reform issues emerge along the way. This alternative offers the advantage of pragmatism and flexibility, but its very open-endedness makes it hard to instill accountability. USAID's Growth Through Investment and Trade program in Indonesia was a case in point. Its scope of work, which also attached high priority to strengthening local analytical and advisory capacity, foresaw the following assortment of achievements as illustrative results:

> More open economy through reduction in tariff rates, tariff dispersion and non-tariff barriers
> Increased non-oil and gas exports
> Moderation of local governments' constraints on trade
> Indonesia in compliance with WTO requirements
> Indonesia actively and constructively participating in the Doha round of negotiations
> Increased private and domestic investment
> Improved telecommunication regulatory regime encouraging foreign investment
> National treatment and market access achieved for foreign investment in services
> Tax administration improved
> Customs administration improved
> Fiscal deficit reduced
> Inflation reduced
> Exchange rate relatively stable and competitive
> Public debt managed well
> Labor policy administered well
> Private sector and other civil society groups actively participating in trade and investment policy discussions and decisions[132]

No one program, of course, can achieve results of such breadth and magnitude. To give focus, a Policy Analysis Council was to recommend "critical" policy issues to address, but its design called for a composition and structure much more akin to an academic organization than to one driven with urgency to address pressing policy concerns. In effect, therefore, the design of the program left things so wide open as to give it almost carte blanche.

A fourth alternative is to compare where a country stands against the Washington Consensus, the Global Competitiveness Index, the Index of Economic Freedom, the Millennium Challenge Corporation selection criteria, etc., to figure out where the country falls short, and to remedy those shortcomings. In short, the approach is priority setting by checklist.

In the limit, the obsession with comprehensive institutional reform leads to a policy agenda that is hopelessly ambitious and virtually impossible to fulfill. Telling poor countries in Africa or Latin America that they have to set their sights on the best-practice institutions of the United States or Sweden is like telling them that the only way to develop is to become developed—hardly useful policy advice! Furthermore, there is something inherently unfalsifiable about this advice. So open-ended is the agenda that even the most ambitious institutional reform efforts can be faulted ex post for having left something out. So you reformed institutions in trade, property rights, and macro but still did not grow? Well, it must be that you did not reform labor-market institutions. You did that too but still did not grow? Well, the problem must be with lack of safety nets and inadequate social insurance. You reformed those with little effect? Obviously the problem was that your political system was unable to generate sufficient credibility, lock-in, and legitimacy for the reforms. In the end, it is always the advisee who falls short, and never the advisor who is proved wrong.[133]

This pointed critique of the checklist approach comes from a review of a self-critique by the World Bank of its experience in policy reform over the prior decade. Interestingly, the Bank itself has become disenchanted with mechanistic blueprint approaches to policy and institutional reform, and is now arguing for experimentation and selective and modest reforms. As Gobind Nankani, the World Bank vice-president who oversaw the review, writes in its preface, "The central message of this volume is that there is no unique universal set of rules . . . [W]e need to get away from formulae and the search for elusive 'best practices.'"[134] Or, as Dani Rodrik sums it up,

Policy reforms of the…Washington Consensus type are ineffective because there is nothing that ensures that they are closely targeted on what may be the most important constraints blocking economic growth. *The trick is to find those areas where reform will yield the greatest return.* Otherwise, policymakers are condemned to a spray-gun approach: they shoot their reform gun on as many potential targets as possible, hoping that some will turn out to be the ones they are really after. *A successful growth strategy, by contrast, begins by identifying the most binding constraints.*[135] [emphasis added]

The World Bank review focuses primarily on macro constraints, but the same concerns apply at a micro level. An exhortation to develop United States-like institutions in Madagascar makes the point:

[E]fficient markets in our economy are based on underlying institutions that economists tend to take for granted. These include property rights, commercial codes, contract law (and its enforcement), forward deliverable contracts and futures markets, insurance and credit markets, Federal and state supported research and extension, and the like. These institutions play a major role in alleviating some of the inherent risk in agricultural markets. They provide safety nets and public goods that individuals cannot obtain independently. When these institutions do not exist or are only rudimentary, markets cannot be expected to work efficiently. In the case of Madagascar, liberalization has expanded production and marketing opportunities for producers and other market participants. However, they have not been able to take advantage of new opportunities in many cases because of infrastructure, information, credit, and other institutional constraints.[136]

Although the exhortation is excellent as an exhortation, the gamut of institutional reforms suggested is so broad that it is unclear where to start. To put it in Rodrik's terms, it fails to point out what constraints are in fact the most binding—a task that obviously requires on-the-ground homework.

Good policies and sound institutions are essential, but policy and institutional reform programs are not necessarily a cost-effective use of resources. The catalog of drawbacks to conventional approaches outlined above may foster the impression that it would be wise for development programs to shy away from policy and institutional reform. That is far from the case. It makes absolutely no sense to throw the baby out with the bathwater. That said, it makes abundant sense to revisit how development practitioners actually go about supporting reform.

For most economists, the contention that development—and the reduction of poverty—depend on good policies and sound institutions has ample evidence to support it and has become almost an article of faith. This book does not dispute that contention. What it does question is making policy and institutional reform **programs** an article of faith. Four years ago, the author participated in the design of a Millennium Challenge Corporation (MCC) program in Mozambique. Interestingly, MCC personnel brought quite different perspectives to different components of the program. For the business development services component, they insisted on a stringent economic analysis to be sure that the corporation's investment would yield a satisfactory economic rate of return. That is very well and good. In contrast, the economic justification of the policy component of the program elicited relatively little concern, as if the goodness of policy and institutional reform were enough, by itself, to justify MCC's involvement.[137] As the drawbacks of conventional approaches attest, however, how one actually goes about policy and institutional reform can make a big, big difference.[138]

What is good for the goose is good for the gander. The same rigor one demands of business solutions to address binding market chain problems applies to policy and institutional reform as well.[139]

The buyer-led approach can provide the ground truth required for identifying binding policy and institutional constraints. Operationally, the starting point of the buyer-led approach is diagnosing the key problems—or opportunities—that affect connector firms and their suppliers. Examples given above focus on problems amenable to business solutions—absence of buyers, poor technology, weak management, lack of access to finance, etc. As one might expect, some diagnoses also surface policy and institutional deficiencies as binding constraints. When that happens, there is no reason that the development practitioner's approach should be any different from what it is in the transactional case: no matter what the nature of the problem is, find the most cost-effective solution and apply it. If that solution is transactional, fine; if it involves policy and institutional reform, fine, too.

Exhibit 2.11 presents the overall approach in schematic form. Overall, the driving philosophy is problem-solving, where solutions are driven by the nature of binding problems.

Exhibit 2.11 Market Chain Problem-Solving Framework

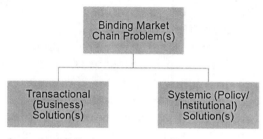

Source: James T. Riordan.

In very general terms, there are two ways to address the problems that stand in the way of market chain growth. The first approach, the "transactional" approach, embodies what people refer to commonly as business solutions. Under the transactional approach, one attacks problems one by one as business propositions. For example, if a client needs finance, it helps him or her access funds from available sources; it does not worry about financial intermediation throughout the whole country. Similarly, if a client needs technical assistance to make a better popsicle, it puts the client in touch with a popsicle production expert; it does not look at the government's vocational education policy and lobby for training programs for all popsicle producers in the country. The vast bulk of examples given above are of this type.

The second approach—the systemic or policy/institutional approach—has to come into play when the binding problem is such that a transactional business solution cannot do the job. A classic example is poor road networks that make affected market chains more costly and less competitive than they would be otherwise. Solving a road problem usually goes far beyond the capability of any one client and requires collective action to influence national or local government transportation priorities. A second example is land tenure insecurity that affects market chain suppliers throughout an entire valley, an expanse that makes the independent, one-by-one approach prohibitive.

Sometimes, a problem may be amenable to resolution either transactionally or systemically. As discussed above, the temptation is to jump to the systemic approach. Its presumed advantage is that it addresses problems across the board and can affect a broad clientele. Its big disadvantage is that often the problems in question are so large, complex, or politically charged that they may be virtually impossible to solve, at least in the short and medium run. Systemic solutions can obviously be far-reaching, but they can be "all or nothing" in character. All other things being equal, therefore, the transactional approach normally is the preference.[140] Why prepare a household vegetable garden with a pneumatic drill when a shovel will do? The bottom line is to be realistic from the start: if the probability of success of a systemic intervention is high, go for it; if not, think twice about embarking on a venture that may have little to show for it in the end.

The beauty of the intelligence emerging from contact with clients under the buyer-led approach is its aptitude for elucidating the binding constraints confronting market chains. Two examples are indicative.

In initial interviews under the Caribbean Open Trade Support program, potential clients shared what they saw as the key constraints to their growth. The constraints covered the waterfront. Most responses touched upon problems amenable to transactional solutions, but some identified policy and institutional issues as well.[141] Program personnel culled the responses to develop a first cut of the policy and institutional issues that the program's policy component might give priority to. By more than a two-to-one margin over its closest competitor, the combined burden of import duties, the country's consumption tax, and its value added tax surfaced as the major policy concern in Antigua-Barbuda. By a similar margin, the burden of Dominica's value added tax and import duties surfaced there. Given the two countries' heavy import dependence, the responses were not surprising, but they did serve to eliminate other issues that might have been "nice" to look at but were clearly of secondary importance to the program's clientele.

After a couple of years of operation, the management of PRA asked its business promotion offices to canvass their clients on the policy and institutional problems of most import to them. To make the process manageable, management instructed the offices to limit themselves to no more than three issues each. Three priorities emerged from the responses: road policy, the non-facilitative posture of the government's phyto-sanitary agency, and the spottiness of secure land titles for small farmers in the highlands of the country.[142] Given the broad swath of the country represented, eliciting ground truth of this kind was key in two respects: first, to furnish a more informed basis for deciding what issues to work on; and, second, to enable the program to get closer to the issues those actually concerned saw as most important.

Bringing policy and institutional focus to a development program is a big plus. By themselves, however, problems do not morph directly into solutions. In fact, the problems identified may be more symptoms than root causes. For that reason, deciding on a course of action typically requires both more precision in defining the nature of the problem and additional analysis, not only economically but in the art of the politically and socially possible. For example, many countries create bureaucratic impediments to setting up businesses, which has prompted a number of reform programs to focus on reducing how much time the process takes and how much it costs. As the data underlying the World Bank's ranking of countries by ease of doing business indicate, the time and the cost of starting a business are clearly problematic in many countries.[143] In some cases, though, especially ex-Soviet Union countries, businesspeople complain, not so much about how much time registration takes or about how many hoops they have to jump through, but about the unpredictability of the whole process. For them, time and money are not so much the issue as the inability to plan ahead and make commitments. The bottom line, once again, is that development practitioners must not only stay micro and do their homework, but concentrate on issues affecting actual business transactions. In recent years, Georgia has received acclaim for its rapid rise up the World Bank's Doing Business rankings. Those involved attribute much of their success to keeping the focus squarely on those private-sector/public-sector interactions of most concern to individual businesses.[144] Ireland embarked on its "Irish-Miracle" growth trajectory by following much the same strategy. In the mid 1980s, when Intel spelled out the concerns that would keep it from investing in the country, the Government of Ireland made addressing those concerns, in essence, the heart of its policy agenda.

Much of the discussion above is big picture stuff. In fact, an increasing body of evidence is materializing— and it obviously affected the World Bank's review of its policy and institutional reform experience—that reform does not have to be enormous to have an impact.[145] As a practical matter, much policy and institutional reform is not—and does not need to be—all-encompassing in scope. In truth, any development program that can help bring about even one major policy change can count itself successful.

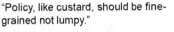

"Policy, like custard, should be fine-grained not lumpy."

"The state of Britain: You've never had it so good," *Economist*, February 3, 2007, p. 12.

This discussion concludes with examples of circumscribed but still significant reforms under programs using key elements of the buyer-led approach:

Peru. When PRA canvassed its clients in the interior of the country, government road policy—both national and local—surfaced as policy and institutional reform priority number one. As PRA did its homework, it eventually adopted a two-pronged attack. The first prong limited itself to a 350 kilometer stretch of road on the lower eastern slope of the Andes known as the Fernando Belaunde Terry (FBT) Highway. As of 2001, the highway was completely unpaved and poorly maintained, a state of affairs that had an especially adverse impact on the Department of San Martín, an area with ample agricultural production potential. Because of the poor shape of the road, produce from San Martín had to take a circuitous route to get to Lima, boosting production costs and lowering the region's competitiveness substantially. PRA had previously pulled together existing cost-benefit analyses of possible infrastructure improvements in the economic corridors it served. Those analyses suggested that even with modest projections of benefits, rehabilitating the highway would likely yield an internal rate of return on the order of 26 percent. As a result, when a broad cross-section of local public officials, businesspeople, and non-governmental organizations—the Tocache Group—approached PRA for help in figuring out a solution to the problem, it was glad to help.

In 2001, a sub-group upped the pressure on the Ministry of Transportation to give the highway higher priority. After some political twists and turns, the Ministry agreed to participate in the search for a solution, and three local businesses, together with PRA, hired a manager to spearhead the initiative. When it became clear that the government would not reallocate central budget monies to the highway, the directorate of the initiative started thinking "outside the box." For years San Martín, together with other Departments in the jungle, had enjoyed an exoneration from taxes applied elsewhere in the country. The objective of the exoneration was to promote development in the region, but by all objective analysis, the measure had not been successful. Little by little the understanding took root that San Martín would benefit more from paying the taxes and earmarking the funds for the highway than by continuing with the status quo. Over the next couple of years, consensus on that score grew in the local community. In 2005, the results became codified in law, and the highway now counts on approximately $14 million annually—not enough to cover the entire cost of rehabilitation, but a start, anyway.[146]

This story is a classic illustration of how policy and institutional reform takes place in the land of the second best. For the orthodox economist, the exoneration from taxes was a distortion, and so is the earmarking that has followed it. If those involved had stuck to orthodox principles, nothing would have happened. The final solution may not be perfect, but it represents the will of those involved—and it works.[147]

The second prong of attack took a broader look at the country's transportation problem, recognizing that current and projected government budgets, even when supplemented with infrastructure loans from the donor community, would not come close to meeting the country's requirements for the foreseeable future. Once again, therefore, it was time to think outside the box—in particular, to explore the potential of public-private partnerships as a way to leverage capital investment by the private sector, both domestically and abroad. Working closely with PROINVERSION, the government's investment promotion agency, PRA helped the government improve Peru's legal, regulatory, and institutional framework to make it more conducive to concessions. Recognizing that the devil is in the details, it also provided "alpha-to-omega" technical assistance, advising the government from the onset of project design through to transaction closure. The assistance in question covered the entire project-life-cycle sequence, including: project identification; financial, technical, and legal structuring; open and transparent competitive tendering; negotiation of concession agreements; and performance monitoring.

In just four years, three major public-private partnership contracts came to fruition. The three partnerships are:

Amazon North Highway Concession. This partnership, valued at $220 million, will improve, rehabilitate, operate, and maintain 960 kilometers of highway between Paita, a port city on the Pacific Ocean, and Yurimaguas, a river port municipality servicing Iquitos in eastern Peru and Brazilian ports of call along the full length of the Amazon river to the Atlantic.

Concession of the South Container Terminal of the Port of Callao. This 30-year, $360 million concession will build and operate a new, state-of-the-art container terminal that will add more than 600,000 TEU (twenty-foot equivalent units) of capacity per year to the Port of Callao, the largest and most important port serving Peru.

Amazon Central Highway Concession. This 30-year, $115 million concession will finance, rehabilitate, construct, operate, and maintain 847 kilometers of national highway linking Lima, on the Pacific coast, Huancayo, in the highlands, and Pucallpa, in the jungle Department of Ucayali.

The Amazon North and Amazon Central highway concessions guarantee the financing, construction, rehabilitation, and long-term operation and maintenance of more than 1,800 kilometers of highway—more than 18 percent of Peru's national highway network. In length, they are the largest road concession projects in the world. The concessions will integrate, along two different routes, the coastal, highland, and jungle regions of Peru, and will connect Peru with Brazil, the region's largest economy. They will reduce transportation costs and travel time significantly, improving the competitiveness of businesses in the regions in question.

All told, USAID spent a little less than $3 million to facilitate the Callao concession. A third party estimates that by 2013 that investment will have brought more than $2.1 billion of benefits to the Peruvian economy.[148]

Tanzania. In the early 2000s, Tanzanian coffee farmers had to pay "nuisance taxes" on the order of 21 percent, a tax burden higher than in any of five "peer" producing countries (Costa Rica, Ethiopia, Guatemala, Kenya, and Uganda). In addition to helping small farmers improve the quality of their coffee, therefore, TechnoServe engaged the Association of Kilimanjaro Specialty Coffee Growers, the Tanzania Coffee Board, and other major actors in the country's coffee industry to push the government to reduce the taxes in question, some of which applied to other agricultural products as well. In 2003, the program succeeded, providing incentives for farmers to reinvest their earnings, become more competitive, and capitalize on business opportunities with major international coffee buyers in ensuing years.[149]

Armenia. For many of the small Armenian businesses that MEDI came in contact with, the binding constraint to expansion of sales, especially export sales, was lack of working capital. As in other emerging economies, banks relied primarily on fixed-asset collateral to secure loans and, as a consequence, focused their attention almost exclusively on large corporate clients. To help solve the problem, MEDI approached the Central Bank and seven commercial banks about their openness to accepting purchase orders as collateral. Each agreed in principle, but also had its concerns. To address them, MEDI helped establish a policy and procedural framework for purchase order financing and provided customized technical assistance to participant banks in how to make the new lending product operational. In just the last few months of the program, participating banks provided 52 loans worth more than $5.8 million to 35 companies, all of which repaid their loans in full and on time, thus establishing a firm foundation for servicing an even greater customer base.[150]

Paraguay. Some policy and institutional reforms can be even more micro. An example from Paraguay, which lends itself readily to portrayal in the market chain framework, is a case in point (see box on next page).

To conclude, the buyer-led approach leans toward applying transactional solutions to clients' binding problems, but there are times when only systemic solutions will do the job. Again, the operative principle at work is to let the nature of the problem determine the appropriate solution. Instead of taking an ivory-tower approach to policy and institutional reform, it makes sense to let policy priorities flow from and be informed directly by intelligence drawn from working with individual businesses. No program can do "policy" across the board. Development practitioners need a ground-truthing filter to sort out the important and the doable from the unimportant and the undoable. The buyer-led approach provides such a filter.

Market Chain Example from Paraguay

Milk distributors and grocery stores in Paraná, a state of Brazil bordering Paraguay, experienced problems in securing a reliable supply of high-quality milk from local sources. Interestingly, governmental authorities supported initiatives to import milk from Paraguay, since Paraguayan milk is higher-quality and less expensive.

Chortitzer, Paraguay's largest milk processor, was hesitant to enter the Brazilian market. Brazilian tax and customs regulations are complex, and the company knew it would need to invest time and money to understand and comply with those regulations. To ease entry, USAID's Paraguay Vende program identified Brazilian buyers willing to buy from Chortitzer and to help it manage the regulations.

Chortitzer's initial shipment of milk encountered difficulty at the border— Brazilian customs officials had never seen milk imported from Paraguay. Together, the buyers in Brazil, Chortitzer, and Paraguay Vende solved the problem, and Chortitzer now exports to Brazil routinely. After one year, its exports of packaged milk surpassed $260,000. More than that, the resolution of the misunderstandings at customs has served as an inducement for other Paraguayan companies to export to Brazil as well.

Final Demand
Brazilian milk distributors, grocery stores

Connector Firm
Chortitzer

Suppliers
Paraguayan dairy farmers

Source: USAID/Paraguay Vende program.

11

Does the Buyer-Led Approach Work?

Previous chapters offer a variety of examples from different countries of how buyer-led programs can help individual market chains expand sales and generate substantial employment. This chapter takes an aggregate perspective, asking whether the composite of all activities in a buyer-led program delivers sizeable numbers of sales and jobs, does so at reasonable cost, and yields an acceptable return on investment. It also shows how the buyer-led approach can deliver results in challenging environments.

Specifically, this chapter consists of two major sections. They show:

How the buyer-led approach delivers ample results cost-effectively, generating a good return; and
How the approach can operate effectively in difficult socio-economic, political, and institutional environments, though admittedly not as effectively as elsewhere.

The buyer-led approach is by no means a panacea. Nor is it written once and for all in stone—it is evolving and improving with applications in new contexts. Still, experience shows that it does succeed in doing what it sets out to do, and does so very well.

Sales and Jobs, Cost-Effectiveness, and Return on Investment

Sales and jobs. Of the various programs applying the approach, PRA has run the longest. It is therefore useful to look at the evolution of its results over time. Exhibit 2.12 shows the time pattern of incremental sales generated under the program.

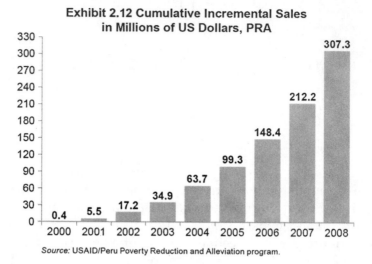

Exhibit 2.12 Cumulative Incremental Sales in Millions of US Dollars, PRA

Source: USAID/Peru Poverty Reduction and Alleviation program.

Once PRA started up, expenditures did not vary dramatically from year to year. As a consequence, the upward trajectory of incremental sales suggests that the longer a program runs, the more bang one can expect from each buck invested in program activities — in other words, that its cost-effectiveness will rise over time. Incremental sales results from other buyer-led programs support that hypothesis strongly. Indeed, the same kind of trajectory appears in buyer-led program after buyer-led program and emerges as a general rule. There are three main reasons for the rising pattern:

"The business best-seller *Good to Great* describes a pattern of success among the U.S.'s top companies as akin to pushing on a large, heavy industrial fly wheel by hand. At first, there is considerable resistance and a great push may generate only a small turn. Increasingly, with each push results in a larger turn, until eventually a small effort results in a rapidly turning fly wheel, working on the principle of energetic momentum. A remarkable characteristic of these top performer companies is that none achieved their status with one dramatic innovation or product. Their sustainable results (over 15 straight years performing 30 percent above the Dow Jones average) were rather due to roll-up-the sleeves commitment and hard work, and a disciplined focus on strategy and execution."

Danilo Cruz-DePaula, "First Annual Work Plan for the USAID Private Sector Competitiveness Enhancement Program in Azerbaijan," Chemonics International Inc., Baku, 2008, p. 4.

Learning from experience. Every development program has start-up costs. It is natural to expect buyer-led programs to start slowly and to pick up steam only after they have actually applied the approach and mastered its nuances.

The way firms grow. Exhibit 2.7 above portrays the step-ladder pattern of the way firms grow. Over time, firms knock off different problems, and jump sequentially from one sales plateau to the next. In one sense, Exhibit 2.12 is the step ladder writ large, that is, the amalgamation of the growth of the program's various client firms.[151]

Graduation of old clients and addition of new ones. Once a buyer-led program has helped a client solve a binding problem, it obviously does not turn on its heel and walk away, but neither does it try to perpetuate a close working relationship. Unless some new pressing problem or opportunity emerges, it makes much more sense for the program to "graduate" the client from intensive attention, and concentrate on new clients that can benefit from program assistance to climb their respective step ladders.

Exhibit 2.13 shows PRA's incremental employment results. As one might expect, Exhibit 2.13 mirrors Exhibit 2.12 to a large extent. The same goes for other buyer-led programs, but, as presaged in Chapter 7, the ratio between sales results and employment results varies from one program to another.

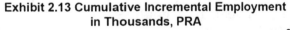

Exhibit 2.13 Cumulative Incremental Employment in Thousands, PRA

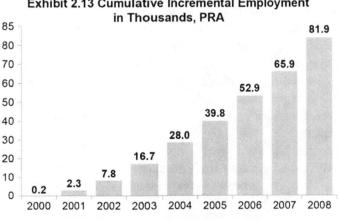

Source: USAID/Peru Poverty Reduction and Alleviation program.

The data in Exhibit 2.13 include the employment generated directly by program clients plus the employment generated in backward-linkage activities—that is, by suppliers as well. The measure of incremental employment is person-year full-time equivalents (FTEs). Operationally, most buyer-led programs collect employment data in person-days and then make the conversion to person-years afterwards. Typically, much of the employment generated by buyer-led programs is seasonal, especially in agricultural pursuits. Working from person-days up allows programs to capture that phenomenon.[152]

The ratio between incremental employment and incremental sales can vary not only among programs but within an individual program's life. For example, the last years of PRA evidenced a pattern of employment generation qualitatively very different from that in the program's early years. Early on, it took roughly $9 to $12 in new sales to generate a person-day of labor. From 2005 on, that ratio rose to the $15:1 to $24:1 range, suggesting, at first glance, that PRA became much less efficient in generating jobs.

The truth is subtler than that. As the PRA final report explains:

> Although it now takes twice as many sales to generate a person-day of labor, it takes half as much labor to generate the same amount of sales—which, all other things equal, suggests that the productivity of labor has risen. If economic theory serves as a guide, this should mean that labor earns more now than it did before. Accordingly, the early years of PRA appear to have generated employment in quantity while the later years have improved productivity.
>
> A close look at businesses supported by PRA suggests that this interpretation is correct. Labor productivity might be expected to have risen in relatively capital-intensive activities like the manufacturing of tiles by Cerámicas KANTU or processing of trout by Piscifactoría de los Andes. But productivity has also risen in primary agriculture. For example:
>
> In the last two years, AiB in Ayacucho has invested heavily in artichokes in Secceslambra and Chiara in Ayacucho, bringing advanced technology to the area for the first

time. Before the arrival of AiB, typical daily wages ranged between S/.8 and S/.15, without social benefits. AiB, a formal company, now pays S/.22 plus social benefits. Given the higher productivity per worker associated with the new technology, AiB could afford to pay the higher wage, which, interestingly, has now become the standard in the area.

With the entry of Frito Lay in Huánuco, potato farmers switched from traditional varieties to capiro, required by Frito Lay for industrial processing. With Frito Lay's assistance, yields have risen dramatically, from eight metric tons per hectare in 2001 to 15 to 18 metric tons currently. Potato farmers now sell—and earn—much more than they did years ago, but the higher production requires proportionally less labor.[153]

Buyer-led programs set incremental sales and employment targets to measure progress against. Not all programs meet their targets each year, but, cumulatively, most either come close to or surpass them. Of course, much depends on the targets one sets in the first place, which, as Chapter 14 describes, is much more art than science.

PRA's targets had their origins in experience under 15 previous USAID trade and investment programs throughout the hemisphere. The PRA Activity Paper divided the programs in question into three categories, successful, moderately successful, and less successful, and chose the successful group as the standard to meet. In coming up with the final numbers, it also relied heavily on experience under USAID/Peru's Microenterprise and Small Producers Support (MSP) program.[154]

Cost-effectiveness. Whether a program meets its targets is indicative. Whether it is cost-effective is another question. The reasons that some buyer-led programs are more or less cost-effective than others are very illuminating, as the following discussion illustrates.

Comparable data exist on the program costs and resultant incremental client sales of buyer-led programs in seven countries—Armenia, Azerbaijan, Bolivia, Kosovo, Nigeria, Paraguay, and

Exhibit 2.14 Cost-Effectiveness of Buyer-Led Programs

Programs	Years of Operation	Incremental Client Sales ($ million)	Associated Contract Costs ($ million)	Incremental Client Sales/ Associated Contract Costs	Main Factors Affecting Results
PRA, Peru	9	307.3	42.3	7.26	Large scale, learning by doing
KCBS, Kosovo	4	165.5	20.2	8.18	Good management, relatively small country
Paraguay Vende	3.5	35.8	4.8	7.45	Rapid start-up, learning from PRA
MARKETS, Nigeria	3.5	105.0	13.0	8.08	Large domestic market, large dynamic client
ABAD, Azerbaijan	2.33	8.8	2.8	3.14	Slow start-up, early closeout
RCA, Bolivia	2	12.0	9.0	1.34	Predominance of permanent crops
MEDI, Armenia	1.25	0.675	0.275	2.45	Pilot program, little time

Source: Chemonics International Inc.

Peru. It is therefore possible to estimate the cost-effectiveness of each program. The findings appear in Exhibit 2.14.[155]

The discussion that follows touches briefly on each program in the exhibit, starting from the bottom and working up.

The USAID/Armenia Micro Enterprise Development Initiative (MEDI) generated results in a very short time. The component of the program applying the buyer-led approach spent $275,000 over a 15-month period. During that time, it facilitated $675,000 in client sales, yielding a ratio of incremental client sales to associated contract costs of 2.45.

How did MEDI deliver the results it did so quickly? As discussed in Chapter 3, the main factor was exemplary management, management that kept its focus squarely on results and stayed disciplined throughout. It also benefited from cross-country learning, taking explicitly into account lessons from elsewhere—Peru and Paraguay, especially.

At first glance, the USAID/Bolivia Rural Competitiveness Activity (RCA) appears the least cost-effective buyer-led program. Over two years, it spent $9 million, generating a modest $12 million in incremental client sales. Two factors contributed significantly to the relatively low sales-cost ratio of 1.34. First, the program works in a difficult environment, facilitating a transition from coca to licit economic opportunities. Second, the most viable economic opportunities in the program's area of influence are permanent crops, that is, crops that typically take two or more years to mature. The results in Exhibit 2.14 do not account for permanent crop investments in the first two years of the program bearing fruit later.

Over a 27-month period, the USAID Azerbaijan Business Assistance and Development (ABAD) program spent $2.8 million and generated $8.8 million in incremental client sales, yielding a sales-cost ratio of 3.14. ABAD supported a broad variety of businesses—rug, nuts, poultry, potato, and watermelon businesses, for example. At its inception, ABAD experienced management problems, which contributed to the program getting off to a slow start. Just as it was starting to gain momentum, the program ended prematurely, preventing it from taking advantage of the benefits of program longevity.

The results from the next three programs demonstrate how, all other things equal, the longer a program runs, the higher the ratio of incremental client sales to associated contract costs one can expect. Each of the programs in question ran roughly twice as long as MEDI, RCA, and ABAD, and each generated sales-cost ratios roughly three times as large.

In its first three and a half years, the USAID/Nigeria Maximizing Agricultural Revenue and Key Enterprises in Targeted Sites (MARKETS) program spent $13 million and generated $105 million in incremental client sales, for a sales-cost ratio of 8.08. The program's key to success has been its focus on high performers, especially a large, dynamic rice processor that expanded its operations significantly by providing assistance to and sourcing product from thousands of small rice farmers.

The cost-effectiveness of the USAID Paraguay Vende program is similar. In three and a half years, the program spent $4.8 million, generating $35.8 million in incremental client sales, for a sales-cost ratio of 7.45. Paraguay Vende, the second buyer-led program, internalized and benefited directly from lessons learned from PRA, on which it patterned itself to a large extent. The program got off to an aggressive start, generating significant results early on. In contrast to PRA, which set up ten business promotion offices in the interior of the country, Paraguay Vende set up three, a less cumbersome logistical task. In addition, the location of Paraguay Vende's economic corridors allowed them to take advantage of export opportunities more readily than their counterparts in Peru.

The USAID Kosovo Cluster and Business Support (KCBS) program benefited from Kosovo's relatively small size, which made it possible to manage the program from the capital of Pristina. KCBS also benefited from strong, disciplined management. Over four years, it spent $20.2 million and generated $165.5 million in incremental client sales, yielding a sales-cost ratio of 8.18. The bulk of the sales came from construction materials, livestock, and fruits and vegetables.

PRA, the first buyer-led program, spent $42.3 million and generated $307.3 million in incremental client sales, yielding a sales-cost ratio of 7.26. It worked initially in ten economic corridors in the interior of the country, but that number fluctuated up and down somewhat during the program's life. The magnitude of the program carried with it a heavy management burden. As the first buyer-led program, PRA also did much learning by doing, especially in the program's early years. On the other hand, the length of the program allowed the program to build considerable trust with clients and achieve impressive results.

Taken together, the cost-effectiveness experience of the seven buyer-led programs dovetails in its programmatic implications. In essence, the major implications are three:

Once more, the longer a buyer-led program runs, the more cost-effective it becomes. Limiting programs to two or three years can be premature, running the risk of missing out on the years that typically yield the most results.

The greater the geographic spread of a buyer-led program, the less likely it is to be as cost-effective as programs limited geographically. Recognizing the management burden a large program imposes is not an argument against scaling up. Far from it. It is simply a flag of caution for program designers not to have unrealistic expectations beforehand.

Solid, disciplined management is essential. Although a less tangible variable than program longevity and program spread, many of the differences in cost-effectiveness among buyer-led programs have to do with the quality of program management.

Return on investment. A study a few years ago reported the programs that different donors considered their best micro and small enterprise programs worldwide. The donors did not define what criteria constituted "best," but PRA appeared first on USAID's list.[156] Although that ranking presumably says something about PRA's return on investment, it is worthwhile to look at return on investment explicitly. If one invests $10 in a development program and get $20 of economic benefits in return, that is one thing. If the return is only $5, it is quite another.

The data from PRA and Paraguay Vende allow for comparable estimation of the internal rate of return to each program. Mathematically, the internal rate of return (IRR) for a program is the value of r that satisfies the following relationship:

$$\sum x_i /(1+r)^{i-1} = \sum c_i /(1+r)^{i-1}$$

or, perhaps more simply,

$$(x_1 - c_1) + (x_2 - c_2)/(1 + r)^1 + (x_3 - c_3)/(1 + r)^2 + \ldots (x_n - c_n)/(1 + r)^{n-1} = 0,$$

where

x_i = the benefit to the program in year i, and
c_i = the cost to the program in year i.

The expenditures made by the two programs correspond to the definition of costs in the internal rate of return formula. Sales, however, do not correspond to the definition of benefits. That is so for two reasons. First, they are the gross sales of program clients, not the value added by them. Second, the sales reported do not take opportunity cost into account. For example, in the absence of the program, the labor employed by PRA and Paraguay Vende clients would likely have engaged in some other, though most likely less remunerative, work. From an economic perspective, it is necessary to net out that counter-factual likelihood to estimate the benefits to the economy for which the program can definitely take credit.[157]

Estimating value added conservatively and opportunity cost liberally, analysts derived internal rates of return for the two programs. For its first seven years, the internal rate of return estimate for PRA came to 33 percent.

This estimate compares very favorably with the few estimates of internal rates of return available for similar programs elsewhere.[158] That said, there are reasons to believe that the estimate in question understates the full impact of the program by a substantial margin. First is the likely conservatism of the assumptions made in the calculations themselves. Second is the omission from the calculations of additional benefits whose magnitude is most likely considerable. The sales from which the benefits in the calculations derive include **only** the direct sales **only** of PRA clients **only** within the economic corridors where PRA works **only** within the current life of the program. They do **not** include:

Sales resulting from income multiplier effects—the additional expenditures of firms and households that have earned more income from PRA-supported activities do not enter the calculus.[159]

Sales of copycats—the results do not account for the sales of the many investors who have seen the success of PRA clients and have decided to invest on their own.

The value added that takes place outside PRA's corridors—PRA calculates its results where it works, that is, in the interior of the country; the results do not include any of the transport and marketing costs required to move final product to Lima or foreign markets, for example.

Sales that are likely to continue beyond the program's life—the calculation shuts off the benefits at Year 7 even though many clients will continue to take advantage of the commercial relationships developed and nurtured under the program.

If anything, therefore, the IRR results reported for PRA do only partial justice to the impact of the program, imbuing even more confidence that the approach can not only deliver results, but deliver them economically.[160]

The IRR calculation for Paraguay Vende yielded an even higher result, 128 percent. Skeptical readers are likely to raise their eyebrows about the magnitude of that estimate, especially since it comes from only three years of operations. So, too, did the author. After going over the calculations carefully, checking the conservatism of all underlying assumptions, and questioning both the veracity of reported sales and whether the program had been instrumental in bringing them about, however, the author found nothing out of order and, in the end, drew perhaps the obvious conclusion: **the rapidity with which a program shows results can make a big, big difference.**

Other analysts performed IRR calculations for KCBS and the Bolivia Trade and Business Competitiveness (BTBC) program, a program with much in common with the buyer-led approach. The analysts used variants of the methodology used for PRA and Paraguay Vende. The results are sensitive to the assumptions they made, but, in general, fall in the neighborhood of the rate of return estimated for Paraguay Vende. To the extent one can generalize from four cases, therefore, it appears the buyer-led approach, when implemented well, can provide a robust return.

To single out one case as a counterpoint, ABAD got off to a very slow start in Azerbaijan. The sluggish beginning resulted from a combination of management problems, its mandate to set up multiple business promotion offices, thus making start-up more painstaking than in a smaller program, and, initially, anyway, lack of clarity on whether ABAD was to be a business development program or a community development program (see the discussion in the next section of this chapter). By its third year, ABAD was beginning to show the buoyancy of sales growth that has characterized buyer-led programs elsewhere. At that point, however, an attempt at an IRR calculation yielded a negative result. Unfortunately, US-AID ended the program early, so it was not possible for ABAD to ratchet up its momentum to the point that the benefits in the out years outweighed the program's start-up costs—highlighting, once again, the importance of getting off to a good start and, equally, the higher unit returns you get the longer a program runs.

Socio-economic impacts. The logic of the buyer-led approach is, first, that increasing sales is a necessary condition to increase jobs and, second, that increasing jobs is a necessary condition to reduce poverty. In neither case is the relationship a sufficient condition. Logically, therefore, the buyer-led approach cannot guarantee reductions in poverty. Still, available evidence—especially from PRA, the most studied of the buyer-led programs—suggests that the approach does indeed reach the poor and has a positive impact on them. A summary of the evidence from PRA appears in the program's final report. A portion of that summary follows:

> Although it is difficult to prove incontrovertibly that PRA has reduced poverty, a substantial body of evidence that has accumulated over the years suggests that PRA has succeeded in reaching large numbers of poor people and has had a significantly positive impact on them.
>
> The first evidence comes from the application to PRA of USAID's Poverty Assessment Tool on PRA's interventions. The tool, designed for USAID by the IRIS Center of

the University of Maryland, estimates the poverty levels of a program's beneficiaries. Specifically, it gauges the extent to which a program reaches the very poor, where the "very poor" means people earning less than $1.00 per day.

PRA distinguishes between program clients and beneficiaries. Program clients typically are processors or traders that enter into formal relationships with the program through business plans. Most times, the processors or traders source from suppliers—typically small producers, particularly farmers. Those small producers are the program's beneficiaries. At the time of the application of Poverty Assessment Tool in late 2007, PRA had 194 active clients who had backward sourcing linkages with 37,800 beneficiaries.

The team applying the assessment tool surveyed 324 randomly selected households throughout the corridors where PRA works. They found an estimated 43 percent of PRA beneficiaries to be very poor. Given that the very poor are a subset of the poor, the results suggest that, even though PRA's immediate clients normally are processors and traders, it has still been quite successful in reaching its ultimate target population.

A second body of evidence consists of the results of case studies conducted by independent third parties. Examples of such case studies include the following:

Impact on the welfare of women manufacturing gold chains in the city of Cajamarca. This econometric study compares women employed by a PRA client in gold chain manufacturing in Cajamarca with a randomly selected control group. The study estimates that PRA support helped raise the incomes of the women and increased the hours they worked by an average of 119 percent and 103 percent, respectively. In absolute terms, the increases in incomes were sufficient to raise the women above Peru's extreme poverty line.

Impact on the welfare of artichoke farmers in the Mantaro Valley. This study uses a quasi-experimental design to compare farmers who produced artichokes for PRA clients with randomly selected control groups. The study estimates that the monthly incomes of PRA-supported artichoke farmers were 30 percent higher than they would have been without PRA support.

Impact on snow pea producers in Ayacucho. Early in the program, PRA helped two clients introduce snow peas in Ayacucho. This study analyzes data from structured interviews with actors working with snow peas, from farmers to exporters. It also compares day laborers working with snow peas with a control group of day laborers working with commercial potatoes, the traditional crop in the area. The study estimates that:

Snow peas generated $351 more in sales per hectare than commercial potatoes

Snow peas generated 269 more person-days of employment per hectare than commercial potatoes

Most of the additional employment went to women

Day laborers working with snow peas earned 15 percent more per month than laborers with commercial potato crops[161]

Preliminary analysis of data from RCA in Bolivia adds an interesting lens to how buyer-led programs can contribute to poverty reduction. According to the principal analyst in charge,

[W]e ask the question about the time and cost required to bring a rural family out of poverty through application of the business model. For this time series analysis we chose client groups from the ARCo [RCA in Spanish] database that received support for developing and implementing business plans, that now no longer receive our support, and have reported sales for at least 3 years, including base line. ARCo support to business plans is limited to one year only, but with some delays and extensions averages about 15 months. Given this initial impulse, rural families with no commercial activities at the beginning reach the poverty threshold in commercial sales in less than 4 years, and the total cost to the project is probably under $2,000![162]

Even if the final analysis of the data—in process as of this writing—shows that the cost to the program is somewhat higher, that would still appear to be a small price to pay to help poor people escape from poverty.

In addition to its contribution to poverty reduction, a buyer-led program can bring about broader socioeconomic effects. The experience of PRA—again, the most studied of buyer-led programs to date—is instructive:

> *Impact on regional gross domestic product (GDP).* The final evaluation attempted to take income multiplier effects into account. Specifically, it estimated the indirect income impacts of PRA activities on the main departments serviced by its ESCs in 2006. Most ESCs appear to have had a sizeable impact on regional agricultural GDP; and Ayacucho, Tarapoto, and Pucallpa appear to have had a visible effect on total regional GDP.
>
> *Demonstration effect.* The final evaluation team also

Estimated Indirect Income Impacts of PRA Activities, 2006

Department (Economic Corridor)	Percentage of Agricultural GDP	Percentage of Total GDP
Ancash (Ancash)	2.13	0.17
Ayacucho (Ayacucho)	8.26	2.35
Cajamarca (Cajamarca, Jaén)	4.58	0.80
Cusco (Cusco)	4.11	0.61
Huancavelica (Huancavelica)	3.26	0.75
Huánuco (Huánuco)	0.84	0.18
Junín (Huancayo)	2.41	0.44
Piura (Piura)	3.55	0.51
Ucayali (Pucallpa)	8.74	1.65
San Martín (Tarapoto)	6.44	1.90

Source: USAID/Peru Poverty Reduction and Alleviation program.

attempted to quantify the extent to which other parties, seeing PRA's successes, replicated what PRA had done. During the relatively brief period of the evaluation, the team identified 25 instances of enterprises or producer associations that had invested in operations similar to those PRA had supported. The tangible evidence of the replication shows up often in sizeable expansions of hectares in crops supported by PRA. Perhaps more significantly, PRA's entry into a given area has frequently induced the entry of additional buyers, increasing competition and the prices farmers receive. When PRA entered Piura, for example, there was only one processor purchasing black-eyed peas. There are now seven.

**Examples of Expansions in Hectares
of PRA-Supported Crops**

Product	Economic Corridor	PRA-supported Hectares	Additional Hectares
Artichokes	Huancayo	375	275
Black-eyed peas	Piura	1,870	400
Amaranth	Cusco	260	80

Source: USAID/Peru Poverty Reduction and Alleviation program.

Changes in thinking about development and how to attack poverty. PRA's demonstration effect has gone well beyond enterprises and producer associations. If imitation is the best form of flattery, then PRA's effect has been profound. Again, to cite the final evaluation:

PRA is changing attitudes and actions on how economic development projects are implemented in Peru. Non-governmental organizations and project implementers are the institutions that most frequently are adapting the PRA market-pull methodology (38 instances). Unexpected by the evaluation team, municipal and regional governments are also observing the increased sales and revenue flowing back to their communities and allocating resources to support business growth (32 instances). In addition, six other instances of organizations, including chambers of commerce, are using the PRA methodology.

Perhaps the most noteworthy example of others' buy-in—literally—into the PRA approach has been the financial and moral commitments that prominent Peruvian institutions have made to PRA. In 2002, Minas Buenaventura celebrated its fifty years of operations in Huancavelica by opening up an ESC [Economic Service Center] that was not independent of PRA but embedded under its management umbrella. Based on the successful experience of Minas Buenaventura in Huancavelica, Antamina made the same kind of commitment in Ancash. In a similar vein, when the government's *Sierra Exportadora* Program was exploring alternatives to bring economic dynamism to the *Sierra* and effectively link poor people there with markets, it concluded that PRA was its best option. Further, rather than attempting to replicate the PRA approach completely on its own, the government joined Minas Buenaventura and Antamina in formalizing a "PRA alliance" with USAID. As a result, PRA is no longer considered simply a USAID program. It enjoys significant Peruvian support, and other interested parties can make commitments to PRA as well, thereby magnifying the overall impact of the program and its approach.[163]

The catalog of socio-economic effects cited here has taken time for PRA to bring about. That, in and of itself, is a significant lesson—and an additional reason for extending successful programs as long as possible. Yes, if a program is not working, by all means cut it off. But if it ain't broke, don't risk ruining it by trying to fix it either.

The time frame required for bringing results about bears on the discussion of transformational development above. There is ample evidence from Peru that PRA has had an effect well beyond its clients and their suppliers. For example, the communities with which Piscifactoría de los Andes has forged relationships are substantially different, both quantitatively and qualitatively, from what they were years ago. The same goes for the local population affected by the dramatic expansion of hectareage in corn and beans in Pucallpa, for the communities participating in the burgeoning artichoke boom near Huancayo, for the farm households now tied into the production of flowers for export in Huaraz, for the many women now working in the jewelry industry in Cajamarca, for the communities affected by the bixina processing plant near Quillabamba, for the once subsistence potato farmers in Huánuco now growing premium potatoes for Frito Lay, etc.

Clearly, none of these examples is comparable to the scale of a Silicon Valley. But neither is any of the examples just a bunch of one-shot sales that, once consummated, wither and die. In an article a few years ago, Michael Porter and Mark Kramer cite the tremendous impact of Nestlé's entry into the milk business in the northern district of Moga in India, showing how the number of suppliers grew from 180 small farmers to more than 75,000, and how their standard of living is now significantly better than in neighboring regions. Interestingly, though, the results in question took place over a period of more than 30 years.[164]

The Nestlé example is arguably an apt point of comparison for understanding the nature of the bottom-up development process taking place under buyer-led programs. The examples from PRA are akin to the Nestlé example in its early years, with some cases more advanced than others, obviously, but all with firm commercial substructures for consolidating and expanding their competitive advantages in the future. Whether all will withstand onslaughts from competitors it remains to see—some will, and some will not. Progress to date may not yet be turning whole economic corridors upside down, but no matter how one looks at it, there is little doubt it is indeed transforming local economies—and in instances like that of Piscifactoría de los Andes, affecting the lives of several communities at once.

The Nestlé example also suggests a way one might go about isolating the impact on poverty of buyer-led programs in the future. Methodologically, the ideal way to isolate the impact of a variable is to control for it over time (before and after) and against a treatment group's peers (in comparison with a control group). As a practical matter, it is rare that a program can set up and implement such a research design.[165] Realistically, therefore, one must decide whether to rely primarily on temporal or cross-sectional comparisons. In India, Nestlé had not conducted a baseline survey at the program's inception in 1962. As a result, the best way for it to assess whether the program had made a difference was through a comparison of its sphere of influence with neighboring regions. By extension, the same kind of approach would make sense in cases like PRA. To sort out the impact of its support to artichoke clients, for example, the relevant comparison would involve looking, first, at the welfare of the communities or valleys now growing artichokes with assistance from the program and, second, at the welfare of communities or valleys with similar ecological characteristics still producing for subsistence.

Adjustments in Challenging Environments

As effective as the buyer-led approach has proven to be, it is not a cure-all. Nor is it equally effective in all circumstances and in all socio-economic, political, and institutional environments.

Complementarity between poverty-reduction and poverty-alleviation programs. As Exhibit 2.1 illustrates, a society's fight against poverty has two fronts, a reduction front and an alleviation front. The focus of this book on poverty reduction is not to belittle the significance of alleviation-oriented social safety net programs. Some of poverty is structural and, as such, not amenable to the sales and job creation programs of the kind described here. As Paul Streeten puts it,

> [T]he poorest 20 percent includes many lame ducks: the disabled, the physically and mentally ill, the handicapped, the old, the unemployable. The charismatic Indian planner Pitambar Pant advocated in the 1960s a minimum-needs strategy that wrote off completely the poorest 20 percent as beyond help. Without going as far as that, special measures are needed to help these people, and commonly recommended policies such as employment creation or access may be of little use.[166]

As discussed in the first section of this chapter, PRA reached a considerable number of Peru's extremely poor households, but far from all. A propos of Streeten's observation, a sizable portion of the country's poorest people benefited—and continues to benefit—more from social safety net than from job creation programs.

The evidence suggests the buyer-led approach can help reduce poverty in its sphere of operation, but by no means all of it.

The role of culture. When development practitioners begin work in a new country, almost invariably they receive the advice, "Remember that this country is unique"—which, put another way, means, "We are different, and you cannot take what you have learned elsewhere and apply it with a cookie cutter here." But just how unique are individual countries? And to what degree do cultural differences among countries affect the transferability of the buyer-led approach from one to another?[167]

Over the years, the development community has displayed some ambivalence about the role of culture in development. At one extreme, some practitioners have argued that the differences between developed and developing countries are so great as to vitiate effective technology transfer. For example, in the aftermath of the Alliance for Progress, Lawrence Harrison wrote:

> The differences between North America and Latin America are enormous, covering virtually all aspects of human life. The North American and the Latin American have differing concepts of the individual, society, and the relationship between the two; of justice and law; of life and death; of government; of the family; of relations between the sexes; of organization of time; of enterprise; of religion; of morality. These differences have contributed to the evolution of societies which are more unlike one another than our past policymakers appear to have appreciated.[168]

If conventional stereotypes were any guide, one might expect anthropologists to share such sentiments. But even forty to fifty years ago, not all anthropologists fit that mold. On the one hand, a number of anthropological studies documented developing country cultures with remarkably high degrees of entrepreneurship.[169] On the other, some even suggested that the similarities among cultures outweigh the differences among them. As Clyde Kluckhohn put it more than 50 years ago,

> The anthropologist for two generations has been obsessed with the differences between peoples, neglecting the equally real similarities upon which the "universal culture pattern" as well as the psychological uniformities are clearly built.[170]

At the other extreme, one might expect economists to embody the opposite stereotype, namely, to argue that only economic forces matter, and that the key to development is "simply" to unleash the universally shared profit motive.

"All the differences on earth are a shadow, compared with the sameness."

Anne Perry, *Highgate Rise* (New York: The Random House Publishing Group, 1991), p. 79.

In fact, most development economists have taken much more measured positions, readily acknowledging culture's significance but, at the same time, failing to integrate cultural considerations fully in their work.[171] Again, as Bauer and Yamey wrote years ago,

> In economically backward societies, there are difficulties in the way of developing and using the entrepreneurial qualities. The force of custom, the rigidity of status, and the distrust of new ideas and of the exercise of intellectual curiosity, combine to create an atmosphere inimical to experiment and innovation. The collectivism of the extended family, the village, the clan or the tribe inhibits innovation because the rewards, if any, have to be shared widely. The innovator disrupts the established order of things in promoting new activities and is therefore often an object of suspicion. The low level of capital also hampers innovation. But these difficulties should not be exaggerated. The influence of foreigners and contact with a money economy have often elicited a response from the adaptable, energetic or ambitious members of native societies.[172]

Experience in implementing buyer-led programs lends credence to this middle ground. Yes, countries definitely are different, but not so different as to negate the power of market forces. Yes, only a limited number of clients will pick up aggressively on market opportunities, but that is true anywhere in the world, not just in developing countries. In the large scheme of things, not everyone is entrepreneurial material, but neither is everyone devoid of entrepreneurial attitudes and talent.

Programmatically, differences among countries obviously mean that one cannot impose a model developed in one place uncritically elsewhere. One must do one's homework and, again, adapt one's tools to the problems one finds. The heart of the buyer-led approach is problem-solving—or, in Easterly's terminology, Searching—and it is especially in culturally challenging environments that practitioners of the approach earn their pay. As a practical matter, protestations that cultural differences stand in the way of solving market chain problems often amount to nothing more than cop-outs and ploys to get off the hook of accountability. Although they may not always succeed, effective problem solvers bring potential solutions to the table, not excuses.

Interestingly, much discussion of culture relates operationally to the distinction drawn above between solving the *problemática* and solving the *problema*. For one who sees the development challenge in cultural terms, everything is all of one piece—that is, you cannot solve anything until you have solved everything. As Michael Harrington put it in *The Other America*, for example,

> "The tendency to blame the system is a convenient way of leaving no one accountable."
>
> E.J. Dionne Jr., "The System at Work," *Washington Post*, June 12, 2007, p. A25.

Perhaps the most important analytical point to have emerged in this description of the other America is the fact that poverty in America forms a culture, a way of life and feeling, that it makes a whole. It is crucial to generalize this idea, for it profoundly affects how one moves to destroy poverty...

Consequently, a campaign against the misery of the poor should be comprehensive. It should think, not in terms of this or that aspect of poverty, but along the lines of new communities, of substituting a human environment for the inhuman one that now exists.[173]

Fascinatingly, almost in the very same breath that Harrington makes his plea for comprehensiveness—that is, for solving the *problemática*—he offers a dramatic example of the power of focusing attention on just one *problema*:

> During the Montgomery bus boycott, there was only one aim in the Negro community of that city: to integrate the buses. There were no speeches on crime or juvenile delinquency. And yet it is reported that the crime rate among Negroes in Montgomery declined. Thousands of people had been given a sense of purpose, of their own worth and dignity. On their own, and without any special urging, they began to change their personal lives; they became a different people. If the same élan could invade the other America, there would be similar results.[174]

Although drawn from a different context, the example cited by Harrington bears directly on the approach for attacking poverty under discussion here. Again, no one denies that poverty is a multidimensional problem. But that is not to say that one has to attack it multi-dimensionally. In other words, describing a problem is one thing; addressing it strategically is another. Just as the focus on integrating buses in Montgomery had significant secondary and tertiary ramifications, so too can the generation of sales and jobs trigger ripple effects, allowing poor households to improve their housing, to access health and education services, to make themselves less financially and physically vulnerable, etc. The developing country taxi drivers referred to in Chapter 5 probably appreciate that point more profoundly than development practitioners themselves.

Applying the buyer-led approach in culturally challenging environments is easier said than done. That said, a combination of ingenuity and patience can often make it work, though not as smoothly as elsewhere. To show how that can happen, this chapter concludes with a discussion of three problematic operating environments that, at first blush, appear inimical to effective application of the approach. The first is an environment in which community ties bind so tightly that they dull private initiative; the second is a program environment that fails to draw clear distinctions between community development and business development; and the third is an atmosphere of entitlement, one found commonly, though by no means exclusively, in post-conflict situations.

Community ties that bind. Human beings live in community. Communities can take many forms—extended families, towns, clans, tribes, ethnic groups, religious groups, etc. To foster harmony, it behooves communities to look to the good of all their members. A savvy community may not give every individual absolutely equal treatment, but it does not exclude anyone consciously either. On the economic front, most developed countries would agree on the principle of equality of opportunity, even though putting that principle into practice may be easier to say than to do. In many developing countries, however, concern for equality extends beyond opportunity and applies also to outcomes. Friedman makes the point with a joke:

> I always remember a joke that Secretary of State James A. Baker III told reporters traveling with him—a joke that Soviet President Mikhail Gorbachev told him. Gorbachev was trying to underscore to Baker how difficult it was for Russia to make the psychological transition to capitalism, after so many years of communism, and he did it with this yarn: A Russian peasant finds a lamp by the side of the road and rubs it. Out pops a genie. The genie tells the peasant he can have any wish.
> The peasant tells the genie, "You know, I have only three cows, but my neighbor Igor has ten cows."
> "So you want twenty cows?" the genie asks the peasant.
> "No," says the peasant, "I want you to kill seven of Igor's cows."[175]

For most people who grow up in the developed world, the joke makes a good story, but nothing more. For most practitioners of development, however, the joke rings very true. In developed countries, most people take it almost for granted that if you work hard, you can get ahead and enjoy the fruits of your labors. In many developing countries, social norms are not so conducive to economic progress. Directly or indirectly, communities apply social pressure on "uppity" members to stay within the reach of the rest of the pack and, if they do succeed in making money, to share the benefits with their peers.

A couple of examples show how such communitarian attitudes can get in the way of the generation of sales and jobs. When the author lived in Cairo years ago, he became acquainted with Marketing Link Program, an admirable initiative launched in the early 1990s by North South Consultant Exchange to support marginalized handicraft producers in different parts of Egypt.[176] Among its other activities, Marketing Link helped a community of Bedouin women secure a purchase order from Oxfam to produce beautiful red- and white-striped bedspreads. Oxfam advertised the bedspreads with photographs in its Christmas catalog. When the community delivered the bedspreads to Marketing Link, however, Oxfam had to reject the order. Why? First, not all the bedspreads had the right colors. Second, not all were of uniform quality.

What had happened? When they received the order, the Bedouin artisans did not really regard it as a business proposition, that is, a contract they needed to honor. Since they were dealing primarily with Marketing Link, and Marketing Link was the creation of a non-governmental organization, they saw the order more as the outgrowth of a charitable initiative and, as a practical matter, an opportunity to generate remunerative work for all the women in the community. Uniformity and quality of work took a back seat to the inclusion of women with less work discipline and, consequently, less opportunity for gainful employment. In the end, therefore, the product they delivered was literally a mixed bag: yes, it included bedspreads that satisfied Oxfam's specifications to a T, but it also included bedspreads of different colors or inferior workmanship.

Had Marketing Link foreseen what was to happen, it might have come up with a creative way to satisfy both Oxfam and the collective interests of the community. By the time it became aware of the problem, however, time had basically run out, and it had no effective recourse.

As Piscifactoría de los Andes expanded its gamut of trout suppliers throughout Peru, it once found itself in a very similar situation. The shores of Lake Titicaca are home to many Aymara Indian communities, which organize themselves in tight-knit, hierarchical fashion. When Piscifactoría floated the idea of setting up a trout processing factory in one of those communities, the chief said he would agree, but only if there were *"trabajo para todos"* —work for everybody. Providing full-time work for everybody was uneconomical, which tempted Piscifactoría to leave things there and walk away. But Piscifactoría and PRA put on their thinking caps and came up with a counter proposal. Piscifactoría explained to the chief that it could not offer everyone full-time employment, but it could break out a number of positions—security and janitorial positions, for example—that the community might want to consider rotating among its members. In that way, everybody would indeed benefit from employment with the factory, but only some of the jobs would be full-time. After some negotiation, the chief agreed, and the scheme has been working smoothly since.

The Piscifactoría example offers two important lessons. First, it demonstrates once more the power of creative problem-solving— again, it is here that development programs demonstrate their imagination and innovation, not in the creation of new and fancy superstructures.[177] Second, it also shows how the buyer-led approach can reach an effective accommodation with communities with a collective bent.

Confusion between community and business development. Government obviously has much to contribute to development. As noted above, though, its proper role encompasses two functions: first, to set clear and transparent rules to facilitate market activity and to enforce compliance with those rules; and, second, to invest in public goods essential for the conduct of private economic activity. Of all the actions that government can take, those are the most basic—and those that typically will have the biggest impact in lowering transaction costs in the economy and making it more competitive.[178]

Although experience worldwide suggests strongly that governments act best when they let private parties decide what to invest in and produce, the allure of taking on a more direct role can be very, very strong. To foster development in their communities, for example, it is not uncommon for local governments to cross the line, confusing, in effect, what is community development with what is business development—and, in the worst of cases, actually acting as a brake on private initiative.

As custodians of public monies, local governments are beholden to their communities to serve the public good. When they set community development priorities—investment in public infrastructure, for example—community members generally expect to have some degree of say, since the funds of all are at stake. In contrast, business investment decisions involve private monies and need not be participatory at all. More than that, they need not respond to everybody's wishes and desires. In an ideal world, in fact, they direct resources to their most efficient economic use, which ultimately is the only way businesses can survive—and private sector jobs continue—in competitive markets. Although communities can have much to do with the nurturing of an environment conducive to business, in the end business plans are business, not community propositions.

Intriguingly, drawing a clear line between community development and business development can be problematic not just for local governments but for donors as well. As their appreciation of institutional concerns has grown, donors have focused increasingly on helping governments do a better job—in fighting corruption, for example—but, willy-nilly, have also encouraged them to stray into territory outside their proper mandate. Two examples highlight the problem.

At its outset, the program description for USAID's Rural Azerbaijan Business Development (RABD) program, later renamed the Azerbaijan Business Assistance and Development (ABAD) program, included the following language:

> The activity will utilize a community development approach to economic development, by mobilizing community members to take an active role in determining market interventions…

The RABD program will assist Azeri communities in identifying constraints to development of private enterprise, assess and prioritize business opportunities, and propose activities to develop these opportunities. USAID envisions the use of a participatory approach to ensure that activities result in the greatest possible benefit to the community as a whole, and that services are demand driven.[179]

In a similar vein, the statement of work for USAID's Areas for Municipal-level Alternative Development (ADAM) program in Colombia read, in part:

[T]he contractor will lead a participatory exercise in which community members will identify the economic activities that they believe have potential...

Based on these discussions, the contractor together with local government officials, the private sector, and the community will sign an agreement that spells out the responsibilities of each. This agreement will be supported by a business plan that identifies the new economic activity or activities to be promoted in the community, specifies the resources (technical, financial, human) required for the effort and their source, provides a financial sustainability projection including estimated volume of production and income and expense projections both during development (when financial development will be provided) and upon completion of outside assistance, identifies capital requirements and probable sources, underlying assumptions, etc.[180]

In short, the designs of both ABAD and ADAM called for local communities to take the lead in identifying what to invest in and produce. In Colombia, in fact, the mechanism took the form of community business plans. As the citations bear plain witness, the approach in each case epitomizes Easterly's description of the Planner.[181]

In Azerbaijan, USAID wanted to shift its focus away from the humanitarian assistance that had characterized its program since the conflict with Armenia in the early 1990s, but given the substantial numbers of internally displaced persons in the country, still did not feel entirely comfortable with letting local businesses—many of them nascent, to say the least—take the lead. Accordingly, it kept the community lens while, at the same time, accentuating business development—an approach that looked defensible on paper but gave rise to serious implementation questions. As things turned out, USAID ultimately decided to focus ABAD on fairly isolated economic corridors at some distance from the principal internal refugee camps, which facilitated the adoption of a relatively undiluted business development approach.

In Colombia, ADAM operates in economic corridors beleaguered by narcoterrorism, which has begotten substantial numbers of internal refugees as well. In addition, assistance goes to communities eradicating existing and agreeing not to plant additional illicit crops.[182] Since all community members are signatories to the agreements, everyone feels entitled to the economic benefits of the program.

Given the peculiarities of each case, it is understandable how the programs' designers would have favored community planning solutions. But once again, it is essential to distinguish between ends and means. To say that one wants to benefit economically as many people in a community as possible is not to say that a community business plan is the best way to bring that outcome about. In fact, this whole book argues that the buyer-led approach is a much more promising road to travel. When development practitioners concentrate, first, on attracting buyers of what communities can produce and, second, on securing the commitment of those buyers to source from the communities in question, the likelihood of generating lasting private sector employment for those communities goes up significantly.

Experience bears that claim out. As a practical matter, community business plans typically give short shrift to the possibility of attracting existing buyers and often look to the formation of enterprises by the members of the communities themselves.[183] Such start-ups usually are fraught with problems. Since nobody has enough—or is willing to invest enough—capital to take a majority stake, many of the enterprises in question have to assume a cooperative or collective form, which often leads to internal squabbles, often over whether to make money or employ people. The differences in interests, coupled with diffusion of accountability and market, production, and management inexperience, make the enterprises' likelihood of survival very low, especially when external assistance retracts its helping hand. All other things being equal, connecting producers in the community with buyers already in the market has much more upside potential. Experience under PRA is a case in point: although PRA has had to invest more time and money in nurturing and consolidating buyer-seller relationships in Peru's co-ca-growing zones than in other areas of the country, its track record exceeds performance in comparable environments elsewhere.[184]

Confusing community and business development is just one way the design of development programs can put a damper on the achievement of results. Another is to pre-select the sectors or clusters that the programs will support. Although sub-optimal, narrowing the playing field that way does have a saving grace, since it is still possible to work connector firm by connector firm within the sectors or clusters chosen. The sunflower oil example from Uganda presented in market chain format above is a case in point. Although Uganda's Investment in Developing Export Agriculture (IDEA) and Agricultural Productivity Enhancement Program (APEP) decided to take a product approach, the implementation strategy they adopted was unambiguously buyer-driven, and the choice of what products to work on depended in large part on the existence of buyers in the market. To a great extent, that was also true of the Market Access and Poverty Alleviation (MAPA) program in Bolivia.

Other design flaws are not so easy to mitigate. Examples include:

Tying assistance to narrowly defined geographic areas, especially when those areas are isolated from markets and have a poor resource base. The refugee resettlement program in Santiago de Pischa discussed in the appendix to this part of *We Do Know How* is a pertinent example. In such cases, it is useful to remember that labor is a mobile factor of production and to think in broader terms geographically.

The same conclusion applies to the application of program eligibility criteria to individual communities (for example, eradicating illicit crops, as in the implementation strategy for ADAM in Colombia). The more tightly defined the geographic area one chooses to work in, the more formidable the challenge of attracting buyers—and the greater the proclivity of management to fixate on short-term palliative solutions (for example, donating livestock or productive inputs). That has certainly been the case in Peru.

Limiting program support to pre-selected solutions. Programs that restrict their support to finance issues, agricultural technology transfer, land titling, cluster formation, steps for registering a business, management training, etc., may all be very useful, but the key problems that impede sales and jobs growth tend to vary considerably from client to client. To address clients' binding constraints, one-size-fits-all solutions do not work, and flexibility of response is essential.

Setting too many objectives. The more targets management has to hold itself accountable for, the greater the danger that it will spread itself too thinly and miss the program's forest for its trees.

Focusing on the sustainability of program-assisted support organizations such as business service providers and producer associations. As argued above, such organizations are means, not ends. Concentrate on what is most important to continue on after your program ends, namely, commercial relationships between market chain buyers and sellers.

Looking to government to contribute materially to market chains. PRA fell into this trap in Peru. Once Peru's Ministry of Agriculture saw that PRA was expanding sales and jobs in rural areas, it looked for ways to board the train, so to speak. In a couple of instances, it agreed to donate excess fertilizer and equipment to connector firms and their suppliers, but its failure to deliver on time put the transactions in jeopardy and tarnished the credibility of the program. Again, the moral of the story is simple: each shoemaker must stick to his shoes. Government can help create a conducive environment for market chains, but it must not form part of the market chains themselves.

Demanding little effective buy-in from clients, contributing to the creation or reinforcing the existence of an environment of entitlement. This fairly common design flaw furnishes a convenient segue to the third potentially problematic environment for the buyer-led approach, discussed below.

Environment of entitlement. An email from a colleague in Bolivia sums up the challenge of working in a situation in which clients see themselves more as deserving recipients of assistance from third parties than active, unsubsidized participants in a market economy:

> The greatest challenge we face...is in the area of desire or commitment...The social-political-historical context is one in which the poor are accustomed to receiving but not paying. It is a context in which the poor often feel that the responsibility to resolve their plight rests more with others and less with themselves. When they participate with a partner, like us, to improve their situation, and benefits do result, they feel (and I really mean they feel deeply) that it is only just that the profits are theirs and the costs are ours. We have worked out some creative ways to break this distorted outlook that are working very well, but it is a challenge we always have to manage...
>
> [O]ur project response has included a number of coordinated efforts, but it basically boils down to pulling the farmer into the business chain and making him aware he is part of the chain and that he is fully exposed to the risks and benefits of that chain.[185]

The entitlement here refers to poor farmers in Bolivia, but neither farmers nor Bolivians enjoy a monopoly on the attitudes expressed. Throughout the world, relatively well off businesspeople as well as their relatively poor suppliers, both urban and rural communities, both men and women, are wont to look to other parties for protection or support, claiming, for a variety of reasons, that some recompense is their due. In 2007, for example, Minneapolis's taxi cartel went to court, arguing that the city had violated its constitutional rights by deregulating entry into the taxi business![186]

The roots of entitlement attitudes are almost legion. In Bolivia, Brazil, Ecuador, and other Latin American countries, indigenous populations hold historical grievances against the non-indigenous parties that secured control over sizeable portions of their countries' productive resource base, especially arable land. In Afghanistan,

Colombia, and Peru, farmers who agree not to plant illicit crops demand that their governments compensate them with productive assets, ideally of comparable value. In Madagascar and Mozambique, small businesses have received business development services for free for so long that they see no reason to pay even a portion of the cost. In Armenia, businesses have seen a number of development programs over-promise and under-deliver, making them reluctant to take advantage of promising outside support unless the programs in question first put their money where their mouths are. In Haiti, the economic embargo of the 1990s drove formerly employed people to look to non-governmental organizations for their livelihood, thereby dampening their sense of self-reliance and feeding the tendency to look to others to solve their problems. In post-Taliban Afghanistan, donors and non-governmental organizations were so anxious for Afghans to see them as supportive that they demanded little quid pro quo. Although the programs in question helped address the country's pressing relief requirements, they also established a precedent for continued subsidization by outsiders.[187] In Kosovo and Sri Lanka, civil strife has created large pockets of economic isolation. As a result of the strife, those affected harbor extreme distrust toward their natural trading partners— and therefore look to non-governmental organizations for succor.[188] In Sierra Leone, ongoing rural insecurity has made people hesitant to invest in agriculture, leading them to migrate to cities and access whatever services they can there. In Azerbaijan, farmers who worked under the Soviet command system long for a return to the safety of making a living without having to worry about finding and satisfying private buyers, much less making investments to improve or differentiate their product to make more money. In Egypt, the centuries-old tradition of bargaining contributes to businesspeople looking at contracts, not as commitments to honor, but as the first stage in an ongoing series of renegotiations in which they push more and more of the burden on to the other party.

Regardless of their origins, entitlement mindsets can make the challenge of nurturing self-reliant market chains daunting. That said, although there are no magic bullets for applying the buyer-led approach in such environments, the task is by no means Mission Impossible.

Experience suggests two conditions for successful application of the buyer-led approach in entitlement environments. First, any solution a practitioner recommends to his or her client must be rock solid. Why? Because the client has options, many of which may demand much less investment on its part.

An example illustrates the conundrum. In 1994, Aquiles Lanao, a pioneer of microfinance in Peru, gave a presentation to the Association of Mothers' Clubs in Ayacucho. His presentation proposed a savings scheme under which club members would set aside a certain amount every week, and gradually increase their assets. After the presentation, the Mothers' Clubs met on their own and decided not to go forward. When they got back to Lanao, he asked why not. Their answer was simple, "We really liked your presentation, but other non-governmental organizations will give us grants, so we can achieve the same result without having to use our own money. So that is what we'll do."

> "Indeed, as a gutsy, old-time missionary friend once told me, 'As a development tool, good intentions are no substitute for continuity or for genuine know-how. Good intentions are not enough. Monkeys picking fleas have good intentions.'"
>
> William and Elizabeth Paddock, *We Don't Know How: An Independent Audit of What They Call Success in Foreign Assistance* (Ames: Iowa State University Press, 1973), p. 82.

The second condition for successful application of the approach in entitlement environments is time. Why? Because clients typically enter the scene with tremendous distrust—especially clients in post-conflict situations—and breaking down that distrust will not occur overnight. The development of the relationship between Piscifactoría de los Andes and SAIS Tupac Amaru discussed above is once again a case in point.

Two additional examples illustrate how the buyer-led approach can work—and even trigger the process of transformational development and mindset change—in entitlement environments:

Uganda. In the sunflower example presented in market chain format above, a sizeable proportion of participating farmers live in the conflict-affected area of Northern Uganda. Despite the insecurity engendered by the conflict, small farmers recognized that adopting the proposed sunflower variety, participating in the program's outgrower scheme, and selling their product to Mukwano made excellent economic sense. In short, the operation met the condition of constituting a solid business proposition, and even though it took a while to work out the kinks, has succeeded in generating substantial benefits for all concerned. As of this writing, a total of 31,300 farmers have participated, generating $5,367,000 for them in gross earnings and an estimated $2,146,800 in net incomes.

Bolivia. USAID's Rural Competitiveness Activity (RCA) operates in Bolivia's Chapare province, one of the country's sources of illicit coca. Since coca is so profitable compared to other crops, most development programs over the years have assumed that they had to underwrite a sizeable proportion of the cost of farmers shifting from coca to licit crops. As one might expect, the heavy reliance of business activity on outside subsidies, together with significant politicization and sporadic outbursts of violence, served to discourage buyers and investors from making long-term commitments there. Recognizing the incongruity and non-sustainability of this state of affairs, RCA decided to bite the bullet and take a consciously commercial bent, including refusing to pay the high levels of subsidy of the past. Unsurprisingly, farmer groups initially voiced strong resistance. As time passed, however, and as RCA succeeded in capturing the interest of new buyers and investors, farmers in the province have come to see the virtue of making long-term commitments to products other than coca. To take just two crops, in one and a half years exports of banana and pineapple rose by an estimated $6.3 and $0.3 million, respectively, which, between them, created the equivalent of approximately 1600 new jobs. But the impact goes well beyond raw numbers. After a visit to the program area, the author put it this way:

> Little by little—that is, transaction by transaction—ARCo appears to have played a significant role in turning the tide, facilitating a gradual shift away from politics and entitlement and toward pragmatism and self-reliance...
>
> In Ivirgarzama...[p]ragmatism was foremost, with a proclivity to go with what works rather than with preconceived solutions. Far from clamoring to take on trading and marketing tasks, most farmers saw the virtue

of developing alliances with buyers. More than that, most look to the project to identify buyers with a predisposition to play a proactive role in their respective market chains, transmitting market signals to their suppliers, even providing them technical assistance and advances of planting materials and other inputs.[189]

To sum up, the buyer-led approach can work effectively, even in what would appear to be unfavorable environments. But making it happen is not easy. It requires persistent, creative, on-the-ground problem solving.

12

Making Language Mirror Thinking

The previous chapters draw sharp contrasts between conventional development practice and the hands-on, business-like approach to attacking poverty proposed in this book. All of which may lead readers to ask themselves, "Are the differences really all that sharp? In his zeal to convince us of the wisdom of the buyer-led approach, does the author create a straw man?"

The differences can be as sharp as the contrasts suggest. As Friedman writes in another context,

> As one senior Arab finance official described this global- ization struggle in his country: "Sometimes I feel like I am part of the Freemasons or some secret society, because I am looking at the world so differently from many of the people around me. There is a huge chasm between the language and vocabulary I have and them. It is not that I have failed to convince them. I often can't even communicate with them, they are so far away from this global outlook…On so many days I feel like I have people coming to me and saying, 'We really need to repaint the room.' And I'm say- ing, 'No, we really need to rebuild the whole building on a new foundation.' So their whole dialogue with you is about what color paint to use, and all you can see in your head is the whole new architecture that needs to be done and the new foundations that need to be laid. We can worry about the color of paint later."[190]

"We have too many high sounding words, and too few actions that correspond with them."

Abigail Adams

David McCullough, *John Adams* (New York: Simon & Schuster Paperbacks, 2001), p. 17.

The following pages present four advertisements for poverty-related positions. They come from four different donors, and are typical of the language development practitioners see and use every day. For one not raised in the development community, reading them probably is like landing on another planet. Granted, the advertisements are only a window into what the organizations in question are all about, but, honestly, one cannot help feeling disappointed by how little light they shed on how the organizations bring the fight against poverty down to earth, what they actually do, and what they hold themselves accountable for.[191]

How do the advertisements relate to the Arab finance official's comment? In essence, the four donors are looking for people to repaint rooms. Nominally, the edifice in question—the challenge of attacking poverty—is the same edifice under discussion in this book. But as a close look at the advertisements reveals, its architectural foundation is quite different.

At its core, this paradigmatic part of *We Do Know How* urges readers not to take the edifice of development practice as given, but to question the underlying architecture of the edifice itself. Given the different mindsets different parties bring to the table, achieving that objective may not be as straightforward as it seems. Yes, all may use the same language, but since everybody's points of reference are different, each interprets what he or she hears in relation to those points of reference. In the worst case, underlying paradigms may diverge so fundamentally that people wind up talking right by each other. As Thomas Kuhn expressed it in *The Structure of Scientific Revolutions,*

> Darwin, in a particularly perceptive passage at the end of his Origin of Species, wrote: "Although I am fully convinced of the truth of the views given in this volume..., I by no means expect to convince experienced naturalists whose minds are stocked with a multitude of facts all viewed, during a long course of years, from a point of view directly opposite to mine."[192]

| Scopes of Work for Anti-Poverty Positions (page 1 of 3) | |

Organization: Asian Development Bank

Positions: Poverty Reduction Specialists

Support implementation of ADB's Poverty Reduction Strategy, specifically in its country and project level operations related to the identification, formulation and implementation of poverty reduction activities. Major activities include identifying poverty related issues and working with project teams to design poverty related aspects of ADB's technical assistance or lending operations in developing member countries (DMC); administering or evaluating such operations; and guiding project teams on practical methodologies for information systems related to poverty monitoring information systems.

Positions: Private Sector Development Specialists

Support implementation of ADB's Private Sector Development (PSD) Strategy and foster PSD through policy dialogue, loans and technical assistance projects. Major activities include assessing the policy, legal and regulatory, and business environment in member countries; providing advice on strategic focus and future interventions to increase private sector investment in ADB's DMCs; and overseeing the departmental PSD portfolio.

Economist, November 8, 2003, p. 18.

Organization: Department for International Development

Position: Poverty and Accountability Adviser

The position holder will be primarily responsible for:

- Working with other advisers to implement DFID Ghana's civil society strategy.

- Building on existing initiatives to promote the voice and rights of poor people.

- Developing DFID support for institutional systems for disseminating GPRS [Ghana Poverty Reduction Strategy] and other targets and on progress towards meeting them and for feeding back client/user experience to policy makers.

- Developing DFID support to public dialogue and coalition building on key reform issues related to the GPRS.

- Working with service delivery teams, particularly in Human Development to identify obstacles to equitable and accessible service provision.

Economist, October 4, 2003, p. 19.

Scopes of Work for Anti-Poverty Positions (page 2 of 3)

Organization: International Fund for Agricultural Development

Positions: Two Country Programme Managers (P-4/P-5)

Under the strategic, policy, and management guidance of the Director, Eastern and Southern Africa Division, the incumbent will be responsible for managing the country programme(s) assigned by the Director. She/He will be required to:

1. Manage the development and impact of medium to long-term **strategies** for IFAD's collaboration with member governments and other stakeholders in rural poverty reduction in the Eastern and Southern Africa Region. This will include the analysis of the dynamics of rural poverty and national rural poverty reduction strategies as well as the building of effective partnerships.

2. Provide leadership in the development of IFAD's **loan and grant financed rural poverty reduction programmes** in borrowing countries; support the implementation of country programmes to ensure effective and sustainable development results; in some cases in collaboration with cooperating institutions; and facilitate the replication and up-scaling of effective innovations.

3. Play a catalytic role in developing **pro-poor rural poverty reduction policies** with the emphasis on enabling the poor and their organisations to advocate pro-poor policy and institutional transformation.

4. Galvanise the outcomes of IFAD-supported investment programmes and dialogue for pro-poor policy change through systematic and evidence-based **knowledge management and learning**.

5. Administer the related budget for cost-effectiveness, and provide coaching and guidance to staff under her/his supervision.

At P-5 level, the incumbent will also:

6. Contribute to regional and departmental strategy and policy development processes, in keeping with the organisational change agenda.

7. Assist resolving complex and politically sensitive problems with governments and cooperating institutions.

Economist, July 16, 2005, p. 23.

Scopes of Work for Anti-Poverty Positions (page 3 of 3)	
Organization: United Nations Development Programme **Position: Director, Poverty Group, Bureau for Development Policy** Poverty reduction is a key priority for UNDP. The organisation's activities in the area of poverty reduction include pro-poor macro-economic policy reforms, globalisation (including trade benefiting the poor), gender mainstreaming, civil society empowerment, and making ICT work for the poor. UNDP supports the formulation of poverty reduction strategies. This involves support to linking poverty reduction strategies to: (a) economic policies for pro-poor growth; (b) budgeting, including expenditures and taxation; (c) national employment strategies; and (d) poverty-focused social security, including safety nets.	The Poverty Group manages several trust funds, including the Thematic Trust Fund for Poverty Reduction, the Millennium Trust Fund and the trust fund for the Integrated Framework for trade in the least developed countries. The Director of UNDP's Poverty Group manages and supervises some 35 Policy Advisers; provides policy advice, mostly to the inter-governmental system in the UN with occasional work at the country level; leads research, drafts and edits corporate reports; helps to mobilise resources and manages various trust funds; co-ordinates inter-agency UN work, including with the World Bank, civil society organisations and bilateral donors; and undertakes public outreach engagements. The Director's major responsibilities include, but are not exclusively confined to, the following: Intellectual Leadership; Partnering; Networking; Management. *Economist*, June 18, 2005, p. 20.

Despite Kuhn's and Darwin's skepticism about communicating paradigm shifts effectively, the way one speaks often reflects the way one thinks. To the extent that development practitioners are open to internalizing the thinking underlying the buyer-led approach, therefore, it behooves them to examine carefully how they speak as well.

Much of the language of development comes from the social sciences. Inadvertently, it has led practitioners to internalize ways of thinking about development at odds with hands-on, business-like approaches to reducing poverty.

It is time to bring development back to speaking plainly, directly, and operationally, and to shed terminology that keeps practitioners above the fray. Three specific examples of vocabulary to shift to in the future include:

Business transactions versus projects. Everybody in development does "projects." Accounting-wise, projects are obviously useful instruments for allocating resources to development purposes. Programmatically, however, projects often become the hallmark of Easterly's Planner: a blueprinting exercise laying out in engineering terms everything development practitioners are to supply. Looked at from the other side of the coin, what projects often do not do is leave enough latitude for the Searching and opportunism that responds to the vagaries of the market and delivers results. It is time to shift focus from projects to **business transactions.** That is where the operational tire hits the road, and creative problem-solving comes into play.

Clients versus beneficiaries, participants, stakeholders, and counterparts. The latter terms come from social science. In practice, the connotation of the first is often paternalistic: development practitioners see "beneficiaries," not as economic agents, not as customers whom it is their job to service, but simply as people who gain from their largesse. For practical purposes, a "participant" or a "stakeholder" can be almost anybody with interests, and, in the end, a "counterpart" is simply someone the development practitioner interfaces with. None of the terms gets at what drives change, which is where attention must go. Both the poor—and, by inference under a demand-driven approach, those who buy from them—merit treatment as **clients.**

> "If we stop thinking of the poor as victims or as a burden and start recognizing them as resilient and creative entrepreneurs and value-conscious consumers, a whole new world of opportunity will open up."
>
> C.K. Prahalad, *The Fortune at the Bottom of the Pyramid* (Upper Saddle River, NJ: Wharton School Publishing, 2005), p. 1.

Contracts versus alliances. The word, "alliance," connotes the coming together of equals. In market transactions, however, demand and supply are not equals: demand is the driver, and supply must accommodate itself to it. Programmatically, the vehicle for linking supply with demand is not alliances but **contracts.**

We Do Know How makes no pretence to constitute a scientific revolution, but it does embody a major shift in mindset that many readers, especially those schooled in conventional development approaches, may be inclined to resist. That said, the language people use steers how they think, which steers how they act. As development practitioners go about changing their thinking, therefore, it behooves them to change how they speak as well.

Appendix to Part II

Fleshing Out A Strategy — What Not To Do

The start-up of a development program is critical since the operational strategy one chooses to adopt at the outset conditions so much of what follows. This appendix gives examples of common strategic mistakes development practitioners make in fleshing out their programs, even when they start with conceptual frameworks along the lines discussed in Chapter 5.

As the reader can see, many of the mistakes reflect the thinking characteristic of Easterly's Planners.

Development practitioners set too many objectives for themselves. As the author was about to enter graduate school many years ago, he received a greeting card from a friend wishing him luck. The front of the card listed sayings like the following:

Keep your nose to the grindstone.
Keep your shoulder to the wheel.
Put your best foot forward.
Keep your eye on the ball.
Keep your ear to the ground.

The message inside said:

Then try to work in that position!

The anomalous position described in the greeting card has its parallel in many development programs. Two examples make the point.

The first is USAID's Market and Trade Development program in Madagascar.[193] The designers of the program spelled out the various results they could expect from program activities and then set them as objectives to achieve during its life. The scope of work for the program is divided into three "results modules," each consisting of three or four parts, each with sub-results to achieve. Although somewhat lengthy, it is worthwhile to list the concatenation of results in its entirety to appreciate just how much of a management burden it places on those charged with implementation:

Market and Trade Development Program in Madagascar (page 1 of 5)

Results Module 1: Increasing the competitiveness of selected product chains

Expected Result 1.1: Ability of Malagasy firms to take advantage of new market opportunities for their products expanded

Expected sub-results:

- Access of firms to critical, regularly updated market and trade information, such as futures markets, freight rates, tariffs and exchange rates improved

- Visibility of Malagasy products on world markets increased

- Participation of Malagasy firms in international trade shows and business events increased

- Trade missions of foreign buyers and investors encouraged

- Business linkages and trade under AGOA [African Growth and Opportunity Act] and other market access arrangements encouraged

Expected Result 1.2: Ability of operators to respond to market demand requirements and meet orders increased

Expected sub-results:

- Capacity of entrepreneurs to monitor and understand market trends, consumer choices, and business practices in foreign countries improved

- Capacity of entrepreneurs to understand what is included in an order (quality requirements, quantity, timing of delivery, payments conditions, packaging, labeling, etc.) improved

- Proficiency of entrepreneurs in dealing with sophisticated or international/ large scale buyers—including in providing samples based on a list of specifications, such as for supermarkets—improved

**Market and Trade Development Program in Madagascar
(page 2 of 5)**

Expected Result 1.3: Operational linkages between stages along selected supply chains strengthened

Expected sub-results:

- Capacity of firms to set up contractual arrangements upstream and downstream to improve efficiency and productivity improved

- Operations and communication flow along selected supply chains rationalized

- Improved production and marketing techniques identified and acquired

Results Module 2: Increasing the capacity and use of business services, financial services, and research institutes

Expected Result 2.1: Capacity of business services providers to deliver to SMEs [Small, Medium, and Micro Enterprises] in targeted supply chains increased

Expected sub-results:

- Capacity of firms and business associations to identify needs and contract for business services improved

- Capacity of business services providers to market their expertise and adapt their range of products to new sectors or new needs improved

- Concerted action between industry groups and private services providers for improving strategic coherence and competitiveness of targeted product chains facilitated

- Outreach of business service providers to more remotely located SMEs improved

**Market and Trade Development Program in Madagascar
(page 3 of 5)**

Expected Result 2.2: Delivery of financial services to SMEs in selected supply chains expanded and improved

Expected sub-results:

- Capacity of firms and business associations to identify and request financial services improved

- Capacity of finance institutions to develop financial services well targeted to the needs of micro, small and medium enterprises in growing sectors improved

- Microfinance best practices promoted

Expected Result 2.3: Research capacity to conduct analysis on applied production technologies, marketing strategies, and policy reforms strengthened

Expected sub-results:

- Local capacity to conduct analyses on production technologies, marketing strategies and policy reforms, and to generate best practices developed

- Relevant market analysis on selected products supported

- Analyses of social and environmental impacts of proposed investments supported

- Research and development of improved processing and handling techniques supported

Market and Trade Development Program in Madagascar (page 4 of 5)

Results Module 3: Improving the enabling environment for private enterprise development and trade and investment

Expected Result 3.1: Main policy and regulatory constraints to increased competitiveness of selected supply chains are addressed

Expected sub-results:

- Regulatory and policy reforms that complement or enhance market incentives adopted and implemented

- Capacity of industry associations and interest groups to lobby in their interests and raise public awareness through media campaign or other means strengthened

- Capacity of firms and other stakeholders in handling specific trade issues that may affect competitiveness, such as new security rules to export to the U.S. increased

Expected Result 3.2: Madagascar's effective participation in key regional trade agreement negotiations and multilateral policy setting discussions enhanced

Expected sub-results:

- Madagascar's effective integration in regional trade groupings such as Common Market for Eastern and Southern Africa (COMESA), as well as those under consideration (Southern African Development Community, SADC, for instance) supported

- Information about trade agreements and multi-lateral policy issues to relevant businesses disseminated

- Assistance to the Government in matters of compliance with the WTO [World Trade Organization] rules and obligations, such as the Sanitary and Phyto-Sanitary (SPS), bio-safety issues or trade in services provided

Market and Trade Development Program in Madagascar (page 5 of 5)

Expected Result 3.3: Market and transport infrastructure constraints addressed

Expected sub-results:

- Public-private sector forums to discuss market and transport infrastructure improvements needed to increase the competitiveness of Malagasy products established

- Economic corridor development approach along transport corridor as a sustainable and comprehensive model of development promoted

Expected Result 3.4: Regulatory and legal constraints to developing rural-based commercial financial services are addressed

Expected sub-results:

- Establishment of a policy agenda conducive to an enabling environment for microfinance development within the banking and financial sector assisted

- Measures to close the gap between microfinance operations and the formal banking sector supported

Source: USAID/Madagascar, "Madagascar Economic Growth Strategic Objective: Statement of Work for Market and Trade Development Program."

Although one could argue that achieving this set of results would contribute to USAID's higher-order objective of market-based, private sector-led growth—including the creation of jobs—just trying to do so could be a management nightmare. All told, there are 32—repeat, 32!—separate objectives for program managers to worry about, with no differentiation in their relative importance. As a practical matter, trying to give attention to all of them is a lose-lose proposition. Not only is the probability of achieving all the results very small, but the very process of trying is almost sure to make program managers miss the forest for the trees. As intellectually elegant as such a framework may be,

> "People cannot see the mountains clearly when they are in the mountains."
>
> Su Dongpo
>
> Qiu Xialong, *A Loyal Character Dancer* (New York: Soho Press, Inc., 2002), p. 178.

it gives practitioners no clear sense of direction, that is, no guidance about how to focus their scarce management time to get the most bang for the buck.[194]

The second example, which has to do with forestry and wood products in Bolivia, tells a similar story.

A few years ago the author traveled to Santa Cruz, Bolivia, on a short-term assignment under a forestry development program. Aware that the author had relatively little experience in forestry, the head of the program suggested he first attend a one-day workshop sponsored by the government committee charged with developing a strategy to enhance the competitiveness of Bolivia's wood and forest products industry. The author agreed, and looked forward to receiving an education in the problems confronting the sector and possible solutions to them. He received an education, all right, but not quite the kind he anticipated.

The first surprise was the composition of the workshop partici-pants. All together, 90 people attended, but only four—four!—came from the industry itself. The rest came from the government, inter-national donors, non-governmental organizations, and consulting firms, or were individual consultants. In short, a workshop direct-ed to the development of a strategy for the sector fell primarily to people who did not belong to it.

A second outcome—perhaps not so surprising in light of the example from Madagascar—was the wide-ranging nature of the workshop's recommendations. Partway through the workshop, the workshop organizers divided the participants into small brain-storming groups to articulate a vision for the sector, to identify its key problems, and to define priority actions to resolve those prob-lems. All together, 29 different sets of actions emerged, venturing far and wide in their scope. Some of them overlapped, of course, and the workshop organizers succeeded in grouping them in eight macro recommendations, but most were so broad as to be vacuous operationally.

A third outcome was the designation of third parties—the gov-ernment, especially—to follow up on the vast bulk of the recom-mendations. Even though the key investment decisions that affect the competitiveness of the wood and forest product sector fall to private parties, most workshop participants looked to government to take the lead.[195] Government can play a constructive role, of course, but when it reaches the extreme exemplified by the workshop, it can actually be counterproductive. In an environment that nurtures Santa Claus thinking—that is, that key decisions and attendant financing are always somebody else's job (or fault!)—there is no way that the self-reliance and entrepreneurship needed to expand economic activity and create jobs is ever going to flourish on more than a minimal scale.

"I also found a new attitude has grown up among these farmers [in Mexico]. The *ejidatario* now considers himself to be 'part of the government's responsibility.' An interesting evolutionary practice! Before the land reform he sat at the door of the *hacendado* waiting for the paternalistic handout. After land reform he must await the largesse of his government."

William and Elizabeth Paddock, *We Don't Know How: An Independent Audit of What They Call Success in Foreign Assistance* (Ames: Iowa State University Press, 1973), p. 167.

The Madagascar and Bolivia examples showcase a mindset that affects most strategy development exercises around the world. Instead of saying A is more important than B, B than C, C than D, etc., most development strategies march to the drummer of the very opposite kind of thinking: be sure not to leave anything out! With competing bureaucracies involved, it can be awkward to say that the mandate of one agency has less importance than another's. Accordingly, if strategy designers have to err on the side of including or excluding an activity, the reaction is almost always to keep it in—sapping thereby the spirit of the exercise itself. Put another way, making everything a priority makes nothing a priority.

Food security strategies are a prime example. The concept of food security is even more multidimensional than the concept of poverty and, with not too much pushing, can morph almost into the concept of development itself. Every few years, most countries prepare food security strategies. In principle there are so many worthwhile things one can do to attack food insecurity that those in charge can justify practically any support activity they can think of. The result is shopping lists of activities. Rarely does opportunity-cost thinking enter the calculus, that is, a recognition that any time you spend a dollar, euro, or yen on one thing, you cannot spend it on something else. To put it another way, there is little appreciation that every good program is not necessarily a high-priority program.

Exhibits 2.15 and 2.16 illustrate the point. Exhibit 2.15 is useful pedagogically for understanding the various elements of food security and their interrelationships. Similarly, Exhibit 2.16 is useful for getting a handle on the diverse determinants of rural prosperity in East and Southern Africa. As aids to learning, they have a purpose. The danger comes when development practitioners make simple translations of the information in question into laundry lists of policies and program actions. The resultant strategies are strategies in name only, not in fact.

In short, most development strategists see their task more as comprehensive diagnosis than as the tough analytical exercise of making programmatic choices. They fail to make the transition effectively from problem description to management parsimony. Instead of applying the KISS principle—Keep It Sweet and Simple— too often they apply the KICC principle—Keep It Cumbersome and Complicated.

Development practitioners launch programs as fishing expeditions. Most development programs commence operations with annual work-planning exercises. Those exercises generally reflect the same failing as the more comprehensive program designs: not leaving anything out. At the inception of a program, its managers do not yet have in-depth knowledge of the program's clients, nor of the specific problems they face. To be sure they cover all the bases, they try to think of all the activities that would appear to be conducive to accomplishing the program's higher-order objectives—and, if in doubt, include them in the work plan. At this stage, it is almost as if all ideas were created equal. Later, of course, the program's managers find out that many of those activities respond to problems that are not terribly important or are not the best way to attack those that are. But by then, it is often too late: the work plan they prepared months before has committed them to carry certain activities out regardless of their impact. So despite protestations from development practitioners that they manage for results, they focus their attention on plans created before they really understand the critical issues.

Programs do of course make adjustments in mid stream, so the scenario above does not have to act as so much of a straightjacket as

Exhibit 2.15 Illustrative Food Security Conceptual Framework

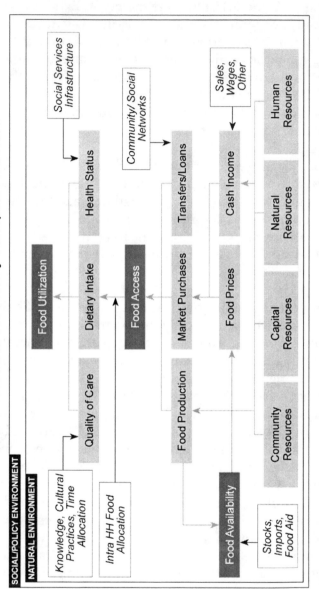

Source: Adapted from Frank Riely, Nancy Mock, Bruce Cogill, Laura Bailey, and Eric Kenefick, "Food Security Indicators and Indicators for Use in the Monitoring and Evaluation of Food Aid Programs," Food and Nutrition Technical Assistance Project, Academy for Educational Development, Washington, D.C., 1999, p. 13.

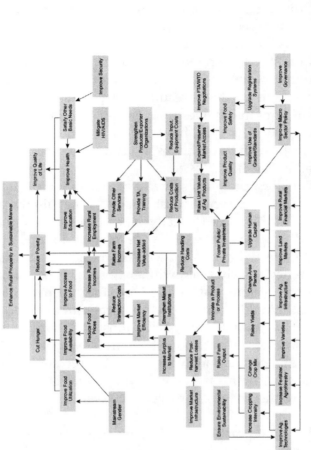

Exhibit 2.16 Framework for Enhancing Rural Prosperity in East and Southern Africa

Source: Adapted from USAID, Regional Economic Development Services Office for East and Southern Africa, "REDSO's Portfolio, IEHA, and SAKSS," Nairobi, Kenya. n.d.

it would appear. But often it does: USAID's Rebuilding Agricultural Markets Program in Afghanistan financed the construction of 145 market collection centers, many of them after experience had indicated most would turn out to be white elephants. Regardless, the basic point is that time-honored procedures for getting programs off the ground often militate against the kind of flexibility good managers require to achieve results. None of this is to say that managers can exempt themselves from the obligation to program their resources wisely. The trick, however, is to combine accountability for final results with flexibility in input use—a theme addressed in some detail in Part III.

Occasionally a program actually breaks out a formal period of up to six months to decide what to do.[196] Intriguingly, an exploratory phase of this kind typically takes place after the agency financing the program has already developed a scope of work for it, various offerors have proposed technical approaches, and the funding agency has chosen a winner to carry it out. After all that groundwork, breaking out a period for study seems anomalous, to say the least. Wouldn't one expect the program to proceed directly to implementation, not to go back almost to ground zero? Even if program managers do not know their clients very well at that point, it certainly appears reasonable to expect agreement on at least an operational paradigm for going forward, that is, a shared vision that if the program does x, it can expect to get y.

Development practitioners let reporting requirements dictate how they organize program activities. Funding agencies generally develop what practitioners know as "strategic objective frameworks," "results frameworks," or "logical frameworks." There are some subtle distinctions among the different methodologies, but in essence the three frameworks delineate the causal relationship between the higher-order objectives that the agencies would like to achieve—higher incomes for poor people, for example—and the intermediate results that the activities they finance can bring about—the transfer of yield-increasing technology to poor farmers, for example. Although not presented diagrammatically, the concatenation of results laid out above for the Market and Trade Development program in Madagascar is a case in point. The framework posits that the higher-order objective of market-based, private sector-led growth will emerge from the three results modules, which in turn will emerge from their respective expected results, which in turn will emerge from their respective sub-results. Although the framework's comprehensiveness tends to dilute management focus, it does allow program designers to articulate clearly the logic underlying the program. It also furnishes a touchstone for defining the kinds of information the agency expects to see during implementation.

At first blush, the reporting requirements derived from strategic objective, results, and logical frameworks would appear a logical choice for organizing program activities, and, in fact, most implementing organizations gravitate in that direction. That is not always wise.

Exhibit 2.17 presents the results framework for USAID's Maximizing Agricultural Revenue and Key Enterprises in Targeted Sites (MARKETS) program in Nigeria. It first shows how the program's objective of expanded economic opportunities in the agricultural sector will contribute to USAID's broader objective of improved livelihoods in selected areas. It then indicates the three Program Intermediate Results (PIRs)—increased productivity, value-added, and marketing—that will contribute to the program objective. Finally, it presents the Key Results Areas (KRAs) that will contribute to each of the PIRs. Like the framework for the program in Madagascar, the results framework for MARKETS holds together nicely: if the program succeeds in bringing about increases in productivity, value-added, and marketing, it is reasonable to expect that more economic opportunities will indeed exist in Nigerian agriculture.

The compact logic of the results framework suggests that it might be appropriate to organize the management of MARKETS along those lines, that is, with one component for increasing productivity, a second for increasing value-added, and a third for increasing marketing of agricultural products—and to have each component report separately on its activities and accomplishments. In fact, organizing the program in that way could be counterproductive. Although the framework makes logical sense, program managers do not know beforehand the relative importance of each intermediate result in expanding economic activity in the

Exhibit 2.17 Results Framework for MARKETS Program in Nigeria

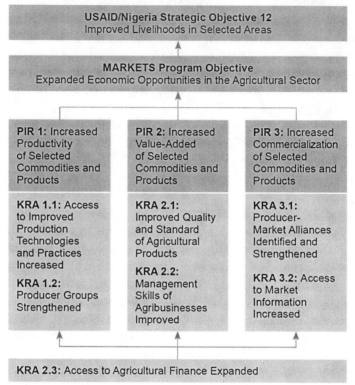

USAID/Nigeria Strategic Objective 12
Improved Livelihoods in Selected Areas

MARKETS Program Objective
Expanded Economic Opportunities in the Agricultural Sector

PIR 1: Increased Productivity of Selected Commodities and Products

PIR 2: Increased Value-Added of Selected Commodities and Products

PIR 3: Increased Commercialization of Selected Commodities and Products

KRA 1.1: Access to Improved Production Technologies and Practices Increased

KRA 1.2: Producer Groups Strengthened

KRA 2.1: Improved Quality and Standard of Agricultural Products

KRA 2.2: Management Skills of Agribusinesses Improved

KRA 3.1: Producer-Market Alliances Identified and Strengthened

KRA 3.2: Access to Market Information Increased

KRA 2.3: Access to Agricultural Finance Expanded

Source: Chemonics International Inc.

agricultural sector. To staff up three components in more or less the same fashion could wind up creating organizational solutions looking for problems. For example, it could turn out that the hypothesized lack of access to high-yielding technology is actually not a significant constraint to the growth of agriculture, but the absence of market opportunities is. On the flip side of the coin, some clients could face constraints in two or three of the areas in question. If the program organized itself in three divisions corresponding to the three PIRs, some clients could wind up with multiple account managers, with all the attendant possibilities for confusion and misunderstanding that balkanized management can bring with it. Part III presents an alternative organizational scheme that can address these potential deficiencies. For now, suffice it to say that the way a program portrays itself logically is not necessarily the best way to organize itself managerially.

Development practitioners' organizing frameworks lead them to view development like a vaccination campaign. The adoption of strategic objective, results, and logical frameworks leads practitioners to look at development more in engineering than in incentive terms. The portrayal of expected results in neatly organized boxes baits them into thinking that their job is simply to program and carry out well defined tasks under each one, and that development impact will almost take care of itself. In reality, **human beings respond to incentives, and if programs fail to incorporate incentives appropriately, all the best engineering in the world will not bring about desired results.**[197]

The following five examples illustrate how practitioners often fail to align operational incentives with desired outcomes:

Program coordinating committees. Many programs set up coordinating committees to give program managers big picture guidance during program implementation. The committees typically consist of prestigious representatives of both the public and private sectors. Just as typically, though, funding agencies see the authority for key implementation decisions as theirs alone. In addition, the very mandate of coordinating committees tends to be nebulous, which leads both program managers and committee participants to view the committees more in public relations than in substantive terms. Most committee members are busy people, and once they see their input is not really affecting much, they tend to lose interest, they attend fewer and fewer sessions, and the committees die of their own weight. In short, there is little real incentive for the members to participate further.

Producer association strengthening. Most small producers cannot plug into national or foreign markets effectively unless they ally themselves with others like themselves. With that end in mind, many programs include components to help them organize into associations. More often than development practitioners might like to admit, the programs spend so much time focusing on setting the associations up as legal entities, developing bylaws, statutes, etc., that the whole process bogs down. Why? Because the basic motivation for associating in the first place gets lost in the shuffle: in the absence of market transactions from which potential members see they can extract economic benefit, there is little incentive for them to engage themselves in a hands-on way.

> "The dilemmas of distributing bednets illustrate some general problems of aid. Donors muster resources, but they fail to align the incentives of the people providing them or benefiting from them. The grand macro-solutions often neglect the nagging micro-foundations."
>
> "The $25 billion question," *Economist*, July 2, 2005, p. 26.

Donor synergy. Most international donors proclaim "synergy" as a conscious objective of their programs, that is, not to act alone but in concert with others. Such proclamations may enjoy credibility on paper, but it is a long way from cup to lip. Not only do donors have different frameworks and priorities, but they are under pressure to look good in their own right. When they can show that other donors are following their lead or adopting their approach, synergy is a wonderful thing. But when the shoe is on the other foot, that is, when a donor winds up subsuming itself under the banner of another, synergy does not look so attractive. Again, there is a practical disconnect between strategic desiderata and on-the-ground incentives.[198]

Organizational sustainability and development of the market for business development services. Many programs select local business service providers to manage the delivery of business development services to clients. Most funding agencies say they would like the organizations they support to be self-sustaining financially after their programs end, prompting development practitioners to coddle their select business service providers with preferential treatment. At the same time, the agencies see the virtue of nurturing the market for business development services more broadly, that is, of facilitating the effective entry of other providers—that is, the providers' competitors—into the market, prompting development practitioners to take more of a hands-off approach. Operationally, therefore, there is a tradeoff between promoting organizational sustainability in the small and developing the market for business service provision at large.

Cost reimbursement contracting. Most funding agencies procure the services of third parties to manage their programs. More often than not, the contractual vehicle is some variant of cost reimbursement: an agency's contractor purchases goods or services (the time of individual consultants, say), bills the funding agency for the cost (incorporating legitimate indirect costs, including profit), and gets reimbursed by the agency for that amount. In its most unadulterated form, how much money the contractor spends bears no relation to performance: the more money the contractor spends, the more it makes. Under such a scheme, the contractor has little incentive to exert discipline over its spending. For example, if a contractor can hire a relatively inexpensive local consultant or a relatively expensive expatriate to carry out a certain task, which option will it choose? The latter, naturally, since the contractor will earn more money that way, especially when it takes into account the airfare and lodging necessary to bring in an outsider. The incentives at work can actually bring about even worse outcomes, motivating contractors to devise tasks for expensive consultants to carry out. No wonder contractors appear to like doing studies so much.

Not all contractual relationships encourage such unbridled spending, but the basic point still pertains: too often there is little relationship between the results a funding agency wants its contractor to achieve and the mechanism it uses to pay the contractor to bring them about. Bill Gates makes the generic point:

> We need a system that draws in innovators and businesses in a far better way than we do today.
>
> Naturally...companies...need to earn some kind of return...It's not just about doing more corporate philanthropy or asking companies to be more virtuous. It's about giving them a real *incentive* to apply their expertise in new ways, making it possible to earn a return while serving the people who have been left out.[199] [emphasis added]

Ideally, funding agencies would pay contractors for the results they deliver, not for the activities they perform. Given the uncertainties inherent in almost all development programs, it is natural for contractors to shy away from such an arrangement. But shying away does not have to mean complete abandonment of the principle of tying pay to results. For example, agencies could reimburse contractors for a large percentage or even all of their before-profit costs, and pay them a premium for the results they actually bring about. For example, the more client sales and attendant jobs a contractor generated, the more money it would make. Chapter 14 discusses how a contractor employing the buyer-led approach can do that with subcontractors. Although there is good precedent for such arrangements outside of development circles, to the author's knowledge no international funding agency has employed such a scheme with development contractors themselves. [200, 201]

In brief, many practices common in development programs often founder on the shoals of inadequate incentives for influencing people's behavior.[202]

Development practitioners take a static, not a dynamic view of development. International development has a number of stylized facts. Among the most salient is the difference in patterns of poverty between rural and urban areas. Most rural areas have higher percentages of poor people than urban areas, and those who are poor in rural areas are generally poorer than their urban counterparts.

In its early days, that is, in the 1960s, the United States Agency for International Development (USAID) operated largely through the vehicle of program loans, that is, loans providing budget support for host country programs. By the early 1970s, a groundswell of dissatisfaction had surfaced about the effectiveness of the approach, especially in benefiting the poor. Accordingly, in 1973 Congress amended the Foreign Assistance Act, instructing USAID to target its programs to benefit the poor directly. In subsequent years, the pattern of foreign development assistance changed dramatically as programs focused increasingly on "basic human needs" and the plight of the "small farmer."[203] Some of that shift in priorities made great sense—it was definitely time to move beyond broad budget transfers—but some was also quite short-sighted.

The principal example of short-sightedness that continues to this day is the over-reliance on statistics as a guide to public policy. Not only do statistics not speak for themselves, but, by definition, they refer to the past. To act on them requires a development paradigm oriented toward the future, which often is lacking.

In the 2001 Presidential campaign in Peru, almost all candidates cited the statistic that micro- and small enterprises make up 98 percent of all enterprises in Peru, and concluded, therefore, that they merit support. Some even went so far as to claim that micro-

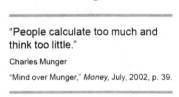

"People calculate too much and think too little."

Charles Munger

"Mind over Munger," *Money*, July, 2002, p. 39.

and small enterprises could be the engine of growth for Peru in the future. Unfortunately, the statistic cited points up the problem, not its solution. In many if not most developing countries, most micro-entrepreneurs would prefer not to be micro-entrepreneurs, but to have a steady job and take home a regular salary. And the claim that micro- and small enterprises can drive development misreads the dynamics of the development process: as discussed above, the driving force for the expansion of micro- and small enterprises normally comes from the demand of larger companies.

Much the same kind of reflection applies to arguments to support small farmers. Throughout the world development practitioners cite currently high percentages of small farmers as the rationale for helping make them better small farmers. In the same vein, some continue to argue that since most small farmers grow basic grains, practitioners should help them grow more basic grains. In both cases, the proponents of support essentially equate the world as it is with where they want to go, thus ignoring evidence worldwide that most small farmers get out of poverty either by becoming larger farmers or by getting out of agriculture altogether. And for those who do stay in agriculture, the route to success is usually not expansion of basic grain production, but diversification out of it.

"Some men see things as they are and say why. I dream of things that never were and say why not."

Robert F. Kennedy, paraphrasing George Bernard Shaw

http://thinkexist.com/quotes/robert_francis_kennedy/3.html.

A personal vignette may be the most compelling way to make the point.

In 1994 the author had the good fortune to make a field trip to Santiago de Pischa, a small town in the highlands of Peru. To get there, he first flew to Ayacucho, the birthplace of the Shining Path guerrilla movement, and then wended his way for over three hours along a tortuously windy and rutted road. The author formed part of a contingent of national government and USAID personnel. The government had just launched a program to resettle internally displaced Peruvians in the locales they had fled years before in reaction to the Shining Path's terror campaign. The intent of the program was noble, to help refugees begin again.

On arrival, the contingent found the village inhabited mostly by elderly women. They hobbled out, ecstatic to receive visitors and press their claims for support. They leaned heavily on the congressman in the contingent, petitioning him for better teachers and health services.

Regrettably, the solutions to Santiago de Pischa's problems were not so straightforward. As the contingent walked around the village and its environs, they made some dispassionate calculations. Dividing available hectareage by the number of households projected to re-inhabit the town, they reached the conclusion that the average household would be able to work only three quarters of a hectare of land. Even if the town adopted the most modern agricultural technology, there was no way that the program could bring it enough economic opportunities for its households to escape from poverty, especially with the nearest market three to four trying hours away. Despite the elderly women's heart-tugging *mística* to re-create their past, the numbers just did not add up. Counter-intuitively, the contingent realized then that they would not find the solution to Santiago de Pischa's problems in Santiago de Pischa. Going ahead with the refugee resettlement program would be simply a palliative, not the way out.

"A traditionalist, Charles Lamb often said that the dale as he had loved it was dying. He knew that the only chance for the young was to get away, and that saddened him. ...The old crafts were dying out because they were uneconomical, and only tourists kept one cooper, one blacksmith and one wheelwright in business."

Peter Robinson, *A Dedicated Man* (New York: Avon Books, 1988), p. 11.

It is one thing to identify and describe who the poor are. It is another to define appropriate programmatic responses to assist the poor in bettering their lot. Very often the place one finds a problem is not necessarily the best place to attack it.

PART III

Putting the Approach into Practice—
Dos and Don'ts

"An idea that doesn't happen is
not an idea at all."

Louis Kahn

"My Architect: A Son's Journey," directed
by Nathaniel Kahn, 2003.

13

Getting Started

The highlands of the Huánuco economic corridor in Peru are ideal potato-growing country. Still, most potato farmers have very small plots, use primitive technology, produce primarily for local wholesale markets—and are poor. Ironically, until very recently most potato chips consumed in Peru—the home of the potato!—came from abroad.

The Capiro potato variety is well suited for industrial processing, especially for chips, and is in high demand. It is also well suited for production in the Huánuco highlands. For that reason, PRA decided to see what obstacles stood in the way of bringing demand and supply together and whether it would be possible to overcome those obstacles at reasonable cost.

Farmers producing for Frito Lay in Huánuco, Peru. *Photo:* USAID/Peru Poverty Reduction and Alleviation program.

Before promoting more production of the Capiro variety, PRA first tied down the demand side. Specifically, program personnel contacted Snacks América Latina SRL, the processor of Frito Lay potato chips in Peru. Snacks América Latina said that if growers could meet quantity, quality, and timing requirements, they would be glad to buy Capiro potatoes from farmers in Huánuco and provide guidance to them on when to plant and how to care for their crop. They also agreed to pay for the farmers' Capiro seed and to sign forward contracts specifying timing, volume, and price. To enable the two parties to capitalize on the win-win opportunity, PRA worked with both buyer and sellers, ensuring that farmers produced to the contracts' specifications and that Snacks América Latina honored its commitments. All told, the area involved came to 400 hectares, an organizational challenge. Under the tutelage of Snacks América Latina, PRA arranged for farmers to receive technical support from planting through to the packaging of potatoes for shipment to the buyer. By working collaboratively with both parties, PRA helped cement a relationship of trust between them, a relationship that continues independently of PRA support.

"Before we plant, the price for potatoes is fixed; a contract is signed between the farmer and the company; and payment is on time. We feel more secure with the investment we are making by agreeing on a fixed price at the beginning of the growing season."

Lucio Ramírez Maíz, farmer, Huanucalla-Pillao, Huánuco, Peru.

"Proyecto PRA Informa," Numbers 10 & 11, USAID/Peru, Lima, Peru, April, 2005.

In its first year, the agreement resulted in almost $1 million in new sales and employment of 57,000 person-days of labor. The next year, production expanded to 550 hectares, and the relationship continues to thrive.

This story from Huánuco illustrates how development programs can make lasting contributions, facilitating mutually beneficial relationships based on trust and performance. The story is not a "model" or a "best practice" to replicate mechanistically elsewhere. It is an example, however, of how bringing problem-solving skills to bear can expand sales, generate jobs, and make currently poor people better off. This third part of *We Do Know How* explains how a development program can organize itself to bring about such results. The book does not offer preprogrammed magic wands—each transaction has its own problems to solve—but it shows that if development practitioners can align everybody's incentives in mutually reinforcing fashion, some very good things can happen.

Part III shows, not how to Plan Easterly's Searcher's job, but how to set things up so that the creative juices of Searchers can take over and deliver results. As Easterly puts it,

"The more one tries to see into the distance, the more generalized things become."

Haruki Murakami, *The Wind-Up Bird Chronicle*, translated by Jay Rubin (New York: Vintage Books, 1997), p. 44.

> [W]e bureaucrats will perform better when we have tangible, measurable goals, and less well when we have vague, ill-defined dreams. We will perform better when there is a clear link from effort to results, and less well when results reflect many factors besides effort. We will perform better when we have fewer objectives, and worse when we have many objectives. We will perform better when we specialize in particular solvable problems, and less well when we try to achieve utopian goals. We will perform better when there is more information about what the customers want, and less well when there is confusion about such wants. We will perform better when the agents at the bottom are motivated and accountable, and less well when everything is up to the managers at the top.[204]

This part of *We Do Know How* lays out an operational framework for putting those basic principles into action.

This first chapter of Part III describes how to set up a buyer-led program. There are five steps involved:

Develop a common, shared framework and vision
Inculcate market chains as an operational framework for action
Formalize a decision criterion like the 5:1 rule
Organize operations geographically
Put a conducive management and organizational structure in place.

Develop a Common, Shared Framework and Vision

Practitioners might be loath to put it so bluntly, but development programs frequently begin as rudderless forays into the unknown. Typically, program participants—that is, funding agencies, management, and key implementation staff—get together, often in a workshop format, to exchange ideas on what they would like to accomplish, brainstorm what activities they might undertake, and flesh out a work plan spelling out what they agree on. To the extent that such workshops foster teamwork and common understandings, they can serve a useful purpose. As a practical matter, though, most start-up workshops suffer from a number of the deficiencies discussed in Part II. Those deficiencies include:

Lack of a development paradigm. Most planning workshops value collegiality and consensus. Accordingly, they tend to give practically everybody an equal voice and, as such, fail to saw off on one strategic direction over another. Anything goes, often at the price of internal inconsistency in what the programs propose to do. To the extent differences surface, the tendency is to paper them over in the work plans.

Inclusion of too many objectives. One corollary of the absence of a development paradigm is the tendency to accommodate all objectives suggested by participants. In its worst form, little differentiation takes place between ends and means—which offers little operational guidance to implementation personnel on how to set work priorities.

Inclusion of too many activities. Like suggestions of objectives, suggestions of activities tend to resemble the proverbial kitchen sink. The operative philosophy appears to be to shoot indiscriminately in all directions in the hope that one or more of the suggested activities will hit the mark. The initial work plan for the Caribbean Open Trade Support program is an example. In it, the planning team proposed 86 activities, 31 of them just for the program's "doing business" component. To its credit, management later pruned the plan down to doable size,[205] but failure to do so at the beginning resulted in personnel rigidities, lack of focus, and delays in delivering tangible results.

In short, most development programs start more with a grab-bag of objectives and activities than with a coherent operational framework with a clear vision for all to rally around.

For the buyer-led approach to be successful, it is essential to swim against the conventional start-up tide. Yes, it is useful to gather personnel together at the beginning of a program, but not to open up what to do and what not to do to all comers. Yes, it is essential to develop an *esprit de corps* around the program, but it is also essential that everyone understand that its whys and wherefores are not up for grabs. In fact, if individuals find themselves uncomfortable with the approach, it is better that they leave the program at the beginning than create frictions and have to sever ties later.

If this line of attack to program start-up appears a bit dictatorial, it is. It starts from the premise that success in generating jobs for poor people has much to do with the approach one adopts, and that compromise on basics is not open for discussion. Yes, of course one has to adapt the buyer-led approach to local circumstances, but not in such a way that adaptation becomes emasculation.

> "The art of leadership is saying no, not yes. It is very easy to say yes."
> Tony Blair
> http://thinkexist.com/quotes/tony_blair.

Exhibit 2.2 presents a generic programmatic strategy for reducing poverty. Exhibit 3.1 shows how PRA took that strategy and turned it into an overarching operational framework to guide its work. The diagram shows both the overall context within which the program operated and the kinds of activities in which it engaged—essentially business development through Economic Service Centers and policy analysis and dialogue informed by the intelligence emanating from the centers—all oriented toward increasing sales, jobs, and incomes and, by extension, reductions in poverty.

> "If you don't know where you are going, you might wind up someplace else."
> Yogi Berra
> http://thinkexist.com/quotes/yogi_berra.

PRA used Exhibit 3.1 primarily internally, although the diagram appeared in presentations to external audiences as well. In 2005,

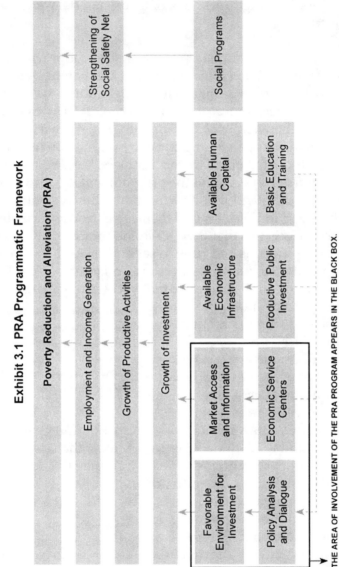

Exhibit 3.1 PRA Programmatic Framework

THE AREA OF INVOLVEMENT OF THE PRA PROGRAM APPEARS IN THE BLACK BOX.

Source: USAID/Peru Poverty Reduction and Alleviation program.

Chemonics International Inc. hired a two-person team to assess the communication strategies of its programs in Latin America and the Caribbean. One of the team's key findings was the degree to which PRA stood out from other programs in its shared sense of mission. Everyone with whom the team spoke, from top to bottom hierarchically, in Lima and throughout the country, could articulate exactly what the program was about and the metric that gauged everyone's performance: sales! The reason for the difference was clear: in contrast to programs that tried to do everything, PRA drilled in to everybody what the program was to focus on right from Day 1.

If designers and participants must agree on one thing at a program's inception, it is what they expect the program to accomplish, not in generalities[206] but in clear, measurable terms. For a buyer-led program, that means increases in sales and jobs. If circumstances dictate, it may make sense to add exports and investment, but one goes beyond those variables at one's peril. Chip Heath makes the point in another context:

> I worked with a nonprofit organization that had *eight* core values. Research has shown that even a few good choices can paralyze people and prevent them from making a decision. How are you going to avoid decision paralysis when you're juggling eight core values? The guiding message of Bill Clinton's first presidential race was, "It's the economy, stupid." There were lots of issues in that race, but you can't keep a complicated campaign organization on track if you try to tackle all of them. You have to pick your battle and win it.[207]

Externally, PRA used a provocative subtitle to distinguish its approach from others in the development marketplace. The subtitle was *"una visión empresarial al servicio del desarrollo,"* which, in English, can have two meanings, "a business vision at the service of development" or "an entrepreneurial vision at the service of development." Either way, the subtitle challenges common perceptions of what development is about. Most Peruvians, like most people anywhere, see development and the fight against poverty primarily as a charitable endeavor carried out by social service agencies and not-for-profit organizations. To speak of "business" in the same breath as "development" or "poverty" is a contradiction in terms. Especially at the beginning, therefore, PRA's subtitle came as a shock. Over time, though, the effect was salutary, broadening people's conceptions of the development process.

Paraguay Vende also developed a diagrammatic framework to convey what it does. In contrast to the more theoretical tenor of the PRA framework, Paraguay Vende's is more operational. Exhibit 3.2 presents the framework, which has three decided virtues:

Placing companies and producers at the core of the diagram draws the viewer's attention to "where the action is." The program's clients are first and foremost companies and producers.

Adjacent to Paraguay Vende's clients appear the four entities with which the program's clients interact directly, the three Economic Service Centers that provide them business development services and the Trade Facilitation Center, at the time the program's policy analysis and dialogue arm.

The remainder of the diagram gives not only the entities involved in running the program, USAID and Chemonics, but also the individuals charged with carrying out different functions, thereby reinforcing their accountability for same.

The title of the program itself, "Paraguay Vende," has also had an impact on people's thinking, both internally and externally. "Paraguay Vende" means "Paraguay Sells," which, in just two words, tells people what the program is about. In the author's experience, no other donor program anywhere has become a brand name in the public domain so quickly.

Exhibit 3.2 Paraguay Vende Programmatic Framework

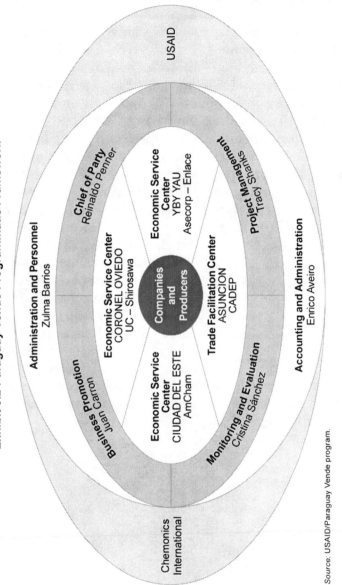

Source: USAID/Paraguay Vende program.

Inculcate Market Chains as an Operational Framework for Action

As useful as diagrams like Exhibits 3.1 and 3.2 are for portraying the overall picture, operationally the devil rears his head in the details. As one might divine from Part II, the meat of the operational details appears in market chains. When launching the buyer-led approach, therefore, it is essential not only to define an umbrella framework that program participants can identify with and internalize, but also to spell out operational parameters to guide their support of market chain clients. Again, the objective of such parameters is not to straightjacket practitioners, but to give them a clear operational development paradigm to guide their work. Experience in various countries bears witness to the creativity and innovation that practitioners can bring to the task once that task homes in on the specific problems constricting a market chain's growth.

"[T]he closer our lives come to the earth, the more real and truthful they become."

Milan Kundera, *The Unbearable Lightness of Being*, translated by Michael Henry Heim (New York: Harper & Row, Publishers, 1984), p. 5.

The discussion in Chapters 7 and 8 is pertinent here, especially the presentation of the concept of the market chain and the kinds of program activities most conducive to supporting it. That said, the diagram in Exhibit 3.3 has proven to be especially powerful pedagogically, and many buyer-led programs have used it. For readers who prefer tables, the key messages appear here in tabular form as well.

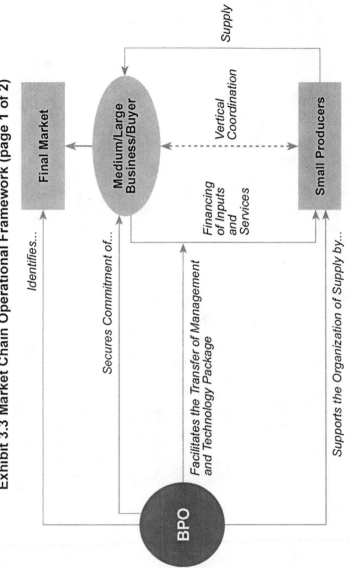

Exhibit 3.3 Market Chain Operational Framework (page 1 of 2)

Exhibit 3.3 Market Chain Operational Framework (page 2 of 2)

Point of Entry	Start with demand, not supply
	Start with connector firms
Strategy	Support market chains, not just individual actors
	Facilitate, do not intervene
Tactics	Capitalize on embedded services
Focus	Focus on sales and jobs, not numbers of clients
	Focus on sales transactions
	Focus on specific problems; do not launch large "projects"
Sequencing	1. Identify final demand in specific terms
	2. Secure commitment of large and medium enterprises
	3. Nurture relationships of trust between larger buyers and smaller suppliers
	4. Organize suppliers to fulfill orders of buyers (quantity, quality, delivery)

Source: Adapted from USAID/Peru Poverty Reduction and Alleviation program and used extensively in other programs.

The framework presented in Exhibit 3.3 is useful not only for learning initially but also for calling to mind later the key operational pointers most practitioners need. In more detail, those pointers include:

Point of entry

Start with demand, not supply. The diagram places the final market at the top of the diagram to reinforce the message that demand is the driver. Suppliers must produce what they can sell, rather than trying to sell what they now produce.

Normally make connector firms your point of entry. In principle, a buyer-led program can work with a final buyer, a connector firm, or suppliers as its immediate client. Given the connector firm's linkage role, it is generally preferable to start there. Starting at one end often makes it hard to appreciate what is going on at the other.

Strategy

Do not look at market chain actors in isolation. Market chain actors are not an island. They meet in market chains. More than that, the problems impeding one actor's growth may lie somewhere else—for example, a processor may have both a market to sell to and adequate production capacity, but not have reliable suppliers to source from.

Facilitate market chains; do not intervene in them. Most buyer-led programs work through Business Promotion Offices (BPOs). A discussion of how to set them up and organize them appears below. Their names vary from country to country, but each performs essentially the same functions. As the diagram illustrates, the job of BPOs is to support market chains, but they ought never form part of them.

Tactics

When possible, capitalize on the embedded services model. Many chains founder because suppliers do not have the financing or the management or technical know-how to produce to potential buyers' specifications. Enlightened connector firms often recognize the problem and jump actively into the breach, advancing funds or providing management or technical guidance directly to suppliers. As the Piscifactoría de los Andes and other examples give testimony, such initiatives can be powerful drivers of sales and job increases, and, all other things being equal, constitute a model worthy of support.

Focus

Focus on generating sales and jobs along the market chain, not the number of clients you attend to. Many development programs set targets for the number of clients they provide assistance to. Under the buyer-led approach, such targets make little sense. Buyer-led programs typically work with a limited number of connector firms as clients, and it is precisely because they focus there that they can induce substantial employment, either within the connector firms themselves or among their suppliers.

A hypothetical example helps make the point. Suppose a development program had the choice of working directly with 500 micro-enterprises or enticing IBM to open up a plant employing 500 people. Under the first option, the program could say it works with 500 clients; under the second, only one. But the employment effect is the same. More than that, operating a plant typically provides opportunities for specialization and scale economies that allow laborers to become more productive and earn more than they could on their own. In such case, a variable many programs treat as an end is in fact simply a means—and deserves treatment as such.

In a similar vein, compare the likely benefits of a program providing technical assistance to individual tomato growers selling to itinerant middlemen or women harvest by harvest with the likely benefits of a program that works with a few connector firms with links to well paying markets, be they local, regional, national, or international. The number of clients in the latter case is smaller than in the former, but the potential for developmental impact is likely many times greater. Not only can connector firms link backward to sizeable numbers of growers, but as examples cited in Part II illustrate, often connector firms are willing to invest in the consolidation of those backward linkages themselves, thereby reducing the need for assistance from a development program and, all other things equal, making the cost-effectiveness of that program all the greater. Again, the moral of the story is to keep one's eye on the prize: sales and jobs expansion is primary; the number of businesses a program counts as clients is secondary.

Focus on sales transactions. Transactions, not studies or meetings, are where the market chain tire hits the road—and where buyer-led programs prove their mettle.

Do not launch large "projects"; solve specific problems. The hallmark of the buyer-led approach is classic problem solving. Starting from the market and proceeding backwards, Business Promotion Offices work with clients to solve whatever problems stand in the way of the expansion of entire market chains. Together, the clients and the offices formalize the actions they shall take in summary Client Growth Plans, described below. The Client Growth Plans not only codify the commitments of the two parties, but contain the baselines against which to measure future achievements. In principle, the services facilitated by the offices can take on a multiplicity of forms. They include but are not limited to: identifying local buyers and nurturing their interest in sourcing from the program's economic corridors; identifying foreign buyers, attracting them, and securing their commitment to source locally; assisting exporters, and the producers from whom they source, in meeting applicable international grades and standards; acquainting local producers with the latest trends in design in international markets; introducing and extending cost-saving technology; assessing enterprises' management practices, and recommending improvements; helping clients organize their accounts to access commercial debt or equity financing; assisting disparate small producers in organizing themselves to produce to the requirements of the market; helping companies register themselves and formalize without trauma; providing technical assistance in regularizing land titles; and putting in place quality control systems to reduce post-harvest losses.

Sequencing

The order in which a program provides services matters, and it matters significantly. Exhibit 3.3 sketches out four different kinds of support a Business Promotion Office can give. Given the primacy of demand, identifying final buyers is first. In other words, before turning to supply-side problems—of which there may be many—a buyer-led program must be sure to tie the demand side down. That does not necessarily mean that the program must identify buyers itself—clients may have buyers lined up already—but at least it must verify that that is the case before moving on to anything else.

Very briefly, the four different kinds of support, in priority order, are:

Identifying final demand in as specific a form as possible. The ideal is to have formal purchase orders in hand, especially in the case of foreign buyers. Orders, from buyers with first names and last names, inject dynamism into the productive system and provide compelling incentives to come to grips with and resolve the multiplicity of supply problems that constrain producers' ability to compete.

Identifying and securing the interest and commitment of large and medium enterprises. To the extent that it makes business sense, the commitment in question may include entering into outsourcing agreements with smaller producers and, in opportune instances, furnishing them financial, management, or technical assistance.

Establishing or nurturing outsourcing relationships, inserting technical assistance and management expertise into the process. This "glue" function lies at the heart of what Business Promotion Offices do. Although technical assistance can take many forms, experience worldwide suggests strongly the critical role that the offices can play as "honest brokers" between parties—large buyers and small sellers, especially—that often enter the scene with deepset prejudices against each other. As stressed in Part II, the building of trust generally is the most basic—and, by altering mindsets, ultimately the most far-reaching—of a buyer-led program's services.

Helping organize producers to deliver the product agreed upon in the quantity, quality, and time frame desired. This task often involves facilitating and consolidating working arrangements among buyers, producer associations, and, when appropriate, third parties with on-the-ground capacity to transfer technical know-how, monitor progress, flag supply problems as they occur, and solve them.

Many buyer-led programs use the case study method to drive home Exhibit 3.3's key messages to new BPO business advisors. The methodology consists basically of three steps:

Step 1. Examine the case. Trainees receive a short case —the problems of a potential client—to analyze. One such case appears in Exhibit 3.4.

Exhibit 3.4 Example, Case Study Exercise, Step 1

> **Case Study: Sunset Cove/Clearview Farms, Antigua and Barbuda**
>
> Sunset Cove is a high-end, luxury resort in Antigua and Barbuda with bookings of tourists lined up for the foreseeable future. Management has established a policy of procuring as many goods and services as possible from local sources, but the flip side of that policy is that those sources must produce to high international standards. As a practical matter, the resort buys many of its supplies from abroad, Europe, especially. The general manager is interested in buying more food and nursery products locally, but has not taken an aggressive posture in contracting with local firms.
>
> The open-air lobby of Sunset Cove is stunning. Among its attractions is the lushness of its foliage, including, in particular, a bounty of orchids, all of which come from Europe. On flowers and foliage alone, Sunset Cove spends $100,000 a year.
>
> About a half mile from Sunset Cove is Clearview Farms, a small-scale fruit and vegetable operation producing entirely for the local market—and the standards thereof. It also has a tiny nursery, which, among other things, produces orchids.
>
> Can the buyer-led program in Antigua and Barbuda help these businesses? What actions would it make most sense for it to support? Can the program make a difference?
>
> This case study comes from real life, but the names and figures are fictitious. The example is for pedagogical purposes only.

Source: James T. Riordan.

Step 2. Define the program's client. The trainees decide who the client of the buyer-led program will be, where the client falls in the market chain, and how the client relates to other actors in the chain. Trainees then enter that information in a blank market chain. A template with a blank chain appears in Exhibit 3.5, and a possible diagnosis of the example case appears in Exhibit 3.6.

Exhibit 3.5 Template, Case Study Exercise, Step 2

Who is the client?
What does the market chain look like?
What is the transaction?

1. Where does the client fit in the market chain?

_____

_____

_____

_____

2. What is the transaction the program might support?

_____

_____

_____

_____

Exhibit 3.6 Example, Case Study Exercise, Step 2

Who is the client?
What does the market chain look like?
What is the transaction?

1. Where does the client fit in the market chain?

The client, Sunset Cove, is the connector firm, the potential glue between high-end tourists and Clearview Farms.

2. What is the transaction the program might support?

Sales of high-quality orchids to Sunset Cove by Clearview Farms.

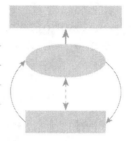

Source: James T. Riordan.

Step 3. Develop a problem-solving strategy. The trainees develop a strategy to address the market chain's key problems, defining the actions the buyer-led program and the client each will take, the sales expected as a result of those actions over the life of the program, the cost to the program of the proposed actions, and an assessment of how projected sales relate to the cost to the program. A template with the different tasks in ordered fashion appears in Exhibit 3.7, and a possible strategy for the example case appears in Exhibit 3.8.

Exhibit 3.7 Template, Case Study Exercise, Step 3

PROBLEM-SOLVING STRATEGY

Problems	Solutions
A.	A.
B.	B.
C.	C.

Expected Results
Increase in sales
Increase in employment

Cost to Program of Solution

Ratio of Increase in Sales to Program Cost

Exhibit 3.8 Example, Case Study Exercise, Step 3

PROBLEM-SOLVING STRATEGY

Problems	Solutions
A. Clearview Farms cannot produce orchids to Sunset Cove's standards	A. Agronomic assistance to Clearview Farms in high-quality orchid production

Expected Results
Increase in sales: $30,000, $60,000, and $75,000 in Years 1, 2, and 3
Increase in employment: One full-time job in Year 1, two in Years 2 and 3

Cost to Program of Solution
1/3 of total cost (shared with Sunset Cove and Clearview Farms) = $10,000 in Year 1 and $5,000 in Years 2 and 3

Ratio of Increase in Sales to Program Cost
8.25:1 ($165,000/$20,000)

Source: James T. Riordan.

Real-life applications of this problem-solving approach naturally are more complex and call for substantially more due diligence than is possible in a training setting, but the basic process is much the same: analyze each client's constraining problems on their own merits, devise possible solutions, and then see whether those solutions are cost-effective. In short, build discipline and accountability for results into what a program does **beforehand**.

Additional case study examples appear in Chapter 17.

Formalize a Decision Criterion Like the 5:1 Rule

The last task in the case study exercise above gives flesh to the 5:1 rule that many buyer-led programs use to bring focus, discipline, and accountability to their work. As the example indicates, the ratio consists of two parts:

Expected increase in sales. This variable refers to the boost in sales that program support will be instrumental in inducing. It includes increases in sales not only in the current year, but in the remaining years of the program's life.

Cost to the program of the solution. This variable refers to the direct costs that the program will incur to help bring about the expected increase in sales. It does not include either fixed direct costs of the program or indirect costs. Nor does it include client costs.

Every time that a buyer-led program entertains the possibility of supporting a client, it goes through the rigor of estimating these two variables. It then takes the ratio of the two and compares it with a cut-off value like 5:1. If the ratio exceeds 5:1, the program moves forward. If it falls short of 5:1, it goes back to the drawing board or decides not to go ahead.

Applying the 5:1 rule looks simple on paper, but very few development programs use anything like it. Why not? The main reason, honestly, is that nobody likes to subject his or her actions to quantitative criteria: it is much more comfortable to do "good" things than to oblige oneself to do cost-effective things. But aside from people's reluctance to hold their feet to the fire, applying the rule has some nuances and implications that are not obvious at first glance.

One is the time dimension for results. The formula limits results to those that will occur during a program's life even though, if all goes well, the results in question—sales—will continue after the program ends. An outside observer may object that cutting off results so abruptly is short-sighted and, as a practical matter, will lead the program to focus only on activities with immediate return. In principle, that critique is valid, but experience in development is so replete with promises of what will occur after programs leave that it is far better to err on the side of accountability, making the programs deliver results, not for Godot, but while they are still around to take the heat.

Three years ago, a colleague of the author pulled together a sample of reports from business promotion programs that Chemonics International Inc. is managing throughout the world. Although the sample was not scientific, he was amazed at how many reports cast what the programs had accomplished in the future—yes, future!—tense. In one report after another he encountered language like, "The development of an official standard for product x will allow producers, processors, and marketers to obtain higher value. This investment will create more wealth for all in the value chain." In short, "Trust us, and you will see results later."

Those involved may object that at the time of writing, program activities had not yet progressed to the point that they could reasonably expect to see measurable outcomes. That may be true in some instances, but extrapolation of results to the future is much more indicative of development-speak than most practitioners would like to admit. In the end, saying that results will come in some undefined future begs accountability—and argues persuasively for building more discipline into thinking through what to do in the first place. The accountable development practitioner makes results, not an article of faith, but something he or she assumes the obligation to accept the credit or take the blame for right from the beginning.

Given the proclivity to shirk accountability, it makes eminent sense to limit the 5:1 rule to the life of the program under question. But doing so does indeed carry with it the danger of ignoring opportunities that require heavy initial investment and do not show results in the short term. Examples include the construction and equipping of factories and planting permanent crops that yield product only after a number of years. Often such investments can not only be lucrative but generate substantial employment for currently poor people. It is important, therefore, for a buyer-led program to build in incentives for practitioners to entertain such longer-term initiatives—and not to confine themselves to short-term opportunities.

There are at least three non-exclusive ways to integrate a long-term perspective. The first, and most obvious, is to design the program to run a goodly number of years—at least five, say—in the first place. As Chapter 11 discusses, evidence from buyer-led programs suggests strongly that the longer you run a program, the bigger the return for your buck. A wise funding agency does not limit its horizon to two or three years, but thinks longer term.[208] Second, some programs—PRA and Paraguay Vende, for example—supplement sales and jobs with a third objective, investment in physical capital and equipment. The rationale for including investment is to oblige practitioners to bring long-term business opportunities explicitly under the tent. If clients make investments in plant or equipment, presumably they are serious businesspeople, thinking beyond immediate returns (in contrast, for example, to traders who invest financially in their operations, but only to manage their cash flow). Third, environments propitious primarily for permanent crops—the economic corridors where USAID's Rural Competitiveness Activity works in Bolivia, for example—may offer relatively few business opportunities from which one can expect results in only one or two years. In such exceptional cases, restricting the estimation of results to the life of the program can indeed be short-sighted. On an exception-that-proves-the-rule basis, and only on an exception-that-proves-the-rule basis, therefore, it may make sense to include an estimate of the discounted present value of harvests a number of years out as acceptable results. Once again, though, when in doubt, err on the side of conservatism—do not abuse the exception to circumvent real accountability.

A further implication of the 5:1 rule is the preference it gives to local, as opposed to foreign, solutions. Helping a client solve a business problem often involves engaging an expert of some kind. Most of the time, a local expert costs substantially less than an expatriate, for whom one typically has to pay not only salary, but travel and per diem costs. All other things being equal, therefore, the denominator of the sales-cost ratio will be lower—and the value of the ratio itself will be higher—when development programs tap local rather than foreign expertise. Instances exist, of course, in which local experts do not have the required qualifications, and it is necessary to look abroad for help. But again, start with the idea that that option will be the exception—do not assume from the get-go that the solution is a foreigner. Working with local expertise makes sense not only philosophically but, much more often than not, on cost-effectiveness grounds, too.

In a similar vein, the higher the proportion of a solution's cost that a client bears itself, the more cost-effective the buyer-led program's support. The same goes for contributions from third parties. In the red quinoa transaction discussed below, CARE provided technical assistance directly to growers, thereby easing the financial burden on PRA's immediate client, the processor, El Altiplano, and the program itself. In many countries, non-governmental organizations specialize in the provision of production assistance to small producers, urban as well as rural, but often their programs founder for lack of market contacts. To the extent that a buyer-led program can identify live buyers for them, a three-way alliance among the buyer-led program's client, a non-governmental organization, and the buyer-led program can be a win-win-win proposition. For everyone's protection, though, it behooves all three parties involved to become signatories of the Client Growth Plan.

Aside from making crystal-clear operationally what must drive the entire program, the biggest virtue of the 5:1 rule is not the value of the cutoff itself, but that it instills rigor and discipline in all program decisions. In and of itself, there is nothing magical about the value 5:1, though it does have decided advantages. Economic theory would argue for estimation of some kind of rate of return, but many development practitioners, especially those working in remote economic corridors, do not have training in such techniques. In contrast, the buyer-led approach's sales-cost calculation generally falls within their ken. More than that, if a business opportunity satisfies the 5:1 rule, the likelihood is high that its rate of return will be more than satisfactory as well.[209] In fact, one can live with cutoffs lower than 5:1 and still have solid returns. In Azerbaijan, the legacy of the Soviet system tends to discourage entrepreneurship, and the basic infrastructure to support economic activity—roads, especially—is spotty. As a result, the designers of the Azerbaijan Business Assistance and Development program decided to go with a ratio considerably lower than 5:1. Much of the same reasoning applies to post-conflict environments like Afghanistan, where physical insecurity, lack of trust, and conflict-engendered entitlement make doing business problematic, to say the least. Again, the key is not so much the exact quantitative cutoff one uses, but that one has enough concern for accountability to use a cutoff at all!

"Nothing is real until you measure it."

Martha Grimes, *The Old Wine Shades* (New York: New American Library, 2006), p. 147.

Originally, the expectation was that PRA would last five years, but it came closer to ten. As a result, one would expect most *ex post* incremental sales/support cost ratios to exceed 5:1 by a considerable margin. That is indeed what happened. For all products, the team conducting the final evaluation of the program estimated the ratio to be 75:1. But that aggregate ratio hides considerable variation among products. As Exhibit 3.9 illustrates, most of the products in which PRA was most cost-effective involve processing activities. In contrast, most of the products in which PRA was least cost-effective are primary products.

Chapter 11 presents results from a number of buyer-led programs, including comparisons of the ratios between net sales and dollars spent. Some of the ratios reported fall below 5:1, which may lead the reader to ask, "If buyer-led programs conform to the 5:1 rule, why are some of the results so low?" The reason is that the ratios reported there are defined differently from the ratios discussed here.

The discussion in this section has to do with how business advisors decide whether to support the market chains of potential clients in specific transactions. In most cases, the decision criterion takes the form of the so called 5:1 rule. If an advisor does the required calculations well, there are solid grounds to expect that by

Exhibit 3.9 Products in Which PRA Was Most and Least Cost-Effective in Providing Support 2000-2007

Products	Highest Incremental Sales/ Support Cost Ratios	Products	Lowest Incremental Sales/ Support Cost Ratios
Jewelry	372	Soybeans	2
Poultry	315	Garlic	4
Flowers and plants	301	Aromatics and medicinal	6
Tourism	290	Natural rubber	6
Spices	262	Honey	10
Household articles and handicrafts	227	Red pepper	13
Bixin	217	Musk	15
Processed foods	210	Forage	15
Ceramic tiles	202	Corn	16
Tara	188	Cereals	19

Source: USAID/Peru Poverty Reduction and Alleviation program Final Report. p. 74.

the end of the program, the incremental sales attributable to the program's transaction(s)-specific support will be at least five times greater than the direct costs of that support (see the first line of Exhibit 3.10). But those costs are not the only costs a buyer-led program incurs. First, there are the other direct costs involved in setting up Business Promotion Offices throughout a country, managing them, monitoring their progress against targets, taking corrective action when necessary, etc. In addition, the organization managing the program has real indirect—overhead—costs to cover. An example is central accounting costs that the organization cannot allocate accurately among its various programs and must therefore apply as a percentage to all of them. Most of the ratios presented in Chapter 11 take all direct and indirect costs into account, comparing them with the sum of all the incremental sales attributable to their respective programs. Although there are no hard and fast guidelines here, it is probably reasonable to expect that after four years of operations, total incremental sales induced by a buyer-led program will exceed its total costs by a factor of at least three to one (see the second line of Exhibit 3.10). Moreover, with more time one can expect the total incremental sales-total costs ratio to grow even larger, gradually approaching and exceeding the 5:1 threshold.

Exhibit 3.10 Reasonable Minimum Expectations for
Incremental Sales/Cost Ratios
over a Four-Year Period

$$\left. \frac{\text{Transaction-specific incremental sales}}{\text{Transaction-specific direct costs}} \right\} 5{:}1$$

$$\left. \frac{\text{Total incremental sales}}{\text{Total direct and indirect costs}} \right\} 3{:}1$$

Source: James T. Riordan.

Organize Operations Geographically

Buyer-led programs organize themselves, not by product, sector, or cluster, but by geography. Chapter 8 lays out a number of specific arguments for doing so. The clinching argument, aside from not pre-picking product, sector, or cluster winners, has to do with building trust, which depends heavily on development practitioners having extended face-to-face contact with their clients. In the end, physical presence is essential, which means that geography is essential.

The preferred methodology for defining how a buyer-led program organizes itself is the construct of economic corridors. This section illustrates how to put that methodology into practice.

Like the 5:1 rule, there is nothing magical about the concept of economic corridors, and demarcating them is much more art than hard science. By definition, economic corridors are spaces in which economic activity naturally takes place, that is, spaces that link rural areas to intermediate cities, and intermediate cities, in turn, to the demands of domestic and international markets beyond. In short, corridors are economic networks within and among which flow goods, services, labor, and capital. Economic corridors fall naturally into hierarchies, with lower-level corridors supplying and, in turn, buying goods and services from higher-level ones. Normally, economic corridors do not conform to political boundaries, but correlate closely with roads and watersheds.[210] All that said, where one corridor begins and ends is not written in stone. In the end, an economic corridor is an organizing device with its roots in economic reality, but also with a certain degree of arbitrariness to it. The specific objectives of a given buyer-led program, and the budget available, often affect their practical demarcation.

Economic corridors are especially suitable for programs oriented toward reducing poverty. Why? Because in very many developing countries, the main reason that poor people are poor is their lack of access to markets. That lack of access can take many forms — for example, the labor market demands certain skills, and the poor lack those skills. More often than not, however, lack of access has a physical dimension to it. Especially in agrarian societies, sizeable proportions of poor people are cut off physically both from buyers to whom they can sell what they can produce and from job opportunities they may be qualified for. To reduce poverty, therefore, it is useful to think in geographic terms, specifically, how to bring the poor more into the commercial mainstream — which leads one naturally to think in economic corridor terms. In fact, the appeal of the economic corridor construct for anti-poverty programs is precisely that it forces practitioners to think through why the poor are not connected to markets and how they can remedy that situation. In general, that remedy can take one of two forms. The first is to bring economic opportunities directly to where the poor live. But the poor often live where economic resources are the most meager, which brings one to the second, at least as frequent, remedy: developing opportunities—typically in cities—to which labor—in economic parlance, a mobile, not a fixed, factor of production—can migrate for work, either permanently or temporarily.

An economic corridor normally includes one, and sometimes two or three, intermediate cities that act as a hub(s) of commercial activity. Such cities not only serve as distribution points for goods entering or leaving the corridor, but typically are home to the businesses that, day to day, constitute the proximate point of demand for—that is, the buyers of—rural goods and services. As a consequence, buyer-led programs normally site their Business Promotion Offices there.

Depending on its size, a corridor can have more than one Business Promotion Office. There is no hard and fast rule for determining how many to set up, but experience suggests the three-to-four-hour rule of thumb. If a business advisor lives more than three or four hours away from a client—a processor, trader, or group of suppliers, for example—it is rare that the advisor will visit that client. Since physical contact lies at the heart of building trust, it behooves a buyer-led program to site its Business Promotion Offices so that business advisors can reach the program's main clients within a three-to-four-hour period.

The discussion that follows shows how two buyer-led programs have used the economic corridor construct to organize themselves geographically. The first is Paraguay Vende and the second is the Micro Enterprise Development Initiative (MEDI) in Armenia. Chapter 17 supplements those cases with examples from Peru, Azerbaijan, Bolivia, and Liberia.

Budget restrictions normally prevent buyer-led programs from establishing physical presence everywhere they would like. As a result, it is necessary to make strategic choices, which in turn makes it necessary to establish criteria for doing so. In the design of both PRA and Paraguay Vende, USAID put two criteria on the table: first, it wanted the programs to go where the poor were; second, it wanted the programs to go where there was economic potential, that is, where, all other things equal, it would be possible to generate economic opportunities for the poor.

In Peru, the designers of PRA first divided the entire country into economic corridors, assigning every district—the equivalent, in United States terminology, of a town—to one corridor or another. Peru has data on extreme poverty by district, which made it possible to rank every corridor in the country by that criterion. Most countries—Paraguay, for example—do not have poverty data disaggregated by district. For that reason, Paraguay Vende's approach to defining economic corridors has more applicability elsewhere.

Paraguay has data on poverty by department—the equivalent of a state in the United States—but not by smaller units. For that reason, the Paraguay Vende design team first applied the desired poverty and economic potential criteria by department, not by economic corridor. The result appears in Exhibit 3.11. The ranking by poverty came from poverty incidence data from a national household survey. In contrast, economic potential refers to the future, not to the past, so existing data do not do justice to the concept. The ranking by economic potential therefore derived from the collective judgment of Paraguayans who know their country well.

Exhibit 3.11 Classification of the Departments in Eastern Paraguay by Economic Potential and Incidence of Poverty

Incidence of Poverty	Economic Potential				
	5	4	3	2	1
5			Caazapá	San Pedro	
4		Canindeyú	Amambay Concepción Caaguazú	Guairá	
3	Itapúa	Ñeembucú		Misiones	Paraguarí
2	Alto Paraná	Central	Cordillera		
1		Asunción			

Source: Economic potential, expert judgment; incidence of poverty, Integrated Household Survey, 2000/01.

The departments that met the two criteria best are those in the northwest portion of the exhibit. In all, there are ten such departments, Alto Paraná, Amambay, Caaguazú, Caazapá, Canindeyú, Concepción, Guairá, Itapúa, Ñeembucú, and San Pedro. Of those, Caazapá was the focus of the German Government's development program at the time, and Ñeembucú is isolated from other departments of interest. The design team therefore decided to concentrate on the remaining eight departments.

The final step was to demarcate economic corridors in the departments in question. The reasoning behind the final decisions, which appear in the map in Exhibit 3.12, ran as follows:

Eastern Economic Corridor. This corridor consists of portions of three departments, Itapúa, Alto Paraná, and Canindeyú. Specifically, it includes districts bordering both sides of the paved highway that runs from east of Encarnación through Ciudad del Este to Salto del Guairá.

Central Economic Corridor. This corridor consists of portions of three departments, Caaguazú, Guairá, and San Pedro. Specifically, it includes districts bordering both sides of the paved highway that runs west-east across Caaguazú, and districts bordering both sides of the paved highway that runs south-north from Villarica through Coronel Oviedo to San Estanislao and beyond into the southern part of San Pedro. This corridor therefore has the form of a cross.

Northern Economic Corridor. This corridor consists of portions of three departments, Concepción, Amambay, and San Pedro. Specifically, it includes districts bordering both sides of the paved highway that runs west-east from Concepción through Horqueta and Yby Yaú to Pedro Juan Caballero, and districts bordering both sides of the paved highway that runs north-south from Yby Yaú into the northern part of San Pedro.

Exhibit 3.12 Demarcation of Economic Corridors in Paraguay

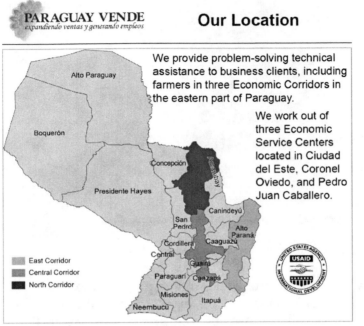

Source: USAID/Paraguay Vende program.

Paraguay Vende has now entered a second phase. During its design, USAID indicated it wanted the program to expand its coverage to the southern part of the country. Still taking into account the characteristics of commercial flows geographically, the implementation team reconfigured its demarcation of economic corridors accordingly—illustrating thereby the flexibility of the construct to meet changing objectives.

In Armenia, USAID had budget to set up operations in only one economic corridor. At the time, USAID had its program heavily concentrated in Yerevan, the capital city, and was anxious to launch a business development program outside its orbit. The question was where.

Available data on sole proprietorships proved the most useful guide for making that decision. Exhibit 3.13 shows the distribution geographically of sole proprietorships across the country. The

**Exhibit 3.13 Geographical Distribution of
Sole Proprietorships in Armenia**

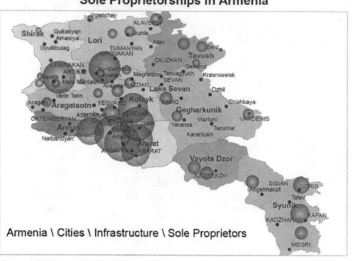

Source: USAID/Armenia Micro Enterprise Development Initiative.

heavy concentration of circles in the middle of the map reflects the dominance of Yerevan. Interestingly, though, the map also reveals relatively sizeable masses of sole proprietorships in the north, a base that a buyer-led program presumably could build upon.

Exhibit 3.14 shows how MEDI acted on that finding. The program demarcated an economic corridor in the north around the road networks connecting its principal cities internally and linking it with Yerevan to the south and Georgia to the north. The corridor consisted not only of the major transportation routes but of their adjoining hinterlands. In the end, the program contracted a local company to manage a buyer-led program from three cities, Gyumri, Vanadzor, and Ijevan (going from west to east, the three places marked with gray-black circles on the map).

Exhibit 3.14 Demarcation of the MEDI North Economic Corridor in Armenia

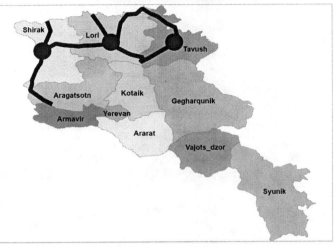

Source: USAID/Armenia Micro Enterprise Development Initiative.

Put a Conducive Management and Organizational Structure in Place

Part II argues strongly against buyer-led programs organizing themselves by market chain functions—agricultural production, agricultural processing, and agricultural marketing, for example— or by product or sector. The rationale for that argument is simple. Until development practitioners actually get their hands dirty working with individual business clients, they simply do not know enough to say that such and such a function is going to constitute such a binding constraint that they should staff up to attack it. Nor do they know beforehand what products really are going to be the winners, which suggests that organizing by products, sectors, or clusters—and staffing accordingly—can be shortsighted and un-economical.

**Exhibit 3.15 Prototype Organizational Structure for a
Buyer-Led Program**

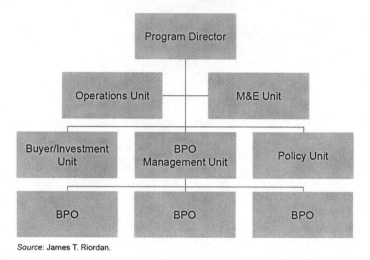

Source: James T. Riordan.

Exhibit 3.15 lays out a prototype organizational structure for a buyer-led program. Like other operational elements of the buyer-led approach, the organization chart is not a straitjacket, but an overall framework that an individual program can adapt to its specific requirements, which, in fact, is what buyer-led programs have done to date.

Leadership for the overall program lodges in the Program Director, who is accountable to the program's funding agency for achieving agreed upon results. More often than not, the funding agency is an international donor organization that contracts out management of the program. The Program Director manages a budget that, within limits, he or she can allocate to bring about desired results. In very broad terms, the Program Director of a buyer-led program does not differ much from managers of programs anywhere. Practically, however, one qualification is paramount: full, and instinctive, commitment to the buyer-led approach and the discipline it calls for. Along the way, strong temptations will arise to deviate from the approach and veer the program off course. The Program Director must captain the ship steadfastly, often steering between Scylla and Charybdis to bring it to port.

Reporting to the program director are three line units:

Business Promotion Offices Management Unit. A buyer-led program normally operates through Business Promotion Offices (BPOs) in its economic corridors. The Business Promotion Offices Management Unit manages the BPOs. The line of command from the Program Director to the BPO Management Unit to the Business Promotion Offices is the "spine" of the program. All other program activities are subservient to it. Experience worldwide bears strong witness to the virtual impossibility of turn-keying the buyer-led approach to third parties. BPOs are highly unlikely to meet their sales and jobs targets without strong central direction and technical monitoring. This unit performs that essential function. In the beginning, the BPO Management Unit provides hands-on guidance and close supervision to BPO staff on how to work with their business clients. Once the BPOs gain experience, the BPO Management Unit's role shifts to backstopping and troubleshooting—and, with input from the program's Monitoring and Evaluation Unit, monitoring performance.

The BPO Management Unit typically consists of a BPO Manager, a BPO Subcontracts Manager, and one assistant for every three to four BPOs under its purview. The inclusion of assistants allows for regular in-person contact with the BPOs, as well as centralized capability to prepare and process scopes of work for international technical assistance when that is required. See Chapter 17 for examples of scopes of work for a BPO Manager and a BPO Subcontracts Manager.

Buyer/Investment Unit. The second line unit identifies and secures the commitment of buyers to source from, and investors to invest in, the program's economic corridors. The driver of the buyer-led approach is buyers. Some buyers may reside physically within a program's economic corridors, but usually much greater opportunities exist outside them, both within a country's capital city and abroad. This unit taps that potential source of dynamism and brings it to bear in support of the program. The Buyer/Investment Unit nurtures relationships with potential buyers domestically and cultivates potential buyers abroad, traveling occasionally to likely foreign markets.

Experience in a number of countries suggests the advisability of focusing initially on promoting sales and pursuing investment aggressively only later. Unless they have worked there before, outsiders, be they domestic or international, are unlikely to invest in many of the economic corridors where buyer-led programs establish presence. Why? Because, investing in an area, even more than sourcing from it, requires trust, and that trust does not develop overnight. Experience under PRA suggests that the best way to promote investment is first, to concentrate almost single-mindedly on convincing outside businesspeople to buy from the program's economic corridors. Once they develop trust with suppliers there—a process that usually takes at least two years and often involves the intermediate step of advancing inputs to suppliers—then generally they are much more positively disposed to put their money down on physical plant and equipment. As PRA's final report puts it,

> If trust is important for buying, it is essential for investing. In PRA's experience with a number of buyer-investors, a three-step process can build relationships that ultimately attract investment. The first step is to interest firms in buying; the second, to interest them in contributing financially to the consummation of sales transactions—by advancing inputs to suppliers, for example; and the third, once the firms have established relationships of trust, is to interest them in investing in physical plant and equipment. Piscifactoría de los Andes in Puno illustrates the process.
>
> Until 2003, Piscifactoría farmed or sourced most of its trout at or near its headquarters in the economic corridor of Huancayo. In that year, with PRA's encouragement and support, it began to explore sourcing relationships with trout suppliers in Puno—Arapa, ATP, and River Fish, for example. As those relationships prospered, Piscifactoría shared its know-how with its suppliers and helped them produce to market requirements. As its confidence in those suppliers, their communities, and local authorities grew, Piscifactoría considered investing in a physical plant and equipment near Lake Titicaca. In 2005, with support from PRA's Cusco-Puno Economic Service Center, Piscifactoría

installed 6 modules with 48 floating cages near the community of Huecalla in the zone of Charcas in the district of Platería in Puno. It also invested $500,000 in a processing plant in the city of Puno's industrial zone. Those investments have substantially boosted Puno's competitiveness in trout, adding value to its natural resources and allowing it to export anywhere in the world. In addition to sourcing from Arapa, ATP and River Fish, Piscifactoría developed sourcing relationships with 16 trout producer associations along the shores of Lake Titicaca. The productivity of those trout producers has risen an estimated 100 percent, and the unit price they receive for their trout is more than 25 percent higher than previously. Efraín Choque, a supplier from the district of Pomata, has increased his production of trout from 10 to 80 metric tons per year. Fidel Chaiña, from the district of Capachica, sells not only to Piscifactoría but to other companies demanding quality product.

Piscifactoría's entry into Puno demonstrates not only how investing can grow naturally out of sourcing, but the impact that one serious, committed, entrepreneurial party can have on a whole region.[211]

The Buyer/Investment Unit typically is lean and mean, with a Buyer/Investment Unit Manager and a hard-driving assistant. See Chapter 17 for an example of a scope of work for a Buyer/Investment Unit Manager.

Policy Unit. Sometimes the key solution to the problems constraining clients' sales growth is systemic, not transactional, in character. For example, the solution may not entail improvements in post-harvest handling, but have to do with government norms and regulations. The Policy Unit works on systemic problems, not across the board, but in support of the transactional support provided elsewhere by the program. For that reason, it is usually unwise to hire high-powered policy/institutional advisors to staff the unit permanently. Again, going in, program managers generally do not know exactly what the nature of the most binding systemic constraints will be. To address a specific policy or institutional issue, it is normally better to hire top-notch talent short term.

Although the BPO Management Unit, the Buyer/Investment Unit, and the Policy Unit perform line functions, the ultimate line units are the **Business Promotion Offices**. As a rule, each Business Promotion office has three business advisors, plus administrative support. In very general terms, the offices perform three functions: they build relationships of trust with local businesses; they identify buyers for the goods and services they can produce; and they help clients resolve whatever supply problems stand in the way of consummating sales transactions. An example of a fleshed out scope of work for Business Promotion Offices—which the program in question calls Business Services Centers—appears in Exhibit 3.16.

Although it is tempting to hire specialists for the Business Promotion Offices, specialists tend to view the world too much through the prism of their own disciplines. Bankers tend to see clients' problems as financial, agronomists see them as agronomic, macroeconomists see them as rooted in policies or institutions, etc. On balance, it is advisable to hire generalists who, ideally, can diagnose clients' most binding constraints more objectively, and then hire short-term specialists to help address the specific problems identified.[212] See Chapter 17 for examples of scopes of work for a BPO Chief and BPO Business Advisors.

> "[D]etails are elemental, and at times trying to acquire, but not in themselves enlightenment. One must know how to read them properly to find their properties of truth."
>
> Matthew Pearl, *The Poe Shadow* (New York: Random House Trade Paperbacks, 2006), p. 196.

In addition to line units, two staff units report directly to the Program Director:

Operations Unit. This unit takes care of the management of the central program office, finance, including accounting, and administration.

Monitoring and Evaluation Unit. The Monitoring and Evaluation Unit collects data from the BPOs on the achievements of their clients, verifies the validity and attributability of those data, and reports the results on a continuing basis to central office management, to the program's funding agency, to the BPOs themselves, and to the public at large. The unit reports directly to the Program

Exhibit 3.16 Example of Scope of Work for Business Promotion Offices (page 1 of 2)

Afghanistan Accelerated Sustainable Agriculture
Program (ASAP) Business Service Centers
Scope of Work

The Business Service Centers (BSCs), which competitively selected subcontractors shall set up and run, shall play the following roles in the ASAP buyer-led approach:

- Identify the technical assistance required by local businesses and producers to increase their sales in accordance with the demands of national and international markets—that is, buyers. The technical assistance can take many forms, affecting sales, distribution, processing, production, etc., all oriented toward increasing clients' sales competitiveness.

- Once identified and ascertained to be qualified, channel technical assistance to clients in the form of first-rate consultants. Ideally, the consultants shall be local, but they may also come from elsewhere in Afghanistan or abroad. The BSCs shall facilitate the delivery of technical assistance only if one can reasonably expect the increase in sales by clients to exceed the cost of the assistance by a factor of at least 3 to 1. The increase in sales and the cost of the technical assistance must be quantifiable. By looking to third-party providers to provide the bulk of assistance, the BSCs shall contribute to the development of business development services markets in their regions.

- Encourage possibilities for small and micro-producers to sell to regional and national businesses under contract, providing preferential treatment to clients open to such alliances.

- Identify obstacles to private investment and, as appropriate, develop program and policy proposals to contribute to the promotion of private investment, the reduction of transaction costs, and regional competitiveness. When necessary, the BSCs shall participate in appropriate institutional networks —with central, regional, and local government entities and chambers of commerce, for example—to put flesh on those proposals and to implement them.

Exhibit 3.16 Example of Scope of Work for Business Promotion Offices (page 2 of 2)

Specific client services the BSCs shall include:

- Facilitate contacts and assist in negotiations between local, regional, national, and foreign buyers, on the one hand, and local businesses and producers, on the other. The BSCs' business promoters shall possess sufficient education and experience to identify promising business opportunities to dynamize the development of their regions, taking into account specific market demands. The technical advisors shall serve as facilitators in buyer-supplier relationships, following the principle of "producing what sells," instead of "selling what is produced," motivating local producers to respond to specific buyer requirements.

- Promote sales.

- Facilitate one-on-one meetings, business-to-business forums, agricultural and trade fairs, etc., to create and nurture mutually beneficial buyer-supplier relationships.

- Help clients diagnose the principal supply problems that stand in the way of their meeting the requirements of buyers, and come up with cost-effective solutions to address those constraints.

- Facilitate the provision of technical assistance to address clients' binding problems.

- Facilitate client access to sources of financing and marketing, legal, transport, insurance, etc., services.

- Provide detailed information to clients on markets, products, and legal issues.

- Generate and disseminate information of interest—for example, regarding markets and business opportunities in their regions.

For the most part, the BSCs shall carry out the activities above client by client. The BSCs shall select clients according to their economic promise, as well as their openness to working with ASAP. That said, the BSCs shall give high priority to identifying and implementing market solutions to poverty in highly marginalized areas.

Source: USAID/Afghanistan Accelerated Sustainable Agriculture Program.

Director, not to the BPO Manager. This arrangement gives the Monitoring and Evaluation Unit semi-autonomy and helps ensure that BPO advisors do not act as both judge and jury. The monitoring and evaluation system not only facilitates reporting of results attributable to the program, but lays the basis for monitoring progress against targets and flagging and addressing problems as they arise. Given its preoccupation with accountability and, as discussed below, its use of monetary incentives, a buyer-led program does not treat monitoring and evaluation as an afterthought—as, in fact, many other development programs do. Serious, ongoing monitoring and evaluation are integral to the buyer-led approach. Chapter 16 discusses the nuts and bolts of the system.

The Monitoring and Evaluation Unit typically consists of a Monitoring and Evaluation Manager, one Monitoring and Evaluation Specialist for every three to four BPOs, and a Monitoring and Evaluation Data Manager. See Chapter 17 for examples of scopes of work for a Monitoring and Evaluation Manager, Monitoring and Evaluation Specialists, and a Monitoring and Evaluation Data Manager.

The prototype organization chart is noteworthy not only for what units and positions it includes, but also for those it does not. Worthy of specific mention are:

Communications. Communications, especially of success stories, is critical to the spread effect of the buyer-led approach. Different programs have adopted different organizational models for communications, and the jury is out on what works best. Some have created a Communications Unit as a separate staff unit or included it as a responsibility of the Monitoring and Evaluation Unit. Others have assigned it to the BPO Management Unit. The two options have their pros and cons. By separating it out, the first option gives communications due importance, but since the program defines communications as a staff function, the BPO Management Unit often tends to regard requests for assistance from the Communications Unit as a distraction if not an imposition and a chore. Under such circumstances, the output of the Communications Unit often fails to convey the "taste and smell" that really tell a story. Under the second option, communications is a line function and therefore part and parcel of the BPO Management Unit's job. The downside, however, is that program people tend to get so caught up in the day to day that they keep putting off documenting their successes, thereby diminishing the potential copycat effect of the program.

Technical specialties. Many development programs establish central program office positions for finance experts, agriculture advisors, etc., on the grounds that the key constraints to address revolve around finance, agricultural technology, etc. The danger is that often programs do not have enough client-by-client intelligence beforehand to make that determination. Sometimes it turns out there is enough real work for the experts in question to take on. But often there is not, which, in effect, turns the experts into stove-piped solutions looking for problems. Again, the moral of the story is straightforward: first, do one's micro homework before staffing up; and, second, take more of a surgical approach to staffing, letting the specific problems the program finds dictate whom to hire for what and for how long.

Gender. Many development programs set up separate staff positions or units to focus on gender-related concerns. The brief of gender specialists normally includes identifying constraints to equal opportunity for women and men, analyzing policy and program alternatives to address those constraints, formulating possible solutions, keeping the program's eyes open to opportunities to involve both women and men, and helping ensure that both women and men benefit from program activities. Although normally very well intentioned, assigning a separate position or unit to focus on gender often turns out not to be worth the money. Why? Because, as a separate function, gender winds up getting treated as an issue apart from mainstream operations. For that reason, buyer-led programs mainstream gender concerns, building them directly into decisions affecting hiring of staff, the selection of what clients to support, and the nature of the support in each case.

Environment. Some development programs treat environmental concerns much the same way they treat gender concerns, and with much the same effect: isolation from mainstream operations with little to show for the effort. Others set up a "bad-cop" Environmental Unit to veto others' ideas—not exactly a healthy relationship. For a buyer-led program, neither outcome is desirable, to say the least. Buyer-led programs aim to consolidate buyer-seller relationships so that they can last after the programs end. As any good businessperson knows, no commercial relationship will sustain itself unless the underlying business is sustainable environmentally. For that reason, buyer-led programs build environmental concerns squarely into operations. Under Paraguay Vende, for example, every Client Growth Plan has an environmental checklist annex (see Chapter 19). The annex, which derives from United States Government regulations, is simple to go through and flags potential environmental problems. It also flags labor issues that could be problematic.[213]

But doing no harm is not the only way to treat environment. Smart businesspeople look not only for ways to avoid environmental evil but to become more competitive economically by doing environmental good.[214] Two examples from Peru illustrate the point:

The first example comes from the Shipibo-Conibo ceramics operation. Traditionally, the community extracted silicon from the crust of a local tree known as *apacharama* to make its pottery stronger and brighter. To harvest the crust, they cut entire trees down. By the time Pier 1 Imports placed its order, the community had already downed so many trees that *apacharama* crust was in short supply. Ingeniously, the technician contracted to facilitate the operation introduced *puritón*, an abrasive derived primarily from rice skin and available commercially, as a replacement. *Puritón* not only eliminated the need to fell trees, but it was cheaper, making the pottery more competitive.

The second example shows how, in conducive circumstances, the buyer-led approach can contribute to the preservation of biological diversity. In Puno, PRA helped induce the President of California-based Quinoa Corporation to place an order for red quinoa, a variety that with the emphasis the market had placed almost exclusively on white quinoa, was actually in danger of extinction. Filling the order required not only production for export but replenishment of seed stock.

14

Setting Up Business Promotion Offices

There are four steps to set up the Business Promotion Offices:

Subcontract with third parties
Select personnel
Set targets and develop an incentive scheme
Facilitate an induction workshop

Subcontract with Third Parties

A buyer-led program normally subcontracts out the operation of Business Promotion Offices to third parties. The third parties typically are local organizations, and can be either for- or not-for-profit. Sometimes they are foreign organizations, but only if they have registered themselves in the countries in question—which, looked at from that perspective, makes them local. Many buyer-led programs encourage the creation of consortia between local and foreign organizations and between for- and not-for-profit entities as a way to bring the best talent to bear. In such an instance, a buyer-led program subcontracts, not with everybody, but with a lead organization. Doing so prevents accountability from becoming diffused. The last thing program management wants is everybody in charge of a BPO and nobody in charge.

Some observers wonder why buyer-led programs go to all the trouble of subcontracting out BPOs. They ask, "Would it not be a lot easier simply to pick good people off the street and make them employees of the lead implementing organization?" The answer is, yes, going that route would be easier, but, most of the time, it would also be suboptimal. Why? There are three reasons.

Recruiting the best people. The first, and most important, reason has to do with finding the best people for the job. In the end, buyer-led programs, like programs anywhere, ride on people. But the people factor is perhaps even more important in buyer-led programs. Given the programs' decentralized structure, BPO personnel are the first and immediate point of contact with clients in the economic corridors. How they interact with those clients has much to do with the programs' success. Accordingly, it is essential not only that central program personnel and BPO staff are on the same wave length, but, given the physical distances typically involved, that central program management have full confidence that BPO staff have the requisite interpersonal skills to develop relationships of trust with clients and have internalized the buyer-led approach thoroughly to implement it faithfully.

Most organizations implementing buyer-led programs specialize in development, not in business. As a result, most of their personnel gravitate toward development people—and when they search for candidates to fill positions in their programs, they tend to look to those circles. Development people are not bad people, of course, but as this book documents throughout, many development professionals have developed mindsets and working habits that, if not inimical to, are far from consonant with a focus on generating private sector sales and jobs. To put it perhaps over-starkly, in staffing the BPOs it is better to err on the side of recruiting businesspeople with an appreciation of development than on the side of recruiting development people with an appreciation of business. All of which implies it behooves buyer-led programs to break out of the box of normal recruiting procedures, widen the net, and look consciously elsewhere.

Subcontracting the BPOs to third parties is an effective way to do that. By developing terms of reference that make very clear what kind of people the program is looking for and putting the procurement out to open bid—for a sample statement of desired business advisor qualifications, see Exhibit 3.17—the program gives offerors incentives to find the right kind of people, thereby broadening the search dramatically and upping substantially the chances of winding up with staff with the characteristics required.[215]

**Exhibit 3.17 Desired Business Advisor Qualifications:
An Example from the Caribbean Open
Trade Support Program (page 1 of 2)**

- *Business sense and experience.* The most effective advisors generally have had a number of years of hands-on experience in the private sector and can communicate effectively with the business community. They understand the businessperson's point of view and can assess intuitively whether a business proposition is worth further probing. They have an idea of what questions to ask to identify the source of business problems and to develop solutions to those problems.

- *Analytical skills.* A business advisor is called upon to prepare Memoranda of Understanding [Client Growth Plans] with client businesses. The MOUs spell out the key problems of clients and how to attack them at a favorable incremental sales-to-cost ratio. Business advisors must have the capacity to quantify the impact of assistance provided to a client, estimate the profitability of an activity, and work closely with clients to close transactions.

- *Problem-solving ability.* Most instances of program support will run into unexpected obstacles and require creative problem solving, on the spot, by the business advisor. It is imperative that business advisors possess a demonstrated capability for effective ad hoc problem solving.

- *People skills.* One of the most important roles of the business advisor is to bring people together and cultivate trust along the market chain so that the commercial relationships in question do not require the continuing presence of the advisor in the future. This is a key element of the buyer-led approach to transaction sustainability.

- *Commitment to making the transaction work.* Most cases of program support will require persistence and extra effort from time to time to keep things moving forward. A high level of energy and professional commitment is essential for a business advisor to achieve sales targets.

- *A robust professional network.* This is a significant asset for developing new opportunities, evaluating potential clients, and making the business community aware of program capabilities and services.

> **Exhibit 3.17 Desired Business Advisor Qualifications:**
> **An Example from the Caribbean Open**
> **Trade Support Program (page 2 of 2)**
>
> • *Integrity and trustworthiness.* These characteristics enable
>   the business advisor to gain the confidence of clients to
>   overcome mistrust and their natural reluctance to enter into
>   difficult business transactions with potentially high returns on
>   investment.

Source: Adapted from USAID/Caribbean Open Trade Support program.

To avoid the onus of an open procurement, some programs think about subcontracting with Chambers of Commerce. But Chambers often differ substantially in their dynamism, vision, and capacity to identify effective business advisors. In Peru, a number of Chambers of Commerce submitted proposals to operate the Economic Service Centers in their corridors, but not one Chamber was successful.

Making feasible the payment of performance bonuses. To motivate performance, most buyer-led programs introduce performance incentive systems. The systems attempt to align the interests and motivation of program personnel as closely as possible with program objectives. Under those systems, if BPO personnel exceed minimum targets for bringing about increases in client sales and jobs, they make more money themselves. Such systems work best under arms-length relationships—a subcontract, for example. As a practical matter, United States Government regulations do not permit prime contractors to use contract funds to pay performance bonuses to their own personnel; they do, however, allow for that possibility for subcontractor personnel.

Spreading the approach. As Chapter 8 argues, the sustainability of Business Promotion Offices is not an objective of buyer-led programs. That said, subcontracting the operation of the BPOs to local organizations can be an effective way to spread the buyer-led approach. In Peru, many Economic Service Center operators originally voiced some skepticism about whether the buyer-led approach would work. When they saw that it did, they became believers and adopted it in their own programs.

"When we came to Ayacucho, we looked like Martians talking about things nobody understood, people did not want to understand or understood badly: VALUE CHAINS, MARKET ORIENTATION, ENTREPRENEURSHIP, COMPETITIVENESS...AND WE WEREN'T GIVING THINGS AWAY...AND WE WANTED TO **HELP THE POOR** THAT WAY?

"Well, things are changing now, there are new organizations taking a business approach, old ones are reinventing themselves."

Hernán Paz, former business advisor, Ayacucho Economic Service Center, personal communication with the author, 2007.

The contractual relationship between the central program office and the operator of a Business Promotion Office is very much *sui generis*. On the one hand, the subcontract sets sales and employment targets for the BPO to achieve. On the other, the subcontract stipulates that the BPO follow a certain methodology to bring those results about. Most people with experience in contracting would argue that you cannot have it both ways: either you give the subcontractor the latitude to allocate subcontract resources as it sees fit to achieve the targets agreed upon, or you forget the targets and simply instruct the subcontractor to do your technical bidding. In fact, experience bears ample witness to the wisdom of having it both ways. On the one hand, taking a hands-off approach and turnkeying the achievement of targets to personnel unskilled in the approach can be a recipe for non-performance.[216] On the other hand, introducing performance bonuses does work, and works very well, even with the methodological restrictions imposed. Yes, local organizations bridle initially at the limitations on what they can do, but the proof of the pudding is in the eating: once subcontractors actually put the approach into practice, they generally find it to their liking.

Governments often find it to their liking as well, and occasionally entertain the notion of implementing similar programs on their own. That option can be problematic, too, not because their enthusiasm is unwelcome, but because managing such programs lies beyond the public sector's core competency. Staffing offices, interacting with client businesses, facilitating their sales growth, etc., all lie down the private sector's alley. More than that, active government involvement can actually be counterproductive. When government starts taking too active an interest in private sector activities, potential clients are wont to smell political motivations, at best, and the coming of the taxman, at worst—both of which can turn them off. Better that government see its role as financier, contracting with entities with the skills to manage a buyer-led program, resisting the temptation to micromanage program activities, but holding contractors firmly to task for final results.

The subcontract between the central program office and the operator of the Business Promotion Office dictates not only the technical approach to follow but whom the operator assigns to staff the BPO. More than that, BPO personnel report technically directly to the Business Promotion Offices Manager, who also approves how much they earn and decides what raises they receive. Most operators find those provisions overly intrusive, seeing their role reduced to little more than establishing an office and administering it. But since the caliber of personnel is a key determinant of the success of a buyer-led program, it is only natural for the central program office to retain the power of the salary purse.[217]

Select Personnel

Procurement instructions normally spell out the criteria by which evaluators will rank proposals. Most buyer-led programs assign about half of the points to the quality of personnel, underscoring the critical importance they attach to the capabilities of the candidates whom offerors put forward. Additionally, most buyer-led program procurement documents call for offerors to present up to three candidates for each business advisor position. If the BPO is going to have three staff, that means that an offeror can propose up to nine people—again, giving the program an ample selection of candidates to choose from.

Most curricula vitae do not give reviewers a good sense of how candidates interact with others and whether they are likely to be effective working independently of day-to-day central program office supervision. In addition to asking for multiple candidates, therefore, most buyer-led programs interview all candidates before

Exhibit 3.18 Examples of Questions for Interviewing Candidates for Business Advisor Positions (page 1 of 2)

Poverty Reduction and Alleviation Program in Peru

The thematic range of possible questions is quite broad, ranging from the conceptual framework of the program to the ideal client, production strategies, marketing, sustainability, technical assistance, financial assistance, etc. Following are examples of questions that one can rework to fit other contexts:

1. (Conceptual framework) The conceptual framework of PRA gives priority to areas with economic potential and high indices of poverty. However, the most vulnerable and aid-worthy populations reside in areas with limited economic potential. Question: If you had the option, would you change the geographic focus of the program, yes or no?

2. (Types of clients) PRA does not draw size distinctions in deciding which clients to work with. Given the program's limited resources, there is a real possibility that the program will work directly more with relatively prosperous clients (solvent businesses) than with poor clients (an owner of a microenterprise, for example). Question: Would you leave the definition of "clients" as it currently stands (and stand by its implications) or would you rework it so as to include solely poorer clients?

3. (Production) Question: Keeping all other variables constant, which type of agribusiness should the program provide support to: 1) one that diversifies production to minimize risk; or 2) one that specializes to increase productivity?

4. (Marketing) Question: Would you endorse a policy of subsidies or tariffs to protect small farmers?

5. (Finance) Question: Do you agree with the imposition of interest rate ceilings on small-scale agricultural loans?

6. (Sustainability) Question: If you had to choose one link of a value chain to provide assistance to, which would it be: 1) producer; 2) middle-man/processor; 3) distributor?

7. (Technical assistance) Question: Choose one of the following as a policy for the program: 1) charge clients the full cost of technical assistance provided; 2) charge on a progressive scale based on level of poverty; or 3) do not charge at all.

Exhibit 3.18 Examples of Questions for Interviewing
Candidates for Business Advisor Positions (page 2 of 2)

In a similar manner one could construct questions concerning
"fair prices," participatory meetings vs. business contracts,
general capacity building vs. specific technical assistance, non-
governmental organizations vs. businesses specialized in providing
technical assistance, rural-urban migration vs. settlements and
rural development, anti-land fragmentation legislation vs. promoting
cooperatives, etc.

Source: Adapted from interview questions developed by Juan Robles of USAID/Peru.

making a final decision. The interviews allow reviewers to see how candidates think on their feet and whether they react to business problems in demand-pull or more traditional terms. Under PRA and COTS, program personnel formulated questions to gauge candidates' programmatic instincts, their ability to probe diagnostically, their presentational skills, their practicality, and their penchant for figuring out creative, market-friendly ways of making things happen. The questions helped identify able candidates in those two programs. In Azerbaijan, with its legacy of decades of central economic planning, asking such questions did not work nearly so well. The interview questions developed in Peru appear in Exhibit 3.18.[218]

Experience is mixed on whether business advisors should come from the economic corridors themselves. Experience in Peru suggests that it is hard for one to be "a prophet in one's own country," and, thus, that it is wise to bring in outsiders as agents of change. In Armenia, however, the fact that advisors came from local communities was essential to opening doors and establishing trust.

Set Targets and Develop an Incentive Scheme

A program that makes itself accountable spells out beforehand the results it proposes to bring about and then holds its feet to the fire to deliver on that pledge. A buyer-led program spells out its proposed results in the form of sales and jobs targets. It first sets yearly and cumulative targets for the entire program and then sets them for the Business Promotion Offices in the economic corridors. Most buyer-led programs also give their BPOs monetary incentives to meet and exceed those targets.

Selecting targets is an art, not a science. Objectives that are easy to achieve are not really targets at all, but neither are pipedreams. The ideal targets are ones that are achievable, but that also challenge managers to push the envelope out farther than might otherwise seem possible.

As discussed in Chapter 11, PRA set its targets by extrapolating from the results of successful trade and investment programs in other countries during the previous decade. It also had the benefit of experience under the Microenterprise and Small Producers Support (MSP) program in Peru itself. The combination of experience before PRA, during PRA, and applying the buyer-led approach in other countries gives buyer-led programs today an empirical base from which to define targets with increasing confidence. As a practical matter, the experience of PRA itself is a useful place to start. Among the programs for which data exist, PRA reflects neither the best nor the worst case. For country environments more conducive than PRA—for example, programs with fewer offices to set up and manage—one can adjust expected performance upward. For those less conducive—for example, countries with severe infrastructure or security problems—one can adjust it downward.

Two examples illustrate how one can go about it. Both use the ratios in Exhibit 3.19 as a point of reference. The ratios give the relationship between total incremental client sales and total program costs for each of the first five years of PRA's life and for the five years as a whole. As one would expect, the ratios rise over time.

Exhibit 3.19 PRA: Total Incremental Sales/Total Cost Ratios by Year and for First Five Years

Year 1	Year 2	Year 3	Year 4	Year 5	Total
0.6546	1.8499	2.4498	2.9894	4.9437	3.2238

Source: USAID/Peru Poverty Reduction and Alleviation program.

The first example comes from the design of a buyer-led program in Northern Mozambique. The Millennium Challenge Corporation ultimately decided not to finance the program, but its design offers a good example, pedagogically, of how to go about setting sales and jobs targets.

The design of the Mozambique program called for it to run five years, with much of the first year dedicated to getting things up and running and much of the fifth year dedicated to closing activities down. The total budget anticipated for the program was approximately $22 million. The anticipated time distribution of expenditures appears in the first line of Exhibit 3.20, reflecting the slow build-up of spending at the beginning and the decline at the end.

Like many of the corridors where PRA works, Northern Mozambique is primarily agricultural. Unlike PRA, the program in Mozambique was going to set up only a few Business Promotion Offices. All other things equal, it was natural to expect the Mozambique program to get off to a more rapid start. At least for the early years, therefore, it appeared wise to project slightly higher sales/cost ratios than performance under PRA would have suggested. Given the preoccupation to close out all program activities by the statutory end of the program's life, however, it appeared advisable to apply a lower, not higher sales/cost ratio in the fifth year. The ratios in question appear in the second line of Exhibit 3.20.

The final line of Exhibit 3.20 gives the final sales targets for the program as a whole and for each year. The targets come from multiplying the numbers in the first two lines of each column.

Exhibit 3.20 Example from Mozambique of How to Set Sales Targets

	Year 1	Year 2	Year 3	Year 4	Year 5	Total
Projected Costs	$1,000,000	$4,000,000	$6,000,000	$6,000,000	$5,000,000	$22,000,000
Projected Sales/ Cost Ratios	0.7	2.0	2.6	3.2	4.5	3.0
Projected Sales	$700,000	$8,000,000	$15,600,000	$19,200,000	$22,500,000	$66,000,000

Source: James T. Riordan.

The second example comes from the Azerbaijan Business Assistance and Development (ABAD) program. In contrast to the approach taken in the Mozambique case, the designers of ABAD took more of a gestalt line of attack. Before getting into year-by-year projections, they asked themselves, "We have $7 million in budget for a four-year program. Geographically, we are going to set up operations outside the economic mainstream. Those areas have uneven if not poor infrastructure. Our clientele grew up in a command, not a market economy. Given all that, how much of an increase in client sales can we realistically expect to induce with our support?"

After some deliberation, the design team concluded that it would be unrealistic to expect more than $2.20 in client sales for every dollar of program expenditure. It therefore set an overall sales target of $15,400,000 and then worked backward to trace out targets that would be reasonable year by year. The result appears in Exhibit 3.21.

Exhibit 3.21 Example from Azerbaijan of How to Set Sales Targets

	Year 1	Year 2	Year 3	Year 4	Total
Projected Costs	$1,750,000	$1,750,000	$1,750,000	$1,750,000	$7,000,000
Projected Sales/ Cost Ratios	0.88	1.76	2.64	3.52	2.20
Projected Sales	$1,540,000	3,080,000	$4,620,000	$6,160,000	$15,400,000

Source: James T. Riordan.

In brief, in Mozambique the designers of the program first looked at what it would be reasonable to achieve year by year and then saw what those targets added up to for the program as a whole. In Azerbaijan, the designers started with a target for the entire program and then looked at the reasonableness of the year-by-year sales/costs ratios that that overall target implied.

The slight variation in the approach in the two examples points up, again, the art vs. science nature of target setting. Yes, there are empirical rules of thumb that a program designer can apply, but judgment is necessary, as is adaptation to the peculiarities of the program context at hand.

The reader may have a gnawing sense of unease about the approach to target setting discussed here. In the end, the methodology involves extrapolating to one country experience gained in others. Would it not be better, one might ask, to develop targets from information from the country itself?

To the extent that development programs set targets at all, that, in essence, is the conventional approach. Typically, the designers of a program take a look at various sectors and ask by how much they can reasonably expect their program to improve those sectors' performance. Perhaps the best way to describe the process is with an example. In preparing its proposal to manage USAID's Market and

Trade Development program in Madagascar, Chemonics International looked at a range of products whose expansion it might support during program implementation. After conducting a "bird's-eye" diagnosis, it culled a set of them—rice, essential oils, fresh and processed fruits and vegetables, ecotourism, and gemstones—for priority support, and estimated—no, guesstimated is the more accurate term—by how much program support might contribute to increasing sales of those products. The non-advisability of picking winners aside, the process of setting targets was largely "black-box" in character. The targets represented the best judgment of individuals who were indeed Madagascar experts, but, in the end, rested on no clear relationship between cause and effect—that is, a statement that if the program does x, it can reasonably expect that, causally, y will result. In the final analysis, therefore, the targets were articles of faith, genuine experts' articles of faith, but articles of faith, nevertheless.

Sometimes the conventional approach takes the process one step farther and, for agricultural products, for example, estimates the number of hectares program activities will support. Rarely, though, does it say exactly what the program will do on that hectareage to make sales go up. The thinking is more, "if we work on that much land, something good will happen," rather than, again, a statement of a causal relationship between an action x and a result y.

Despite the conventional approach's drawbacks, a Malagasy is likely to feel much more comfortable with data from his or her own country than with data from Peru, of all places. More than that, a Malagasy is likely to critique setting targets from buyer-led program data from other countries on the very same grounds that the author critiques the conventional approach—namely, as an article of faith. But there is a key difference. If a program is going to adopt buyer-led principles in a given country, it is logical to look at what experience elsewhere tells about the efficacy of that approach. And if a goodly number of countries reveal similar patterns of results (y) from application of the same approach (x), then the faith required to set targets goes down considerably. In short, buyer-led programs rest on a development paradigm, and that development paradigm—with variations, of course—works in various contexts.

The logic of the buyer-led approach is that sales drive jobs, so, operationally, most buyer-led programs attach highest priority to achieving sales targets. But most programs set jobs targets, too.

In program environments with ample scope for promoting and nurturing outsourcing arrangements between connector firms and suppliers, jobs typically bear a relationship to sales that, if not entirely stable, is not terribly volatile either. Under Paraguay Vende, for example, it took an estimated $9.88 of client sales to generate a person-day of labor in Year 1, $7.22 in Year 2, and $8.92 in Year 3. The overall average was $8.25. Under PRA, it took approximately $10.50 of client sales to generate a person-day of labor up through 2003; through 2005, it took approximately $12.20—an increase, obviously, but not a dramatic one.

Prior to commencing work, it is difficult to predict just how much advantage a program can take of outsourcing possibilities. In setting employment targets, therefore, designers of new buyer-led programs generally err on the side of caution. In programs where outsourcing appears to offer promise, they apply, not the best-scenario ratios from Paraguay Vende, but the conservative end of the spectrum from PRA. Specifically, in both the Mozambique program and the Accelerated Sustainable Agriculture Program in Afghanistan, for example, designers divided agreed upon sales targets by 12 to derive employment targets.

Some program environments offer relatively limited scope for outsourcing—for example, programs that focus on products with limited backward linkages or island economies accustomed to importing the bulk of their production inputs. In such cases, one has to lower one's employment expectations, applying divisors considerably higher than 12, at least in the programs' early years.

Again, setting targets, whether for sales or for jobs, is not a mechanistic numbers exercise. It requires judgment. The same goes for the distribution of global targets among a program's economic corridors. Going in, program managers expect some corridors to perform better than others and therefore factor in those expectations.

**Exhibit 3.22 Distributing Targets Among Economic
Corridors: An Example from PRA**

Results Projections 2001

Projected Results Net Sales and Days Worked by Economic Corridor		
Economic Corridor	Net Sales U.S. $	Number of Days Worked
Huancayo	500,000	45,920
Cajamarca	600,000	55,084
Huánuco	750,000	68,850
Tarapoto	600,000	55,250
Cusco	150,000	14,130
Huaylas	450,000	41,000
Puno	350,000	31,866
Jaén	250,000	23,220
Pucallpa	400,000	37,000
Ayachuco	250,000	23,200
Total	4,300,000	395,520

Source: USAID/Peru Poverty Reduction and Alleviation program.

Exhibit 3.22 gives a real-life example, the targets that the man-agement of PRA set for its offices in 2001. In setting them, PRA took into account differences among economic corridors in productive infrastructure, market access, entrepreneurship, and capacity to organize supply. The differences in targets reflect not only differ-ences in those factors, but differences in when the Economic Service Centers began operations. For instance, most people would expect Cusco to perform above average, but the office in Cusco was the last of the centers to come on line and had just commenced operations.

As the program went on, some Economic Service Centers performed above expectations and some below. All in all, the factor that most distinguished the high performers from the rest of the pack was not the natural resources of the economic corridors (although they were not unimportant), but the caliber of center personnel. For those centers that exceeded expectations, management generally upped their targets in subsequent years, raising the bar to incentivize even higher performance. For those that fell short of expectations, management generally did one of two things. Either it recognized it had set the bar too high and lowered targets accordingly or it took corrective action—changing personnel, if necessary—to bring the laggard offices up to par.

Once PRA was up and running, management asked the Economic Service Centers to propose their own sales and jobs targets each year. Interestingly, most centers came in with ambitious numbers, and more often than not, management had to chew the recommended targets down. Given the performance incentives they could expect to receive (see the discussion below), one might have expected the centers to lowball their numbers, but that is not what happened: optimism—and pride vis-à-vis their peers—overrode narrow self-interest!

Most buyer-led programs have instituted some kind of a performance incentive system to align the interests of BPO personnel with program objectives and boost the likelihood of achieving high results. PRA adopted a relatively straightforward approach, tying performance bonuses to increases in client sales. Other programs added different, sometimes complicated wrinkles. The bottom line of that experimentation suggests once more the wisdom of the KISS principle, Keep It Sweet and Simple. The discussion that follows describes how PRA's system worked.

In brief, the key characteristics of the system were:

> "Call it what you will, incentives are what get people to work harder."
>
> Nikita Khrushchev
>
> http://thinkexist.com/quotes/nikita-khruschev.

If an Economic Service Center met its client sales target for the year, each of its business advisors received $1000. To put that number in context, a typical business advisor earned between $1500 and $3000 a month. As a result, even the floor bonus of $1000 was "real money."

If the center exceeded its target by a predetermined percentage, each business advisor received more than $1000. In 2004-05, the scale was as follows:

% over the target	$ per person
>200	3000
175 – 199	3000
150 – 174	2200
125 – 149	2000
>100	1800
75 – 99	1600
50 – 74	1400
25 – 49	1200
0 – 24	1000
<0	0

Source: USAID/Peru Poverty Reduction and Alleviation program.

PRA management budgeted $3000 per center per year for performance bonuses. Some centers met their targets; others did not. When most centers exceeded their targets, management shifted funds from other uses to cover the shortfall—a nice problem to have.

Each advisor in the center received the same amount. At one point, PRA experimented with a bonus system that differentiated among center personnel, and the experiment backfired. Differentiated bonuses prompted selfish behavior: "if you're away on vacation, why should I help your client?" The same bonuses for everybody prompted teamwork and cooperation: "we're all in this together, so I'll be glad to help out."

In Armenia, the expectation of the same bonus for all prompted MEDI North's business advisors to discuss, critique, and suggest ways to improve each other's work. In one instance, colleagues convinced an advisor to add promising high-performers to his portfolio of lackluster clients. The advisor in question had gotten into a bit of a rut and was starting to throw good money after bad. His peers challenged him, successfully, to branch out.

Even though all advisors received the same performance bonus, PRA still could differentiate among them at salary increase time. In short, PRA was able to have it both ways, that is, it had one mechanism to incentivize collective behavior and one to incentivize individual behavior.

To incentivize teamwork and collaboration among centers, all of the program's business advisors received a separate performance bonus if the program as a whole met its global target for the year. In PRA, the amount varied from year to year. In Paraguay Vende, it was 30 percent of the total bonus pool.

The performance bonus scheme also included a provision to incentivize the organization subcontracted to run the center: five percent of the amount received by its business advisors.

PRA made its quantitative formula known to all beforehand. At the moment of truth, that is, at the end of the year, there was no allowance for qualitative ifs, ands, or buts. All advisors knew that walking in.

PRA paid the bonuses agreed to on time. Particularly in the first year, doing so sent an important message to all advisors that management was indeed serious about putting its money where its mouth was.

The PRA performance incentive system provided incentives for business advisors not only to deliver results but to report them, once again aligning their interests with those of top management. In the end, "data talk," and advisors received their bonuses only if their results saw the light of day and the Monitoring and Evaluation Unit deemed those results attributable to their work.

An additional incentive to top-flight performance is pride in the face of peer pressure. Most buyer-led programs make public the results of their different Business Promotion Offices, thereby fomenting informal competition among them. When business advisors know that others will compare the results of their work with those of their peers, they have even more reason to go the extra mile.

Needless to say, the specifics of performance incentive systems will vary from country to country and from program to program. That said, the mutually reinforcing elements of the PRA system are a logical point of departure for designing such systems.

Facilitate an Induction Workshop

Once a buyer-led program has selected the operators of its Business Promotion Offices, it normally conducts an "induction workshop" for the new business advisors. The word, "induction," appears advisedly, in that the point of the workshop is consciously to induct new personnel into the program's mindset and operational procedures. The induction workshop shares with new advisors the thinking underlying the buyer-led approach, spells out the policies and procedures they are to follow to put the approach into practice, and gives them a chance to put what they learn to the test.

As the buyer-led approach has evolved and matured, practitioners have refined the content and format of induction workshops. Experience suggests that the ideal workshop last about four days, with two days dedicated to classroom instruction and interaction, and two spent in interviews with potential clients. The classroom portion relies heavily on case studies and encourages lateral discussion and presentation. The two days of classroom interaction do not necessarily have to be back to back. The interview portion provides an opportunity for advisors not only to make contact with live candidate clients, but to apply what they learn in the classroom and receive immediate feedback on how they go about it. Each day ends with a wrap-up summary of concepts presented and principal points discussed.

The content of the classroom portion of the induction workshop consists of an introduction to the basics of the buyer-led approach followed by four interconnected operational modules. The four modules appear in logical and sequential order in Exhibit 3.23. They cover what business advisors do day to day.

Exhibit 3.23 Induction Workshop: Operational Modules

What Business Promotion Offices Do Day to Day: An Overview

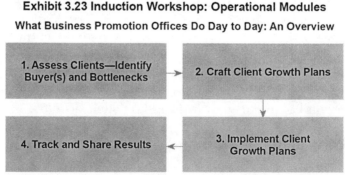

Source: Joseph Jordan and James T. Riordan.

Exhibit 3.24 presents one way to divide up the introduction and the four operational modules into morning and afternoon sessions over the two classroom days. The discussion that follows outlines each session in turn.

Exhibit 3.24 Induction Workshop: Classroom Sessions

	Morning	Afternoon
Day 1	Introduction: Basics of the Buyer-Led Approach	Operational Modules 1 and 2: Assessing Clients and Crafting Client Growth Plans
Day 2	Operational Module 3: Processing Client Growth Plans and Drafting and Implementing Scopes of Work	Operational Module 4: Making Monitoring and Evaluation Real and Communicating Results

Source: Joseph Jordan and James T. Riordan.

Day 1, Morning Session, Introduction. This first session of the workshop conveys didactically the paradigmatic underpinnings of the buyer-led approach and key operational principles for business advisors to internalize and follow. The introduction presents the big picture and sets the framework and tone for the rest of the workshop. Content-wise, the presentation of the approach normally draws heavily from the material presented in Part II, using examples to convey key concepts and operational implications. As one might expect, the principal themes include:

The meaning of "demand-driven"
The concept of the market chain
Solving problems transaction by transaction
Accountability for results

Among the key operational implications are the following, which come verbatim from the opening session at an induction workshop in St. Lucia:

Build on market incentives; do not build production capacity for its own sake
Operationally, demand means a buyer with a first name and a last name

Large and small enterprises are allies, not rivals
City and countryside are allies, not rivals

Build trust—it is the most important service
Your point of entry is individual connector firm transactions, not sectors or products
Tailor solutions to the *problema*; do not jump to the *problemática*
Pre-picking sectors can come at high cost
When possible, promote contracting to generate jobs
Focus on the sustainability of market chains, not yourself
Communicate success stories

Make your measure of success sales and jobs
Set targets
Build in incentives to meet them
Hold yourself accountable
Do continuous, serious monitoring and evaluation
Think of cost-effectiveness and return on investment
Manage with discipline, applying the 5:1 rule

Day 1, Afternoon Session, Operational Modules 1 and 2. After the theory of the morning, the afternoon session dives directly into case study exercises. The exercises in question include or are similar to the Sunset Cove/Clearview Farms example given above and the case study examples in Chapter 17. Workshop participants break up into small groups. Each group first defines who its client shall be and how that client relates to other actors in the market chain. It then develops a strategy to address the market chain's key problems, defining the actions the buyer-led program and the client each will take, the sales expected as a result of those actions over the life of the program, the cost to the program of the proposed actions, and an assessment of how projected sales relate to the cost to the program—that is, whether the transaction satisfies the 5:1 rule. Using the format of Exhibits 3.5 and 3.7, the groups report their findings in plenary session, critiquing and learning from each other.

Case study exercises have proven especially useful in countries with a history of heavy state intervention—countries of the ex-Soviet Union, for example. Business advisors' appreciation of market forces may come more from books than from personal experience, which makes it imperative that workshop facilitators minimize theory and deal with basics in direct, applied fashion.

In some programs, it has proven useful to use local cases—that is, from the countries in question—so that participants can see better the relevance of the exercises to their work. In other programs, it has proven useful to use examples from other countries to broaden the horizons of participants.

Later in the afternoon, the workshop participants take the process one step farther. Using the same case study examples, they draft Client Growth Plans for the transactions in question. The content of the Client Growth Plans, and instructions for preparing them, appear in Chapter 15.

Day 2, Morning Session, Operational Module 3. It is one thing to craft a Client Growth Plan; it is another to process it so that it can take effect. The morning session of the second classroom day therefore goes through the procedures required to approve and make Client Growth Plans operational. As Chapter 15 discusses, different buyer-led programs delegate different degrees of authority to their BPOs. Before they go into force, however, all Client Growth Plans, regardless of program, must meet a number of exacting criteria, many of which fall under the purview of monitoring and evaluation. This session of the induction workshop dedicates considerable time to those criteria. The Monitoring and Evaluation Unit of the Caribbean Open Trade Support program developed a checklist formalizing them, which the Poverty Reduction by Increasing the Competitiveness of Enterprises (PRICE) program in Bangladesh took and refined some more. A generic version of the checklist appears in Exhibit 3.25.

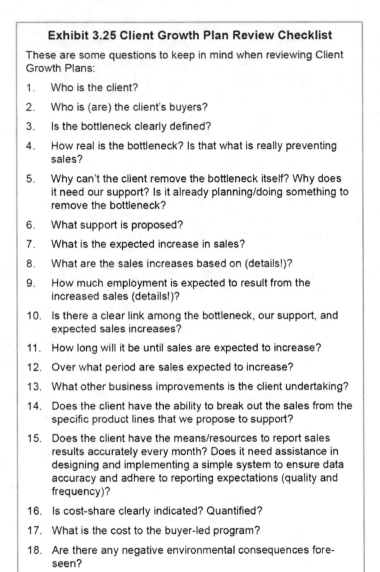

Exhibit 3.25 Client Growth Plan Review Checklist

These are some questions to keep in mind when reviewing Client Growth Plans:

1. Who is the client?

2. Who is (are) the client's buyers?

3. Is the bottleneck clearly defined?

4. How real is the bottleneck? Is that what is really preventing sales?

5. Why can't the client remove the bottleneck itself? Why does it need our support? Is it already planning/doing something to remove the bottleneck?

6. What support is proposed?

7. What is the expected increase in sales?

8. What are the sales increases based on (details!)?

9. How much employment is expected to result from the increased sales (details!)?

10. Is there a clear link among the bottleneck, our support, and expected sales increases?

11. How long will it be until sales are expected to increase?

12. Over what period are sales expected to increase?

13. What other business improvements is the client undertaking?

14. Does the client have the ability to break out the sales from the specific product lines that we propose to support?

15. Does the client have the means/resources to report sales results accurately every month? Does it need assistance in designing and implementing a simple system to ensure data accuracy and adhere to reporting expectations (quality and frequency)?

16. Is cost-share clearly indicated? Quantified?

17. What is the cost to the buyer-led program?

18. Are there any negative environmental consequences foreseen?

Source: Adapted from USAID/Caribbean Open Trade Support program.

Many Client Growth Plans call for buyer-led programs to procure consulting assistance to help solve key client problems, which means that business advisors must know how to prepare clear scopes of work to facilitate that process. Accordingly, this

---

Exhibit 3.26 Draft Scope of Work

This Document Is a Template to Share with a Client When Developing a Scope of Work

[Insert nature of work]
[Insert name of client]

1.	Expert	[Insert name of expert if appropriate]
2.	Position	[Insert position name]
3.	Period of Performance	[Insert time frame of assignment]
4.	Level of Effort	[Insert level of effort]
5.	Client Growth Plan Reference	[Insert Client Growth Plan reference]
6.	Business Advisor	[Insert name of business advisor]
7.	Background	[Insert a brief background of the client and a description of proposed support—should be between 2-3 paragraphs]
8.	Objectives	[Describe the objective of the assignment—should be between 2-3 paragraphs]
9.	Tasks	[Insert as many bullets as needed to describe necessary tasks of the assignment]
10.	Deliverables	[Insert as many as needed to describe deliverables of the assignment]
11.	Reporting	The consultant will report to [name of client] and [name of business advisor], or their designee(s).
12.	Nature of Contract	[Insert any other details relevant to SOW]

Source: USAID/Afghanistan Accelerated Sustainable Agriculture Program.

classroom session normally includes a third case study exercise. Building on the Client Growth Plans prepared the day before, workshop participants spell out the specifics of the assistance called for. In doing so, they normally use a template like Exhibit 3.26.

Day 2, Afternoon Session, Operational Module 4. The buyer-led approach to monitoring and evaluation differs substantially from other, more commonly known approaches. For that reason, the afternoon session of the second classroom day describes how monitoring and evaluation is not a stand-alone activity, but one that folds directly into operations, buttressing the program's commitment to delivering results and holding itself accountable for same. It also spells out business advisors' reporting requirements. With a performance incentive system in place, advisors have a compelling reason to comply with those requirements. A detailed description of the buyer-led approach to monitoring and evaluation appears in Chapter 16.

The second afternoon session also emphasizes how communication of success stories is integral to the buyer-led approach, which, again, has definite implications for what business advisors do.

During the interview portion of the induction workshop, the new business advisors meet with a variety of local businesses to explore the possibility of their becoming clients of the program. In the interviews, the new advisors jump directly from theory to action, applying in real life what they have just learned in the classroom. Workshop facilitators accompany the advisors in the interviews and give them feedback right after, thereby increasing the likelihood that they "get" the approach. Experience suggests it is wise to schedule no more than four interviews a day, two in the morning and two in the afternoon. Some induction workshops give the participants templates to guide the interviews. The one developed by the Caribbean Open Trade Support program appears in Exhibit 3.27. Its intent is to serve as a guide, not as a questionnaire to fill out in the presence of the respondent.

Good interviewing is essential to diagnose potential clients' key problems correctly. For that reason alone, the interview portion of an induction workshop is very, very important. In many countries, it is common for businesspeople to say their biggest problem is lack of financing. In-depth questioning often reveals that lack of financing is a symptom, not the root cause. Business advisors must recognize that possibility and keep probing to get at interviewees' most binding constraints.[219]

An example from Armenia illustrates the point. On making contact with a local furniture company, a MEDI business advisor learned it was having trouble fulfilling orders. A business development services program sponsored by another

"How can we be effective if we do not know where the greatest need lies?"

Anne Perry, *Traitors Gate* (New York: Ballantine Books, 1995), p. 109.

donor had met with the company some time before and, taking the company at its word, had diagnosed the problem as lack of financing. It therefore helped the company prepare a business plan to secure a bank loan. In fact, the root problem was not lack of money, but poor management. The company had a variety of customers with a variety of requirements, and it did not know how to specialize and schedule production.

Lest the obvious get lost in cataloguing the induction workshop's content, a less tangible but no less important objective of bringing participants together in workshop format is the development of an *esprit de corps* among all business advisors, an identification of all involved with the objectives of the entire program, and a willingness to see themselves not as separate, isolated agents, but parts of a coherent, unified whole. Once the workshop ends, it is essential that all involved shed their individual organizational affiliations, seeing themselves as representatives not of organization x but of buyer-led program y.

As one might expect, each buyer-led program has its peculiarities, and induction workshops must take those peculiarities into account. For that reason, the description of the various sessions above is not a straightjacket, but simply a place to start in designing a workshop for a new program. The agendas of two actual induction workshops appear in Chapter 18.

Exhibit 3.27 Template for Interviews with Potential COTS Clients (page 1 of 4)

Contact information for the company

Name of the Company: _____

Address: _____
Web site: _____

Name of interviewee: _____
Interviewee's position: _____

Phone: _____
Fax: _____
Email: _____

General information on the company

In what year did the company begin operations? _____

What is the company's legal status? _____

Is the company engaged in...

Primary production? _____
Processing? _____
Trading (reselling)? _____
Tourism? _____
ICT? _____
Other services? _____

What do you sell?

_____
_____
_____

The company's market

Roughly, what percentage of your customers are:

Local? _____
Regional? _____
International? _____

Exhibit 3.27 Template for Interviews with Potential COTS Clients (page 2 of 4)

If you have customers locally, who are your top buyers?

_____
_____
_____

If you have customers regionally, who are your top buyers?

_____
_____
_____

If you have customers internationally, who are your top buyers?

_____
_____
_____

Does your company sell...
Directly? _____
Through agents(s)? _____
Why do buyers purchase what you offer? _____
What distinguishes what you offer from what your competitors offer?

_____

Are you interested in expanding your sales?_____

If yes, whom would you sell to?

_____
_____
_____

How would you go about reaching these customers?

_____
_____
_____

Have you taken any steps already? _____
If yes, what?

_____
_____
_____

Exhibit 3.27 Template for Interviews with Potential COTS Clients (page 3 of 4)

Do you join forces with other companies? _____

If yes, with whom and how? _____
_____
_____

Information on production and backward linkages

In non-dollar terms, how much did you sell the last 12 months?
_____

How much of that did the company produce itself?
_____

If not everything, where did you get the rest?
_____
_____
_____

From whom did you buy your primary inputs?
_____
_____
_____

Does your business vary seasonally? _____

If yes, what are your best month(s)? _____

Please describe the company's infrastructure, machinery, equipment, and land. _____
_____
_____

At approximately what percentage of capacity do you use these fixed assets? _____

Are grades, standards, or certifications important in your business?
_____

If yes, which ones apply, and what have you done? _____
_____
_____

If you had more buyers, could you deliver? _____

If not, why not? _____

Exhibit 3.27 Template for Interviews with Potential COTS Clients (page 4 of 4)

Baseline data

What were your sales the last 12 months? $ _____

During the last 12 months, how many people did you employ on average ...

Full-time?_____ How many were family? _____

Part-time? _____ How many were family? _____

Top problems

If the government could change one thing, what change would most help you increase sales? _____

What are the top three business problems that prevent you from growing, or business opportunities that will allow you to grow?

A. _____
B. _____
C. _____

Potential solutions to top business problems

What actions are the most cost-effective solutions to those problems, or responses to those opportunities?

A. _____
B. _____
C. _____

If these actions were successful, by how much would sales grow ...

This year? $ _____
Next year? $ _____
The year after that? $ _____

Source: USAID/Caribbean Open Trade Support program.

15

Selecting and Working with Clients

This chapter discusses the following:

How to select clients to work with
How to structure relationships with clients
What makes a good business advisor?
Attacking systemic problems

Select Clients to Work with

In most buyer-led programs, the Business Promotion Offices' first task after the induction workshop is to prepare Annual Operating Plans. The plans in question value quality over quantity and typically are executive in style. The primary objective of the plans is not to lock the advisors into preprogrammed activities for the rest of the year. Since new business opportunities can come up at any time—and since unforeseen events can wipe out what one considers a "sure thing," the specifics of Annual Operating Plans can be out of date almost as soon as their ink is dry. No, the Annual Operating Plan has two purposes: first, to test whether the business advisors really internalize the buyer-led approach; and, second, to provide an empirical basis for the negotiation of corridor-specific targets for the upcoming year. Far from putting a damper on creative opportunism, the point of the Annual Operating Plan exercise is simply to keep advisors' "eyes on the prize" so that they can deliver results. The Annual Operating Plans may have the name of plans, but they are more the tools of Easterly's Searchers, not Planners.

Different buyer-led programs have experimented with different templates for Annual Operating Plans (see Chapter 19 for an example), but the core task is to take a first crack at selecting potential clients, using information along the lines of that outlined in Exhibit 3.27. Normally, Business Promotion Offices have about 30 days to prepare their plans. During that period, they make contact with as many potential clients—again, normally connector firms— as possible, diagnose their key bottlenecks as best they can, craft possible solutions, and take a first stab at estimating an incremental sales-cost ratio in each case. The Annual Operating Plan consolidates the information that results from that work and summarizes it in a table like Exhibit 3.28.

Exhibit 3.28 Business Promotion Offices' Annual Operating Plans: Core Information

Clients in order of priority	Problem(s)	Solution(s)	Expected new sales, life of program	Expected cost to program	Sales/cost	Expected new jobs, life of program	Comments
1.							
2.							
....							
n.							

Source: James T. Riordan.

Upon receipt of a BPO's Annual Operating Plan, personnel from the program's management office—at a minimum, the BPO manager, the Monitoring and Evaluation Manager, and their staffs— visit the BPO and, together with the business advisors, scrutinize the plan in detail. They also meet with the potential clients the BPO considers most promising. In internal meetings they ask the business advisors probing questions about each case proposed for support. Given the tendency for advisors to revert to supply-push thinking, they grill the advisors especially hard on whether there are real live buyers for the transactions in question. They also prod to ascertain, first, that the team has diagnosed clients' problems correctly and, second, that the proposed solutions are not just nice things to do but zoom in on the problems identified.

"A typical marketing paradox is that buyers, such as supermarkets and processors, complain about inadequate supply while farmers complain about lack of markets. Clearly the buyers have not been too active in seeking out new suppliers, while farmers have lacked the skills and resources to identify new markets and the ability to take advantage of identified markets through value addition activities such as grading, cleaning, sorting, packaging, bulking, and primary processing. Organizations working to link farmers to markets need to contact agrifood companies, traders, retailers and exporters and identify their product shortages. This should really be the first step of any programme to develop linkages."

Andrew W. Shepherd, "Approaches to linking producers to markets: A review of experiences to date," Agricultural Management, Marketing and Finance Occasional Paper, Food and Agriculture Organization of the United Nations, Rome, Italy, 2007, pp. 11-12.

Most induction workshops make "demand-driven" a cracked record, if not a mantra, emphasizing the imperative to start at the market, not with the producer, and that operationally, the "market" means buyers with first names and last names. It may strike the reader as strange, then, that a month later, top management still feels compelled to harp on the same message. Although one might prefer it otherwise, experience bears strong witness to supply-push thinking dying hard. In program after program, first-year Annual Operating Plans keep surfacing with proposals to expand production capacity before tying down demand. The reasoning in the first four examples in Exhibit 3.29 is typical, which explains why the demand-driven message requires constant reinforcement.

Exhibit 3.29 Examples of Common Arguments for Program Support

Argument for Program Support	Should the Program Move Ahead?
"Russians like our tomatoes. The demand is there. Please help us expand tomato production."	No
"Statistics suggest demand for tomatoes is growing in Russia. Please help us expand tomato production."	No
"I saw in a donor report that demand for tomatoes is up in Russia. Please help us expand tomato production."	No
"We could increase sales if we had better yield. Please bring us an expert to help us increase yield."	No
"A tomato processor says he will buy my tomatoes if we can improve the quality. Can you bring us an expert to help us improve quality?"	Yes!

Source: James T. Riordan.

The reader may object that the test of identifying a buyer with a first name and a last name is too stringent. Take the case of Frito Lay, for example. Frito Lay did not know the name of everybody who would buy its potato chips, yet PRA worked with them to expand potato production. In fact, there is a big difference between the Frito Lay transaction and the first four examples above. The key to the Frito Lay transaction was not the relationship between Frito Lay and potato chip consumers, but that between Frito Lay and its suppliers. In that relationship, Frito Lay was the buyer, not the seller. More than that, it had committed itself to source from the potato growers in Huánuco, and was sufficiently well capitalized to absorb the loss if the deal fell apart. In the first four examples above, the proposed client is the seller, not the buyer. In the absence of information to the contrary, it is irresponsible to assume that the client can absorb the loss if the tomatoes do not sell. The buyer-led approach certainly does not rule out supporting clients in making incursions into new markets, but not when those markets are defined nebulously and the clients in question are so close to the edge financially that they cannot absorb the risk.

For clients close to the edge to make more money, knowing exactly what a specific buyer wants can have significant consequences, as the following examples illustrate.

> Members of the [Bolivian producers'] associations learned a lot from buyers about the products, product quality, and amounts that the buyers are willing to buy and the prices they are willing to pay. The Chipamaya Cheese Producers had been making cheeses of 300 to 500 grams and selling them in local markets. They met with Charito, an agro-marketer, and Charito agreed to buy 50 cheeses a week at an excellent price, but only if they were 1-kilogram cheeses, which is the most popular size with consumers. The Compuerta Fish Producers raise fresh trout in cages in Lake Titicaca. They met with Ricafruit, an agro-processor, which wanted to buy smoked trout. Ricafruit offered to train the Compuerta producers to smoke their trout, and they signed a two-year contract at a very good price for all the trout that the Compuerta producers could smoke.[220]

At the end of the day, the principal determinant of whether a buyer-led program supports a given client is the associated transaction's incremental sales-cost ratio. All other things equal, the program will give highest priority to those transactions with the highest ratios, and not support any with ratios below a predetermined cutoff value like 5:1.

The straightforwardness of the 5:1 rule contrasts dramatically with conventional practice. First of all, most programs select sectors to give priority to before they select individual clients to work with or specific transactions to support (if they do). Second, most programs take a multiplicity of criteria into consideration, often grouping them in high, medium, and low categories, and, in some instances, forming indices from them. The selection criteria below come from a broad range of programs in Azerbaijan, Bangladesh, Central America, East Timor, Guyana, Madagascar, Moldova, Mozambique, and Serbia. Collectively, they give the reader a view of the waterfront of criteria in common use.

Programs typically give priority to sectors, products, or businesses with at least some of the following characteristics:

Established presence—and, ideally, leadership position—in local or international markets
Existence of an ample market—that is, a large number of buyers—to sell to
Markets with growth potential
Demonstrated potential to increase exports
Existence of niche markets for clients to differentiate their goods and services from others'
Goods and services with unique properties
Potential for sales and income growth
Profitability and sustainability
Return on client investment
Likelihood of results in the relatively near term
Potential to generate jobs, either directly or through backward linkages
Potential to generate jobs for women
Potential for women-owned enterprises to benefit
Potential to generate jobs for young people

Potential to generate jobs for currently marginalized ethnic groups

Potential to develop or expand backward linkages, especially with small and micro-enterprises or broad-based producer associations

Existence of value-added opportunities

Established processing and production base

Number of processors and suppliers of raw materials

Relative ease of transferring production, post-harvest, and processing technology

Ability of businesses to manage more sophisticated operations

Relative ease of labor acquiring required skills

Ability to deliver quality product at competitive prices

Ability to meet tight production deadlines

Commitment by management to make improvements to tap broader markets

Commitment by management to introduce new technology to become more productive and competitive

Commitment by management to shoulder a substantial portion of the cost of improvements

Commitment by suppliers to make improvements

Opportunities to incorporate international product quality standards and labor practices

Contribution to environmental protection and sustainable management of natural resources

Suitability of the natural resource base

Existence of production, transport, processing, and marketing infrastructure

Existence of a legal and regulatory environment favorable to business

Inclusion of geographical areas with high levels of poverty, yet with potential for business growth

Government interest in a sector

Sectors, products, or businesses not assisted actively by government or donor programs

Existence of programs that can provide synergy and carry out complementary activities

Likely cost-effectiveness of program support

Likelihood of program assistance having a spread effect

Ease of implementation of program activities
Feasibility of delivering effective technical assistance
Data availability and openness of clients to sharing information
Opportunities to contribute to improved enterprise governance
practices and reduced corruption

No one program uses all these criteria, of course, but many do take as many as a dozen of them into formal consideration. As discussed above, setting multiple objectives is not recommended management practice. The same goes for criteria for selecting clients. In practice, development practitioners can tie themselves up in knots looking for the perfect sector, product, or business to work with.[221] No one sector, product, or business is likely to satisfy every criterion postulated, which suggests the advisability of taking a portfolio approach, all under the aegis of the 5:1 rule. Just as stock brokers have holdings with short- and long-term maturities, with low and high risk, etc., so too does the skilled practitioner of the buyer-led approach diversify his or her portfolio of clients. Most development program funding agencies want to see results as soon as possible. It therefore makes sense to secure early wins while, at the same time, nurturing opportunities with potentially dramatic results in the medium term. In a similar vein, it is wise to work with businesses that traditionally hire women while, at the same time, looking at opportunities where women do not work now but conceivably could in the future. In short, the overall guiding criterion is cost-effectiveness, but under that umbrella lies ample scope for attending to other concerns of interest.

A frequent retort to applying the 5:1 rule is that it "creams" clients, that is, it takes the best and leaves the rest to fend for themselves. The use of the pejorative term, "creaming," creates the impression that the 5:1 rule is discriminatory, which in fact, it is not. First, setting aside illegitimate businesses, the rule excludes absolutely no business *a priori*. It simply looks for those opportunities that will contribute the most to expansion of sales and, all other things equal, jobs—precisely what the program purports to achieve. Again, working with one firm that satisfies the 5:1 rules applies absolutely no exclusivity. Any business that meets that criterion is eligible. Second, buyer-led programs have to be sensitive to the charge of facilitating the creation of monopolies. They therefore go out of their way to counteract that tendency. How? By consciously bringing as many businesses as possible under the tent—that is, if a program supports a business in a given sector, by figuring out ways for other businesses in that sector to meet the 5:1 rule, too. The more really is merrier. Third, very often the real constraint to a program expanding its client base is not that any one business is so much more efficient than its peers, but a matter of risk aversion. Many entrepreneurs are hesitant to invest in improvements in their businesses until they see that a similar business has done so successfully. In the extreme case, the conventional logic of development practitioners actually gets flipped on its head: it is not a question of how many businesses a program chooses to work with, but how many businesses choose to work with the program. Development practitioners like to believe everybody likes to work with them; that is not necessarily the case, especially when the programs in question—buyer-led programs, for example—skimp on subsidies.

James Butcher, who was the Director of the MEDI program in Armenia, put the process of selecting clients in overall perspective as follows:

> From our point of view no product is "good" or "bad," which means that we don't encourage advisors to target one sector or another. We even shy away from open-ended debates about which sectors have the most potential. Instead, we focus on the complexities of each individual opportunity linked with an actual buyer. After the buyer(s) is (are) identified, we might have a discussion about our client's competitive position and the sector, but this discussion is almost always initiated and encouraged only after a buying opportunity is identified. This is just one way of encouraging our advisors and ourselves to "keep our eye on the ball," which in the end is finding buyers and helping suppliers in our corridor satisfy their demand.[222]

Structure Relationships with Clients

At the conclusion of the review of its Annual Operating Plan, a Business Promotion Office normally receives the green light to craft Client Growth Plans with and for a number of clients. Client Growth Plans go by different names in different programs—Business Plans and Memoranda of Understanding, for example. Whatever one calls them, in all programs they constitute the administrative trigger for buyer-led programs to provide clients' market chains concrete support.

Client Growth Plans have gone through a variety of iterations as the buyer-led approach has spread from PRA to a gamut of other programs around the world. Exhibit 3.30 presents a recent version, a template for Client Growth Plans used by the Competitive Enterprise Development program in Albania. Although not necessarily a "model" for future programs, it does take into account lessons learned in programs to date. For its part, Exhibit 3.31 is an actual Client Growth Plan, the Business Plan for PRA's client, Curtipiel SAC. Although PRA Business Plans generally are wordier than Client Growth Plans elsewhere, the example gives the reader a good sense of the thinking that goes into a Client Growth Plan and the various issues that come up for consideration before a buyer-led program and its client sign on the dotted line.

The Client Growth Plan is a "contract" between a buyer-led program and a client. It formalizes the relationship between the two parties. Not only does it codify in writing the diagnosis they have made of the client's problems, the solutions they believe will solve those problems, and the results that are likely to follow. It also spells out exactly what the two parties will do going forward—that is, it commits both the program and the client to specific actions. The Client Growth Plan may not be enforceable in a court of law, but it is more than a casual handshake. Both parties give their word to do their parts, and sign the plan to confirm their commitment.

The Client Growth Plan is also a tool for monitoring performance and for confirming the attribution of results to program actions. In verifying sales and jobs results, Monitoring and Evaluation Units look not only at the validity

> "[I]f you mean to achieve something, you need to have very precise actions in mind."
>
> Anne Perry, *The Whitechapel Conspiracy* (New York: Ballantine Books, 2001), p. 299.

of the numbers but whether there is a *prima facie* case that observed effects resulted from what the two parties did. For that reason, it is essential that the plan make that *prima facie* case right at the beginning, that is, that it spell out the logical connection between what the parties to the plan agree to do and what they expect will come out the other end. To the degree possible, it is essential to rule out speculation after the fact that the results happened by accident, coincidence, or serendipity.

All Client Growth Plans contain statements of problems, solutions, expected results, and the actions the two parties will take. Most also spell out the commitments of the two parties concerning data — that the client will provide them, and that the program will treat client-specific data confidentially. Some plans include the baseline data on sales and jobs explicitly; others incorporate them by reference from elsewhere. As noted above, Paraguay Vende also annexes an environmental checklist to take environmental and labor issues specifically into account. The checklist appears in Chapter 19.

At the beginning of a buyer-led program, the Business Promotion Offices Manager keeps a tight rein on the preparation of Client Growth Plans, insisting that no plans go forward until the Monitoring and Evaluation Unit has reviewed them carefully and he or she has looked at them personally. Under the Micro Enterprise Development Initiative in Armenia, for example, management rejected 13 of the first 18 Client Growth Plans submitted. As Business Promotion Offices gain more experience, the Business Promotion Offices Manager generally loosens up the reins. That is especially true in large programs — PRA, for example — where insisting that the Manager review every single Client Growth Plan would make him or her a bottleneck to getting things done. In large programs, some degree of delegation is essential. In programs of smaller scale, the danger of the Business Promotion Offices Manager becoming a bottleneck is not so severe. Even after more than four years of operation, the overall Program Director of Paraguay Vende signed every Client Growth Plan personally.

Practice is split on who should be the signatory. Some argue that it behooves the Business Promotion Office Chief to sign, since, operationally, the accountability for transforming a Client Growth

Plan into results rests with the Business Promotion Office, not with the program as a whole. Others argue that the Program Director should sign all Client Growth Plans, not only for quality control, but to accentuate to all that the buyer-led program really is a program, not simply a collection of balkanized entities doing their own thing.

Exhibit 3.30 Client Growth Plan Template, Albania
(page 1 of 6)

Plani i ZHKN për Rritjen e Klientëve	CED Client Growth Plan
Projekti i USAID-it për Zhvillimin Konkurues të Ndërmarjeve ka si qëllim të avancojë rritjen e qëndrueshme ekonomike gjerësisht në Shqipëri. Ky projekt do të ndihmojë ndërmarrjet jo-bujqësore për t'u bërë më konkuruese dhe të rrisin shitjet e tyre. Gjithashtu, ky projekt do të ndihmojë në krijimin e punësimit fitimprurës. Projekti do t'i arrijë këto objektiva përmes zgjerimit të tregtisë dhe investimeve, rritjes së produktivitetit të ndërmarrjeve dhe krijimit të një fuqie të përmirësuar punëtore.

Projekti ZHKN u ofron kompanive kliente shërbime të zhvillimit të biznesit, për t'i ndihmuar ato të rrisin shitjet dhe nivelin e punësimit. Me anë të një mbështetjeje të përshtatur, të përqendruar dhe efikase në aspektin e kostos, projekti ZHKN i ndihmon kompanitë të luftojnë problemet që pengojnë rritjen e tyre. ZHKN dhe [Emri i Firmës Kliente] këtej e tutje i referuar si Klienti, bien dakord me termat dhe kushtet e vendosura në vijim. | USAID's Competitive Enterprise Development (CED) Project seeks to advance sustained, broad-based economic growth in Albania. It will help non-agricultural enterprises become more competitive and increase their sales. It will also help create gainful employment. The project will achieve those objectives by expanding trade and investment, increasing enterprise productivity, and improving workforce development.

CED provides business development services to client firms to help them increase their sales and expand employment. With tailored, focused, cost-effective support, CED helps firms attack the problems that prevent them from growing. CED and [Name of Client], hereinafter referred to as the Client, agree to the terms and conditions set out hereunder. |

Exhibit 3.30 Client Growth Plan Template, Albania
(page 2 of 6)

Historik	Background
Informacion i Përgjithshëm:	**General information:**
[Përshkrim i saktë i: sektori ku punon Klienti; lloji i biznesit ku angazhohet Klienti; mallrat që prodhon ose shërbimet që ofron; viti kur Klienti ka filluar aktivitetin; statusi ligjor; tregjet kryesore ku Klienti kryen shitjet; kanalet e shpërndarjes që përdor; burimet kryesore furnizuese]	[Concise description of: sector in which Client works; type of business Client engages in; goods it produces or services it provides; year Client began operations; legal status; primary markets Client sells to; distribution channels it uses; primary suppliers it sources from]

**Exhibit 3.30 Client Growth Plan Template, Albania
(page 3 of 6)**

Të dhëna bazë		Baseline Data	
Gjatë 12 muajve të mëparshëm/ During the preceding 12 months			
Shitje (në LEK)/ Sales in LEK	[...]		
Punësimi (në ditë pune)/ Employment (in workdays)	[...] (meshkuj)/ (men)	[...] (femra)/ (women)	[...] (total)
Pengesat kryesore për rritjen dhe zgjidhjet e propozuara: [Pengesat kryesore (jo më shumë se tre) në rritjen e shitjeve; zgjidhjet e propozuara për tejkalimin e pengesave dhe për rritjen e shitjeve]		Principal constraints to growth and proposed solutions: [Principal constraint(s) (no more than three) to increasing sales; proposed solution to remove constraint(s) and increase sales]	
Pengesat/Constraint		**Zgjidhja e Propozuar/Proposed Solution**	
1. [...]		[...]	
2. [...]		[...]	
3. [...]		[...]	
Qëllimi i Planit të Rritjes së Klientit Pengesa(-t) kryesore për rritjen e shitjeve, që do të luftohet(-n) nga ky Plan për Rritjen e Klientit është (janë): [.............]		**Scope of Client Growth Plan** The principal constraint(s) to increasing sales that this Client Growth Plan attacks is (are): [.............]	
Angazhimi i ZHKN Nën këtë Plan për Rritjen e Klientit, Projekti ZHKN angazhohet të ndihmojë Klientin të tejkalojë pengesat përmes: • [Veprimit 1] • [Veprimit 2, nqs është e nevojshme] • [Veprimit 3, nqs është e nevojshme]		**CED Commitment** Under this Client Growth Plan CED commits itself to help the Client remove the constraint(s) by: • [Action 1] • [Action 2, if necessary] • [Action 3, if necessary]	

**Exhibit 3.30 Client Growth Plan Template, Albania
(page 4 of 6)**

Angazhimi i Klientit	Client Commitment
Nën këtë Plan për Rritjen e Klientit, vetë Klienti angazhohet për: • [Veprimin 1] • [Veprimin 2, nqs është e nevojshme] • [Veprimin 3, nqs është e nevojshme] • Të konstatojë dhe të vërë çdo muaj në dispozicion të ZHKN-së rritjen e shitjeve, prodhimin, punësimin, dhe investimet që janë realizuar si pasojë e këtij Plani për Rritjen e Klientit. • Të ndjekë rekomandimet e ndihmës eksperte teknike që i jepet Klientit në kuadrin e këtij Plani për Rritjen e Klientit. • Të pajtohet me të gjitha kërkesat rregullatore e ligjore, duke përfshirë këtu standardet për mjedisin, shëndetin, punën dhe sigurinë, siç urdhërohen nga autoritetet kombëtare. • Të mos fajësojë ZHKN-në për ndonjë humbje ose dëmtim që Klienti mund të pësojë nga zbatimi i rekomandimeve të ofruara përmes këtij Plani për Rritjen e Klientit.	Under this Client Growth Plan, the Client commits itself to: • [Action 1] • [Action 2, if necessary] • [Action 3, if necessary] • Ascertain and make available to CED each month the increases in sales, production, employment, and investment that have taken place as a result of this Client Growth Plan. • Heed the recommendations of expert technical assistance provided to the Client under this Client Growth Plan. • Comply with all legal and regulatory requirements, including environment, health, labor, and safety standards mandated by national authorities. • Hold CED harmless against any losses or other damages that the Client may incur by implementing recommendations arising from this Client Growth Plan.

Exhibit 3.30 Client Growth Plan Template, Albania
(page 5 of 6)

Rezultatet e Pritshme	Expected Results
Veprimet e ndërmarra në kuadër të këtij Plani për Rritjen e Klientit priten të rezultojnë në: • Rritjen e shitjeve të [...] • Rritjen e punësimit të [...] (meshkuj) [...] (femra) [...] (total)	The actions taken under this Client Growth Plan are expected to result in: • Increased sales of [...] • Increased employment of [...] (men) [...] (women) [...] (total)
Periudha e Zbatueshmërisë	**Effective Period**
Ky Plan për Rritjen e Klientit është në fuqi nga data e nënshkrimit nga të dy palët, deri më [Datën].	This Client Growth Plan is effective from the date of signature by the two parties until [Date].
Raportimi dhe Mirëbesimi	**Reporting and Confidentiality**
Klienti do të koordinojë të gjitha aktivitetet e këtij Plani për Rritjen e Klientit me Menaxherin e Zhvillimit të Biznesit të ZHKN-së, [Emri i Konsulentit te Biznesit].	The Client will coordinate all activities under this Client Growth Plan with CED's Business Development Manager, [Name of Business Advisor]
Nëpërmjet këtij dokumenti ZHKN për pjesën e tij, pranon të mbajë sekret të gjitha të dhënat për shitjet, prodhimin, punësimin dhe investimet, të raportuara nga Klienti dhe të kufizojë përdorimin e tyre nga personeli i ZHKN-së dhe USAID-it. ZHKN do ta trajtojë të gjithë informacionin e dhënë në besim të plotë. ZHKN mund të kërkojë një verifikim të pavarur të të dhënave, në mënyrë që të dokumentojë dhe të sigurojë integritetin e tyre. Klienti pranon të bashkëpunojë me ZHKN-në, në mënyrë që të verifikojë rezultatet e raportuara.	For its part, CED hereby agrees to keep all sales, production, employment, and investment data reported by the Client confidential and restrict its use to CED and USAID personnel. CED will treat all information disclosed in full confidence. CED may request independent verification of data in order to document and ensure their integrity. The Client agrees to cooperate with CED in order to verify reported results.

Exhibit 3.30 Client Growth Plan Template, Albania
(page 6 of 6)

Të Ndryshme	Miscellaneous
Secila palë mund t'i japë fund këtij Plani për Rritjen e Klientit duke i dhënë 5 (pesë) përpara njoftim me shkrim palës tjetër. Të gjitha aktivitetet e ZHKN-së i nënshtrohen angazhimeve të financimit të USAID.	Either party may terminate this Client Growth Plan by giving five (5) working days prior notice in writing to the other party. All CED activities are subject to the ongoing funding commitments of USAID.
Nënshkrimi i palëve Të dyja palët në këtë Plan për Rritjen e Klientit firmosin dy kopje.	**Signatures of the Parties** The two parties to this Client Growth Plan sign two copies.

[Emri I Klientit]/[Name of Client Business]
Adresa e Klientit/Client Address

Name:
Title:

Signature: _____
Date Signed: _____
Place Signed: _____

Zhvillimi Konkurues Sipërmarrës në Shqipëri (ZHKN)
Rruga "Pjetër Bogdani", Bld. 36/1, Ap.5-6, Kati i Dytë,
Tiranë, Shqipëri 1000

Albania Competitive Enterprise Development (CED)
Pjeter Bogdani Str., Bld. 36/1, Ap.5-6, 2nd Floor
Tirana, Albania 1000

Name:
Title: CED Director

Signature _____
Date Signed: _____
Place Signed: _____

Source: USAID/Albania Competitive Enterprise Development program.

Exhibit 3.31. Client Growth Plan Example, Peru (page 1 of 6)

Puno Economic Service Center
Business Plan

Business advisor*: Luis Torres Zenteno

Name of client: Curtipiel SAC
Product: hides
Date: August 2004

---

1. Diagnosis of the business

1.1. The company (30 lines maximum)

1.1.1. Type of organization (incorporated company, producer association, individual, etc.):

Closed Incorporated Company (SAC).

1.1.2. Partners or owners of the business and percentage of participation:

- José Iturriaga   85%
- Marco Barrenechea   5%
- Claudia Iturriaga   10%

1.1.3. Time the business has been in existence (existing, new, expansion):

Curtipiel was founded in 2000.

1.1.4. Nature of the business and marketing channels:

a) Goods or services the company produces or markets:

Sheep wool
Merino sheep hides

b) Marketing channel (direct, with distributors, etc.):

Direct

1.1.5. Market opportunities this business takes advantage of to be profitable:

*Member of the Economic Service Center responsible for the client.

**Exhibit 3.31. Client Growth Plan Example, Peru
(page 2 of 6)**

The company has clients for this product, a business it has been in for several years.

1.1.6. Seasonality of the business:

The Company plans on buying product all year long.

1.1.7. Scope of the business (local, regional, national, etc.):

Export-oriented business.

1.1.8. Investment in fixed assets by the company in infrastructure, machinery, equipment, and land:

Approximately US$350,000.

1.2. The product or service (30 lines maximum)

1.2.1. Description of the product or service:

Puno is the country's main livestock Department, and for the specific case of sheep, it has 27% of the sheep population of the country. For that reason there are enough sheep hides for the company to supply itself here and meet the demand it has abroad.

1.2.2. Advantages of the product or service for which it is bought or preferred:

We have sheep of the Merino breed, which is what the company currently demands, and because of the climatic conditions in the Department of Puno (cold) the hides do not decompose since they have excellent quality.

1.2.3. Competitiveness factors: price, quality, differentiation, volume, market niches, seasonality, etc. (advantages compared with competitors):

The product is competitive because there is adequate volume for regular supply year round, and the price remains stable.

1.2.4. Unit costs of production for the good or service **(attach cost table):**

1.3. Demand (30 lines maximum)

1.3.1. List the main buyers of the good or service in the current market:

**Exhibit 3.31. Client Growth Plan Example, Peru
(page 3 of 6)**

Currently the product is only bought by intermediaries who get their supply in weekly community fairs. Once they have collected enough volume, they take it to Lima to be resold to hide export companies.

The clients of the Company are:

Grupo Yerver
Genis Antel SA
Brespel

1.3.2. Estimation of demand for the product or service in the current market (monthly or yearly volume):

The company calculates it could buy an average of 120,000 soles of hides a month.

1.4. The market (30 lines maximum)

1.4.1. Identification of competitors:

The companies that dedicate themselves to the same product are:

- Jorge Gonzáles Quintanilla
- Industria Peletera Artesanal
- Curtiembre La Pisqueña
- Dimas Mesías Inga
- L Pelle Export

1.4.2. Price and volume fluctuation in the target market:

In Puno, the current purchase price of the product is S/. 8 per hide.

1.4.3. Commercial market opportunities:

Currently the prospects for the hides business are positive since due to world preference for natural products, the demand for hides is going to be growing since more and more automobile upholstery is using less synthetic material, and leather is taking its place. In addition, demand will be growing for leather for garments.

1.5. Problems that limit the development of the business
(30 lines maximum)

Exhibit 3.31. Client Growth Plan Example, Peru
(page 4 of 6)

Describe the three main problems:

a)   Dispersion of supply: the slaughter of sheep in Puno is done at home since there is little done in slaughterhouses; as a result, it is difficult to bring supply together.

b)   There is no training in the slaughtering of sheep or in the conservation of hides to have quality hides for sale.

c)   Absence of a "hides bank" in which community members can store hides to sell in volume.

d)   Weak organization to supply volume with quality.

2. Business Plan

2.1. Objective of the Business Plan

The main objective consists of training and contributing to the organization of sheep producing communities in techniques of slaughtering, preservation of hides in "fresh salt" or "dry salt," which are the two ways hides have higher prices, and, in addition, organizing the communities to sell hides in bulk since in this way the company could buy them directly without going through many intermediaries.

2.2. Company mission

To obtain hide supplying communities that will be loyal to the company so that it is a business for several years.

2.3. Description of the proposed business

Enter into the hides business in Puno directly, for which it will first be necessary to train communities to supply product in accordance with the company's standards and then to organize them to supply their product in volume.

3. Strategy of the Economic Service Center and commitments of the client (30 lines maximum)

3.1. Support strategy of the Economic Service Center with the client

Give technical assistance to the communities in techniques of hides preservation in "fresh salt" and "dry salt," and then organize them so they can supply the company with volume.

Exhibit 3.31. Client Growth Plan Example, Peru (page 5 of 6)

3.2. Commitments of the Economic Service Center and their relationship to the priority problems (rank the three main ones)

a)   Identify and organize communities to supply their product together.

b)   Technical assistance for the communities in the slaughtering of sheep and hides preservation.

c)   Seek to create "hides banks" in the communities.

3.3. Commitments of the Client in relation to the actions of the Economic Service Center

a)   Buy the hides supplied by the communities in accordance with the market price.

b)   Support the technical assistance in hides preservation.

c)   Provide the "know how" to establish hides banks.

3.4. Expected results** and main activities of the Economic Service Center

a)   Begin to gather hides from the communities at the beginning of 2005.

b)   That at least 50% of the hides turned in by the communities at the end of 2005 be preserved in "fresh salt" or "dry salt."

c)   Have at least one hides bank working in the communities in 2005.

3.5. Time table of sales and investments (at least for 1 year)

(develop this table on a separate page)

**Concrete and verifiable achievements obtained from the implementation of the activities.

Exhibit 3.31. Client Growth Plan Example, Peru
(page 6 of 6)

Concept	Sales in Last Quarter (Oct-Dec04)	Projected Sales and Investments (S/.)				
		Quarter 1 (Jan-Mar05)	Quarter 2 (Apr-Jun05)	Quarter 3 (Jul-Sep05)	Quarter 4 (Oct-Dec05)	Total
Product	Hides					
Sales S/.	0	200,000	350,000	370,000	400,000	1,320,000
Investments	0	0	0	0	0	0

Source: USAID/Peru Poverty Reduction and Alleviation program. Curtipiel SAC's Business Plan used with permission.

Over time, some of the clients that emerge from the first Annual Operating Plan exercise succeed in tackling their key problems, increase their sales, and graduate from the buyer-led program. Others move on to second-generation problems, and collaboration with the program continues. Still other clients' Client Growth Plans do not work out as expected, and those clients drop out. As a result, the portfolio of Business Promotion Offices is never static. Successful Business Promotion Offices are perpetually in the hunt both for new clients and for buyers looking for goods and services that either existing or new clients could potentially supply.

How do business advisors go about identifying new clients and buyers? To use Easterly's terminology, not by Planning but by active Searching. Effective business advisors do not spend a lot of time in their offices. Most of their time they are out, scouring for business opportunities wherever they can find them—and once they have found them, keeping at it to ensure the deals close.[223] Such an aggressive posture is especially important at the inception of a program. In their first two months of operations, the four advisors in the MEDI North Office in Armenia made contact with 196 businesses. By the end of the third month, they had drafted 18 Memoranda of Understanding (Client Growth Plans), five of which went into force during that period.

Gregory Kruse describes how PRA business advisors spent their time as follows:

"Good ideas are common—what's uncommon are people who'll work hard enough to bring them about."

Ashleigh Brilliant

http://thinkexist.com/quotes/ashleigh_brilliant.

"A crow starves sitting, but finds flying."

Icelandic proverb

Arnaldur Indriðason, *Jar City: A Reykjavik Thriller*, translated by Bernard Scudder (New York: Picador, 2004), pp. 197-98.

The business advisors' most important task is identification of potential business deals. The advisors search for business opportunities through personal business networks, through presentations and meetings with business groups, by knocking on doors of companies that do or could do business in the corridor, and by following up on leads provided by advisors in other centers or the Lima office. The advisors need to know the business community of their corridor, and regularly contact local firms to introduce themselves and expand their network of contacts. They also identify national level enterprises that trade in products of the corridor.

The "market-driven" approach of the PRA Program means that the business advisors look for qualified buyers ready and able to pay for product or services producible in the corridor.

Real business opportunities take many forms. Sometimes a local firm will literally walk in the door of the center looking for a specific form of assistance, such as identification of a market, improvement of packaging, or help with an industrial process. In other cases, buyers may be seeking products that the corridor can supply. They may be firms that operate at a regional or a national level, or exporters. On occasion, a buyer is looking for a product not currently available in the corridor but one that is similar to local products or that utilizes local materials.

In each case, the business advisor must rely on his or her analytical skills and business sense to evaluate both the business opportunity and the client. In fact, evaluation of the client is the first priority, because even the best business deal will succeed only through the commitment and capability of the person who is trying to make it work.

In the process of developing a Business Plan, a business advisor makes contact with the principals of a potential buyer firm and its managers, and sometimes with its suppliers, customers, or even its bank in order to evaluate the buyer's reputation and ensure that the business opportunity is real from the demand side. To the extent possible, the advisor attempts to secure a firm commitment from a potential buyer for a quantity of a specified product at a specified price.

On the supply side, the advisor identifies local producers and contacts them to determine their interest. The advisor must evaluate whether they are capable of fulfilling the buyer's requirements, or if they could become capable with some technical assistance, access to capital, or other assistance. Their business experience, location, and existing production capacity are factors the advisor must investigate to make this determination. The evaluation must look carefully at the quality and characteristics of local products in comparison with the needs of the buyer, together with costs of production, packaging, and transport.

If the deal appears workable, the advisor brings the parties together to help negotiate the terms of their relationship, playing the role of "honest broker" in the exchange of information, facilitating communication, and smoothing over differences. There is often a significant element of mistrust between the parties that the personal assurances of the business advisor can help overcome. The assurances usually include the advisor's word to monitor the transaction through to completion, making himself or herself available as problems arise and "guaranteeing" that both parties keep their part of the deal and are treated fairly.

Sometimes the services of an expert consultant are required. It is the role of the business advisor to determine the need for such services, draft terms of reference for the consultant, and manage the relationship between the consultant and the client.

Approval of the business plan by the project's head office unleashes the assistance process, which follows no formula or logic other than that dictated by the circumstances of the deal. It is invariably a bit different in every case and the creativity of the business advisors comes into play as they attempt to make the deal work for all parties, and forge lasting linkages and business relationships in the process.[224]

Different buyer-led programs have developed different ways to address different program-specific requirements. A number of years ago, most of the development community in Armenia bought into the conventional wisdom that local large firms were a world unto themselves, vertically integrated, and averse to sourcing from third parties. When the Micro Enterprise Development Initiative suggested promoting sourcing agreements between large and medium enterprises, on the one hand, and small and micro-enterprises, on the other, it encountered considerable skepticism. Before going full steam ahead with the buyer-led approach, therefore, it first designed and paid for a survey of firms in four regions of the country. Contrary to the expectations of many, the survey results demonstrated considerable scope for outsourcing as a tool to expand small and micro-enterprise sales and jobs. Some of the information from the survey later proved useful for identifying buyers and clients, but its principal benefit was convincing skeptics of the advisability of putting the buyer-led approach into practice.

In Paraguay, most promising business opportunities involve exporting. For that reason, Paraguay Vende developed a questionnaire to assess the export readiness of potential clients (see the template in Chapter 19). When clients do appear ready, oftentimes the program helps them prepare company profiles to share with potential importers abroad. A company profile presents a succinct picture of the client—ideally, with photos—and spells out the kinds of goods and services it can provide. Typically, it consists of four sections:

General information on the company: name, location, contact information, year operations began, legal status, owners, director/ manager, human resources, plant and equipment, sales history, main export markets, references, etc.

Information about the product: principal product, use and applications, technical specifications, packaging, etc.

Conditions of production: origin and life of machinery and equipment, normal capacity of facilities, current level of utilization, source of raw materials, storage capacity, international certifications, etc.

Conditions of sale: primary export contact, terms of sale commonly used, export sales agents, providers of export services (banks, brokers, agencies, etc.), packaging, estimated delivery time, promotion policies, etc.

The company profile tries to resolve the chicken-and-egg problem often inherent in exporting. The idea is not for a client to sell what it has already produced, but to show potential buyers that it is capable of producing product—whose specifications the buyer will ultimately determine—that meets international standards. Looked at another way, the profile is a tool for marketing in the true sense— a way to elicit what the buyer wants—not a manifestation of the supply-push dictionary definition of marketing attacked in Part II.

The challenge of cracking export markets leads many development practitioners to think of international fairs, and sponsoring client businesses to participate in them. Even when clients go well prepared—which often is not the case—it can take three years or more to cultivate contacts to the point of consummating sales. Normally other strategies are more cost-effective, especially ones that facilitate buyers and sellers meeting each other in business-to-business, one-on-one, face-to-face formats. As the author put it in a report in Paraguay,

> The Searcher vs. Planner paradigm is especially germane to the establishment of market linkages ...Although we might like to think otherwise, identifying and securing the commitment of buyers to source from target suppliers is not something development professionals can plan like a vaccination campaign. Searching for buyers obviously requires organization, but, in the end, searching is searching. More than that, it is hard work. In the author's experience, there is no magic formula for identifying and tapping new markets. If any-

"'Nought is given 'neath the sun,
Nought is had that is not won.'"

Swedish hymn

Dag Hammarskjöld, *Markings*, translated by Leif Sjöberg and W.H. Auden (New York: Alfred A. Knopf, Inc., 1964), p. 103.

thing, the formula is persistence—that is, refusing to give up.

That said, experience does suggest that some market linkage strategies are more conducive than others to making the search successful. On the negative side of the ledger, experience in Paraguay and elsewhere suggests that facilitating the attendance of client business at international fairs is not a high-payoff strategy, especially if one is anxious to show results in the relatively near term (that is, one or two years). On the positive side of the ledger, three other strategies appear especially appropriate:

Identifying and bringing buyers to Paraguay—in contrast to the other way around. Foreign buyers often start with negative preconceptions about local suppliers. Bringing them to meet potential suppliers face to face on their own turf often can help allay those preconceptions and build trust.

Organizing road shows—that is, trips abroad to meet one on one with prospective buyers. To be successful, road shows require substantial preparation, first, in setting up the right appointments, and, second, in readying inexperienced local businesses to present themselves credibly in a foreign environment.

Identifying sellers abroad—that is, parties who can act as agents for local producers in identifying buyers and consummating deals. The advantage of working through agents is their knowledge of markets abroad and the preferences of buyers. Normally agents work on commission, which helps align the incentives of the two parties to succeed.[225]

Some programs place such stress on expanding exports that they overlook the potential of import substitution, that is, producing and selling goods currently imported. As part of the induction workshop of the MARKETS program in Nigeria, participants visited a local supermarket (see Exhibit 3.32). As they walked the aisles, they found a number of goods that Nigerians could produce but that came from abroad. They also found a number of goods from local processing companies. In both cases, the presence of the products on the shelves gave advisors signals about demand: the supermarket would never have bought the goods in question if it did not believe it could sell them. In the instance of imports, a logical first step for business advisors is to ask supermarkets whether they would buy locally if local producers could match their imports in quantity, quality, and timely delivery. If the answer is yes, then the advisors can delve to see why local producers have stayed on the sidelines. There may be good reasons that local producers are not competitive, but then again, there may not. If not, a potential opportunity exists for generating sales by producers that would not take place otherwise. The task of identifying and organizing producers to meet supermarkets' requirements may be a challenge, but, in the end, that is what a business advisor's job is all about: solving problems and making things happen.

Exhibit 3.32 A Sampling of Products for Sale in a Nigerian Supermarket

Photo: Joseph Jordan and Oscar Rizo-Patrón.

In the instance of products already processed in country, the point where business advisors start may be different, but the process to follow is much the same. The labels on the merchandise in a supermarket normally give contact information about processors, whom business advisors can contact to see if they want more product.

Starting by going to the local supermarket—or, more generically, with something known and at hand—not only is a more cost-effective market identification strategy than expensive market studies, but it also allows fledgling business advisors to get their feet wet with something they are comfortable with. That strategy certainly worked in Armenia. By starting with businesses they knew, advisors gained the confidence to venture forth later into uncharted territory.

A key element of the relationship between a buyer-led program and its client is who pays for what. In a buyer-led program, business advisors spend most if not all of their time identifying business opportunities, building trust between buyers and sellers and with themselves, helping clients figure out how to break operational log-jams, and as program-supported transactions unfold, backstopping clients to ensure that the transactions come to consummation. As a rule, those services—referred to elsewhere in this book as "facilitation," "honest brokering," and "*acompañamiento*"—are ones that neither buyers nor sellers—walking in, at least—are willing to pay for. Whether for lack of information on markets, technology, etc., insecurity-induced risk aversion, perpetually changing government norms and regulations, a bad taste from the past, or whatever other reason, it is common for buyers and sellers to shy away from promising business opportunities. To put it in the parlance of economists, a "market failure" is at work, making the transaction costs of market entry prohibitively high.

From a theoretical perspective, what buyer-led program Business Promotion Offices try to do day to day is lower those transaction costs. By definition, therefore, the heart of their work is a public, not a private good—which, put another way, means that it makes no sense for buyer-led programs to insist on clients paying for their services. Interestingly, that conclusion is not just theory. Around the world, the repeated failures of Business Promotion Offices to recover substantial portions of their operating costs from user fees provide solid empirical evidence that that strategy does not work.

When buyer-led programs talk about cost-sharing with clients, the discussion concerns the conventional business development services—agricultural extension, environmental management services, training in cost-saving management techniques, introduction of new technology, etc.—that Business Promotion Offices help arrange for but do not normally provide directly themselves. Those services are private, not public goods—and in a frictionless, perfectly functioning market, one would expect clients to pay their full cost.

In fact, most of the markets where buyer-led programs work are far from frictionless and do not function perfectly. The very reasons that make connector firms and their suppliers unwilling to pay for facilitation and honest brokering spill over to conventional business development services, making clients reluctant to pay full freight. To nudge things along, therefore, buyer-led programs typically bear a portion of the cost of those services. The issue then is what proportion of those costs should the program bear, and what proportion should the client bear?

Many programs are tempted to set up rigid cost-sharing schedules as a function of the price tag of the assistance provided and the size of the client receiving or channeling it. The danger is that such schedules can become almost ends in themselves, with programs winding up managing for process, not for results. Experience suggests the wisdom of maintaining flexibility, as the following considerations show:

Keep the objective clear: it is increasing sales and jobs. Getting clients to pick up a high proportion of the costs of conventional business development services is a way for a buyer-led program to save money and free up resources for other promising opportunities. The more strapped a program financially, in fact, the greater the proclivity to up the ante. But one can push the zeal to save money to extremes and actually jeopardize the results one wants to obtain. Suppose, for example, that a wealthy company is unwilling to pay what a buyer-led program would normally expect a company its size to contribute, but the potential return on the technical assistance at issue is an enormous increase in sales and jobs. In such cases, it may be counterproductive to dig in one's heels "on principle"; doing so could forfeit sizeable gains.

Clients must "own" the assistance they receive. In many developing countries—Armenia is a case in point—donor-sponsored business support programs offer business development services to clients gratis. Many clients are skeptical of that practice and wonder about the "catch"—that is, if there is a hidden agenda at work that they may have to worry about later. As businesspeople, they know that "you get what you pay for," and therefore have misgivings about the kind of services they can expect to receive. And that is the point. If firms receive support for free, what right do they have to demand that its providers target it to their individual needs? In contrast, once they put their own money on the line, they have more of a stake in its success and can be more demanding. In short, they can be honest-to-goodness clients, not "beneficiaries."

> "Donors must also be answerable to the people they claim to help. The Samaritan should not cross the road unless the injured traveler by the wayside can hold him to account for dressing his wounds and providing a roof for the night. Otherwise donors offer what they want to give, not what the poor can use, and they have little incentive to follow through on any charitable gesture they might make."
>
> "Development aid: In praise of small things," review of Easterly, *The White Man's Burden*, *Economist*, April 1, 2006, pp. 68-69.

In an environment in which it is common for programs not to charge for services, some recommend that client contributions be success-based, that is, that a client pay nothing up front but compensate a service provider after it succeeds—if it does—in increasing the client's sales. Although that alternative is appealing in that it puts pressure on the service provider to deliver, the pressure is entirely one-sided. Anyone will pay for manna from heaven after the fact. For outside support to bear fruit, the client must make some kind of commitment beforehand. Only in that way will it have a real incentive to care about the assistance it receives, monitor it closely, and demand results. If it is unwilling to contribute at all, a buyer-led program has no other alternative than to doubt the seriousness of the client and walk away.[226]

A uniform and consistent client contribution requirement policy is appealing in theory, but complicated in practice. Realistically, one cannot expect a small or micro-enterprise to pay the same for a service as one of the largest companies in a country. Some graduation of client contributions is necessary. By the same token, the longer a client receives support from a program, the more one would expect that client to pay as time goes on. But size of client and time in program are not the only confounding factors. Consultant costs can vary widely, for example, even for basically the same services. Not only can the difference in the fees of local and international consultants be substantial, but the costs of local consultancies can differ widely depending on whether payment of travel and per diem is required. Accordingly, a percentage-of-total-contribution formula—perhaps the most appealing option in theory—can result in very different contributions for similar services.

How clients contribute can have serious management, accounting, and financial implications. If a buyer-led program accepts cash contributions from clients, good accounting practice normally calls for it to set up a separate account for the purpose intended. Setting up a separate account adds to the program's management and accounting burden. More than that, it can create cumbersome tax obligations, depending on the financing agency's regulations and host-country laws. Experience suggests the advisability of buyer-led programs and their clients not "pooling" payment for the services of third parties, but each paying for different things. For example, some buyer-led programs pay the costs of bringing a consultant to a country, but local clients pick up all local costs—local transportation, hotels, meals, etc.

Where a buyer-led program's money goes and who receives the assistance in the end can be two very different things. Some observers of buyer-led programs accept intellectually the development logic of starting with connector firms, not with suppliers, but voice considerable disquiet about how that logic plays out in practice. Why? Because connector firms tend to be more prosperous than their suppliers, and working with them as clients makes it look like buyer-led programs are supporting the "rich"—an especially anomalous position for an approach to development that purports to help the poor. Looked at from that perspective, buyer-led programs do indeed have an image problem, but much more often than not, the image is image, not reality. Take the bean operation on the Ucayali River, for example. One of PRA's clients was La Procesadora, a relatively prosperous Peruvian agricultural processing company. PRA did indeed "subsidize" La Procesadora's operation in the area. But what did the subsidy go for? To pick up a portion of the cost of tailoring production practices to the peculiarities of that agro-ecological environment and extending those production practices to the many small farmers who actually planted and grew the beans. Yes, La Procesadora benefited from the subsidy—it made money. Proportionally, however, one could argue that the farmers benefited even more. All of that aside from the transaction-induced jump in the local wage rate, which had a spread effect beyond the transaction per se.

The La Procesadora example is not at all atypical. Just about every time a buyer-led program supports the application of the embedded services model of business development, allying itself with a relatively prosperous connector firm, the bulk of the benefit goes to the connector firm's suppliers, the very population the program tries to reach. All of which illustrates the far-reaching adage cited above: the place where you find a problem is not necessarily where it makes sense to attack it!

In cases where the connector firm acts in essence as the channel to reach poor suppliers, arguments that prosperous clients should contribute proportionally more than poorer ones—a proposition most people would endorse—becomes much less cut and dried than one would expect at first bounce, reinforcing once again the advisability of not setting hard and fast rules for client contributions, but letting the operational objective—increasing sales and jobs—carry the day.

To sum up, the ultimate objective of sharing costs with clients is to maximize, not client contributions, but sales and jobs. Flexibility, not mechanistic formulas, is called for. That said, there definitely has to be some real contribution on the part of the client. Ownership is essential. Finally, practical considerations suggest the wisdom of the client and the program paying for different things—an example, again, of the KISS principle in action.

Handling the cost-sharing issue in this way may be very well and good, but, some would argue, the danger still exists that Business Promotion Offices will take advantage of their privileged position in a corridor to provide conventional business development services themselves and crowd out existing providers in the market. There are four different factors that militate against that eventuality. Taken in tandem, the first two constitute the most powerful safeguards:

Incentives. The first safeguard is the program's performance bonus scheme. Any time a business advisor spends providing conventional business development services is time he or she could spend developing and nurturing new business opportunities that could translate into new sales and jobs and, potentially, more money for the advisor. In other words, providing conventional business development services comes at an opportunity cost.

Specialized nature of conventional business development services. As a rule, buyer-led programs hire generalists as business advisors. Since good business development services typically are very situation-specific, not one-size-fits-all, most of the time buyer-led program advisors would not be qualified to provide the conventional business development services required even if they wanted to. One of PRA's early clients was Tutti Fruti, a small ice cream business in the city of Jaén. Tutti Fruti was able to sell everything it produced. The owner was anxious to expand, but realized he needed to improve the quality of his popsicles, which were grainy in texture, to expand his market share significantly. After scouring the market for sources of qualified expertise, PRA identified an ex-Nestlé technician whose specialty was popsicle production. The technician spent two weeks in Jaén, explaining to the owner what equipment made sense and what processes to adopt. At the end of the consultancy, the owner purchased the equipment, applied the processes, and opened up two subsidiaries, one in the neighboring city of Bagua and the other in the city of Loja in Ecuador. By doing so, Tutti Fruti became PRA's first multinational client (!), a modest success that would never have come to pass if the Economic Service Center in Jaén had tried to provide the technical assistance itself. When one gets down to the nitty-gritty, the question of whether to outsource conventional business development services to third parties very often turns out to be a non-issue.

Policy. Business Promotion Offices are under orders to outsource conventional business development services to third parties. It is a matter of policy.

Budgeting. The budgets for Business Promotion Offices contain a line item earmarked for third-party support.

A final issue affecting the relationship between a Business Promotion Office and its client is the kind of services the program is open to finance, either directly or through third-party providers. As the examples throughout this book illustrate, most buyer-led programs limit their services to a combination of facilitation/honest brokering and conventional business development services, where the latter term includes what many refer to as technical assistance. Put negatively, buyer-led programs normally do not provide grants for plant and equipment, that is, for physical capital. There are a number of interlocking reasons for that limitation:

Counteracting supply-side bias. Including grants for physical capital as a program option tends to feed the preconception that all a business needs to grow is more plant and equipment, which in turn depends on financial capital. Experience in buyer-led programs suggests that that diagnosis is often flawed. It also points up the wisdom of staying away from supply-side schemes — "projects" — and focusing on business transactions.

Distinguishing between serious and not so serious clients. Most businesses are likely to react more positively to a business advisor with money in hand than to an advisor armed with essentially nothing more than good will and an offer to help them solve their problems. At the beginning, therefore, buyer-led program business advisors normally have a tough sell. All other things equal, however, the clients that demonstrate a willingness to work with a buyer-led program are likely to be more serious businesses than those looking primarily for a handout. Yes, having no money makes a business advisor's job harder, but his or her resultant portfolio of clients is likely to consist of businesses whose future expansion rests on a solid foundation. On bad days, PRA personnel may have rued their inability to entice clients easily. On more dispassionate days, though, they were the first to admit that not having grant money was one of the best decisions that went into the program's design. That was true even when it did turn out that lack of financing was indeed a major constraint and the client and the program had to find creative ways of securing funds through existing market channels.

Fomenting full-fledged business ownership. Observers schooled in economic theory often raise the objection that a subsidy is a subsidy, so what is the big deal if a subsidy goes to pay for plant and equipment or goes to pay for business development services? Theoretically, there may be no big difference, but operationally the two are apples and oranges. Experience worldwide bears witness to the value of sweat equity in the development of an enterprise. Plant and equipment that entrepreneurs have saved and sweated to finance have a very different value from capital stock they have received either free or at a deep discount. Once more, the issue is ownership, meaning full identification by owners with the business as theirs. The only way that happens is when owners invest their own money in the business's plant and equipment—in other words, when they assume serious risk. Only with such exposure can one be certain that owners have the motivation to do what it takes to make sure the business not only stays afloat but makes money. When development programs allow "owners" to play with grant money, they pave the road to white elephantdom.

Letting the problem determine the solution, not vice-versa. Most development programs with grant programs set up separate funds for that purpose and assign personnel to manage them. Most grant program managers find themselves under strong pressure to "move the money"—often regardless of whether a grant is the appropriate response to a client's problems. Under that kind of pressure, grant programs can become like fishing expeditions. The one buyer-led program that experimented with grants bears witness to that tendency. Day after day, the grants manager of the Azerbaijan Business Assistance and Development program kept asking, "Where can I spend this grant money usefully?" Most buyer-led programs never ask that question, but rather, "What is (are) the client's major constraint(s) to growth, and what tool is best to address it (them)?" Too many grant programs not only create conflicting incentives but become ends in themselves, measuring their success by how much money they spend, not by what the money brings about.

Many donors and development practitioners have become inured to managing grant programs and find the suggested limitation on use of funds hard to accept. And, in fairness, it is not as if grants always lead to white elephants. In recent years, for example, TechnoServe has run grant competitions to identify entrepreneurs with viable business ventures. The Bolivia Trade and Business Competitiveness program sponsors business plan competitions to the same end. The Accelerated Sustainable Agriculture Program in Afghanistan made small grants averaging only $2,500 to 250 small agricultural input stores around the country. The result is a functional network with national coverage. In each of those cases, grant amounts have been relatively small, which, put another way, means that the programs in question have swum successfully against the tide and kept grant money in proper perspective. **As a practical matter, the recommendation to avoid grants is not a doctrinaire stricture, but guidance based on how development programs normally work. Yes, there are exceptions to prove the rule, but not enough to justify the exceptions as the rule.**

What Makes a Good Business Advisor?

Good business advisors need not be Supermen or Wonder Women, but they do need to know how to be Easterly Searchers. Day in and day out, good business advisors take the meaning of "demand-driven" seriously, exercise discipline in selecting what clients and transactions to support, work collegially with clients in a way that builds trust, focus single-mindedly on solving specific binding market chain problems, and follow through to ensure that promising opportunities in fact translate into results. The advisors may not always succeed, but not for want of trying. When the going gets tough, good business advisors do not roll over and play dead but figure out how to make things work, thinking "outside the box," if necessary. In sum, they work hard and solve problems.

"My dear friend, clear your mind of can't."

Samuel Johnson

Source: http://thinkexist.com/quotes/samuel_johnson.

There is no magic formula to become a good business advisor. For recruiting purposes, the qualifications described in Exhibit 3.17 are a place to start. For readers who like checklists,

---

Exhibit 3.33 Keys to Success for PRA Business Advisors

Although every client has different problems, and the types of assistance required vary accordingly, there are common elements that are the basis for the program's success. These may be characterized as follows:

- Focus on Demand—the advice to clients in the corridor is, "Produce what you can sell, don't sell what you produce." For the business advisors, the corollary is, "Find the buyer and assist clients in the corridor to deliver; don't promote the products of the corridor in the hopes of finding a market."

- Qualify the Proposed Assistance—evaluate program costs and increases in client sales to ensure that the latter will be at least five times the former.

- Qualify the Client—on both the demand and supply side, evaluate the capabilities, seriousness, level of commitment, and resources of the players in the deal, to ensure that program recommendations show results.

- Qualify the Deal—analyze the value proposition for both the buyer and the seller to ensure that the deal is profitable and attractive, and therefore sustainable without ongoing program support.

- Support the Business Relationships—facilitate communication, information flow, understanding, signing of contracts, and resolution of problems and conflicts to enable the development of a commitment on both sides to pursuing the business in the future.

- Support the Profitability of the Deal—technical assistance can be the key to identifying the most attractive markets, expanding sales, improving product quality and cutting costs, so that corridor products are competitive and corridor businesses are profitable and have a future.

- Plan for Disengagement—the Economic Service Centers are by definition temporary institutions, and the role of the business advisor is to facilitate a viable, long-lasting business relationship and then fade away.

Source: Gregory Kruse.

Exhibit 3.33 may be useful. That exhibit lays out in ordered fashion the various tasks that go into an advisor's job. Although written for PRA, the checklist has applicability elsewhere.[227]

For those who like to learn from examples, Exhibit 3.34 may be helpful. Written by Suzanne Savage, the first Business Services Director of the Azerbaijan Business Assistance and Development

Exhibit 3.34 How to Work with Buyers and Producers, Azerbaijan (page 1 of 3)

We start with the buyer

We first talk to buyers of products that are currently produced or could be produced in the economic corridors to identify the gaps between what buyers want and what they are getting.

We try to facilitate forward contracts to ensure guaranteed sales for the producer and guaranteed input supply for the processor.

We work primarily at the bottom of the market chain, focusing on farmers, processors, and others who produce inputs for larger businesses, and do not focus on retail or consumer business— although we encourage businesses all along the supply chain to maintain intimate knowledge of what end-buyers want.

1. **Finding a producer to fill specific buyer needs**
    Example: A company is searching for tomato and pomegranate concentrates typically not produced here. The owner exports to Europe and is willing to pay a very high price per ton if a processor can produce them at the level of concentration required. He does not have resources to seek out all processors, explain what he needs, collect samples, and test the product. Through its marketing centers, ABAD has gotten samples from processors and the buyer is now testing the samples.

2. **Organizing production supply of many producers**
    Example: A Baku-based milk company requires fresh milk supply, but does not have resources to organize hundreds of small dairy farmers. ABAD is assisting with the procurement of collection stations, determining locations for collection stations based on the location of farmers, and assisting farmers to increase yield of milk with training in animal feeding and milking.

3. **Ensuring reliable, consistent supply to buyers**
    Example: A wine producer has a significant requirement for grapes. Although the country has a lot of vineyards, a large portion of the grapes are rejected by the vineyards because of disease, failure to harvest at the right time for required sugar content, and other production problems. ABAD is communicating the requirements to growers, and providing assistance to instruct them in techniques that result in a more consistent supply.

Exhibit 3.34 How to Work with Buyers and Producers, Azerbaijan (page 2 of 3)

4. **Modifying production to meet buyer needs**
    Example: Tomato processors in Masali reject huge quantities of tomatoes delivered by farmers because the varieties are more suitable for eating, not processing. In addition, all farmers tend to plant tomatoes at the same time and harvest at the same time, which limits the processing season and processors' revenue. ABAD is working with local tomato farmers to test new varieties that are more appropriate to tomato processors' needs and ripen earlier, thereby extending the processing season.

5. **Reducing processors' input costs by developing input supply locally**
    Example: A flour mill purchases wheat from Ukraine and Russia because the varieties of wheat required are not grown within Azerbaijan. ABAD identified farmers willing to plant the specific variety the flour mill wants, and facilitated a contract to ensure the sale/supply.

Exhibit 3.34 How to Work with Buyers and Producers, Azerbaijan (page 3 of 3)

For producers

We do not work with producers to increase yield or quality unless it is to meet a specific buyer's needs.

6. **High-value product has no market within Azerbaijan, but could have good potential outside the country**
Example: A company that finished its first production of rose oil in Zagatala is capable of increased volume as well as extending its line of production to include other essential oils. If it is able to find buyers, additional farmers will be identified to plant crops specifically for this purpose. ABAD is working to identify specific buyers of essential oil, their packaging, quality and pricing requirements, and their willingness to enter into contracts with the Zagatala company. ABAD will provide assistance to farmers to maximize production.

7. **Reduce farmers' production losses by producing only what will sell**
Example: A watermelon farmer in Salyan had seven of his 25 tons of watermelon rot because the market was over-supplied. ABAD identified a buyer willing to sign a contract for 80 tons of an early-ripening variety of watermelon. ABAD is helping the farmer procure seeds and will provide growing assistance to the farmer to ensure success of the new crop.

8. **Capturing new business opportunities by filling gaps in the supply chain and producing what the market wants, with guaranteed sales**
Example: A vineyard manager is responsible for planting hundreds of hectares of new vines in Guba. He is unable to secure a sufficient supply of posts to support the trellises, as they are produced in very small supply in a location six hours away from Guba. He is aware of farmers' intentions to plant thousands of new hectares of vineyards in the next two years, and knows that poles last only a few years, which means both an increased and perpetual demand for posts. The vineyard owner is able to finance 50 percent of the cost for the vineyard manager to start producing posts in Guba. ABAD is contributing the other 50 percent of the cost to begin production, which will employ a minimum of 10 people.

Benefits—bridge the trust gap, matchmaking specific buyer to specific producer, assist producers in producing what buyers want.

Source: Suzanne Savage.

program, the examples give a glimpse into the reasoning that went into her decisions of what to support and what not to support at the beginning of the program.

Although every Client Growth Plan is unique, there are a number of programmatic issues that come up frequently, both within a program and across programs. This section concludes with a discussion of some of those issues, together with tips on how to address them. The list of issues is not exhaustive, but sufficient to give the reader a sampling of the thinking that practitioners of the buyer-led approach bring to different kinds of problems.

Graduating clients vs. developing long-term relationships. The *modus operandi* of the buyer-led approach is problem-solving. Business advisors help clients solve specific business problems that prevent them from increasing sales and, directly or indirectly, expanding jobs. Once clients solve their problems, the business advisors have no role to play. Buyer-led programs do not form part of market chains, and unless new problems emerge that clients cannot address on their own, it is time for the buyer-led programs to move on. This problem-solving philosophy runs counter to much community development practice, in which outside organizations commit themselves to long-term relationships with "their" communities. When organizations with backgrounds in community development venture into business development, the temptation is strong for them to do much the same thing. The very sustainability of business relationships, however, depends on outside organizations limiting their support to one-shot infusions of assistance and, otherwise, letting economic forces do their thing.

All that said, some business problems can take some time to solve. In contrast to the couple of months it took Nutreina and Teresa Romero to enter into a buyer-seller relationship, for example, some transactions take years to consummate. The red quinoa operation in Puno, Peru, is a case in point. Since red quinoa was in danger of extinction, it took a couple of years just to generate enough seed to plant enough red quinoa to start meeting Quinoa Corporation's requirements.

Cooperation among development programs vs. operational independence. Donor organizations like to tout the virtue of "synergy" among their programs, but incentives do not always exist to make synergy work. An example that did work is the red quinoa operation. Plot sizes in the quinoa-growing area near Lake Titicaca average only one quarter of a hectare. Quinoa Corporation had ordered eight containers of red quinoa from El Altiplano, PRA's immediate client, which meant that filling the order was going to be a tremendous technical and organizational challenge. As fate would have it, CARE had developed its own quinoa program in the area and had a number of quinoa experts on its local staff. When CARE learned of the order for red quinoa, it was highly motivated to jump in and help make the transaction work, making its extensionists available to the operation and lowering substantially the costs that El Altiplano and PRA had to incur. As time went on, El Altiplano took over the lion's share of technical assistance, thereby lowering the dependency on CARE and increasing the likelihood of the sustainability of the connector firm-supplier relationship.

Synergy works when the incentives of interested parties align themselves in mutually reinforcing harmony. Regrettably, that does not happen as a matter of course. In Peru, PRA was good at identifying buyers, and local private voluntary organizations were good at extending production assistance. In principle, therefore, alliances between the two looked like marriages made in heaven, with each party playing to its strength and saving the other money. The alliance between PRA and CARE worked very well in Puno, but similar alliances did not always bear fruit. Why not? For a number of reasons. First, and most importantly, most of the time PRA and its collaborating partners failed to put their agreements to collaborate in writing, either as part of clients' Business Plans or separately. Both parties presumably acted in good faith, but the absence of written agreements led to misunderstandings—and, in the worst cases, to "blame games" afterwards. The moral of the story is to spell out commitments on paper, ideally in Client Growth Plans. Second, and this point relates to the first, the two parties had different senses of urgency for getting things done. In one instance, one partner had promised to run the operation by its microfinance arm and secure a loan for small farmers for fertilizer. By the time the fertilizer arrived, it was too late in the growing season to be of use. Third, sometimes organizations' urge to get their names in the limelight created antibodies, undermining the initial openness of partners to collaborate.

Despite looking nice on paper, synergy can degenerate into too many cooks spoiling the broth. Unless lines of accountability are crystal clear, the fewer actors the better.

Although undesirable, one can understand why development programs put up walls around themselves. Sometimes, though, the designs of the programs themselves make things worse. In Azerbaijan a few years ago, USAID developed one program to foster linkages between connector firms and the buyers of their goods and services and another program to foster linkages between connector firms and their suppliers. In other words, instead of seeing market chains as wholes, it cut them in two. What was the result? Two separate contractors wary of each other and chary about sharing information on "their" clients. At more or less the same time, USAID/Mali took things one step farther, letting one contract for forward linkages, a second contract for backward linkages, and a third contract for finance—creating the kinds of operational rigidities discussed in Part II. The bottom line? Keep support for market chains whole; do not dismantle it into separate pieces.

Arm's-length vs. close relationships with local governments. When a buyer-led program shows that it can deliver results, local governments take notice. When local governments take notice, it is common for them to invite business advisors to local government meetings. As advisors spend more and more time in government meetings, they spend less and less time with current and potential clients and buyers, thereby becoming less effective in what they are paid to do.

Meeting frequently with governors, mayors, and their staffs can be a heady experience for business advisors, giving them a sense of importance in the local community. Before they know it, though, advisors can wind up spending undue amounts of time on issues that bear only a tangential relationship to solving the business problems of their clients. Again, focus, focus, focus! To the extent that a local government, either by exercising its regulatory power or by investing in public goods, can contribute to the expansion of client sales, the time an advisor spends with local government officials is well worth it. To the extent that is not the case, however, it is better that advisors stay on the sidelines and focus on the specifics of clients' business problems.

An example of how buyer-led program-induced local government action can contribute to the expansion of client sales and jobs comes from Paraguay Vende. In 2004, a foreign investor came to the city of Ciudad del Este to explore the possibility of opening up a plastics factory there. The city referred the investor to Paraguay Vende to discuss details. Guided by Paraguay Vende, the investor found what it believed to be an ideal site on the outskirts of the city. The only problem was access. The site was located just off a sandy dirt road about 200 meters from the main thoroughfare. To construct the factory, the company was going to have to bring heavy trucks in and out, which the sandy dirt road would not support. Paraguay Vende personnel therefore approached the mayor, showing how the company's plans to invest $15 million would generate significant sales and jobs for the municipality in the future and arguing that it was well worth the municipality's while to cobblestone the 200 meters to make the investment happen. The mayor agreed, the investment went forward, and the factory has hired people and is now up and running.

Transactions vs. projects. Throughout, this book argues strongly for keeping one's programmatic focus on individual business transactions, resisting the temptation to do "projects" or to solve the problems of sectors, clusters, or countries all at once. For one in the trenches, the temptation to finance projects can be so daunting that the message is worth repeating here. Every development program receives proposals out of the blue soliciting financial support. More often than not, the proposals bear the hallmarks of projects—minimal or no treatment at all of who will buy the good or service in question, a capital-intensive production scheme heavily dependent on third-party financing, and a scale of operations such that one cannot do anything unless one does everything. Often, proponents talk a good game and package their ideas slickly, which can make it difficult to say no. But a good buyer-led program must hold firm, probing to identify the buyer, the key problem constraining growth in sales, and the most cost-effective way to solve that problem. No one is opposed to thinking big, but the adage, "think globally, act locally," has special applicability here.

In recent years, the word, "scaleability," has come into vogue in development circles, reflecting the concern of funding agencies that what they sponsor transform itself into something more than patches of green. Even before an idea has proven itself on a small scale, many ask the question, "If it works, how can we scale it up." Interestingly, the terminology used reveals the thinking of the Planner. Yes, development programs can make people aware of business ideas that work. But they cannot program their spread like a vaccination campaign. Rather, an idea must pass the market test: does the idea make good enough business sense that it makes sense for others to jump in? There is a whole literature on the diffusion of innovations to suggest that that process does not happen overnight, but depends on a number of factors that determine its course.[228]

> "Poirot is not concerned with nations. Poirot is concerned with private citizens."
>
> Hercule Poirot
>
> "One, Two, Buckle My Shoe," *Agatha Christie's Poirot*, Series Four, directed by Ross Devenish, 1992.

A recent book relates a story that highlights the different mindsets project-oriented and business-oriented practitioners bring to development:

> "Don't sell the skin till you've caught the bear."
>
> Peter Lovesey, *The Headhunters* (New York: Soho Press, Inc., 2008) p. 205.

[V]illage development projects have consistently failed as a mechanism of economic development. The basic problem is this: When you find a need, do you "design a project" or "start a business"? These are two very different ideas from two different worlds of action. For example, in 2006, a group of business students traveled to Kenya to help out a Millennium Development Village...The Village had a technology program that designed a cheap lantern that the village could make and sell. The staff of the village asked the business students for a marketing plan. Right away, the students found an entrepreneur nearby who sold a similar lantern for a fraction of the price. The business students proposed that the Village become a marketer of that cheaper lamp to other villages, and make a profit that way. The entrepreneur agreed. The Village technology program said no. It wanted to make and sell its own lamp.[229]

Low-hanging fruit vs. start-ups. Like projects, start-ups can be tempting propositions for buyer-led program business advisors to support. Supporting the emergence of new businesses definitely has its attractions, especially from an equity perspective. The typical start-up is strapped for cash, and helping someone of relatively modest means make the transition from laborer to entrepreneur is very appealing. Alas, most start-ups do not fare well—available data from Bolivia, for example, indicate that four of five new businesses close down within two or three years[230]—often for the same reasons that make projects unattractive. Perhaps the most common failing—unsurprisingly—is not tying down demand beforehand, though the heavy dependence on third parties for financial support is often a critical determinant as well.

The inference to draw from this discussion is not to rule start-ups out of court, but to subject every client—new or old—to the test of something like the 5:1 rule. If a proposed transaction passes the test, then there is no reason not to go full-speed ahead. Much more often than not, the transactions that pass through the filter successfully will be those of established businesses. Some use the disparaging term, low-hanging fruit, to refer to those business opportunities that will yield the highest return for the least expenditure of resources. But what is objectionable about that? Although extending a helping hand to a budding Horatio Alger has its allure, the job of buyer-led programs is to generate as many jobs as possible in as cost-effective way as possible.

Specialization vs. complete vertical integration. Throughout the world, small farmers are wont to complain that the middlemen and women who buy their produce pay them less than what they are entitled to receive. In Latin America, a common term for market intermediaries is "coyotes," which conveys well the sense of exploitation many small farmers feel. To redress what they see as

an unfair situation, it is common for small farmers to ask development programs for support to help them market their product on
their own, that is, to help make them coyotes themselves. Unfortunately, the track record of such attempts is poor. First, coyotes'
margins generally are not nearly as exploitative as outsiders would
like to think, especially when one factors in the impact of often hor-
rid roads, for example, on intermediaries' operating costs. Second,
when small farmers venture into marketing, it is normally completely alien territory: without having passed through the school of
hard knocks of experience, they wind up marketing their products
very inefficiently and losing money. In the end, specialization is a
good thing, not a bad thing. Better that farmers focus on improving
what they know how to do well than plunging into the unknown
and losing money in the bargain.

> "The owner of Elvin 2 Potato Company Agagulu Huseynov said 'These days, farmers have to not only grow produce; they also have to be skilled business people... [W]e are learning how to restructure our farming practices to meet the demands of the market economy.'"
>
> Jamil Bayramov, "USAID provides support to farmers in southern Azerbaijan," editor@cbnextra.com, November 8, 2006.

Some development professionals find the suggestion that farmers
stay down on the farm morally un-
tenable. For them, such a position
appears to condemn small farmers
to the lowest point on the totem pole
in perpetuity, producing commodities for others to add value to later.
But that need not be the case at all.
Even for those who produce "just"
commodities, the promotion of the
entry of more intermediaries into the market can boost competition for their produce and the prices they receive. More than that,
the embedded services model of outsourcing discussed throughout
this book bears witness to how buyer-led programs can help small
farmers add value to primary production and, by satisfying the
quantity, quality, and timeliness requirements of demanding buyers, receive more money. The growers who supply Frito Lay with
potatoes, the fishermen who sell trout to Piscifactoría de los Andes,
the small farmers who grow artichokes for AGROMANTARO, etc.,
no longer fit the development stereotype of "small farmers." Learning by doing, they now resemble more commercial businesspeople
satisfying the requirements of their customers—and, again, earning
more in the process.

Working with a mix of suppliers vs. just small producers. In their yearning to create jobs for the poor, some development programs make a point of working only with small suppliers. Although well intentioned, such a strategy can be counterproductive. In practice, pragmatism is in order.

One of PRA's first clients was a feed company in Huánuco. The company required 200 hectares of corn, but from experience, was wary of relying just on small farmers. PRA therefore facilitated a "package deal." It first identified two reliable medium-sized farms that could meet roughly one half of the company's requirements. It then brought small farmers on board, helping them produce to the same quantity, quality, and timeliness yardsticks as their larger counterparts. In essence, the inclusion of the two medium-sized farms was the "price of admission" to make the broader transaction go. Working just with small producers would have been a non-starter.

Spineless artichokes are new to Ayacucho, and production there began only in 2006. Nutreina, an agro-processing company, first rented land to manage itself. It also helped finance the input costs of an association of small farmers that wanted to join the operation. Most of those farmers were used to growing traditional varieties of potatoes, which do not require anywhere near the constant attention and technical know-how that artichoke production does. Most obtained poor yields from their artichokes, and Nutreina had to assume the loss.

In 2007, a second company, AiB, learning from Nutreina's experience, rented 73 hectares of land to manage completely on its account. It compared yields with cuttings and seedlings, experimented with different planting densities, and conducted soil and water analysis to identify the practices that worked best. PRA bore a portion of the technical assistance costs and, perhaps most importantly, helped ease the entry of AiB into an area highly suspicious of outsiders.

A year later, local farmers saw with their own eyes that it was possible to grow artichokes successfully in the area, that artichokes generated farm income more or less continuously over a two-year period, that they generated employment for the community, and that it was profitable enough to pay labor good wages with full social benefits. Only then, therefore, with the evidence from the initiative of a large company to look at, did local farmers shift into artichokes in a serious way. Interestingly, AiB gave the farmers cuttings to ease their entry and assigned technicians to supervise production on their holdings—a win-win proposition.

Tourism and handicrafts vs. other goods and services. Although this book urges development practitioners not to pre-pick sectors or products to work with, transactions in tourism and handicrafts have special characteristics worthy of mention. There are exceptions, but much development practice in tourism suffers from the "build-it-and-they-will-come" mindset. In country after country, the thinking of tourism proponents tends to run along the following lines: "Demand is not the problem. It is that our attractions are not attractive enough. If we had more and better facilities, accommodations, etc., tourists would come and enjoy them." In other words, more and better supply would attract additional demand.

Just as supply-push thinking can have negative repercussions elsewhere, it can in tourism. White elephant hotels throughout the world bear witness to what can happen if one is not careful.

A bedrock of the buyer-led approach is that one cannot take demand for granted, but must identify the buyer(s) before engaging in supply-side activities. In tourism, that is easier said than done. Since demand normally is so diffuse, there is indeed a chicken-and-egg problem: how does one know what "the buyer" wants when there are so many of them? But unless one gets at least some approximation of what tourists are looking for—as opposed to what one might like tourists to look for—the investments of buyer-led program clients could come to naught. It is one thing for a big player like the Marriott Corporation to take the risk that tourists will not materialize; it is quite another for a tiny family-owned hotel in Timbuktu—more the kind of client a buyer-led program works with—to do so. All of which makes it incumbent on development practitioners, as well intentioned as they may be, not to lead that client down the primrose path.

One way for a buyer-led program to get at what tourists are willing to pay for is to solicit input from the foreign tour agencies that specialize in sending tourists to its country as well as from tour agencies in the country itself. In these days of direct on-line reservations, tour agencies are obviously not the only source of market-tested intelligence on tourist preferences, but certainly not one to minimize either. Tapping into the intelligence of tour agencies has the virtue that the agencies' livelihood depends on their attuning themselves to what tourists really are looking for. Not only do they need to learn what tourists want before they go on a trip, but often they receive useful feedback afterwards on what they liked, what they did not like, whether they would make a return trip, and, if so, for what.

Even when tour agencies turn out to be solid conduits for delimiting the kinds of tourism activities a buyer-led program might support, it often takes considerable time from the time a client makes an investment until it sees a marked increase in sales. Good business advisors take that expected lag into account, do not put all their eggs in the tourism basket, and balance out their support for tourism activities with support for other transactions with much quicker returns.

An additional factor differentiating work in tourism from work in other sectors is the multiplicity of actors typically involved. As Danilo Cruz-DePaula described his work in sustainable tourism in the Dominican Republic,

> [S]takeholders are extremely varied and many of the key stakeholders are outside the traditional supply or value chain (tour operators, hotels, etc.). In fact, many of them have not thought of themselves as having anything to do with tourism when in fact they are central to it (municipalities, environmental NGOs). You have to have some type of instruments for bringing these folks together and make them see their interdependence.[231]

Unlike businesses in some other sectors, most tourism businesses cannot operate independently of the environment around them—indeed, their very viability often depends directly on it. Put another way, working in tourism generally involves what economists call "externalities," which can have both positive and negative ramifications. It also makes industry—or cluster—approaches to solving clients' growth problems more attractive than in other sectors (see the discussion associated with Exhibit 2.8 in Part II). All other things equal, though, the involvement of more actors can make the achievement of concrete results increasingly iffy and push off even farther into the future the time such results will materialize. All of which argues, again, for caution about getting involved in tourism in the first place—and if you do, for keeping your focus squarely on specific transactional problems as a way to assure that what you do does not diffuse itself into activities with little real return.

Like support of tourism businesses, support of handicraft businesses has a number of attractions. Not only do handicrafts, like tourism, offer the promise of generating quality employment for currently poor people; often they can contribute to the preservation of artisans' cultural traditions and heritage. But, again, handicraft transactions are normally not quick turn-around propositions. Just figuring out what customers want often requires sending samples and getting feedback and requests for changes—a process that can repeat itself not once but a number of times.

In summary, both tourism and handicrafts are alluring development-wise, and often it makes good sense to support specific transactions. In each case, however, a long lag can occur between initial activities and results, which, experience shows, many development practitioners are not prescient enough to recognize at the beginning. A word to the wise, therefore: do not rule out support for tourism and handicraft transactions *a priori*, but when you do get involved, know what you are getting into.

Cutting your losses vs. throwing good money after bad. Despite all attempts to winnow out losing business propositions and to make the transactions a buyer-led program does support successful, some do not bear fruit. When a transaction runs into trouble, it is tempting to invest more in the operation to save it. Sometimes that strategy makes sense, but sometimes a business advisor has to face up to reality and recognize that, for whatever reason, the transaction will not work.

Most development programs—buyer-led programs included— are quick to broadcast their successes, not their failures. No buyer-led program can expect to bat 1.000. The author once asked a representative of Fundación Chile, a pioneering organization known internationally for its success in creating and disseminating innovative busi-

> "[A] true expert was one who admitted there weren't any answers."
>
> Colin Cotterill, *Anarchy and Old Dogs* (New York; Soho Press, Inc., 2007), p. 9.

nesses, what percentage of its business investments have failed. The respondent said about half. As a point of comparison, in 2008 PRA calculated the percentage of its clients that had fallen by the wayside. Coincidentally, that figure turned out to be 50 percent—though, interestingly, the percentage was much higher early in the program than later, presumably reflecting the experience the program gained in deciding which clients to support in the first place.

In implementing a buyer-led program, one needs to be realistic, recognizing that some opportunities will not pan out. A good business advisor focuses on opportunities with high-probability payoffs in sales and jobs, minimizing the time and energy spent in propping up laggards.[232]

Getting your hands dirty vs. doing a study. Some business advisors think too much, trying to dot every i and cross every t before making decisions. Business opportunities require due diligence analysis, of course, but sometimes development professionals let fear of failure paralyze them into inaction. In such instances, perfection can become the enemy of the good. In principle, there is always more information one can gather to inform decisions, but at some point, the cost of acquiring more information can outweigh the benefit of same, and one has to bite the bullet and act. Experience suggests the wisdom of resisting the temptation to over-think things: in the event something untoward happens along the way, there is generally scope for making mid-course adjustments.

Following through vs. focusing just on demand. The buyer-led approach puts so much of a premium on tying down demand that sometimes its practitioners fall into the trap of thinking that once a buyer makes a purchase commitment, the job of the business advisor is done. Nothing could be farther from the truth. The success of buyer-led program-supported transactions typically hinges on the follow-through, especially in helping suppliers meet buyer requirements. Put another way, the success of this very much demand-driven approach depends directly on what happens on the supply side! A business advisor that neglects the supply side does so at his or her peril.

Shortly before its conclusion, an independent third party conducted a final evaluation of PRA. During it, the agricultural agronomist on the evaluation team observed that PRA had provided much closer and more effective agricultural extension than traditional supply-side programs—a very intriguing finding, to say the least.

One particular kind of follow-through is common enough to merit special mention. Under the embedded services model, connector firms provide inputs to suppliers with the understanding that they will subtract the cost of those inputs from the market price of the final product at the time of delivery. Sometimes the delivery price is spelled out in a formal contract between buyer and seller; sometimes it is not. Regardless, when the time comes for delivery, it is common for other buyers to approach the suppliers, offering them the going market price, not discounted for the cost of the inputs. Many suppliers find the proposition to "cut and run" very tempting—especially when the going market price turns out to be considerably higher than that agreed to at the beginning of the operation. In societies without strong contract protection, the original connector firms have essentially no recourse against such eventualities.

When rule of law is weak, the buyer-led program business advisor is often the only neutral party that can gain the trust of the two parties to a deal and hold the fledgling relationship between buyer and seller together. In PRA's first year, the program earned its stripes precisely by resolving a problem of that kind. An agricultural processing firm had advanced inputs to bean producers in Cajamarca. Between planting and harvest, the market price for beans rose to a level much higher than either party had anticipated months before, when they signed a contract to seal the deal. At first, the processing company took the position that a contract was a contract, and they would pay the bean growers exactly what they had agreed to, not a penny more. Since the price had risen so much, the bean growers told the company its offer was exploitative and threatened to go elsewhere. To keep the possibility of a long-term relationship intact, PRA intervened as the honest broker, eventually getting each party to back away from its initial bargaining position, and move forward together. If PRA had stayed on the sidelines, there is little doubt that the whole deal would have fallen apart.

The Cajamarca bean example is typical of a phenomenon that takes place worldwide. Not just in Peru, but anywhere, a good business advisor accompanies buyers and sellers right through to the end. As Part II argues forcefully, transactions require trust, and this is one instance in which that truism is especially *à propos*.

Results vs. process. Some buyer-led programs put so much stress on getting Client Growth Plans signed that the implementation of the plans becomes almost an afterthought. Again, keep the focus on results, not on process, and follow through to the end.

"I" vs. "we." Some development programs place such emphasis on cooperation, collaboration, and coordination—the three Cs—that accountability becomes diffuse and everybody is in charge and nobody is in charge. A good business advisor accepts full accountability for the performance of his or her clients. He or she gladly helps others, but with the understanding that each program-supported business transaction has its buck stop with one advisor.

Specifics vs. generalities. In development circles, it is common to hear statements like, "this country does not have any entrepreneurs" or "there are no niche markets out there with buyers willing to purchase the small quantities our clients can supply." Such sweeping generalities, which often amount to pretexts for inaction, are antithetical to the buyer-led approach. Not only does the approach focus on specifics, but it adopts the mindset of the Searcher precisely to prove such statements wrong.

Respecting clients vs. preaching to clients. Last, but certainly not least, good business advisors recognize that clients normally know much more about their businesses than they ever will. Good business advisors do not preach to their clients but facilitate deals, helping clients get to the essence of their problems and working creatively with them to solve those problems.

Attacking Systemic Problems

As this book notes throughout, sometimes clients' binding constraints are not business problems in the normal sense of the word, but ones that call for systemic solutions. The systemic solutions in question typically have to do with issues of policy, especially laws, norms, and regulations governing economic activity.

As Part II argues, a buyer-led program does not enter the policy arena lightly. Development experience is rampant with examples of programs spending lots of time and energy on policy concerns and, in the end, having very little to show for it. Support for policy activities, just like support for business activities, requires due diligence beforehand, that is, an assessment whether the program can realistically expect to be successful in helping bring about desired policy change at reasonable cost. How, operationally, does a buyer-led program do that?

> "Never measure the height of a mountain, until you have reached the top. Then you will see how low it was."
>
> Dag Hammarskjöld, *Markings*, translated by Leif Sjöberg and W.H. Auden (New York: Alfred A. Knopf, Inc., 1964), p. 7.

In essence, there are two key steps. The first is to determine whether a critical mass of clients exists to justify the program getting involved. Is the initial client's problem an isolated case or are there other businesses both interested in and likely to benefit from the policy change in question? Is there enough interest and commitment for them to form a coalition to work on the issue? The second step is to estimate whether the economic benefits resulting from the policy change are likely to be large enough to justify the cost. Realistically, would the blood, sweat, and tears involved be worth it?

Buyer-led programs have gone about identifying clients' key policy constraints in different ways. As Chapter 10 explains, PRA canvassed its Economic Service Centers, culling what business advisors had ascertained from individual contact with clients throughout the country. For its part, COTS consolidated the opinions potential clients had expressed in exploratory interviews. The two approaches allowed the programs to identify the policy issues of most importance to clients, but, in and of itself, did not gauge the degree to which clients would commit themselves to work for change. In Peru, three of PRA's clients spearheaded the creation of the Tocache Group to lobby the central government to finance the rehabilitation of the Fernando Belaunde Terry Highway. That evidence of commitment, together with the high priority that emerged for roads from PRA's canvassing of its centers, made road policy a natural point of focus for the program. Chapter 10 discusses how that focus played out in practice.

The formation of a coalition of businesspeople willing to work for policy change is desirable, but not always essential to leverage government action. For example, there was no need for a coalition of businesspeople to lobby the city of Ciudad del Este to pave the 200 meters of access road to the proposed site of the $15 million plastics factory. The numbers spoke for themselves, and Paraguay Vende was able to prompt government action with a very modest investment of time and energy on its part.

More often than not, effecting change for just one company is not so easy. In Peru, a slaughterhouse in Arequipa received a purchase order for alpaca meat from an exotic food company in Germany. The plant was HACCP (Hazard Analysis and Critical Control Point) certified, but, according to the norms of the Peruvian phyto-sanitary agency, alpaca is a wild animal, and for that reason illegal to export. PRA approached the agency to see if it would be possible to amend the regulation in question, but soon realized that doing so would be an uphill battle whose cost might not compare favorably with the exports likely to result.

Although no buyer-led program has done so to date, the ideal mechanism for weighing benefits against costs would be what notionally one could call a "Multiple Client Growth Plan." The multiple client plan would resemble Client Growth Plans in that it would formalize the financial commitments of the buyer-led program and its client partners to solve the policy problem at hand, as well as the benefits—sales and jobs, for example—that the parties expect to result. Short of such formality, a good buyer-led program cannot afford to make the goodness of the proposed policy change an article of faith—it must make some attempt, even a back-of-the-envelope attempt, to quantify and compare benefits and costs. In Peru, previous studies suggested strongly that the rehabilitation of key roads would have high economic rates of return. The existence of such analyses made the decision to go forward relatively stress-free. Admittedly, it is difficult to know with exactitude beforehand just how much a program will need to invest and for how long. To err on the side of conservatism, it may be wise, therefore, to discount expected benefits by the program's best "guesstimate" of the operation's probability of success, and, thus, prevent enthusiasm for change from blinding proponents to the difficulties involved.

Organizationally, a buyer-led program's Policy Unit is the logical candidate to lead the policy charge. At the beginning of the program, no one knows for sure exactly which policy issues will assume importance, which, again, suggests that the staffing of the Policy Unit be "lean and mean" at the outset. Once policy priorities become clear, however, it makes arrant sense to bring in experts specifically to address those issues—again, letting the problem determine the solution, not vice-versa. Such a strategy would appear common sense, but it stands in contrast to practice in other programs. Many development programs propose to build capacity in the private sector to lobby government for change, but almost in isolation from the specific issues that call for lobbying. Experience suggests the wisdom of focusing on the what first, and then staffing up accordingly.

16

Tracking and Sharing Progress

This final chapter of Part III discusses how to:

Make monitoring and evaluation a management tool
Communicate with the public, especially success stories

Make Monitoring and Evaluation a Management Tool

A colleague of the author once canvassed a group of development professionals on the first words that come to their minds when they hear the term, "monitoring and evaluation." In alphabetical order, the responses included "analysis," "baseline," "burdensome," "client requirement," "data," "database," "impact," "indicators," "metrics," "milestones," "number-crunching," "outputs," "qualitative," "quantitative," "questionnaires," "reporting," "results," "surveys," and "targets." Notable by their absence were two words that lie at the heart of the buyer-led approach to monitoring and evaluation, "accountability" and "management."

Like most such systems, buyer-led program monitoring and evaluation systems collect data, process them, analyze them, and report results in user-friendly form to program funding agencies. Under the buyer-led approach, however, monitoring and evaluation is first and foremost a management tool. It compels buyer-led programs to make themselves accountable for meeting agreed-upon targets, it helps them identify early on the problems that stand in the way of meeting those targets, and it suggests ways to solve them. Monitoring and evaluation is embedded in a buyer-led program's operations; it is not an isolated data-crunching operation. In buyer-led programs, most business advisors eschew the development profession's knee-jerk reaction to monitoring and evaluation as an infringement on the "real" work of development. With performance incentives in the offing, self-interest leads advisors to care very much about program accomplishments.

> "If we really want to do work that makes a difference, work that has some effect, then we have to know whether it is working. ...And if you do it well, you don't only want to know what works; you want to know how it works."
>
> Judith Rodin, Rockefeller Foundation
>
> Jon Gertner, "For Good, Measure," The Money Issue, *New York Times*, nytimes.com, March 9, 2008.

Exhibit 3.35 summarizes the key elements of monitoring and evaluation under the buyer-led approach.[233] The basic unit of measure is the clients of the Business Promotion Offices. As discussed above, most times clients are connector firms, but, depending on the case, they can also be those firms' suppliers. In contrast to programs that rely on statistical data from third parties or that collect survey data themselves, buyer-led program performance data derive directly from clients. When a business advisor crafts a Client Growth Plan with a potential client, he or she also establishes a client-specific baseline. The baseline typically consists of the client's sales and attendant employment over the previous 12 months. Some buyer-led programs also break out export sales and investment, and most disaggregate employment data by gender. For ease of exposition, the discussion here limits itself to sales and jobs. Each month after the

Exhibit 3.35 Basic Elements of Monitoring and Evaluation Under the Buyer-Led Approach

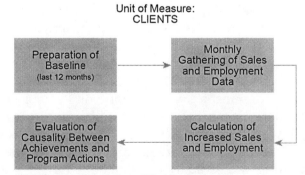

Unit of Measure: CLIENTS

- Preparation of Baseline (last 12 months)
- Monthly Gathering of Sales and Employment Data
- Calculation of Increased Sales and Employment
- Evaluation of Causality Between Achievements and Program Actions

Source: USAID/Peru Poverty Reduction and Alleviation program.

Client Growth Plan goes into effect, the business advisor reports the client's gross sales and direct employment the previous month. The Monitoring and Evaluation Unit verifies all data from the Business Promotion Offices, both the baseline and the data reported each month. It also looks at attribution, assessing the causality between program actions and results in relation to the development logic laid out in the Client Growth Plans. Finally, it systematizes results in user-friendly form to facilitate tracking and informed decision-making.

The discussion that follows describes the work of the Monitoring and Evaluation Unit in detail.

Reviewing Client Growth Plans. The Client Growth Plan defines the relationship between a buyer-led program and its client. Before the Client Growth Plan goes into effect, the Monitoring and Evaluation Unit reviews it, not only for the plausibility of the data therein, but for its development logic, that is, whether the program actions proposed in the plan are likely to bring about the hypothesized results in a cost-effective way (see Exhibit 3.25). If the plan holds water, the Monitoring and Evaluation Unit signs off on it. If not, the unit withholds its clearance and requests that the business advisor and client in question tighten it up or, in the extreme case, go back to the drawing board.

Verifying baselines. Baselines are the values of indicators of interest before any program actions take place. They give development practitioners snapshots against which to measure progress in the future. In a buyer-led program, the "zero moment" occurs when the business advisor and the client sign the Client Growth Plan. Shortly thereafter, the Monitoring and Evaluation Unit meets with the client to verify the baseline in question (for an example of a baseline data form, see Chapter 20).

Verifying monthly sales and employment results. Every month, Business Promotion Offices report the gross sales and direct employment of their clients the previous month to the Monitoring and Evaluation Unit. In some buyer-led programs, the BPOs report the results by email, which the Monitoring and Evaluation Unit enters in the program's data base. Other programs use a Web-based interface, which allows business advisors to enter their clients' results directly into the system on line, thereby eliminating the burden of and potential error associated with double entry. Either way, the data entered initially are provisional until the Monitoring and Evaluation Unit reviews them.

At the beginning a buyer-led program, business advisors and monitoring and evaluation personnel alike usually are skeptical that clients will share sales and employment data with program personnel—and if they do, whether the data will be accurate. Throughout the world, businesspeople fear the tax man and, as a result, are skittish about potentially sensitive information wending its way into a tax authority's hands. The nickname Peruvians give to SUNAT, their tax collection agency, says it all: the Gestapo!

Interestingly, this initial concern has rarely played itself out in practice. Why?

First, Client Growth Plans stipulate that buyer-led programs will treat client sales and employment data as confidential. Buyer-led programs have taken that stipulation seriously and stuck to it.

Second, for monitoring and evaluation purposes, buyer-led programs ask only for data on gross sales and employment. They do not ask for profits, which could be problematic.[234]

Third, willingness to share information depends on trust. No magic wand can create client trust overnight, but advisors can foster and build it over time. A key ingredient in building client trust is compliance with the provisions agreed to in Client Growth Plans. In the end, the best way for buyer-led programs to nurture trust is to honor their commitments and help clients achieve contemplated sales increases. Nothing succeeds like success, and nothing builds trust like results. Indeed, clients that hold data close to the chest at the beginning often come full circle at the end: success makes them so proud of their accomplishments that, far from wanting to hide their light under a bushel, they want the whole world to know— and wind up looking to buyer-led programs to help them publicize what they have done!

Fourth, a buyer-led program asks only for sales and employment data related to the line of business it is supporting, which may make up only a fraction of a business's total operations. As a hypothetical example, suppose that a buyer-led program in Bangladesh has a well established shrimp processor-exporter as a client and that its major problem is a paucity of buyers. Suppose that the buyer-led program succeeds in identifying a new customer in Romania willing to purchase all the shrimp the company can supply. Suppose, finally, that the company has never exported to Romania before. For purposes of monitoring and evaluation, the buyer-led program can define the "business" it is supporting as "exports to Romania." By that definition, the baseline is zero, and the new sales attributable to program support are the totality of the company's exports to Romania. Everything else—for monitoring and evaluation purposes, anyway—is irrelevant.

Interestingly, it is easier to draw the distinction between "business" and "line of business" in Spanish than in English. In English, the word, "business," can refer both to a company as a whole and to the various activities in which it engages. In Spanish, a company—*empresa*—can have many lines of business—*negocios*. For monitoring and evaluation purposes, it is the *negocio* that is of interest, not the *empresa*.

As a rule, Monitoring and Evaluation Specialists visit the Business Promotion Offices assigned to them once a quarter and meet with each client two or three times a year. The specialists coordinate their visits with BPO staff who prepare their agenda and schedule meetings with their clients.

Most clients are leery about sharing their books, especially at the beginning of a program. As a consequence, Monitoring and Evaluation Specialists cannot always verify directly the data reported by business advisors, but must bring more nuanced, imaginative approaches to the task. As discussed in Part II, the skills of a financial analyst generally lend themselves more to that task than those of conventional monitoring and evaluation practitioners. In any event, periodic meetings with the client are essential, typically with the owner or manager of a connector firm. Since owners and managers are busy people, the meetings usually are brief, lasting no more than 15 to 20 minutes. In the meetings, the Monitoring and Evaluation Specialists probe to ascertain the veracity of data, to confirm that the support of the program has been instrumental in bringing results about, and to bring to light any problems that are hindering progress. They also solicit suggestions as to how the program can improve.

Monitoring and Evaluation Specialists normally ask clients for their sales figures in writing, ideally as official, sworn declarations. If necessary, the specialists can cross-check data with other sources. In the case of agricultural products, for example, production and sales data must square with the area harvested and the level of technology used. Another way to verify data is to check with a client's buyer. In the case of exports, it may be possible to cross-check customs records.

Once the Monitoring and Evaluation Unit verifies sales and employment data with clients—and makes any necessary modifications—the data become definitive. Monitoring and Evaluation Specialists prepare trip reports after their site visits. The typical trip report includes people and places visited, documentation of the activities the Business Promotion Office has carried out for its clients, the results verified, and recommendations and conclusions. It also documents potential problems for management's attention.

For readers with a penchant for flowcharts, Exhibit 3.36 illustrates the work of the Monitoring and Evaluation Unit step by step.

Exhibit 3.36 Flow Chart of Responsibilities of Monitoring and Evaluation Unit

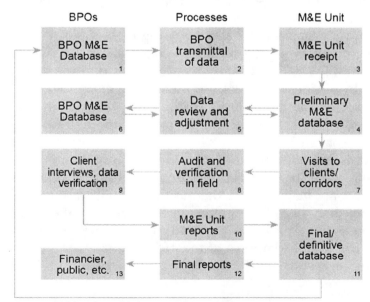

Source: USAID/Peru Poverty Reduction and Alleviation program.

To insulate the Monitoring and Evaluation Unit from pressures to apply less than due rigor in its verification of results, some buyer-led programs have pondered the advisability of outsourcing monitoring and evaluation to a third party. In principle, such an arrangement would guarantee operational independence. In practice, however, it could also build in too much hands-off formalism into the relationship between the Program Director and monitoring and evaluation personnel—and, in the process, undercut the fluidity of open communication required to spot operational problems early and address them in close to real time. For key management decisions, good managers do not want to wait on formal reports from outside personnel. They want information when it is fresh, so that they can solve problems when they are fresh. On balance, experience suggests that it is better to keep monitoring and evaluation in house. The proviso, of course—and it is a big one—is that the Program Director commit himself or herself to maintaining the integrity of the semi-autonomous relationship between the Monitoring and Evaluation Unit and the rest of the program.[235]

Together with periodic reports from the Business Promotion Offices on the operational challenges they face, the intelligence provided by the Monitoring and Evaluation Unit helps inform management decisions like the following:

Identification of personnel for priority management attention. Buyer-led program monitoring and evaluation systems allow program managers to identify underperforming Business Promotion Offices and business advisors. Indicators include repeated failures to meet targets and gravitation toward conventional supply-push development strategies. Many business advisors internalize the approach intellectually, but, initially, at least, are unable to put it into practice. The buyer-led program approach to monitoring and evaluation can help program managers identify such individuals and take remedial action sooner rather than later.

Maintenance of focus on program objectives. At one point, a chief of one of PRA's Economic Service Centers was inclined to dismiss one of his business advisors because of poor organization and work style. But the data from the monitoring and evaluation system showed that the advisor in question was responsible for most of the client sales facilitated by the center. Instead of dismissing the advisor, therefore, the chief gave him the opportunity to improve his work habits, and he continued to exceed sales and jobs targets.

Continuation or termination of relationships with clients. Buyer-led monitoring and evaluation systems also are key for determining whether or not to continue assistance to clients. Program managers need to know whether clients comply with the terms of their Client Growth Plans, and when they do, if the actions in question are bringing about results. If results are not forthcoming, it may be time for both parties to reassess strategy and, in the worst case, agree not to throw good money after bad.

"Success depends on knowing what works."

Bill Gates, Co-Chair, Bill and Melinda Gates Foundation

"When Will We Ever Learn? Improving Lives through Impact Evaluation," Report of the Evaluation Gap Working Group, Center for Global Development, Washington, D.C., 2006, p. ii.

Rarely do development programs have the knowledge base ready at hand to make tough management decisions like these informedly and expeditiously. The buyer-led approach to monitoring and evaluation is definitely an exception to the rule.

Calculating increased sales. Although some cases give rise to the need for more nuanced treatment,[236] calculating increased (or "incremental" or "new") sales is generally straightforward. The basic formula is:

Increased sales = gross sales - baseline sales

A hypothetical example used in a number of induction workshops illustrates the procedure:

The first step is creating the baseline, that is, the sales of the client's line of business during the previous 12 months. If the line of business is very seasonal, it generally makes sense to go back and construct the baseline month by month. If the line of business is not very seasonal, then assigning each month 1/12 of total sales during the last year normally suffices. The example assumes that the line of business has not been seasonal and it is possible to represent the baseline as follows:

Mar 2005	Apr 2005	May 2005	Jun 2005	July 2005	Aug 2005
100	100	100	100	100	100
Sept 2005	Oct 2005	Nov 2005	Dec 2005	Jan 2006	Feb 2006
100	100	100	100	100	100

Source: Joseph Jordan.

Once the buyer-led program and its client sign a Client Growth Plan and the parties begin to take the actions agreed to, the Business Promotion Office meets with the client each month to register total sales for the line of business in question. In the example, the monthly sales are as follows:

Mar 2006	Apr 2006	May 2006	Jun 2006	July 2006	Aug 2006
150	120	100	135	180	110
Sept 2006	Oct 2006	Nov 2006	Dec 2006	Jan 2007	Feb 2007
100	175	150	150	120	110

Source: Joseph Jordan.

Under the assumption that sales have increased as a result of the actions taken (more on that below), it is possible to calculate the increases in sales attributable to the program by subtracting the baseline amounts from the sales for the corresponding months a year later. In the example at hand, the resultant computation is:

Mar 2006	Apr 2006	May 2006	Jun 2006	July 2006	Aug 2006
50	20	0	35	80	10
Sept 2006	Oct 2006	Nov 2006	Dec 2006	Jan 2007	Feb 2007
0	75	50	50	20	10

Source: Joseph Jordan.

Estimating increased employment. Calculating increased employment is more complicated than calculating increased sales. Why? Because, in principle, at least, the increases in employment one has to account for take place at two different levels in a market chain, within the client connector firm and among its suppliers.

Methodologically, calculating the increase in employment that takes place in a client connector firm is identical to calculating the increase in its sales: create a baseline of the employment that took place in the line of business during the previous 12 months, collect data on total employment in that line of business every month thereafter, and calculate the increases in employment attributable to the program as the month-by-month differences between the two.

Getting a handle on increases in employment among a connector firm's suppliers is not so easy. In Peru, for example, it is not at all rare for a connector firm to source from hundreds if not a thousand or more small suppliers. The sheer number of suppliers makes it prohibitive cost-wise to collect data on employment from each and every one. A more economical approach is called for.

One option would be to survey a sample of each connector firm's suppliers, but depending on how many clients a program has, the costs of going that route could mount up quickly.[237] A second option, which PRA and other buyer-led programs have adopted, is to apply employment coefficients derived from technological relationships. Again, perhaps the best way to explain how the approach works is with an example:

> A client firm buys, processes, and sells potatoes. Suppose that the client sells 40 metric tons of processed potatoes, that potato yields in the zone average 20 tons per hectare, that it normally takes 280 person-days to grow and harvest a hectare of potatoes there, and that it normally takes five person-days for the firm itself to process a metric ton of potatoes in its plant. Under those assumptions, it is possible to estimate the employment content of the sale as follows:

280 person-days/hectare x 2 [40/20] hectares =

560 person-days

5 person-days/metric ton x 40 metric tons =

200 person-days

Total   760 person-days

The example demonstrates the applicability of the coefficient methodology for estimating employment not only among a connector firm's suppliers but within the connector firm itself. Most buyer-led programs use it to estimate only the backward linkage portion of employment, but PRA applies it to the client connector firm as well.

In essence, a technological employment coefficient gives the employment required to generate a certain quantity of production. In the case of agriculture, the coefficients often appear in per-hectare form. Sometimes a connector firm knows from how many hectares it is sourcing; often it does not. In the latter case, the logic of the calculation, as in the example, has two steps: so much production requires so much hectareage, and so much hectareage requires so much employment.

Where does a buyer-led program get the coefficients to apply this approach? PRA financed three coefficient studies, one for primary agriculture, one for agricultural processing, and one for non-agricultural pursuits. In each case, technical experts scoured available sources of information, and condensed it in tabular form. Each study cost about $10,000, a relatively small investment for a multi-million dollar program. The resultant coefficients, especially for agriculture, were very much location- and technology-specific. As one might expect, programs that do not cover as broad a spectrum of goods and services as PRA can derive the coefficients it requires more economically.[238]

The natural unit of measure for expressing the technological relationship between employment and production is person-days. Using that measure also makes sense for economic activities that are seasonal in nature, especially agricultural activities. Of course, measuring employment initially in person-days does not rule out the possibility of converting person-days to full-time equivalents

(FTEs) later, though, remarkably, little uniformity exists from one country to another on just how many person-days make up an FTE.

Assessing Attribution of Causality

The Client Growth Plan is the point of departure for assessing whether observed results are attributable causally to the support of a buyer-led program. The Client Growth Plan lays out the development logic of the relationship between the buyer-led program and its client: "If we do x, we expect a y increase in client sales to result." The first check for attribution of causality, therefore, is whether the two parties have done x. If they have not, then there is no way the program's Monitoring and Evaluation Unit can allow the program to take credit for the results in question.

Three real-life examples make the point:

PRA and a textile client signed a Business Plan. It identified lack of buyers as the client's principal constraint. In the plan, PRA committed itself to finding the company new buyers. It did not succeed in doing so. Even though the client's sales went up, PRA's Monitoring and Evaluation Unit did not accept the results as attributable to the program.

In another Business Plan, PRA and its client identified lack of access to raw materials as the client's major problem. Instead of addressing the client's raw material constraint, however, PRA arranged for a training course for the company's sales staff. Sales went up, but PRA's Monitoring and Evaluation Unit refused to accept the results as attributable.

A litchi exporter was one of the first clients of the Market and Trade Development program in Madagascar. Over the first year of its life, the program helped the client improve litchi quality and build relationships of trust with small farmers. At the end of the year, those involved wanted the program to take credit for what they had done. In their haste to get going, however, the parties had not formalized anything in writing. As a consequence, there was no solid baseline to measure progress against and no empirical basis for saying that the program's support had contributed causally to subsequent sales. As a result, the program's Monitoring and

Evaluation Unit refused to include any of the litchi exporter's sales in the results attributable to the program.

The fact that a Business Promotion Office does "something" is not enough to make the case for attribution of causality. What the Business Promotion Office does has to square with the commitments it made in the Client Growth Plan and contribute causally to solving the problems identified therein.

Normally if a Business Promotion Office and its client adhere to the action strategy laid out in the Client Growth Plan and the actions in question contribute to overcoming the major problems identified in the plan, the Monitoring and Evaluation Unit will recognize the increase in sales that results as attributable. Normally, but not always. Suppose, for example, that client sales go up in monetary but not in real terms, and the reason for the jump in prices is market forces outside the management control of either the client or the program. In such case, the results would not be attributable, but, clearly, that kind of scenario is much the exception that proves the rule.

In the end, the job of the Monitoring and Evaluation Unit here is not to obtain absolutely indisputable proof of attribution or to play "gotcha" with the Business Promotion Center for pushing the envelope of causality. Rather, it is simply to give an honest answer to the following question: "Objectively, is it reasonable to believe that by executing the terms of the Client Growth Plan, the program and the client helped bring about sales results that would not have occurred otherwise?" If the Monitoring and Evaluation Unit can answer that question in the affirmative, then the program can take credit for the results in question. If the answer is negative, then the opposite is the case.[239]

When buyer-led programs collaborate with third parties—other development programs, financial institutions, non-governmental organizations, government agencies, etc.—as a way to leverage scarce resources and get more bang for their buck, the question often arises as to which party can take credit for results. The temptation often is to split the results fifty-fifty, that is, to say that the buyer-led program brought about half of total sales and jobs and the collaborating partner the other half. That answer may be a practical way out, but it is much too ad hoc, and begs the whole question of causality. Again, the key criterion for attribution is whether the **program** took the key steps to solve a problem that stood in the way of observed results coming to pass—**regardless of who actually put the solution into practice**. If the program really was the catalyst that made the difference, then it should have no qualms about taking credit for the entire increase in sales and jobs. On the other hand, if it simply helped out on something that was going to happen anyway, the attribution should be zero.

Three examples illustrate the logic.

Example 1. In discussions with a potential buyer-led program client, it becomes clear that poor technological practices are its principal constraint to future growth. As the program looks around for sources of technical assistance to address the constraint, it finds that a sister development program has appropriate people on board and is willing to assign them to assist the client. The collaborating partner provides the technical assistance, but since the buyer-led program identified the problem and took the initiative to correct it, there is no reason that it should not take full credit for the increases in sales and jobs that result (in economese, the value of the marginal product it induced by its action).

Example 2. In discussions with another potential client, the buyer-led program finds that lack of access to financing is the binding constraint. It introduces the client to a local bank and helps it meet the bank's requirements to secure a loan. Although the bank provides the loan, the program is the one that took the make-it-or-break-it steps to solve the problem in the first place and, once again, can take credit for the entirety of the sales and jobs that result.

Example 3. In discussions with a third potential client, the buyer-led program finds that it is about to expand its factory and, specifically, to hire an industrial architect to design the layout. The program offers to pay for the architect, and the client agrees. In this instance, the expansion was going to take place anyway, and all the program did was pick up a portion of the cost that the client would have borne in any case. As a consequence, the increase in sales and jobs that the program can attribute to itself from the increase in factory space is zero.

One final point. It is of interest to note how a buyer-led program's approach to attribution of causality—in fact, its whole approach to monitoring and evaluation—dovetails with the discussion of how businesses grow in Part II. Exhibit 3.37 replicates Exhibit 2.7, but adds time and monetary dimensions to it. The horizontal axis makes explicit that the firm solves its problems over time. The vertical axis makes explicit that as it solve its problems, its sales normally rise. Building on the discussion above, the shaded section represents what a Monitoring and Evaluation Unit could attribute to a buyer-led program if the program came on the scene when the firm encountered Problem 2, it helped the firm solve that problem, and the firm would not have solved the problem otherwise. Under the assumptions that client sales go up and all other things stay the same, what the program can claim as attributable to its support is the increase in sales that the firm now enjoys times the number of years over which that increase lasts—in theory, *ad infinitum*; in real life, of course, much less than that.

Exhibit 3.37 How Firms Grow—and the Connection with Monitoring and Evaluation

Sales	**Problem 4**	Bigger market demands collaboration with others. Firms band together, form cluster.
	Problem 3	A regulatory agency raises objections. Companies lobby for and effect policy change.
	Problem 2	The buyer demands higher quality. The company improves its workmanship.
	Problem 1	A leather company has a limited market. It finds a new buyer, but of a new design. It adjusts its design and expands production.

Source: James T. Riordan.   Time

Exhibit 3.37 also illustrates another key point stressed above: a buyer-led program does not have to stay with a client forever in order to keep taking credit for results. If a program helps solve a problem once and for all, and, as a result, the firm is able to maintain its sales at a higher level indefinitely, there is no reason that the program cannot take credit for that increase indefinitely. Again, the job of a buyer-led program is to facilitate solutions of problems; it is not to form part of a market chain. More than that, the quicker a program can help a client solve a binding problem, the better. From an opportunity-cost perspective, the sooner a program can wrap up its support to one client and attend to other clients, the more results it can bring about.

Managing information. The Monitoring and Evaluation Unit organizes and administers the data that come from the Business Promotion Offices. Having a user-friendly database allows program management to track results in close to real time and to take corrective action, if necessary. It also allows the program to analyze what is happening, break it down in different ways, and respond to requests for reports agilely and rapidly.

When PRA started up, it created its database in MS Access and developed special software, SISMONITOR, for data entry, data analysis, and generation of reports. When other buyer-led programs followed suit, they found it easier to start from scratch than to adapt SISMONITOR to their own, sometimes idiosyncratic ends. Some of the programs found it made sense to use Access, but others found it easier to work in Excel. As discussed above, some programs made their systems Web-based to facilitate communication and reduce error.

The data demands of a buyer-led program do not call for the skills of rocket scientists. For an experienced database developer, constructing a buyer-led program database is a fairly straightforward proposition. And for a good systems analyst with exposure to Access and Excel, administering it is straightforward as well. Although database software may not transfer readily from one program to another, it is replicable at reasonable cost.

Communicate with the Public, Especially Success Stories

For many connector firms and their suppliers, the decision to engage in a business transaction often hinges on whether others they know have already done something similar successfully. Sometimes a good sales pitch can sway businesspeople to go ahead, but in the end, a sales pitch is really nothing more than promises, promises. In contrast, when businesspeople see peers who have already succeeded, a common reaction is, "I can do it, too." The copycatting that has taken place under PRA and other buyer-led programs is evidence of that phenomenon. It also has broader implications for how buyer-led programs communicate, not only with the organizations that finance their work, but with the public at large, especially businesses of different kinds and sizes.

Most development programs communicate with their constituencies. More often than not, though, they stress what they plan to do much more than what they have done. Bulletins reporting on planning workshops are a common case in point. Even programs that report accomplishments often play up more the services they have facilitated than hard-and-fast evidence that they have made a difference in people's lives. For example, a case study of the Equitable Rural Economic Growth Activity in El Salvador reports the results of the program as follows:

> Several of the rural organizations assisted through this activity are still active and are delivering valuable services to their members/clients. The type of services delivered include: agricultural processing, purchase and sale of inputs, and training on organic and other production techniques. Thirteen credit unions provide credit to rural clients. But perhaps the project's most lasting impact was changing attitudes in rural communities and organizations by helping farmers think and act like entrepreneurs.[240]

Better service delivery and changes in farmers' attitudes are not insignificant achievements, but in and of themselves give little indication of whether farmers are really better off than they were before.

Buyer-led programs consciously make a point of reporting, not the number of people who have participated in training courses, for example, but the increases in sales and jobs that the programs' support has helped bring about. They report such results in both aggregate form and personal vignettes. The vignettes illustrate how the increases in sales and jobs have affected individual client households' lives. In the end, it is final results that talk, give development programs their credibility, and make others want to work with them.

A practical manifestation of such a communications strategy is Paraguay Vende's series of informational bulletins (see Exhibit 3.38). Not only has the bulletins' content consisted primarily of success stories, but Paraguay Vende has striven to make their layout and design attractive and of professionally high quality. PRA did much the same. All other things equal, readers pay more attention to something that catches the eye than to inexpensive material.

**Exhibit 3.38 Examples of Paraguay Vende
Informational Bulletins**

Photo: James T. Riordan.

Paraguay Vende stands out for another reason. Although some programs write up their accomplishments, few describe why it is that those accomplishments came about. In other words, they report facts and stories, not the how and why behind them. The Paraguay Vende final report is a notable exception to that rule.[241]

Some programs develop Web pages as their primary form of communication. That may be a good strategy for communicating with funding agencies, which like to see their programs on line, but experience suggests it is not effective—initially, at least—for reaching potential connector firm clients and their suppliers. Even though the world is becoming increasingly electronic, it is unwise to assume that potential clients will go to the trouble of searching for program information on line. Many people, even sophisticated business people, prefer to have something polished and professional physically in their hands. Starting with about its ninth bulletin, PRA shifted from just electronic copy to hard copy as well, and made sure the print versions got out to the business community. In retrospect, that decision was a turning point in getting the program recognized widely.

Reporting success stories is very well and good, the reader may object, but what about a program's early days, that is, when it does not yet have success stories to share? Clearly, informational materials are essential, but experience suggests caution is in order. If a program over-promises at the beginning, it can raise expectations to levels impossible to meet later and damage the program's reputation long term. All other things equal, it is advisable to maintain a low communications profile at the outset and focus on the implementation challenge of getting some quick successes out the door. Once those success stories are in hand, then it makes sense to move aggressively into the public domain, using direct, plain language—not development jargon—to convey what the program has done. Once the success stories become known, experience often bears witness to a marked change: instead of program personnel having to run around knocking on potential clients' doors, potential clients start knocking on their doors. Nothing speaks more to the seriousness and worth of a program than past success.

Exhibit 3.39 presents the "fact sheet" that the Caribbean Open Trade Support program has used to acquaint potential clients with the kinds of business advisory services it provides. The fact sheet is not flashy, but it conveys clearly what the program does, how and under what conditions it does it, and why.

Focusing on final results also applies to communications with funding agencies. Good funding agencies take the mantra, "managing for results," seriously. Yes, they hold their implementation partners accountable, but instead of micromanaging their activities, they keep their eye squarely on a very limited number of big picture results. USAID/Peru is a good example. In PRA's early years, USAID/Peru asked its implementation contractor to report results every six months. The format of the report was one table: sales, jobs, and investment broken down by economic corridor. Period.

**Exhibit 3.39 Fact Sheet, Caribbean
Open Trade Support Program (page 1 of 2)**

≡USAID
FROM THE AMERICAN PEOPLE

**Caribbean Open Trade Support (COTS):
Business Advisory Services**

What is COTS? Caribbean Open Trade Support (COTS) is a program funded by the United States Agency for International Development (USAID). COTS is designed to enhance private sector competitiveness by increasing company sales, reducing administrative barriers to doing business, and developing trade opportunities. COTS' primary activities are currently in Antigua and Barbuda and in Dominica.

What support does COTS provide to private sector firms? COTS provides business advisory services to client firms to increase sales. COTS assists clients to identify and remove constraints inhibiting sales growth through focused and cost effective support. Specific support from the project is tailored to removing the constraint or "bottleneck" that inhibits a specific business transaction. Services range from business mentoring and networking assistance to providing local, regional, or international consultants.

How does COTS deliver services? In Dominica, COTS works through ICMS Ltd., a local business service provider, to deliver advisory services to clients in cooperation with the COTS team. In Antigua and Barbuda, COTS directly provides and manages advisory services through its staff and network of consultants. Each client has a business advisor who is responsible for working with the client to eliminate constraints that inhibit growth. Although specialized consultants may be brought in, the business advisor serves as the key point of contact for the client firm, and monitors and manages any intervention with the firm. Confidential data shared between clients and COTS is not shared with third parties. However, publicly available information and the general nature of COTS' interventions may be shared with other economic development partners.

What is the cost of services provided by COTS? COTS requires that firms receiving assistance share information about sales, investment, employment, and production generated by the provided services. COTS also requires that firms receiving assistance share in the cost of each intervention.

Does COTS provide any kind of financing? COTS does not offer any kind of direct financial assistance for clients. However, COTS may assist clients in identifying and developing potential sources of finance.

**Exhibit 3.39 Fact Sheet, Caribbean
Open Trade Support Program (page 2 of 2)**

When does COTS deliver services? COTS works with a client based on the potential level of increased sales that will reasonably result from COTS' investment and client commitment to remove a constraint. After a constraint is identified for removal the business advisor calculates the amount of sales that would reasonably result from the removal of the constraint following program support. Once the business advisor and the client agree upon an intervention and the commitment of each party to remove the identified constraint, the business advisor puts this into an agreement for signature by both parties.

Why does COTS offer services to private sector firms? COTS offers business advisory services to firms to increase sales and competitiveness. At the end of the program, COTS envisions a more vibrant private sector that is more entrepreneurial, globally competitive, entering new markets, offering new products and services, expanding employment opportunities, and channeling new investment to expand business activity.

How does COTS measure success? COTS' success is measured by the increase in sales and investment that program activities generate.

Contacts

COTS Antigua	COTS Dominica
Gambles Medical Center	42-2 Kennedy Avenue
St. John's, Antigua	Independence Street
Phone: 268-460-2687	Roseau
Fax: 268-562-6687	Commonwealth of Dominica
	Phone: 767-440-4884
	Fax: 767-440-4887
Inquiries: info@usaid-cots.com	

PART IV

Examples

"Rules make the learner's path
long, examples make it short and
successful."

Seneca

http://thinkexist.com/quotes/seneca

Inculcate Market Chains as an Operational Framework for Action

Exhibit 4.2 presents a variation of the market chain framework for Paraguay where cooperatives play a major role.

Exhibit 4.2 What Do We Do?

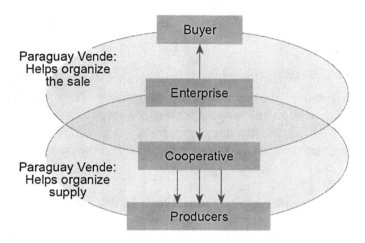

Source: USAID/Paraguay Vende program.

17

Getting Started

This fourth part of *We Do Know How* contains materials that have proven of use in different buyer-led programs. They include examples and variations of forms and templates discussed in Part III as well as other, supplementary material.

The structure of Part IV mirrors the chapters of Part III.

Develop a Common, Shared Framework and Vision

Exhibit 4.1 presents an umbrella framework used in the Micro Enterprise Development Initiative (MEDI) in Armenia.

Exhibit 4.1 Business Promotion Offices' Role

BPOs identify buyers of products and services

BPOs assist clients in consummating transactions

Demand for production is identified

Demand pulls supply

Client produces what it can sell

BPOs facilitate technical assistance and financing solutions to enable firms to produce to buyers' specifications.

Source: Adapted from James W. Butcher, "Business Development Services: Setting Up and Operating a BDS Center," AMIR Business Development Services Conference and Workshop, USAID/Jordan, Amman, 2005.

Sometimes, supporting market chains requires taking additional links into account. Exhibit 4.3 presents a framework that a program in Uganda developed for that purpose.

Exhibit 4.3 Integrated Enterprise Growth Support Model, Uganda Support for Private Enterprise Expansion and Development Program, 2003

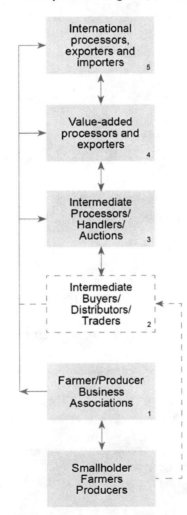

Source: USAID/Uganda SPEED.

Exhibit 4.4 presents a framework for assisting market chains used under the Azerbaijan Business and Development (ABAD) program.

Exhibit 4.4 Assistance Process Overview

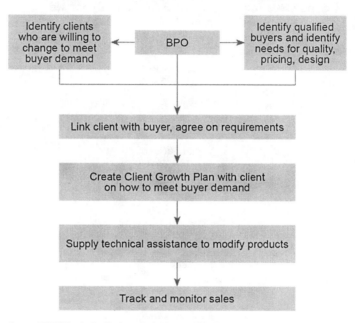

Source: USAID/Azerbaijan Business Assistance and Development program.

Exhibit 4.5 summarizes guidance given to ABAD advisors.

Exhibit 4.5 Induction Workshop Conclusion

Source: USAID/Azerbaijan Business Assistance and Development program.

Exhibits 4.6 through 4.10 present case study examples that have proven useful in start-up workshops to inculcate the operational approach.

Exhibit 4.6 Case Study Example, Azerbaijan

Case Study: ABC Company

One of the Azerbaijan program's Business Promotion Offices has contacted ABC, a large and financially solvent juice processing plant. The company is selling everything it produces. It could sell more. To expand production, it needs more raw material, that is, fruit. The quality of local produce is not up to ABC's standards, so it is about to sign a contract to import fruit from a New Zealand firm—both new varieties and ones that Azeri farmers could produce. The plant's manager is not against sourcing locally, but is worried about working with new, unknown local suppliers. In the past, small producers have preferred to sell first at fresh markets and only second to the processing facility, normally bringing it second-rate, poor-quality produce.

At the same time, a number of the program's Business Promotion Offices have been in contact with fruit producers in their respective economic corridors. Many used to export to Russia and are now without stable buyers. Over the last five years, they have decreased production volumes but still have excess production after each year's harvest. They complain that they are not able to sell in local markets and local processors always pay late. They know that they have to invest in new or update existing irrigation systems. They know little about improved farming techniques and by how much they could increase their yields. The local vocational agricultural school has just closed its doors, which means that it is no longer training farmers or cultivating demonstration plots.

Could the Business Promotion Office(s) help here? Who would be the program's client(s)? What actions would it make most sense to support? Can the program make a difference?

This case study comes from real life, but the names and details are fictitious. The example is for pedagogical purposes only.

Source: James T. Riordan.

Exhibit 4.7 Case Study Example, Bangladesh

Case Study: Khulna Water

Khulna Water processes and exports shrimp. It has been in business for more than two decades, but its sales have been stagnant for a number of years. Its plant is up to international standards and can process five metric tons of shrimp per day, but it operates at only 25 percent of capacity. The company has 80 permanent and 160 seasonal workers. It has buyers in the United States (2/3) and Europe (1/3), but its shrimp is low-quality, so they buy from Khulna Water at a low price. The combination of low prices and idle production capacity means that the company's profit margin is small, even in good years.

Khulna Water's biggest problem is lack of quality raw material— that is, shrimp. Discriminating—and high-paying—buyers require traceability, that is, the ability to track shrimp from farm to factory and ultimately to the consumer. The traders who supply Khulna Water buy shrimp wherever they can get it, and do not worry about traceability. The only way Khulna Water can guarantee traceability to its customers is by developing close-knit relationships directly with shrimp farmers, which is a labor-intensive proposition.

Khulna Water can process fin fish in addition to shrimp, but it does not have a well established network of fin-fish suppliers. To make fin fish a major portion of its business, it would also need to invest in special plastic boxes, which would be expensive.

Last year, it tried to solve its shrimp traceability problem by working directly with 350 shrimp farmers. All went well until the moment of delivery, when the shrimp farmers demanded payment immediately in cash. Even though Khulna Water had ready buyers, it did not have a purchase order in hand. As a result, the company could not obtain bank financing to pay its suppliers, so the shrimp farmers sold their product elsewhere at a lower price. This year, a Japanese client has expressed interest in buying high-quality shrimp, but has not yet given Khulna Water a firm commitment. Given its experience last year, the company is reluctant to invest time and energy in forging close relationships with suppliers only to have them sell to traders at the last moment. The financing problem aside, supplier loyalty is a major problem. In fact, many processors feel obliged to invest in schools in farmer communities to secure their allegiance.

Can the buyer-led program in Bangladesh help this business? What actions would it make most sense for it to support? Can the program make a difference?

This case study comes from real life, but the names and figures are fictitious. The example is for pedagogical purposes only.

Source: James T. Riordan.

Exhibit 4.8 Case Study Example, Bolivia

Case Study: Buenavista Rubber Harvesters Association

The Buenavista Rubber Harvesters Association has 600 members. Its principal occupation is harvesting natural latex from rubber trees. The subsequent production process is rudimentary: members press the rubber manually and dry it in the open air. Neither the harvesting nor the production of the rubber produces any residues, and the association is committed to reforestation.

Production is currently 30 tons a year, which the association sells in its entirety in dried laminate form. Production falls far short of national demand, estimated at 200 tons a year. Approximately 20 industries—among them producers of tires, shoes, and vehicle and machine implements and parts—all use natural rubber as raw material and satisfy their demand almost completely with imports.

Specific problems of the association include:

- The primitive production process results in considerable losses of raw material.
- Deficiencies in quality make the price the association receives for its rubber less than that of imported rubber.
- The quality of the rubber produced by the association varies greatly from one member to another.

Since domestic supply does not satisfy their requirements in either quantity or quality, leading companies in rubber-using industries have expressed a willingness to invest both in plantations and in machinery and equipment.

Could the buyer-led program in Bolivia help here? Who would be the program's client? What actions would it make most sense to support? Can the program make a difference?

This case study comes from real life, but the names and figures are fictitious. The example is for pedagogical purposes only.

Source: James T. Riordan.

Exhibit 4.9 Case Study Example, Dominica

Case Study: Bay Oil Cooperative

Dominica produces 85 percent of the world's bay oil, and Bay Oil Cooperative, established in 1972, accounts for 90 percent of that. Bay oil is used primarily for cosmetics. It derives from bay leaf, which is plentiful in Dominica. The cooperative's processing plant has four employees, but it sources from up to 650 members who harvest bay leaves from trees near where they live. There are a number of other tropical plants in Dominica that, with relatively minor adjustments to its equipment, the cooperative could process into oil as well. To date, the bay oil business has been sufficiently robust that it has not ventured much into other products.

Recently, a British study has raised some health questions about bay oil. Although it appears the risk applies only to cases of use in extremely high quantities, the study has sent shock waves through the market. The cooperative can produce up to 160 barrels of oil a year. Following historical patterns, it produced 120 barrels last year. It appears that its normal buyers will purchase only 45, leaving it an unsold inventory of 75 barrels. A local buyer-led program has made contact with the management of Bay Oil Cooperative, which has brought this set of affairs to the program's attention.

Could the buyer-led program help here? What actions would it make most sense to support? Can the program make a difference?

This case study comes from real life, but the names and figures are fictitious. The example is for pedagogical purposes only.

Source: James T. Riordan.

Exhibit 4.10 Case Study Example, Kosovo

Case Study: Quarry Mining Companies

One day, a business advisor from a buyer-led program in Kosovo was driving along a major road. On one three-kilometer stretch, he noticed large quantities of flat stone piled on the side. He stopped for a look. He discovered hundreds of hectares on either side quarried for beautiful decorative stone.

He started asking questions and searched the Internet for prices of flagstone. He found that prices in Kosovo are ridiculously low—the wholesale price of flagstone is $360 per cubic meter in the European Union and only $70 per cubic meter at the Kosovar mines. The mines currently sell 85 percent of their production domestically. Apparently, most stone exports pass through former peacekeepers "in the know" who ship it out of the country through informal channels.

Subsequent discussions with local mines have revealed that they use very primitive equipment. After they quarry stone, they may leave it outside for years before selling it.

Could the buyer-led program help here? Who would be the program's client? What actions would it make most sense to support? Can the program make a difference?

This case study comes from real life, but the names and figures are fictitious. The example is for pedagogical purposes only.

Source: James T. Riordan.

Organize Operations Geographically

As Chapter 13 discusses, PRA and Paraguay Vende went about defining economic corridors in similar fashion. The big difference is that PRA first defined economic corridors for the entire country and used poverty and economic potential criteria to choose which corridors to work in, whereas Paraguay Vende first applied poverty and economic potential criteria to the country's departments and then defined economic corridors within and among the departments it determined of high priority.

Exhibit 4.11 shows the classification of economic corridors in Peru by connection to extreme poverty and economic potential. In contrast to the corresponding exercise for Paraguay, many more places appear clearly in the northwest quadrant of the table, which suggests that poverty and economic potential do indeed go together sometimes, which in turn can facilitate the selection of what corridors to work in. The initial ten corridors where PRA worked are Ayacucho, Cajamarca, Cuzco, Huancayo, Huánuco, Huaylas, Jaén, Pucallpa, Puno, and Tarapoto. Visually, those economic corridors appear in the map in Exhibit 2.10. As one might expect, over time there have been some additions to and subtractions from the initial list of corridors given priority.

In designing its Azerbaijan Business Assistance and Development program, USAID had objectives similar to those of its counterpart in Armenia. In Armenia, USAID wanted to get a business development program going outside Yerevan. In Azerbaijan, USAID wanted to help get the economy moving in areas relatively untouched by the dynamism of the oil industry and the construction of the pipeline from Baku west to the Georgian border. Given the peculiar shape of the country, the ABAD team decided to concentrate on Azerbaijan's "fingers," as the light areas in Exhibit 4.12 indicate. Programmatically, ABAD focused on linking those lower-hierarchy economic corridors with the burgeoning demand of the pipeline corridor, as well as with markets abroad. It gave particular emphasis to agriculture, arguably the sector most cut off from the dynamism elsewhere in the economy and home to a high proportion of poor people.

Exhibit 4.11 Classification of Economic Corridors in Peru by Economic Potential and Connection with Poverty

Economic Potential

Connection with Extreme Poverty	5	4	3	2	1
5	Cuzco Jaén	Huánuco Pucallpa	Ayachucho Cajamarca Puno	Chachapoyas	Conchucos Huancavelica
4	Tarapoto	Huaylas Iquitos			
3	Arequipa Chimbote Huancayo Ica Tambopata Tacna Trujillo Tumbes				
2	Cañete Huacho				
1	Chiclayo Piura				

Source: Ministry of the Presidency, "Elementos para el Desarrollo de las Ciudades Intermedias en Apoyo a la Lucha Contra la Pobreza Extrema," final draft, Lima, Peru, 1996.

Exhibit 4.12 Demarcation of Economic Corridors in Azerbaijan

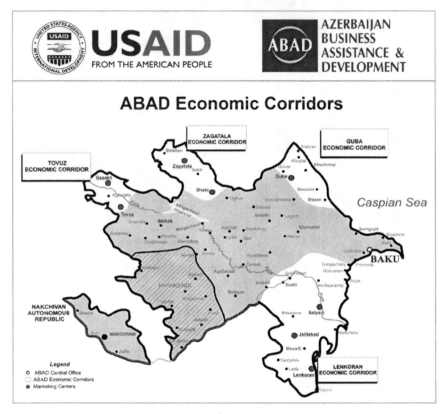

The economic corridors of USAID/Bolivia's Rural Competitiveness Activity (RCA) almost define themselves. RCA looks to generate sales and jobs in licit economic activities in areas that are a source of coca. Almost all coca production in Bolivia takes place in two large valleys that, by their very nature, form economic corridors. The corridors in question appear in Exhibit 4.13.

Exhibit 4.13 Demarcation of Economic Corridors in Bolivia

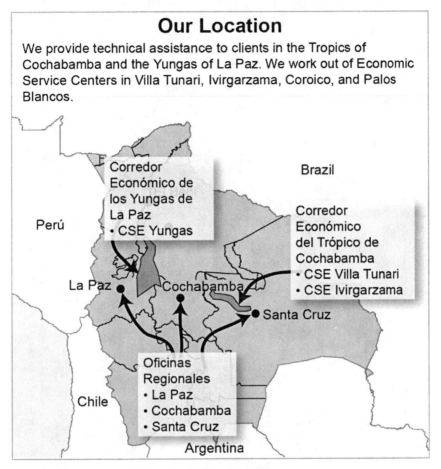

Our Location

We provide technical assistance to clients in the Tropics of Cochabamba and the Yungas of La Paz. We work out of Economic Service Centers in Villa Tunari, Ivirgarzama, Coroico, and Palos Blancos.

Corredor Económico de los Yungas de La Paz
• CSE Yungas

Brazil

Corredor Económico del Trópico de Cochabamba
• CSE Villa Tunari
• CSE Ivirgarzama

Perú

La Paz

Cochabamba

Santa Cruz

Oficinas Regionales
• La Paz
• Cochabamba
• Santa Cruz

Chile

Argentina

Source: USAID/Bolivia Rural Competitiveness Activity.

In designing a buyer-led program for Liberia, Mercy Corps relied on county data to define and rank economic corridors in a manner similar to Paraguay Vende. The economic corridors appear in Exhibit 4.14, and the ranking of the corridors by level of poverty and economic potential appears in Exhibit 4.15.

Exhibit 4.14 Economic Corridors in Liberia

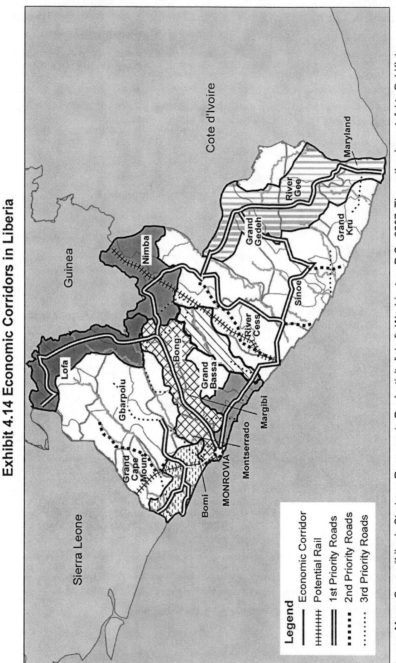

Source: Mercy Corps, "Liberia Strategy: Recovery to Productivity," draft, Washington, D.C., 2007. The author is grateful to Pol Klein for sharing this material.

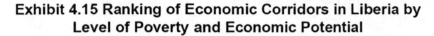

Exhibit 4.15 Ranking of Economic Corridors in Liberia by Level of Poverty and Economic Potential

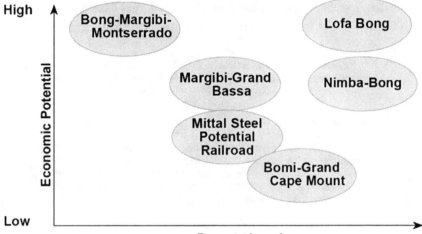

Source: Mercy Corps, "Liberia Strategy: Recovery to Productivity," draft, Washington, D.C., 2007. The author is grateful to Pol Klein for sharing this material.

Put a Conducive Management and Organizational Structure in Place

The following is an example from Afghanistan of a scope of work for a Business Promotion Offices Manager.

**Exhibit 4.16 Terms of Reference, National Director
Afghanistan Accelerated Sustainable Agriculture Program
Business Service Centers
(page 1 of 2)**

Job Summary

The National Director will support the successful delivery of business services through the BSCs to speed sales and employment growth in rural areas of Afghanistan. The objective of this position is to give programmatic and technical direction and to exercise oversight to ensure the BSCs meet their sales and employment targets.

Specific Duties and Responsibilities:

This position will require strong supervisory, communication, and marketing skills to complete the tasks associated with this position's broad responsibilities, which include:

- Conduct a transparent and open competitive bidding process to select the subcontractors to operate the BSCs.
- Select and guide the personnel designated to manage the BSCs.
- Prepare and submit a composite annual work plan for all BSCs.
- Negotiate and assign sales and employment targets to the BSCs.
- Evaluate the performance of the personnel of the BSCs each year.
- Guide the BSCs in the preparation of their annual work plans.
- Evaluate the technical activities of the BSCs and their use of resources, and reassign resources if required to obtain desired results.
- Evaluate and approve requests from the BSCs.
- Give technical support to the BSCs to fill the orders identified by the Buyer and Investment Identification Advisor.
- Provide close guidance, encouragement, and advice for BSC staff as the centers shift from start-up mode to shepherding business deals.
- Conduct continuous monitoring, mentoring, and coaching of BSC staff during implementation.
- Assist with the creation of market linkages between small and medium enterprises and commercial enterprises with established markets.
- Supervise central office technical program staff in supporting the BSCs and enabling them to meet their sales and employment targets.
- Update and advise ASAP's Program Director on successes and issues as required.
- Give public presentations of the program.
- Promote agreements with interested groups such as public sector entities, private companies, and small producers.

**Exhibit 4.16 Terms of Reference, National Director
Afghanistan Accelerated Sustainable Agriculture Program
Business Service Centers
(page 2 of 2)**

Location

ASAP Central Office, Kabul.

Reporting and Work Coordination

The National Director will report to the ASAP Program Director and will carry out his/her job in close coordination with the Buyer and Investment Identification Advisor and the Subcontracts Manager.

Source: USAID/Afghanistan Accelerated Sustainable Agriculture Program.

The following is an example from Afghanistan of a scope of work for a Business Promotion Offices Subcontracts Manager.

Exhibit 4.17 Terms of Reference, Subcontracts Manager Afghanistan Accelerated Sustainable Agriculture Program Business Service Centers

Job Summary

The Subcontracts Manager will oversee the administration of the Business Service Centers.

Specific Duties and Responsibilities:

Under the direction of the National Director, the Subcontracts Manager will:

- Train the personnel of the BSCs in the administrative procedures called for under their subcontracts.
- Explain USAID regulations to the BSCs, especially what expenses are eligible and not eligible for reimbursement.
- Review and approve the BSCs' monthly invoices.
- Track those expenses against budget.
- Monitor the aggregate budget of all BSC subcontracts.
- Manage the files of administrative communications and expenses.
- Visit the BSCs every two months to check original documentation and local procedures.

Location

ASAP Central Office, Kabul.

Reporting and Work Coordination

The Subcontracts Manager will report to the National Director and will carry out his/her job in close coordination with ASAP's Finance, Administration, and Contracts Unit under the direction of the ASAP Deputy Program Director.

Source: USAID Afghanistan Accelerated Sustainable Agriculture Program.

The following is an example from Afghanistan of a scope of work for a Buyer/Investment Unit Manager.

**Exhibit 4.18 Terms of Reference, Buyer and Investment Identification Advisor
Afghanistan Accelerated Sustainable Agriculture Program**

Job Summary

The Buyer and Investment Identification Advisor will facilitate and nurture sustainable commercial relationships between local businesses and producers, and national and international buyers. He/she will promote and facilitate investment in Afghanistan.

Specific Duties and Responsibilities:

Under the direction of the National Director, the Buyer and Investment Identification Advisor will:

- Identify buyers and conduct follow-up activities to "close the deal" between those buyers and local suppliers. Such activities will include monitoring the shipment of samples, field visits, etc.
- Backstop the BSCs in interacting with clients, developing promising business opportunities, helping farmers meet buyer requirements, etc. This function will require periodic trips to the regional offices.
- With the BSCs, identify, structure, and monitor consultancies to help clients overcome supply bottlenecks and consummate deals.
- Evaluate and approve consultant activities when required.
- Give public presentations of the program.
- Promote private investment in Afghanistan, especially in the regions serviced by the BSCs.

Location

ASAP Central Office, Kabul.

Reporting and Work Coordination

The Buyer and Investment Identification Advisor will report to the National Director and will carry out his/her job in close coordination with the BSCs.

Source: USAID Afghanistan Accelerated Sustainable Agriculture Program.

The following is an example from Afghanistan of a scope of work for a Business Promotion Office Chief.

Exhibit 4.19 Terms of Reference, Center Chief
Afghanistan Accelerated Sustainable Agriculture Program
Business Service Centers

Job Summary

The Chief of a Business Service Center will provide programmatic and technical leadership in the facilitation of business services to clients in his/her region to ensure that the BSC meets its sales and employment targets.

Specific Duties and Responsibilities:

Under the direction of the National Director, the Center Chief will:

- Develop an annual work plan for the regional BSC. The work plan will indicate how the BSC will meet the sales and employment targets established by the National Director.
- Approve delivery of technical assistance to BSC clients to help them overcome whatever bottlenecks prevent them from producing to the specifications of buyer orders.
- Develop his/her portfolio of clients capable of expanding sales, employment, and investment.
- Develop and nurture a relationship of trust with those clients.
- Ensure that the BSC's business promoters report client sales and employment each month to the ASAP central office monitoring and evaluation system.
- Give guidance to his/her business promoters.
- Evaluate the performance of the business promoters continuously.
- Decide how the BSC will use its resources to meet its targets.
- Recommend reassigning BSC resources if necessary.
- Evaluate and approve requests from the business promoters.
- Promote agreements at the regional level with public sector entities, private companies, and small producers.

Location

An ASAP Business Service Center in one of the regions of Afghanistan (e.g., Herat, Mazar).

Reporting and Work Coordination

The Chief of a Business Service Center will report to the National Director, and will carry out his/her job in close coordination with the Buyer and Investment Identification Unit Director.

Source: USAID Afghanistan Accelerated Sustainable Agriculture Program.

The following is an example from Afghanistan of a scope of work for BPO Business Advisors.

Exhibit 4.20 Terms of Reference, Business Promoters Afghanistan Accelerated Sustainable Agriculture Program Business Service Centers

Job Summary

The Business Promoters of a Business Service Center will assist client businesses and producers in their region to expand their sales and generate employment.

Specific Duties and Responsibilities:
Under the direction of the BSC Chief, the Business Promoters will:

- Find private clients capable of expanding sales, employment, and investment.
- Develop and nurture a relationship of trust with those clients.
- Identify the bottlenecks that prevent client businesses and producers from growing.
- Develop client-specific business plans to help them overcome the bottlenecks identified.
- Provide technical assistance to BSC clients to help them overcome whatever bottlenecks prevent them from producing to the specifications of buyer orders.
- Identify providers of technical assistance in the local market.
- Report client sales and employment each month to the ASAP central office monitoring and evaluation system.
- Request technical support from the National Director or the Buyer and Investment Identification Advisor.
- Write up success stories that ASAP can communicate to the business community at large.

Location

An ASAP Business Service Center in one of the regions of Afghanistan (e.g., Herat, Mazar).

Reporting and Work Coordination

The Business Promoters will report to the Chief of the BSC and will carry out their jobs in close coordination with the Buyer and Investment Identification Advisor.

Source: USAID Afghanistan Accelerated Sustainable Agriculture Program.

The following is an example from Afghanistan of a scope of work for a Monitoring and Evaluation Manager.

Exhibit 4.21 Terms of Reference, Monitoring and Evaluation Director
Afghanistan Accelerated Sustainable Agriculture Program

Job Summary

The Monitoring and Evaluation Director will manage all activities related to the collection, verification, attribution, and analysis of data on ASAP's two principal results indicators, client sales and the employment associated with them. The Monitoring and Evaluation Director will also contribute to the preparation of internal and external reports.

Specific Duties and Responsibilities:

Under the direction of the ASAP Program Director, he/she will:

- Manage the program's monitoring and evaluation system.
- Supervise the team's Monitoring and Evaluation Specialists and Monitoring and Evaluation Data Manager.
- Program sales and employment targets for the program as a whole and for each year.
- Prepare monitoring and evaluation reports—quarterly, semiannual, and annual—for internal use and for USAID.
- Provide guidance for the preparation of all reports—client baselines, monthly sales and employment reports, etc.—that the BSCs must submit to the Monitoring and Evaluation Team.
- Oversee the verification of the data provided by the BSCs and the analysis of the attributability of the results to program support.
- Monitor progress against targets on a continuing basis.
- Prepare terms of reference for special studies to estimate the impacts of specific instances of program support on economic well-being.
- Represent the program before USAID and other audiences.

Location

ASAP Central Office, Kabul.

Reporting and Work Coordination

The Monitoring and Evaluation Director will report directly to the ASAP Program Director, and will carry out his/her job in close coordination with the National Director.

Source: USAID Afghanistan Accelerated Sustainable Agriculture Program.

The following is an example from Afghanistan of a scope of work for Monitoring and Evaluation Specialists.

Exhibit 4.22 Terms of Reference, Monitoring and Evaluation Specialists
Afghanistan Accelerated Sustainable Agriculture Program

Job Summary

The Monitoring and Evaluation Specialists will verify results data in one-on-one meetings with program clients. They will also assess whether the results are attributable to program support.

Specific Duties and Responsibilities:

Under the direction of the Monitoring and Evaluation Director, the Monitoring and Evaluation Specialists will:

- Assess and make recommendations on the content of client business plans to establish a foundation for the attribution of results.
- Verify in the field the data reported by the BSCs.
- Evaluate the attributability of results to BSC activities.
- Introduce SISMONITOR into the ASAP monitoring and evaluation system (SISMONITOR is the software to track clients' sales and employment).
- Manage SISMONITOR.
- Prepare and submit reports on data verification trips.
- Participate in the preparation of selected impact assessment and other case studies.
- Participate in the preparation of reports for internal use, as well as for USAID.
- Orient BSC personnel in the rationale for and implementation of ASAP's buyer-led approach.

Location

ASAP Central Office, Kabul. The Monitoring and Evaluation Specialists will travel regularly to the regions serviced by the BSCs. Monitoring the development of baselines and business plans, verifying results data with clients, orienting BSC personnel, etc., will require them to spend at least 50 percent of their time outside of Kabul.

Reporting and Work Coordination

The Monitoring and Evaluation Specialists will report to the Monitoring and Evaluation Director and will carry out their jobs in close coordination with the BSCs.

Source: USAID Afghanistan Accelerated Sustainable Agriculture Program.

The following is an example from Afghanistan of a scope of work for a Monitoring and Evaluation Data Manager.

Exhibit 4.23 Terms of Reference, Monitoring and Evaluation Data Manager
Afghanistan Accelerated Sustainable Agriculture Program

Job Summary

The Monitoring and Evaluation Data Manager will maintain SISMONITOR, the software to track the results of the program, and generate all the reports that program management requires to assess the performance of the BSCs and take management decisions.

Specific Duties and Responsibilities:

Under the direction of the Monitoring and Evaluation Director, the Monitoring and Evaluation Data Manager will:

- Maintain SISMONITOR, resolving any functional or operational problems that may occur.
- Support other members of the Monitoring and Evaluation Team in loading and updating data and in receiving data from and sending data to the BSCs.
- Load baseline and monthly sales and employment data.
- Generate monthly, quarterly, semiannual, and annual reports on sales and employment by client, by BSC, by product, etc.
- Update the data base of clients.

Location

ASAP Central Office, Kabul.

Reporting and Work Coordination

The Monitoring and Evaluation Data Manager will report to the Monitoring and Evaluation Director and will carry out his/her job in close coordination with the Monitoring and Evaluation Specialists.

Source: USAID Afghanistan Accelerated Sustainable Agriculture Program.

18

Setting Up Business Promotion Offices

Facilitate an Induction Workshop

Exhibits 4.24 and 4.25 present the agendas of the classroom portions of induction workshops conducted in St. Lucia and Afghanistan, respectively.

**Exhibit 4.24 Saint Lucia Business Development
Induction Workshop (page 1 of 2)
Monday, November 12, 2007**

8:30 am – 9:00 am	Welcoming Address
9:00 am – 9:15 am	Overview of Workshop and Schedule for Week
9:15 am – 10:00 am	The COTS Approach:The Basics
10:00 am – 10:30 am	Coffee Break
10:30 am – 11:15 am	The COTS Approach: Application of the Basics
11:15 am – 11:45 am	Question and Answer and Discussion
11:45 am – 12:00 pm	Instructions for Group Exercise After Lunch
12:00 pm – 1:00 pm	Lunch
1:00 pm – 2:00 pm	Developing Client Growth Strategies: Case Study Examples—Groups
2:00 pm – 2:45 pm	Reporting and Discussion–Groups
2:45 pm – 3:00 pm	Coffee Break
3:00 pm – 3:30 pm	Converting Strategies into MOUs: How-To
3:30 pm – 4:15 pm	Converting Strategies into MOUs: Case Study Examples—Groups
4:15 pm – 4:45 pm	Reporting and Discussion—Groups
4:45 pm – 5:00 pm	Reflections, Wrap-Up, and Plans for Day Two

**Exhibit 4.24 Saint Lucia Business Development
Induction Workshop (page 2 of 2)
Tuesday, November 13, 2007**

8:30 am – 8:45 am	Review of Day One and Introduction to Day Two
8:45 am – 9:00 am	Preparing MOUs: Highlights of Group Exercise from Day One
9:00 am – 9:30 am	Criteria and Procedures for Reviewing MOUs
9:30 am – 9:45 am	Construction of Baselines
9:45 am – 10:00 am	Coffee Break
10:00 am – 10:30 am	Preparing SOWs: How-To
10:30 am – 11:15 am	Preparing SOWs: Case Study Examples—Groups
11:15 am – 11:45 am	Reporting and Discussion—Groups
11:45 am – 12:00 pm	Highlights of Group Exercise
12:00 pm – 1:00 pm	Lunch
1:00 pm – 1:15 pm	Review of Morning and Introduction to Afternoon
1:15 pm – 2:00 pm	Translating SOWs into Action: Procurement
2:00 pm – 2:15 pm	Managing Implementation of SOWs
2:15 pm – 2:30 pm	Firm Impact Monitor—Overview
2:30 pm – 2:45 pm	Weekly Sales Monitoring
2:45 pm – 3:00 pm	Coffee Break
3:00 pm – 3:30 pm	Monthly Entry
3:30 pm – 4:15 pm	Sharing Our Successes
4:15 pm – 4:45 pm	Question and Answer and Discussion
4:45 pm – 5:00 pm	Reflections, Wrap-up, and Plans for Wednesday–Friday

Source: USAID/Caribbean Open Trade Support program.

Exhibit 4.25 ASAP Buyer-Led Approach
Induction Workshop (page 1 of 2)
Sunday, March 16, 2008

9:30 am – 9:35 am	Welcome and Introduction of USAID Representative
9:35 am – 11:00 am	Remarks by USAID Representative & Presentation on Ethics Issues
11:00 am – 11:15 am	Break
11:15 am – 11:30 am	Introduction to Workshop
11:30 am – 12:15 pm	The Buyer-Led Approach: The Basics
12:15 pm – 1:00 pm	Lunch
1:00 pm – 1:45 pm	The Buyer-Led Approach: Application of the Basics
1:45 pm – 2:15 pm	Q&A and Discussion
2:15 pm – 2:30 pm	Instructions for Group Exercise
2:30 pm – 3:30 pm	Developing Client Growth Strategies: Case Study Examples—Breakout Groups
3:30 pm – 4:00 pm	Reporting and Discussion—Breakout Groups
4:00 pm – 4:15 pm	Break
4:15 pm – 4:45 pm	Converting Strategy into Business Plans: Case Study Examples—Breakout Groups
4:45 pm – 5:15 pm	Reporting and Discussion—Breakout Groups
5:15 pm – 5:30 pm	Reflections, Wrap-Up, and Plans for Day Two

Exhibit 4.25 ASAP Buyer-Led Approach
Induction Workshop (page 2 of 2)
Monday, March 17, 2008

9:00 am – 9:15 am	Review of Day One and Introduction to Day Two
9:15 am – 9:45 am	Client Services: Developing Scopes of Work
9:45 am – 10:30 am	Group Exercise
10:30 am – 10:45 am	Break
10:45 am – 11:15 am	Group Exercise Report Out
11:00 am – 11:30 am	Processing Business Plans and SOWs
11:30 am – 12:00 pm	Q&A and Discussion
12:00 pm – 1:00 pm	Lunch
1:00 pm – 1:15 pm	Introduction to Afternoon Session
1:15 pm – 2:00 pm	Making M&E Real: Managing BSCs for Success
2:00 pm – 2:15 pm	Transitioning to the New M&E System
2:15 pm – 2:45 pm	Q&A and Discussion
2:45 pm – 3:00 pm	Break
3:00 pm – 3:15 pm	Telling Our Story: Communicating to the Public
3:15 pm – 3:30 pm	Telling Our Story: Communicating with USAID
3:30 pm – 4:00 pm	From Workshop to Work Plan: A Preview
4:00 pm – 4:15 pm	Wrap-Up

Source: USAID Afghanistan Accelerated Sustainable Agriculture Program.

Exhibit 4.26 is an example from Albania of a Client Growth Plan Checklist.

Exhibit 4.26 Client Growth Plan Checklist,
Competitive Enterprise Development, Rritje Albania

Client(s):	Business Advisor:		Industry:	
1. Who are the Client's buyers?				
2. Complete the cost-effectiveness analysis for each constraint: Binding Constraints Solutions Estimated Cost to CED Estimated Cost to Client (cost-sharing) Increase in Sales Increase in Jobs Estimated Cost-Effectiveness of CED Support				
3. Is the identified constraint really what is preventing sales?				
4. Why can't the Client remove the bottleneck itself? Why does it need our support?				
5. Is there a clear link among the bottleneck, support, and expected sales?				
6. What is the expected timeframe of support to address the constraint?				
7. How long will it be until sales are expected to increase?				
8. For how long will sales increase?				
9. What are the results of the environmental checklist? (attach completed environmental checklist to this CGP checklist)				
10. Does the Client have the ability to break out the sales for the product lines that we propose to support?				
11. Can the Client report sales results accurately each month?				
12. What kind of assistance does the Client need to ensure data accuracy and adhere to reporting expectations (quality and frequency)?				

Date: _____   Approved by: _____

Source: USAID/Albania Competitive Enterprise Development program.

19

Selecting and Working with Clients

Select Clients to Work With

Exhibit 4.27 presents the instructions given to Bolivia's Rural Competitiveness Activity's Economic Service Centers on how to prepare their Annual Operating Plans.

Exhibit 4.27 Example of Annual Operating Plan Instructions (Part 1 of 5)

**Bolivia Rural
Compettitiveness Activity**

**Guidelines
for
Annual Operating Plans 2006**

(due November 30, 2005)

Exhibit 4.27 Example of Annual Operating Plan Instructions (Part 2 of 5)

USAID
FROM THE AMERICAN PEOPLE

Introduction
(not to exceed 1 page)

Objective of Economic Service Center

_____

_____

_____

_____

_____

_____

_____

Exhibit 4.27 Example of Annual Operating Plan Instructions (Part 3 of 5)

USAID
FROM THE AMERICAN PEOPLE

Business Profile: Description
(not to exceed 1 page for each potential client)

1. The market chain.
   Where does the client fit?

_____

_____

_____

2. The business.
   What is the transaction?

_____

_____

_____

_____

**Exhibit 4.27 Example of Annual Operating
Plan Instructions (Part 4 of 5)**

USAID
FROM THE AMERICAN PEOPLE

Business Profile: Analysis
(not to exceed 1 page for each potential client)

1. Client

2. Problems	3. Solutions
A.	A.
B.	B.
C.	C.

4. Expected Results
- Increase in Sales
- Increase in Employment
- Investment
- Number of Families Involved

5. Cost to RCA of Solution

6. Ratio of Increase in Sales to RCA Cost

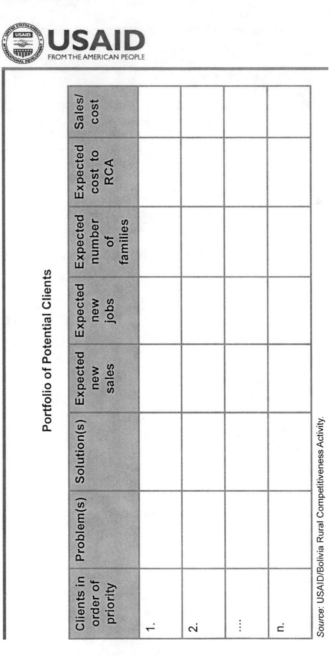

Exhibit 4.27 Example of Annual Operating Plan Instructions (Part 5 of 5)

Portfolio of Potential Clients

Clients in order of priority	Problem(s)	Solution(s)	Expected new sales	Expected new jobs	Expected number of families	Expected cost to RCA	Sales/cost
1.							
2.							
...							
n.							

Source: USAID/Bolivia Rural Competitiveness Activity.

Exhibit 4.28 presents the result of estimating incremental sales-cost ratios to select clients under the Azerbaijan Business Assistance and Development program.

Exhibit 4.28 Portfolio of Clients in Azerbaijan: Projected Incremental Sales-Cost Ratios, by Client

Corridor	Client's name	Product	Projected Sales Increase	Projected Employment Increase	Cost to Solve Problem	Sales to Cost Ratio
Guba Economic Cooridor	Client A	apple	$300,000.00	5700	$10,600.00	28.30
Guba Economic Cooridor	Client B	macaroni, flour	$1,172,880.00	3800	$5,000.00	234.58
Guba Economic Cooridor	Client C	meat	$84,780.00	760	$14,500.00	5.85
Lankoran Economic Cooridor	Client D	flour mill, animal feed	$227,187.00	1520	$14,810.00	15.34
Lankoran Economic Cooridor	Client E	furniture	$239,040.00	3800	$16,000.00	14.94
Lankoran Economic Cooridor	Client F	tomato for export	$5,000.00		$436.00	11.47
Lankoran Economic Cooridor	Client G	animal husbandry	$41,619.00	2280	$910.00	45.74
Lankoran Economic Cooridor	Clieint H	bakery	$77,431.00	13840	$13,000.00	5.96
Tovuz Economic Cooridor	Client I	lime stone bricks	$100,993.00	6650	$21,000.00	4.80
Tovuz Economic Cooridor	Client J	confectionery	$13,558.00	570	$336.00	40.35
Tovuz Economic Cooridor	Client K	grapes	$12,000.00	2074	$1,015.00	11.82
Tovuz Economic Cooridor	Client L	gravel and sand	$3,792,480.00	13300	$30,000.00	126.42

Source: USAID/Azerbaijan Business Assistance and Development program.

Structure Relationships with Clients

Exhibit 4.29 presents the template the Azerbaijan Business Assistance and Development program used for Client Growth Plans, which it called Client Development Plans.

Exhibit 4.29 Client Development Plan Template
Azerbaijan Business Assistance
and Development Program

CLIENT DEVELOPMENT PLAN	MÜŞTƏRININ BIZNES İNKIŞAF PLANI
Date:	Tarix:
Business Advisor:	Biznes Məsləhətçisi:
Client:	Müştərinin adı:
1. Client profile (description of business, market they sell to, strategy for growth)	1. Müştəri haqqında məlumat (biznesin təsviri, satış bazarları, inkişaf strategiyası)
2. Annual revenue (by product or service if more than one)	2. İllik gəlir (məhsul və ya İllik xidmətlər üzrə)
3. Buyers and their specific requirements (price, packaging, variety, quality, size, etc.)	3. Alıcılar və onların xüsusi tələbatları (qiymət, qablaşdırma, növ, keyfiyyət, ölçü və s.)
4. Is buyer willing to make a commitment or sign contract?	4. Alıcı öhdəlik götürməyə və ya müqavilə bağlamağa hazırdırmı?
5. Hindrances to meeting buyer demand	5. Alıcının tələbatının ödənilməsinə mane olan amillər
6. Actions Marketing Center will take to help meet buyer demand	6. Alıcının tələbatının ödənilməsinə kömək etmək üçün Marketinq Mərkəzinin fəaliyyətləri
7.Client commitments to Marketing Center	7. Müştərinin Marketinq Mərkəzi qarşısında götürdüyü öhdəliklər
8. Expected results from Marketing Center activities (including financial projection showing calculations)	8. Marketinq Mərkəzinin fəaliyyətlərindən gözlənilən nəticələr (hesablamalar əsasında hazırlanmış maliyyə proqnozları daxil olmaqla). Hesablamalar göstərilməlidir.
9. Signature	9. İmza
Business Advisor:	Biznes Məsləhətçisi:
Client:	Müştəri:

Source: USAID/Azerbaijan Business Assistance and Development program.

Exhibit 4.30 presents the template Paraguay Vende used for Client Growth Plans, which it called Business Plans (the original is in Spanish).

Exhibit 4.30 Business Plan Template, Paraguay Vende

USAID | PARAGUAY VENDE
DEL PUEBLO DE LOS ESTADOS UNIDOS DE AMÉRICA   PROMOVIENDO DESARROLLO ECONÓMICO

Business Plan			
Business Strategy, Products, and Markets			
Business			
Products & Services			Prepared by
Markets			
Diagnosis of Opportunities			**Actions**
Buyers			
Client			
Intermediaries			
Suppliers			
Work Plan			
Action 1			In Charge of
Action 2			In Charge of
Action 3			In Charge of
Action 4			In Charge of
Results			
Results to Monitor			

Product	Schedule of Projected Sales (in USD, by year)					Total
	Base Year Sales	2007	2008	2009	2010	
	mo.-yr - mo.-yr	mo.2007 - Dec. 07	Jan.08 - Dec.08	Jan.09 - Dec.09	Jan.10 - May 10	

Name of client	Advisor, CSE	Director, CSE	Dir., Paraguay Vende
			Date:

Source: USAID/Paraguay Vende program.

Exhibit 4.31 presents the form Paraguay Vende annexed to its Business Plans to address environmental and labor issues (the original is in Spanish).

Exhibit 4.31 Environmental Checklist, Paraguay Vende (page 1 of 10)

PARAGUAY VENDE
expandiendo ventas y generando empleos

ENVIRONMENTAL REVIEW FORM

ECONOMIC SERVICE CENTER: **DATE:**

1. Description of the Client:

Name:
Location of the business:
Type of business:
Describe the production process, indicating clearly those stages in which raw material contaminants can be used and those in which waste or other kind of contamination can be generated.
Possible support from Paraguay Vende:
Will herbicides, fungicides, or any other kind of pesticides be used in any stage of production? If yes, describe the activity.

**Exhibit 4.31 Environmental Checklist, Paraguay Vende
(page 2 of 10)**

2. Description and Analysis of the Site:

Description of the locality (size, topography, uses, buildings, access roads, public services, etc.):

Describe briefly the status of the environment in the place where it is proposed to give support: inventory of bodies of water and factors that may affect the soil, water resources, air, and human health.

Are there sources of contamination? (describe)

( ) Water runoff

( ) Solid waste

( ) Other

**Exhibit 4.31 Environmental Checklist, Paraguay Vende
(page 3 of 10)**

3. Checklist of Environmental Considerations:

Review carefully the following Environmental Guidelines; they are the basis for assessing impacts well and for describing adequately both impacts and mitigation measures to implement. Point out what impacts are possible and possible mitigation measures related to the support proposed.

Fill in each box using the following ratings:

P =   Positive environmental effects are present
L =   Low level of negative environmental effects
M =   Medium level of negative environmental effects
H =   High level of negative environmental effects
I =   The level of impact is uncertain
NA =   A rating is inapplicable or unnecessary

Exhibit 4.31 Environmental Checklist, Paraguay Vende (page 4 of 10)

SOIL

Environmental Impact	Currently	In the Future
Possibility of erosion (from cropping practices)		
Exposed soils (from crop preparation)		
Soil compaction (because of livestock)		
Loss of organic material (reduction of vegetation coverage)		
Chemical contamination (fertilizers, pesticides)		
Deterioration or depletion of the organic layer due to plowing (especially with intensive weeding)		
Progressive reduction of soil fertility because of the lack of crop rotation		

4. Discussion of environmental considerations: For each L, M, or H rating, explain:	5. Impact mitigation measures and increasing the benefits: Describe the mitigation measures to use for each impact foreseen, and who will be responsible for them.
Nature and severity of the expected impact. Based on what is identified above, describe the type of impact and its intensity	
Areas that will be affected. Based on what is identified above, describe the magnitude of the impact	
Groups or individuals that will probably be affected. Based on what is identified above, describe who will be affected and how much	

**Exhibit 4.31 Environmental Checklist, Paraguay Vende
(page 5 of 10)**

WATER RESOURCES

Environmental Impact	Currently	In the Future
High consumption and reduction of water volume		
Reduction of water retention capacity		
Interruption of water flow (damming, detours)		
Water contamination (fertilizers, pesticides, waste, etc.)		
Contamination from runoff of liquid residues or untreated water		
Contamination from solid waste runoff		
Loss of humidity from agricultural use		
Sedimentation of water bodies		

4. Discussion of environmental considerations: For each L, M, or H rating, explain:	5. Impact mitigation measures and increasing the benefits: Describe the mitigation measures to use for each impact foreseen, and who will be responsible for them.
Nature and severity of the expected impact. Based on what is identified above, describe the type of impact and its intensity	
Areas that will be affected. Based on what is identified above, describe the magnitude of the impact	
Groups or individuals that will probably be affected. Based on what is identified above, describe who will be affected and how much	

**Exhibit 4.31 Environmental Checklist, Paraguay Vende
(page 6 of 10)**

AIR

Environmental Impact	Currently	In the Future
Generation of dust		
Air contamination from particle or gas emission		
Generation of noise		
Generation of odors		
Smoke from burning waste, harvest residues, or grasses		

4. Discussion of environmental considerations: For each L, M, or H rating, explain:	5. Impact mitigation measures and increasing the benefits: Describe the mitigation measures to use for each impact foreseen, and who will be responsible for them.
Nature and severity of the expected impact. Based on what is identified above, describe the type of impact and its intensity	
Areas that will be affected. Based on what is identified above, describe the magnitude of the impact	
Groups or individuals that will probably be affected. Based on what is identified above, describe who will be affected and how much	

Exhibit 4.31 Environmental Checklist, Paraguay Vende (page 7 of 10)

HUMAN HEALTH

Environmental Impact	Currently	In The Future
Water-borne diseases (infectious vectors)		
Diseases caused by use of agrochemicals		
Other possible causes of illness or accidents		
Use of dangerous materials (toxic agro-chemicals, corrosives, explosives, medical/pharmaceutical material, etc.)		
Possibility of accidents due to restricted areas, machinery use, unprotected areas, etc.		

4. Discussion of environmental considerations: For each L, M, or H rating, explain:	5. Impact mitigation measures and increasing the benefits: Describe the mitigation measures to use for each impact foreseen, and who will be responsible for them.
Nature and severity of the expected impact. Based on what is identified above, describe the type of impact and its intensity	
Areas that will be affected. Based on what is identified above, describe the magnitude of the impact	
Groups or individuals that will probably be affected. Based on what is identified above, describe who will be affected and how much	

**Exhibit 4.31 Environmental Checklist, Paraguay Vende
(page 8 of 10)**

6. Environmental Decision Recommended:

	No significant negative environmental impacts are expected; the analysis of the appropriateness of Paraguay Vende support can continue **(No impact)**
	Environmental impacts can be eliminated or reduced to acceptable levels through impact mitigation measures foreseen and agreed upon in this evaluation; the analysis of the appropriateness of Paraguay Vende support can continue **(Minor impacts)**
	Significant environmental impacts are likely and require additional environmental study; a Project Environmental Evaluation will be prepared
	Environmental impacts are likely, and neither their mitigation nor new alternatives are feasible; Paraguay Vende will not support this business

Exhibit 4.31 Environmental Checklist, Paraguay Vende
(page 9 of 10)

7. Checklist of Labor Rights (ADS 225.3.2)

Fill in each box using the following ratings:
C = Complies
N = Does not comply
I = Uncertain or not verifiable
NA = A rating is inapplicable or unnecessary

Theme	Component	
Right of Association (ILO 87; ILO 98)	The company respects the right of its employees to form unions, and to be members of a union of their choosing, as well as to bargain collectively.	
	The company guarantees non-discrimination against the representatives of their personnel, and that those representatives have access to the workers in their place of work.	
Forced Labor (ILO 29; ILO 105)	The company does not use or sponsor the use of hard labor, nor does it require that its personnel leave in its keeping "deposits," or identity documents, when they start work with the company.	
Child Labor (ILO 138; Law 213)	The company does not use or support the use of laborers less than 15 years old (except for family enterprises and professional schools).	
	The company does not use or support the use of laborers less than 18 years old in dangerous or unhealthy work.	
	The company does not use or support the use of laborers less than 18 years old after ten o'clock at night or before six o'clock in the morning.	

Exhibit 4.31 Environmental Checklist, Paraguay Vende
(page 10 of 10)

7. Checklist of Labor Rights (ADS 225.3.2) – Continued

Theme	Component	
Working Conditions (ILO 155; Law 213)	The work week does not exceed 48 hours and personnel have at least one day off during every seven days worked.	
	Salaries paid are equal to or higher than the minimum established by law.	
	The company establishes a safe and healthy work environment, and takes adequate measures to prevent accidents and injuries caused during or associated with work activity.	
	The company maintains hygienic bathrooms for the use of all its employees, guaranteeing access to potable water and, when appropriate, installations with adequate sanitary conditions for food storage.	
Explain each N, I, or NA rating.		

Review conducted by:

Source: USAID/Paraguay Vende program.

Exhibit 4.32 presents the questionnaire Paraguay Vende used to assess the export-readiness of potential clients (the original is in Spanish).

Exhibit 4.32 Questionnaire for Exporters, Paraguay Vende (page 1 of 4)

PARAGUAY VENDE
expandiendo ventas y generando empleos

QUESTIONNAIRE FOR EXPORTERS

Company:	Date:
Name:	
Position:	

1. Analysis of the company

Export experience

1. The company has exported in the last five years:
☐ Sporadically   ☐ Never   ☐ Yes*

*Give details on principal markets:

_____

_____

_____

_____

_____

2. The company has personnel with export experience:
☐ Yes*   ☐ No

*How many: _____ (_____)

3. The company has a foreign trade department:
☐ Yes   ☐ No

4. The company masters English:
☐ Yes*   ☐ No

*Who: (position(s))

_____

_____

_____

**Exhibit 4.32 Questionnaire for Exporters, Paraguay Vende
(page 2 of 4)**

5. Who makes the sales decisions in the company:
☐ Manager   ☐ President*   ☐ Board**   ☐ Others***

*How often is he or she present: _____   (_____)

**How often does it meet: _____   (_____)

***Indicate their positions: _____

Export strategy and access to technology and information

6. The company has well-defined objectives, targets, and strategies to expand into foreign markets.
☐ Yes*   ☐ No

*Explain actions: _____
_____
_____

7. In its business plan, the company has budgeted for the costs of developing the export market, market studies, site visits, shipment of samples, brochures, development of a website, etc.
☐ Yes*   ☐ No

*Explain actions: _____
_____
_____

8. The company has participated in international fairs in the last five years:
☐ Yes*   ☐ No

*Indicate which: _____
_____
_____

Exhibit 4.32 Questionnaire for Exporters, Paraguay Vende
(page 3 of 4)

9. The company has promotional material such as:
Catalogues, brochures:
☐ Yes   ☐ No

Web site:
☐ Yes   ☐ No

10. The company has:
Fax and telephone:
☐ Yes   ☐ No

Email:
☐ Yes*   ☐ No

*☐ Personal accounts   ☐ Company account

Financial solvency

11. The company has the capacity economically to enter the export market:
☐ Yes*   ☐ No

*Indicate sources of financing:

_____

_____

_____

2. Product analysis

12. The company has a product that has sold successfully in the domestic market:
☐ Yes   ☐ No

13. This product has little room to grow in the local market:
☐ Yes   ☐ No

**Exhibit 4.32 Questionnaire for Exporters, Paraguay Vende
(page 4 of 4)**

---

14. The company is cognizant of the norms for packing, packaging, labeling, foreign regulations, quality standards, and cultural preferences in foreign markets:
☐ Yes*   ☐ No

*Indicate which markets:

_____

_____

_____

15. The company has the capacity to increase production to absorb international sales:
☐ Yes*   ☐ No

*How much: _____   (_____) Indicate unit of measure.

16. The product has quality certifications:
☐ Yes*   ☐ No

*From where: _____

Issued by whom: _____

Source: USAID/Paraguay Vende program.

Tracking and Sharing Progress

Make Monitoring and Evaluation a Management Tool

Exhibit 4.33 presents the form PRA uses for collecting client baseline data.

Exhibit 4.33 Baseline Data Form, Peru, PRA
(page 1 of 3)
Format 1
Client Baseline

General Information About the Client

Self-Generated Code:	01	DO NOT FILL IN

Location

Economic Corridor:	02	
Department:	03	
Province:	04	
District:	05	
Town:	06	

General Data About the Client

Name of the Client:	07	

Legal Status:

Individual (1) Company (2)	08	
Name of Representative:	09	
DNI or RUC:*	10	

*Equivalent of social security or registration number

Exhibit 4.33 Baseline Data Form, Peru, PRA
(page 2 of 3)

Data on the Company or Economic Unit

Product or Service:	11	
Unit of Measure:*	12	
Stage in the Economic Chain:	13	

Indicate one of the following options:
a) Primary production
b) Transformation
c) Marketing
d) Other services (including tourism)

Date of the baseline:	14	

Baseline of Sales and Production

Employment Factor	15	DO NOT FILL IN

*Unit of measure in which the product or service is expressed when it is marketed

Exhibit 4.33 Baseline Data Form, Peru, PRA
(page 3 of 3)

Sales and production of the client during the last twelve months:

16	Year and Month[1]	Sales (S/.)	Production[2]	Sales Price (S/.)
	1[3]			
	2			
	3			
	4			
	5			
	6			
	7			
	8			
	9			
	10			
	11			
	12			
	Total			

Business Facilitator[4] | 17 | |

[1]Indicate month and year

[2]Quantity produced in the unit defined in (12)

[3]Month immediately prior to the date the Economic Service Center began operations with the client

[4]Member of the Economic Service Center responsible for the client

Source: USAID/Peru Poverty Reduction and Alleviation program.

Communicate with the Public, Especially Success Stories

Exhibit 4.34 presents examples of PRA informational bulletins.

Exhibit 4.34 Examples of PRA Informational Bulletins

Photo: James T. Riordan.

Notes

Foreword

[1] Lyndon B. Johnson, White House Conference on Education, Washington, D.C, 1965.

Chapter 1
Attacking Poverty: Do We Know How?

[2] William and Elizabeth Paddock, *We Don't Know How: An Independent Audit of What They Call Success in Foreign Assistance* (Ames: Iowa State University Press, 1973).

[3] Ibid., pp. 299-300.

[4] Examples of strident indictments along the way include Graham Hancock, *Lords of Poverty: The Power, Prestige, and Corruption of the International Aid Business* (New York: Atlantic Monthly Press, 1989); and Paul Vallely, *Bad Samaritans: First World Ethics and Third World Debt* (Maryknoll, NY: Orbis Books, 1990).

[5] See William Easterly, *The Elusive Quest for Growth: Economists' Adventures and Misadventures in the Tropics* (Cambridge, MA: MIT Press, 2001); and *The White Man's Burden: Why the West's Efforts to Aid the Rest Have Done So Much Ill and So Little Good* (New York: Penguin Press, 2006).

[6] Virginia Postrel, "The Poverty Puzzle," *New York Times,* nytimes.com, March 19, 2006.

[7] See Jeffrey Sachs, *The End of Poverty: Economic Possibilities for Our Time* (New York: Penguin Press, 2005).

[8] See William Easterly, "The Big Push Déjà Vu: A Review of Jeffrey Sachs's *The End of Poverty: Economic Possibilities for Our Time,*" *Journal of Economic Literature*, XLIV (March, 2006), pp. 95-105.

[9] William Easterly, "4 Ways to Spend $60 Billion Wisely," *Washington Post,* July 2, 2006, p. B2.

[10] For more on this point, see Abhijit Vinayak Banerjee, "Making Aid Work," *Boston Review*, July/August, 2006.

[11] Thomas Friedman, *The Lexus and the Olive Tree* (New York: Anchor Books, 2000), p. 442.

[12] Alan García Pérez, "Draft Speech of Alan García Pérez, President of the Republic of Peru, to the Institute for International Economics," September 21, 2006, pp. 2-3.

[13] See World Bank, *Globalization, Growth, and Poverty: Building an Inclusive World Economy* (New York: Oxford University Press, 2002).

[14] USAID, "Securing the Future: A Strategy for Economic Growth," Washington, D.C., 2008, pp. 6-7.

[15]Friedman, op cit, p. 163.

Chapter 2
What Is the Buyer-Led Approach?

[16] Pol Klein, personal communication with the author, 2007.

Chapter 3
If We Do Know How, Why Do We Not Act Accordingly?

[17] See www.elsevier.com/wps/find/bookdescription.cws_home/600083/description#description.

[18] See www.aidtoartisans.org.

[19] Some observers will be quick to point out that Africa has received massive infusions of aid over the years. But, as Glenn Hubbard and William Duggan argue persuasively, those infusions have not added up to the equivalent of a Marshall Plan. The Marshall Plan focused on the restoration of business as an engine of growth, and businesspeople ran it. Much of aid to Africa has gone through governments and non-governmental organizations, and has focused on social programs. See Glenn Hubbard and William Duggan, "Why Africa needs a Marshall plan," *Financial Times*, FT.com, June 5, 2007. See also Carol Pineau, "The Africa You Never See," *Washington Post*, April 17, 2005, p. B2; and Moises Naim, "Demise of a Metaphor: Why the Marshall Plan's success is not so easy to repeat," *Washington Post*, November 4, 2007, p. 6.

[20] TechnoServe, solicitation, n.d.

[21] Clive Crook, "Capitalism: The Movie: Why Americans don't value markets enough—and why that matters," *Atlantic Monthly*, March, 2006, p. 46.

[22] "The good company: Companies today are exhorted to be 'socially responsible'. What, exactly, does this mean?" *Economist,* January 22, 2005, p.11.

[23] "Meet the Hard-Nosed Do-Gooders: A New Generation of Graduates Is Finding Market-Based Solutions for Problems in the Nonprofit World—and Getting Paid for It," Inside Business, *Time,* January, 2006, p. A24.

[24] For example, one of the principal recommendations of the report (James T. Riordan, "A Strategy to Integrate Small Farmer Initiatives and Expand Export Agriculture in Nicaragua," report submitted to Asociación Nicaraguense de Productores y Exportadores de Productos no Tradicionales (APENN), Managua, Nicaragua, 1997) was:

Action programs under this element of the strategy would be limited to products currently produced predominantly by small and medium farmers and products that are amenable to small and medium farm production in identified areas. The products in question would be high-value, and oriented either for export or to replace imports. Examples of programs eligible for support could include:
- Organic coffee and sesame production
- Ginger, malanga, and vegetable production
- Coffee production (p.7).

Chapter 4
Planning, Searching, and the Rest of the Book

[25] Easterly, *The White Man's Burden*, pp. 5-6.
[26] See Gregory F. Robison, "The Cultural Challenge of Supporting Enterprise," *Grassroots Development*, XVII (No. 2) and XVIII (No. 1), 1994, 23-34.

Appendix to Part I
Excerpts from "The Cultural Challenge of Supporting Enterprise"

[27] Ibid.

Chapter 5
Where to Start – Poverty, Jobs, Sales, and Market Demand

[28] Susan E. Rice, "We Must Put More on the Plate to Fight Poverty," *Washington Post*, July 5, 2005, p. A13. For a country-specific study concluding that terrorism has its roots in poverty, see Quy-Toan Do and Lakshmi Iyer, "Poverty, Social Divisions and Conflict in Nepal," Working Paper 07-065, World Bank, Washington, D.C., 2007. For a cross-country analysis that fails to concludes that poverty is a contributing factor, see Alberto Abadie, "Poverty, Political Freedom, and the Roots of Terrorism," *American Economic Review*, XCVI (No. 2, May, 2006), 50-56.

[29] Much of the discussion that follows borrows heavily from James T. Riordan, Enrique Vásquez H., Roberta van Haeften, Fred L. Mann, and Carlos Figueroa A., *Attacking Poverty: A Market Approach* (Lima, Peru: Universidad del Pacífico, 2003).

[30] David Gordon, "Indicators of Poverty and Hunger," presentation, Expert Group Meeting on Youth Development Indicators, United Nations, New York, 2005.

[31] See Abhijit Vinayak Banerjee, Roland Bénabou, and Dilip Mookherjee (eds.), *Understanding Poverty* (New York: Oxford University Press, 2006).

[32] http://www.oup.com/us/catalog/general/subject/Economics/Developmental/?view=usa&ci=9780195305203.

[33] "Education has been and always will be a principal line of escape for the children of the poor." Arnold C. Harberger, "The View from the Trenches: Development Processes and Policies as Seen by a Working Professional," in *Frontiers of Development Economics: The Future in Perspective*, edited by Gerald M. Meier and Joseph E. Stiglitz (New York: World Bank and Oxford University Press, 2001), p. 544.

[34] For more on such interactions, see Ravi Kanbur and Lyn Squire, "The Evolution of Thinking About Poverty: Exploring the Interactions," in Meier and Stiglitz (eds.), op cit, p. 184.

[35] Allison Coppel and Kirsten Olsen, "Community Engagement Models for the Extractives Industry in Developing Countries," external version, Stanford Graduate School of Business, Palo Alto, California, 2006, p. 8.

[36] Luca Barbone, "Foreword," in Pierella Paci and Pieter Serneels (eds.), *Employment and Shared Growth: Rethinking the Role of Labor Mobility for Development* (Washington, D.C: World Bank, 2007), p. ix.

[37] "Pro-Poor Growth: A Guide to Policies and Programs," USAID/Washington, Washington, D.C., 2005, p. xvii.

[38] Stefan Dercon, review of Gary S. Fields and Guy Pfeffermann (eds.), *Pathways Out of Poverty: Private Firms and Economic Mobility in Developing Countries* (Washington, D.C.: International Finance Corporation, 2003), in *Journal of Economic Literature,* XLIII (June, 2005), 508.

[39] Aneel Karnani, "Microfinance Misses Its Mark," *Stanford Social Innovation Review,* V (Summer, 2007), 38.

[40] Some would argue that financial capital should appear explicitly as well. Clearly, investment requires money, but one could also argue—as here—that finance constitutes one of the markets under the rubric of "access to functioning markets." In the end, including finance implicitly or explicitly is a question of taste.

[41] "Economics focus: Secret sauce: China's rapid growth is due not just to heavy investment, but also to the world's fastest productivity gains," *Economist*, November 14, 2009, p. 90.

⁴² For more on the concept of total factor productivity, see Diego Comin, "Total Factor Productivity," New Palgrave Dictionary of Economics, Second Edition, edited by S. N. Durlauf and L. E. Blume, 2008, http://www.dictionaryofeconomics.com/search_results?q=total+factor+productivity&edition=current&button_search=GO.

By definition, increasing total factor productivity also means increasing value added, which still others suggest as the appropriate North Star for development programs of this kind.

⁴³ At the last session of USAID's conference, "Competitiveness in the Next Decade," in Kyiv, Ukraine in 2009, a speaker concluded with the reflection that productivity drives competitiveness, implying that it behooved future USAID programs to focus on increasing productivity. Unfortunately, he failed to ask the question, "What drives productivity in the first place?"

⁴⁴ Note the determinative role of demand in this example. A recent book offers the provocative thesis that the reason the industrial revolution took place in Britain and not somewhere else comes down to demand. See Robert C. Allen, *The British Industrial Revolution in Global Perspective* (New York: Cambridge University Press, 2009).

⁴⁵ "The Peru Poverty Reduction and Alleviation (PRA) Program," USAID/Peru, Lima, 2008, p. 55.

⁴⁶ James T. Riordan and David L. Tacker, "Interim Impact Evaluation of PL-480, Title I, Section 108 Program in the Dominican Republic," Annex F, LAC TECH II Agriculture and Rural Development Technical Services Project Evaluation Team, Santo Domingo, Dominican Republic, 1995, p. 5.

⁴⁷ Vicki Moore, "Lessons Learned on Implementation of Competitiveness Activities," USAID, Washington, D.C., 2002.

⁴⁸ Some point to product branding as an example of a value-adding strategy for which a focus on individual transactions is inappropriate. But developing a brand is typically not only an expensive but an iffy proposition—which argues for knowing what you are getting into right from the beginning and setting clear targets to monitor progress against over time. Once development programs begin helping businesses—or countries—develop brands, inertia can take over, leading them, in the worst case, to throw good money after bad. In the end, a product branding strategy cannot abstract from sales. A brand may bring a business or a country tremendous pride and identity, but if developing it does not translate into increases in revenue, is it worth it?

Years ago, a Belgian priest spearheaded the creation of a trout canning company in southern Peru. The company, Arapa, is named for a lake that connects to the much larger Lake Titicaca. The Arapa canning company operates on the shore of Lake Arapa, and gets its raw material—trout—

from fishermen with small, relatively primitive cages in the lake. The company provides the fishermen fingerlings and fishfood, and the fishermen deliver the trout to the factory. Arapa's first big client was a buyer in Australia who viewed the relationship more as a charitable venture than as a business proposition. It paid Arapa above-market prices for its fish, which the company canned with its own label, and the company was content to operate as a low-volume, high-margin business. After a while, the Australian company severed the relationship, leaving Arapa operating at 20 percent capacity. At that point PRA made contact with Arapa, and agreed to try to find it a new buyer. It succeeded in capturing the interest of Santa Isabel, a major supermarket chain then owned by Ahold. But Santa Isabel stipulated two conditions: first, they would use their own brand name (Bell's), not Arapa's; and, second, they would pay much less per can than the Australian company did. At first, of course, Arapa did not like either of the conditions, the first because it supposedly took away the company's "identity," the second because it forced the company to shift its whole business strategy from a low-volume, high-margin operation to a high-volume, low-margin operation. After some time, however, Arapa gradually came to see the wisdom of selling to Santa Isabel under those conditions, and that commercial relationship continues today.

[49] Vicki Moore, op cit.

[50] Much of the discussion that follows borrows heavily from James T. Riordan, "One Buyer at a Time," *Stanford Social Innovation Review*, V (Winter, 2007), pp. 48-55.

Chapter 6
What Does "Demand-Driven" Really Mean?

[51] "The Peru Poverty Reduction and Alleviation (PRA) Program," pp. 59-60.

[52] William Perreault, Jr. and E. Jerome McCarthy, *Essentials of Marketing*, 10th ed. (New York: McGraw-Hill Irwin, 2006), p. 16.

[53] Economists also learn Say's Law, named after the French economist Jean Baptiste Say (1767-1832). The popular expression of Say's Law, "supply creates its own demand," does not appear in Say's writings. A more accurate interpretation of Say's Law is that overproduction may be possible in individual markets, but, overall, an economy-wide glut is impossible if all markets function freely.

[54] Friedman, op cit, p. 10.

[55] See USAID/Europe and Eurasia, "Moldovan Fashion Maven Takes on Milan," http://www.usaid.gov/locations/europe_eurasia/press/success/2007-09-prog.html#top, 2007; and USAID, "Moldovan Company's

Rise in Productivity Yields New Clients," Program E-Spotlight, Issue 12, September 19, 2007.

[56] For an eloquent description of the dynamism that cities can impart to the countryside, see Frank Ellis and Nigel Harris, "New Thinking About Urban and Rural Development," Keynote Paper for DFID Sustainable Development Retreat, University of Surrey, Guildford, UK, 2004.

[57] For an example in which information on—and recommendations of—buyers forms an integral part of a market study, see Gonzalo Miranda, "Report on Brazilian Market Access for Raspberries and Onion," Market Access and Poverty Alleviation Program, USAID/Bolivia, Cochabamba, Bolivia, 2003. Fintrac Inc. advertises its market surveys as one of its signature products, and their quality is definitely better than most. See, for example, "The U.S. Market for Fresh Asparagus," Market Survey #01, Farmer Training and Development Program, Millennium Challenge Account of Honduras, La Lima Nueva, Cortés, Honduras, December 2006. Even there, though, information on buyers appears not in the text, but in an annex. For an example of a production-oriented market study (where, again, information on buyers appears in the appendices), see International Programs Office, College of Agricultural and Environmental Sciences, University of California, Davis, "Rehabilitating Agriculture in Afghanistan: Horticultural Market Survey," Davis, California, 2003.

[58] Dell has made personalization of demand the core of its business strategy, making each of its computers to order. Decisions on what computers to produce rely not on what the company projects will sell, or would like to sell, but on what customers have already committed to buy.

Chapter 7
Market Chains, Building Trust, and Job Creation

[59] Reuben E. Slone, "Leading a Supply Chain Turnaround," Reprint R0410G, *Harvard Business Review*, October, 2004, p. 3.

[60] Olaf Kula, Jeanne Downing, and Michael Field, "Globalization and the Small Firm: An Industry Value Chain Approach to Economic Growth and Poverty Reduction," microREPORT #42, USAID, Accelerated Microenterprise Advancement Project—Business Development Services, Washington, D.C., 2006, p. 11.

[61] USAID, "Value Chain Approach to Poverty Reduction: Equitable Growth in Today's Global Economy," Accelerated Microenterprise Advancement Project—Business Development Services, Washington, D.C., n.d., p. 3.

[62] Even proponents of value chains are quick to acknowledge that "the real world can be much messier" than textbook descriptions of value chains

would imply—thus suggesting, once again, that development practitioners would be wise to keep their feet on micro ground. See Raphael Kaplinsky and Mike Morris, "A Handbook for Value Chain Research," International Development Research Centre, Canada, n.d., p.52.

[63] Much of the discussion that follows borrows heavily from Riordan, "One Buyer at a Time."

[64] Gerald Schmaedick, Michael Glover, Antonio Tacchino, Iván Mifflin, Pedro Flores, and Renso Martínez, "A Qualitative Assessment of the Poverty Reduction and Alleviation Program of USAID/Peru: January, 2003," Checchi & Co. International Consulting, Task Order #814, Evaluation IQC, under Contract No. AEP-I-00-00-00022-00, Washington, D.C., 2003, Volume I, p.17.

[65] A taxonomy of business development services in a recent journal article does not even mention facilitation or honest brokering. And although it includes marketing, it leans more toward the dictionary definition discussed above than to identifying buyers. See Merten Sievers and Paul Vandenberg, "Synergies through Linkages: Who Benefits from Linking Microfinance and Business Development Services?" *World Development*, XXXV (No. 8, 2007), 1342-43. Other sources where one would expect to see explicit mention of facilitation and honest brokering and does not are: "AMAP BDS Knowledge and Practice Task Order: Lexicon," microNOTE #6, USAID, Washington, D.C., 2005; and United Nations Economic Commission for Europe, "Entrepreneurship and SME Development: Index of SME Development," http://www.unece.org/indust/sme/ece-sme. htm, 2006. Interestingly, in an investigation of business development services programs around the world, M.B.A. students from the Stanford Graduate School of Business found it difficult to use conventional categories to compare the buyer-led approach with other programs, and treated it separately in the text. See Laura Commike, Allison Coppel, Rory Eakin, Mar Higuera, Bhavika Vyas, and Steve Walsh, "Small & Medium Size Enterprises: *What will drive future growth?*" Stanford Graduate School of Business, Palo Alto, California, 2005.

[66] James T. Riordan, "Trade and Economic Growth," presentation, "Aid to Trade" Conference, Alexandria, Egypt, 1999. See also R.C. Feenstra, "Integration of Trade and Disintegration of Production in the Global Economy," *Journal of Economic Perspectives*, XII (No. 4, 1998), 31-50.

[67] See "Genera Nestlé 650 mil empleos en América Latina," EFE, El Universal, Geneva, Switzerland, March 8, 2006.

[68] Ironically, maybe the most compelling examples of how outsourcing can generate employment are illicit ones: cocaine market chains sourcing from small coca producers in Bolivia, Colombia, and Peru, and opium market chains sourcing from small poppy producers in Afghanistan.

For better or worse, just like the Shipibo-Conibo ceramics example, they dramatize the vigor of market incentives. See "Afghan Poppies Sprout Again: Production Nears Record Levels, Worrying Anti-Drug Officials," *Washington Post,* November 10, 2003, p. A16.

[69] For still additional examples of outsourcing relationships in developing countries, see Andrew W. Shepherd, "Approaches to linking producers to markets: A review of experiences to date," Agricultural Management, Marketing and Finance Occasional Paper, Food and Agriculture Organization of the United Nations, Rome, Italy, 2007, pp. 45-55.

[70] "The Peru Poverty Reduction and Alleviation (PRA) Program," pp. 63-66.

Chapter 8
Principles for Supporting Market Chains

[71] See Michael E. Porter, *The Competitive Advantage of Nations* (New York: Free Press, 1990).

[72] "Clustering for Competitiveness," KIAsia News Bytes, No. 80, September, 2005.

[73] See, for instance, the Bolivia wood and forest products industry example in the appendix to this part of the book.

[74] For an overall assessment of USAID's experience with competitiveness programs, see The Mitchell Group, Inc., "Promoting Competitiveness in Practice: An Assessment of Cluster-Based Approaches," Washington, D.C., 2003. For an assessment of a specific case, see INOTEH Consulting, "Evaluation Report for Macedonian Competitiveness Activity," Skopje, Macedonia, 2006.

[75] "But [while] man has almost constant occasion for the help of his brethren,...it is in vain for him to expect it from their benevolence only. He will be more likely to prevail if he can interest their self-love in his favour, and show them that it is for their own advantage to do for him what he requires of them. Whoever offers to another a bargain of any kind, proposes to do this. Give me that which I want, and you shall have this which you want, is the meaning of every such offer; and it is in this manner that we obtain from one another the far greater part of those good offices which we stand in need of. It is not from the benevolence of the butcher, the brewer, or the baker that we expect our dinner, but from their regard to their own interest. We address ourselves, not to their humanity but to their self-love, and never talk to them of our own necessities but of their advantages." Adam Smith, *An Inquiry into the Nature and Causes of the Wealth of Nations*, edited by W.B. Todd, based on the 1784 Edition,

Volume 2 of *Glasgow Edition of the Works and Correspondence of Adam Smith*, edited by D.D. Raphael and Andrew Skinner (Oxford: Clarendon Press), pp. 26-27. To put it another way, one can not program an exchange—or investment—like a vaccination campaign; it is a function of incentives.

[76] For an entertaining treatment of this point, see Eliyahu M. Goldratt and Jeff Cox, *The Goal: A Process of Ongoing Improvement* (Great Barrington, MA: North River Press, 2004).

[77] Subject to the proviso, of course, that they honor the confidentiality of the information that is proprietary to each business.

[78] Most programs prepare bulletins—frequently both electronic and hard-copy—to acquaint funding agencies, potential clients, and the public at large with what they are doing. More often than not, the bulletins concentrate on what the programs are going to do in the subsequent few months. Strategically, it generally makes more sense to advertise what they have accomplished already. New clients react much more enthusiastically to past success than to promises, promises, promises. See Chapter 16.

[79] Copycatting—or what Paul Krugman calls "a cascade of followers"—appears to have been a key ingredient in Ireland's growth boom over the last two decades. See Paul Krugman, "Good News from Ireland: A Geographical Perspective," in *International Perspectives on the Irish Economy*, edited by Alan W. Gray (Dublin: Indecon Economic Consultants, 1997), p. 50; and James Burnham, "Why Ireland Boomed," *Independent Review*, VII (No. 4, Spring, 2003), 554. For a more comprehensive discussion of copycatting under PRA, see Chapter 11.

[80] The 2003 mid-term evaluation of PRA estimated the economic impact on the Ucayali region of the program's support of individual market chains. It found that sales induced by PRA made up almost 13 percent of regional agricultural GDP at the time. It also estimated that, under conservative assumptions, that percentage would rise to almost 22 percent in five years. See Schmaedick et al., op cit, Annex 11.

[81] "The Peru Poverty Reduction and Alleviation (PRA) Program," pp. 71-72.

[82] Schmaedick et al., op cit, p. 52.

[83] José Iturríos, "elementos para la discusión sobre un crecimiento 'pro-pobre,'" email to USAID, February 1, 2006. For more on the relationships among markets, transaction costs, and opportunities for the poor, see Eleni Z. Gabre-Madhin, "Market Institutions, Transaction Costs, and Social Capital in the Ethiopian Grain Market," Research Report 124, International Food Policy Research Institute, Washington, D.C., 2001; and David Stifel, Bart Minten, and Paul Dorosh, "Transactions Costs and Agricultural Productivity: Implications of Isolation for Rural Poverty in Madagascar," Markets and Structural Studies Division Discussion Paper

No. 56, International Food Policy Research Institute, Washington, D.C., 2003.

[84] Interestingly, the most dynamic cluster the author has seen at work—the budding artichoke cluster in Peru—does not even call itself a cluster. But all the systemic interactions one would expect to see among the four determinants of Porter's diamond are there in spades.

[85] "Identification of Lead Firms—Team Final Report," USAID, Caribbean Open Trade Support Program, Saint John's, Antigua, 2006, p.1.

[86] For research concluding that firm-specific factors are more important than industry structure in explaining variations in performance, see Rifat Kamasak, "Firm Specific versus Industry Structure Factors in Explaining Performance Variation," Eurasia Business and Economic Society Conference, Istanbul, Turkey, 2010.

[87] At one point some observers touted East Asia's success in picking winners, but even there the batting averages of the countries in question turned out not to be all that high. For a case study, see Jaime Aristy Escuder, "Frente al Statu Quo: Ganadores Derrotados," Hoy, Santo Domingo, Dominican Republic, September 17, 1996, p. 2D. For recent examples of governments' lack of success in promoting entrepreneurship, see "Schumpeter: Fish out of water: Policymakers are turning their minds to the tricky subject of promoting entrepreneurship," Economist, October 31, 2009, p. 78.

[88] The lumpiness of these results should not come as a surprise. It is natural to expect a relatively limited number of medium and large enterprises to account for the lion's share of employment and economic activity, especially when one considers outsourcing as part of the equation. To reiterate, the end objective of a development program may be to make the "little guy" better off. But that does not mean the little guy is the place to start work. Find out where the economic dynamism—that is, the demand-pull—lies, and capitalize on it, bringing small and micro enterprises in under the market tent.

[89] At the beginning of the last decade, the European Union stipulated that all its automobile manufacturers treat whatever leather they use with organic tanning agents. Worldwide, there are four such agents. One of them comes from tara, a bush that grows basically in only two countries, China and Peru. Tara tannin contains practically no coloring, leaving bright, light resistant leather. The new regulation caused demand for tara tannin to rise dramatically, prompting a number of companies to commence or expand operations in northern Peru, boosting the derived demand for labor to harvest tara in the field as well.

[90] Bixin is a natural red colorant derived from the achiote tree.

[91] R. Glenn Hubbard and William Duggan, The Aid Trap: Hard Truths

About Ending Poverty (New York: Columbia University Press, 2009), p. 84.

[92] In the 30th anniversary issue of *Money* in 2002, the magazine examined which stocks had done well and which had done poorly since 1972. The best-performing stock was Southwest Airlines, a dramatic exception in an otherwise anemic industry. Had analysts restricted their sights to industries, Southwest Airlines would never have even hit their radar screen. See Jon Birger, "The 30 Best Stocks," *Money*, Fall, 2002.

[93] In Honduras, the service Fintrac's clients find most important is access to markets. See Fintrac Inc., "SDE en el Sector de Agronegocios: Optimizando Impacto," presentation, VI Foro Interamericano de la Microempresa, Guatemala, Guatemala, 2003. See also "Las tendencias del empleo juvenil en nuestro país," *El Comercio,* Lima, Peru, July 16, 2000, p. b1.

[94] Jonathan Morduch, "The Microfinance Promise," *Journal of Economic Literature*, XXXVII (December, 1999), 1569-1614, takes stock of experience in microfinance up to that point. It concludes:

[T]he promise of microfinance should be kept in context. Even in the best of circumstances, credit from microfinance programs helps fund self-employment activities that most often supplement income for borrowers rather than drive fundamental shifts in employment patterns. It rarely generates new jobs for others, and success has been especially limited in regions with highly seasonal income patterns and low population densities. The best evidence to date suggests that making a real dent in poverty will require increasing overall levels of economic growth and employment generation. Microfinance may be able to help some households take advantage of those processes, but nothing so far suggests that it will ever drive them.

For a more recent critique, see Karnani, op cit. See also, Abhijit Banerjee, Esther Duflo, Rachel Glennester, and Cynthia Kinnan, "The miracle of microfinance? Evidence from a randomized evaluation," an unpublished paper by the Abdul Latif Jameel Poverty Action Lab, Department of Economics, Massachusetts Institute of Technology, Cambridge, MA, 2009.

[95] Matthew Stewart, "The Management Myth," *Atlantic Monthly*, June, 2006, 86-87.

[96] Many development practitioners, seeing small farmers as their principal clientele, castigate local banks for failing to lend to agriculture, and gravitate toward systemic solutions to make lending more open and agile. Ironically, almost anywhere one goes in developing countries, banks are awash with cash and looking to lend. Although it is a hard pill to swallow, many agricultural projects simply are not competitive—even after one take banks' strong risk aversion into account. More often than

not, banks' disinclination to lend is a symptom of something much more fundamental. Interestingly, the willingness of buyer-led programs to help farmers address fundamental competiveness problems can serve to tip the balance, making the ventures in question much more attractive in banks' eyes.

[97] Jorge Mesinas, "Informe Final de Prácticas Profesionales," unpublished paper, Harvard University, Cambridge, Massachusetts, 2005, p.3.

[98] The discussion in this section borrows from James T. Riordan and Adam Noyce, "The Sustainability of Business Development Services in Developing Economies: What Do We Want to Sustain and Why?" Eurasia Business and Economic Society Conference, Istanbul, Turkey, 2010.

[99] http://en.wikipedia.org/wiki/Sustainable_development.

[100] Bureau for Latin America and the Caribbean, U.S. Agency for International Development, "Making Markets Work for the Rural Poor: An Agenda to Advance Broadly Based, Sustainable Rural Economic Growth in Latin America and the Caribbean," Washington, D.C., 1994, p. 11.

[101] Note the coincidence with the dynamics of the formation of clusters. Once, again, demand is the driver.

[102] "Fostering Small Business Growth: Micro Enterprise Development Initiative Final Report," USAID/Armenia, Yerevan, 2006, p. 46.

[103] For an example of a business that has continued to flourish years after it received support from a development program, go to www.oyanca.com. Oyanca began producing soapstone, ceramics, and paper under USAID's Agricultural Reconstruction and Assistance (ARAP) program in Nicaragua, which ended in 2002. It continues to thrive, exporting to Marshall Fields and Target. As a former participant in ARAP put it, "If this is not sustainability, then I don't know what is." James Johnson, "Sustainability," email to Chemonics International Inc., October 6, 2005.

[104] Jeanne Downing, USAID/Washington, email, Microenterprise Learning Information and Knowledge Sharing, December 14, 2005.

[105] Some—the Millennium Challenge Corporation, for example—object to connector firms as the point of entry for development assistance, arguing that it should go directly to those most in need of it, that is, the poor. In the embedded services model, the connector firm is much less the recipient of assistance than the channel through which it reaches poor suppliers. And, again, who better to channel it than the party with a vested commercial interest in doing it right?

[106] In Guatemala, applying the "more-buyers-the-merrier" strategy resulted in nearly 30 percent increases in prices for small wood producers. See "Developing bargaining power in Guatemala," http://chemonics.com/projects/default.asp?content_id={C04A0AA0-581C-4E39-9894-6EED4AC35658}, Chemonics International Inc., Washington, D.C., 2003.

[107] Again, conventional business development services include such actions as identifying new buyers for clients, helping them develop business plans to obtain bank financing, introducing them to new technology, improving their internal management systems, etc.

[108] See John E. Lamb and Bruce Brower, "Agribusiness Development Centers," Chemonics International Inc., Washington, D.C., 1999.

[109] Fintrac Inc., "Jump-Starting BDS Markets in Honduras: When Direct Provision Makes Sense," VI Foro Interamericano de la Microempresa, Guatemala City, Guatemala, 2003, p. 1.

[110] James T. Riordan, "Azerbaijan Business Assistance and Development Project: Recommendations for Strengthening Its Marketing Centers," Chemonics International Inc., Washington, D.C., 2005.

[111] Suzanne Savage, "Short Term Sales and Marketing Technical Assistance," Albania Small Business Credit and Assistance Project, Tirana, Albania, 2005, pp. 6-7.

[112] For a case in point, see USAID/Kazakhstan, "Request for Proposal (RFP) No. EG115-06-007—Kazakhstan Small Business Development (KSBD) Project," Almaty, Kazakhstan, 2006, p. C-7.

[113] See Katherine W. McKee, Director, Office of Microenterprise Development, USAID/Washington, "Context and Evolution of BDS," presentation, Business Development Services Conference 2005: Shaping Jordan's Industry with International Best Practices, USAID/Jordan, Amman, 2005.

[114] The author has interviewed numerous applicants for numerous positions over the years. At the risk of sounding facetious, he has found an inverse correlation between the number of training courses listed in a curriculum vitae and an applicant's orientation toward achieving results. The author has nothing against learning, obviously, but as a general rule, the longer the list of training courses listed, the shorter the list of the applicant's practical accomplishments.

[115] The agreement was the first in the world under USAID's Global Development Alliance (GDA) program.

[116] An understudy of Frank Lloyd Wright once suggested that he manage the construction of a building on the East Coast from his base at Taliesin West in Arizona. Wright replied, in effect, "You don't solve an architectural problem at 2000 miles away. You have to go to it."

[117] Seminal references on economic corridors include: Avrom Bendavid-Val, "Rural-Urban Linkages: Farming and Farm Households in Regional and Town Economies," *Review of Urban and Regional Development Studies*, No. 2, 1989; Ricardo Vergara, "La Ciudad y el Campo: ¿Una Danza Eterna?" *Debate Agrario*, No. 13, Lima, Peru, 1992; Alberto Paniagua V. and Héctor Nogales S., "Bolivia: Bases para una Política de Desarrollo Rural

Regional," draft, Documento de Campo 52, Proyecto MACA/PNUD/ FAO, Apoyo a la Gestión Técnico-Normativa del MACA, La Paz, Bolivia, 1993; and Ministry of the Presidency, "Elementos para el Desarrollo de las Ciudades Intermedias en Apoyo a la Lucha Contra la Pobreza Extrema," final draft, Lima, Peru, 1996. Interestingly, the underlying theme of this literature—economic integration—emerges as the fundamental guiding principle in *World Bank, World Development Report 2009: Reshaping Economic Geography* (Washington, D.C.: World Bank, 2009).

Chapter 9
Making Accountability Real

[118] The author acknowledges with gratitude the singular contributions of Joseph Jordan to this chapter and to Chapter 16.

[119] See Evaluation Gap Working Group, "When Will We Ever Learn? Improving Lives Through Impact Evaluation," Center for Global Development, Washington, D.C., 2006, http://www.cgdev.org/content/ publications/detail/7973.

[120] The penchant to measure performance by activities rather than by outcomes not only applies to individual programs but can characterize a development program as a whole. See Stewart Patrick, "U.S. Foreign Aid Reform: Will It Fix What Is Broken?" Center for Global Development, Washington, D.C., 2006, p. 16; and USAID, "Strategic Goal 5: Economic Prosperity and Security," Washington, D.C., 2007, http://www.usaid.gov/ policy/par06/ps_so2_sg5.html.

[121] James A. Baker, III, Lee H. Hamilton, et al., "The Iraq Study Group Report," Washington, D.C., 2006, p. 62.

[122] See Inter-American Development Bank, "The case of the Information Technology Rio Program (Río Informático) in Brazil," VI Foro Intermericano de la Microempresa, Guatemala City, Guatemala, 2003. For a dissenting view on the advisability of investing in information technology, see "The real digital divide," *Economist*, March 12, 2005, p. 11.

[123] See for example, USAID/Bolivia, "Request for Proposals (RFP) No. 511-04-018, USAID/Bolivia Rural Competitiveness Activity, Amendment No. 2," La Paz, Bolivia, 2004, p. 19.

Chapter 10
Solving Systemic Problems: Policy and Institutional Reform

[124] Peter T. Bauer and Basil S. Yamey, *The Economics of Under-Developed Countries* (Chicago: University of Chicago Press, 1957), p. 172.

[125] See World Bank, *Assessing Aid: What Works, What Doesn't, and Why*

(New York: Oxford University Press, 1998); and William Easterly and Ross Levine, "Tropics, Germs, and Crops: How Endowments Influence Economic Development," National Bureau for Economic Research Working Paper No. 9106, Cambridge, MA, 2002.

[126] See Easterly, *The Elusive Quest for Growth*.

[127] See John Williamson, ed., *Latin American Adjustment: How Much Has It Happened?* (Washington, D.C.: Institute for International Economics, 1990).

[128] For a more elegant enunciation of this point, see T.N. Srinivasan, "Global Competitiveness: Developing Country Perspectives," conference presentation, Revisiting Egypt's Competitiveness: The Road Ahead for Building Leading Sectors, Cairo, Egypt, 2004.

[129] Martin Wood, "Business Operating Environment," email to USAID, August 10, 2006. The extent to which local advisors can influence policy is also open to question. See "On deaf ears: Does India's government pay any heed to its economic advisers?" *Economist*, March 6, 2010, p. 94.

[130] James T. Riordan and J. David Flood, "Lessons Learned from USAID Support of Agricultural Policy Reform in Ecuador and How They Compare with Lessons Learned Elsewhere," draft, USAID/Ecuador, Quito, Ecuador, 1996, pp. IV-3, IV-8.

[131] A major achievement of a policy program in Peru in the late 1980s, in fact, was dissuading a minister from following his instincts. The Minister of Agriculture at the time was politically astute, energetic, and quick to grasp the nuances of policy issues. He also was impetuous. One afternoon he got the idea of setting a floor price for potatoes throughout the country and decided to announce his decision to Congress that evening. En route by car from the Ministry to Congress, the minister's principal advisor had ten minutes to convince him that such a move would be folly. He succeeded, and the program averted a big mistake, highlighting an oft overlooked lesson, that sometimes the doing of good is much less important than the prevention of evil.

[132] See USAID/Indonesia, "Growth through Investment and Trade (GIAT): Scope of Work," Jakarta, Indonesia, 2003, p. 22.

[133] Dani Rodrik, "Goodbye Washington Consensus, Hello Washington Confusion? A Review of The World Bank's *Economic Growth in the 1990s: Learning from a Decade of Reform*," *Journal of Economic Literature*, XLIV (December, 2006), 980.

[134] World Bank, *Economic Growth in the 1990s: Learning from a Decade of Reform* (Washington, D.C.: World Bank, 2005), p. xiii.

[135] Rodrik, op cit, 982. Interestingly, this is essentially the same point Goldratt and Cox, op cit, makes for firms.

[136] Patricia Kristjanson and Jerry Martin, "More Than Free Markets Are

Needed: The Case of a Peasant Millionaire in Madagascar," *Choices,* 4th quarter, 1991, p. 21.

[137] "Reformers in several [post-Communist] countries have reported that they have *never* seen an economic benefit analysis to support legal reforms." Wade Channell, "Lessons not Learned: Problems with Western Aid for Law Reform in Postcommunist Countries," Rule of Law Series, Number 57, Carnegie Endowment for International Peace, Washington, D.C., 2005.

[138] Hubbard and Duggan take the Mozambique program to task for its traditional approach to development. See R. Glenn Hubbard and William Duggan, *The Aid Trap: Hard Truths About Ending Poverty,* pp. 97-98.

[139] For a relatively rare example of an analysis of the economic impact of business reforms after the fact, see Nathan Associates Inc., "The Impact of USAID-Funded Private Sector Development Programs on Mozambique's Private Sector," USAID/Mozambique, Maputo, 2008.

[140] This preference runs directly counter to conventional wisdom. "[G]iven the high return from policy change, ...donors should not work at the firm or cluster level unless they are also somehow addressing the policy problems too." USAID, "Enterprise Growth Initiatives: Findings of a New USAID-Funded Report by Snodgrass & Winkler," EG technical Briefing, No. 7, Washington, D.C., 2004.

[141] In fact, the template for the interviews included a question on the topic. To give focus and avoid opening up a Pandora's box of complaints about the government, the question read, "If the government could change one thing, what change would most help you increase sales?" The template appears in Chapter 14.

[142] This last priority meshes with the growing consensus worldwide on the significance of property rights. "The answer that is now accepted, virtually without dispute, is that secure and enforceable property rights are the lifeblood of an efficient free-market economy." Shahid Yusuf and Joseph E. Stiglitz, "Development Issues: Settled and Open," in Meier and Stiglitz (eds.), op cit, p. 230. See also Hernando de Soto, *The Mystery of Capital: Why Capitalism Triumphs in the West and Fails Everywhere Else* (New York: Basic Books, 2000). Still, regularization of property rights is no silver bullet, and programs focusing on property rights alone can miss constraints that may be more binding—all of which argues, again, for one's doing one's micro homework. See John Gravois, "hey, wait a minute—The De Soto Delusion: Peruvian Economist Hernando de Soto's ideas for helping the poor have made him a global celebrity. Now, if only those ideas worked...," http://slate.msn.com/id/2112792, 2005.

[143] See http://www.doingbusiness.org.

[144] See "Georgia: Opened for Business—Georgia Business Climate Reform Final Report," USAID/Georgia, Tbilisi, 2009.

[145] See Edward Glaeser, Rafael La Porta, Florencio Lopez-de-Silanes, and Andrei Shleifer, "Do Institutions Cause Growth?" National Bureau of Economic Research Working Paper No. 10568, Cambridge, MA, 2004; and Ricardo Hausmann, Lant Pritchett, and Dani Rodrik, "Growth Accelerations," National Bureau of Economic Research Working Paper No. 10566, Cambridge, MA, 2004.

[146] The balance is foreseen to come from a public-private partnership. See below.

[147] "[I]n the end, all policy economics represents cost-benefit analysis in some form or other. But we are here distinguishing between the rather ivory-tower, utopian pursuit of the 'conditions for an optimum' and the down-to-earth, pragmatic questions of whether a given policy change moves us up or down, or which of two or three plausible alternatives will move us up the most. To answer these kinds of question, we must turn to what I call the 'economics of the nth best.' This really translates into the application of the basic tools of applied welfare economics in a setting with a considerable number of distortions, all but one or two or three of which have to be taken as given as one analyzes today's (or this year's) policy moves." Harberger, op cit, pp. 543-44.

[148] See James W. Fox, "The Callao Port Concession: A USAID Home Run," presentation, USAID Economic Growth Officers Workshop, Washington, D.C., 2007.

[149] See TechnoServe, "'Business Solutions to Rural Poverty' Theme of TechnoServe's Annual Meeting," World: A Newsletter for Friends of TechnoServe, Summer/Fall, 2003, p.3.

[150] Most of the clients in Armenia were urban. For an example of the successful application of purchase-order financing in rural areas, see Ramiro Ortega Landa, "Value Chain Financing in Rural Bolivia: Introducing Purchase Order Financing," USAID/Bolivia, La Paz, n.d.

Chapter 11
Does the Buyer-Led Approach Work?

[151] Exhibit 2.7 posits that once a firm solves a binding problem, it continues on its new sales plane *ad infinitum*. In practice, of course, that is not the case. For reasons beyond their control—a downturn in demand, for example—sales may decline. With a jump in demand, they can also increase.

[152] Interestingly, different countries use different conventions to convert person-days to person-year equivalents. In Peru, the National Statistics and

Information Institute uses a factor of 180 to convert rural person-days to person-years, and a factor of 220 to convert urban person-days to person-years. When PRA converted its employment results, it used a factor of 200, which, if anything, underestimates the program's employment effect, given the high proportion of agriculture-related pursuits in PRA's client portfolio.

[153] "The Peru Poverty Reduction and Alleviation (PRA) Program," pp. 16-17.

[154] See USAID/Peru, "Poverty Reduction and Alleviation Activity (527-0387)," Lima, Peru, 1998.

[155] The discussion in this section borrows from James T. Riordan, "Are Business Approaches to International Development Cost-Effective? A Cross-Country Analysis," Oxford Business and Economics Conference, Oxford, England, 2010.

[156] See Donald Snodgrass, Lara Goldmark, Jenny Pan, Tsitsi Makombe, Matthew Rees, and Jennifer Sebstad, "Inventory and Analysis of Donor-Sponsored MSE Development Programs," microREPORT #15, USAID, Accelerated Microenterprise Advancement Project, Washington, D.C., 2005, p. 79.

[157] An economic perspective is different from an accounting perspective. From an accounting perspective, the sales reported by PRA and Paraguay Vende are attributable in full to PRA and Paraguay Vende: as noted above and discussed in detail in Chapter 16, a key function of a buyer-led program's monitoring and evaluation unit is to verify independently that it is highly unlikely reported results would have taken place otherwise. An accounting perspective asks what happened and whether the result observed would have taken place without the program. An economic perspective goes one step farther: it asks what value the result added to the economy, netting out what clients, and the labor associated with them, would likely have done—but in fact did not do—had the program not come along.

[158] See, for example, the estimates for programs in Ecuador, Guatemala, and Uganda in Krishna Kumar, "Generating Broad-Based Growth Through Agribusiness Promotion: Assessment of USAID Experience," USAID Program and Operations Assessment Report No. 9, Washington, D.C., 1994, pp. 38-42.

[159] Recipients of income typically demand new goods and services, which generates additional income, which then sets off an additional round of spending, and so on, and so on. The standard methodology for estimating these rounds of impacts is input-output analysis. Although the concept sounds very simple, the methodology can become arcane and time-consuming to implement.

The input-output literature draws distinctions among direct, indirect, and induced impacts. Direct impacts are the increases in sales or income that result directly from program support. Indirect impacts are those resulting from the derived demand for inputs required to bring about the direct impacts. Induced impacts are the expenditures by the households receiving additional income somewhere along the way. The latter two impacts are both backward linkages, though sometimes empirical results refer only to one or the other, which can lead unsuspecting readers to draw erroneous conclusions.

Not surprisingly, empirical estimates of backward linkages (here, the sum of indirect and induced impacts) can vary widely, though maybe not nearly so widely as one might think. Input-output studies of different countries and sectors suggest that most backward linkage multipliers hover in the neighborhood of 2, that is, that every dollar of economic benefit leads to an additional dollar of benefit elsewhere in the economy. It also suggests that it is rare for a multiplier to be less than 1.8. As a conservative rule of thumb, therefore, it is probably reasonable to assume that for every dollar of direct benefit induced by a buyer-led program, $.80 of additional benefit takes place elsewhere.

For examples of studies providing empirical estimates of backward linkage multipliers, see USAID/Peru, "Research Brief: A Pro-Poor Analysis of the Artichoke Value Chain in Peru," Greater Access to Trade Expansion Project, Lima, Peru, 2007; Eamon Henry and Reem Goussous, "Conduct Economic Impact Study for Tourism Sector—Phase 1 & 2: Final Report," USAID/Jordan, Achievement of Market-Friendly Initiatives and Results Program, Amman, Jordan, 2004; and Andrew Scarborough, "Calculating the Multiplier Effect of Targeted Households' Annual Increases in Income on Bolivia's Gross Domestic Product—Stage II: Oregano, Onion, Grape and Berry Programs," USAID/Bolivia, Market Access and Poverty Alleviation Program, 2005. For references on input-output methodology, see Łucja Tomaszewicz, "New I-O Table and SAMs for Poland," draft, XIII International Conference on Input-Output Techniques, Macerata, Italy, 2000; Bureau of Economic Analysis, "Benchmark Input-Output Accounts of the United States, 1992," http://www.bea.gov/bea/an/io1992/maintext.htm; and Thijs ten Raa and José M. Rueda-Cantuche, "Output and Employment Input-Output Multipliers on the Basis of Use and Make Matrices," 45th Congress of the European Regional Science Association, Amsterdam, 2005.

[160] TechnoServe talks about the "ripple effect" of its work, where the ripple includes not only copycat effects but the investment by client businesses in quality-of-life improvements in their communities. TechnoServe gives an example from Nicaragua (TechnoServe, "'Good News' from Tanzania and Nicaragua," email, August 18, 2004):

[O]nce a business begins to generate increased economic activity in a community, the business itself can support other quality-of-life improvements—without support from TechnoServe or reliance on donors or aid of any sort. (So many improvements that depend on external aid are not self-sustaining, often disappearing once the aid flow ceases.) TechnoServe's ultimate objective is to help create these "ripple effects," where one good business leads to another, and where businesses become the engine driving community improvements. Here's an example of that latter "ripple":

In December, members of the Pueblo Nuevo Cooperative presented their community health clinic in Jinotega, Nicaragua, with $1,500 worth of medical equipment, including examination tables and scales, as well as special medicines for patients with diabetes and asthma...Pueblo Nuevo's members used part of their profits from the 2002/2003 coffee season to make these purchases.

This season, Pueblo Nuevo was able to hire 330 seasonal and full-time workers, based on projections of 500,000 pounds of coffee produced and $500,000 in earnings. (Last season, Pueblo Nuevo produced 300,000 pounds, earned $300,000, and employed 270 workers.) And Pueblo Nuevo's members, still thinking about what they can do for their community, are in discussions with a potential partner—a private-sector company—about working together to construct a new school for Jinotega.

It all starts with the businesses: growing them, strengthening and expanding them, helping them adjust to new market conditions and take advantage of new opportunities.

[161] "The Poverty Reduction and Alleviation (PRA) Program," pp. 12-14. The term, "beneficiary," which Chapter 12 urges development practitioners to drop from their vocabulary, comes from the PAT methodology. The references for the case studies cited are: Pedro Mateu and Jean Vilca, *Modelo de medición de impacto sobre el bienestar objetivo y subjetivo: Un análisis de caso del Proyecto de Reducción y Alivio a la Pobreza (PRA)*, Documento de Trabajo 62 (Lima, Peru: Universidad del Pacífico, 2004); Gonzalo Talavera Forlin, "Medición del impacto del proyecto PRA sobre el bienestar de los productores de alcachofa en el Valle del Mantaro," Universidad del Pacífico, 2004; and "Oscar Chaquilla, "Evaluación de impacto del holantao en Ayacucho," Lima, Peru, 2005.

[162] Preston Pattie, personal communication with the author, 2009. Additional commentary from that communication is also of interest: "Data for ARCo clients was taken from the project database which routinely gathers inputs from Economic Service Centers and the Monitoring Unit at modest cost. This is in stark comparison to the millions spent on elaborate information systems that sometimes prove unwieldy."

[163] "The Poverty Reduction and Alleviation (PRA) Program," pp. 15-19.

[164] See Michael E. Porter and Mark R. Kramer, "Strategy and Society: The Link Between Competitive Advantage and Corporate Social Responsibility," *Harvard Business Review*, www.hbr.org, December 2006, p. 11.

[165] USAID's Market Access and Poverty Alleviation program in Bolivia is such a rarity, though the measure of success used is income, not a broader definition of poverty that likely would appeal more to the methodological purist. To assess the impact of the program on the income of its client farmers, MAPA designed and conducted annual surveys for both treatment and control groups. To isolate impact effectively, MAPA not only calculated the differences in income between program-introduced crops and traditional crops; it also compared MAPA clients against a control group of farmers with similar characteristics. This approach netted out natural increases in productivity and income that would reasonably have occurred without program assistance. At the end of five years, MAPA's activities are estimated to have contributed to a 24 percent net increase in income for its clients. Two less rigorous studies come up with similar findings. Talavera, op cit, estimates the incomes of PRA-supported artichoke growers to exceed their peers' by 30 percent. Matthew Edwardsen and Mark Wood, "Hybrid Sunflowers: Dramatically Increasing Ugandan Farmers' Income," *Africa Journal*, Summer, 2007, p. 31, estimates the incomes of Ugandan sunflower growers to have increased by nearly 30 percent as a result of support from USAID's APEP program.

[166] Paul P. Streeten, "Comment," in Meier and Stiglitz (eds.), op cit, p. 87.

[167] Despite countries' pleas for individual treatment, a specialist in country marketing notes wryly, "almost every country claims to be a crossroads or a gateway (or both) and presents itself as a 'land of contrasts.'" "National branding: A new sort of beauty contest," *Economist*, November 11, 2006, p. 68.

[168] Lawrence E. Harrison, "Waking from the Pan American Dream," *Foreign Policy* (Winter, 1971-72), p. 164. For a recent entreaty to look to culture first, see David Brooks, "Questions of Culture," Op-Ed, *New York Times*, February 19, 2006.

[169] See, for example, Sol Tax, *Penny Capitalism: A Guatemalan Indian Economy* (Chicago: University of Chicago Press, 1963).

[170] Clyde Kluckhohn, "Universal Categories of Culture," *Anthropology Today*, edited by A.L. Kroeber (Chicago: University of Chicago Press, 1953), p. 515.

[171] For more on this latter point, see V.W. Ruttan, "Institutional Innovation and Agricultural Development," *World Development*, XVII (No. 9, 1989), 1385.

[172] Bauer and Yamey, op cit, p. 103. For similar middle-of-the-road positions, see Albert O. Hirschman, *The Strategy of Economic Development* (New Haven: Yale University Press, 1958), pp. 11-24; Gustav F. Papanek, "Economic Development Theory: The Earnest Search for a Mirage," in *Essays in Economic Development and Cultural Change in Honor of Bert F. Hoselitz*, edited by Manning Nash, *Economic Development and Cultural Change*, XXV (Supplement, 1977), 274; and Gerald M. Meier, "The Old Generation of Development Economists and the New," in Meier and Stiglitz (eds.), op cit, p. 31.

[173] Michael Harrington, *The Other America: Poverty in the United States* (Baltimore: Penguin Books Inc., 1962), pp. 156, 164.

[174] Ibid., p. 164.

[175] Friedman, op cit, p. 154.

[176] In 1999, the trade and marketing activities of the marketing link program shifted to the Egypt Craft Center, which has since changed its name to Egypt Craft Center/Fair Trade Egypt.

[177] For an innovative approach to linking sequestered Pakistani women embroiderers with buyers, see Mennonite Economic Development Associates, "Behind the Veil: Access to Markets for Homebound Women Embroiderers in Pakistan—Final Report," Islamabad, Pakistan, 2008.

[178] Roads are probably the most common example given of public goods that reduce market transaction costs. There also are less obvious examples of public goods one can invest in for the same end. Facilitation of commercial linkages—that is, the creation and nurturing of trust between buyers and sellers with a patent predisposition not to work with each other—is one.

[179] USAID/Caucasus-Azerbaijan, "Program Description (Revised): Rural Azerbaijan Business Development," Baku, Azerbaijan, 2004, pp. 1, 3.

[180] USAID/Colombia, "Request for Proposal 514-05-009," Bogota, Colombia, 2005, p. 13.

[181] To be fair, not all programs confuse community and business development. By distinguishing clearly between the roles of public sector and private sector parties, USAID's Local Economic Development in Ukraine program (ULED) has helped Ukrainian city governments attract investment, promote business development, and create jobs. See Ukraine Local Economic Development Program, "ULED Tool Kit," USAID/ Ukraine, Kiev, 2009.

[182] Coca and poppy.

[183] In Bolivia, municipalities lobbied for and recently won access to "productive" monies. The decree does not define what "productive" means. Although some municipalities are looking carefully before they leap, many are gravitating toward either funding joint ventures with

existing companies or starting up new companies, clearly crossing the line between public and private sector activity.

[184] PRA had to adjust its expectations to the reality of coca-growing zones. PRA estimates its cost-effectiveness in coca-growing zones to have been only three fourths of its cost-effectiveness elsewhere. Nevertheless, it was still larger than what ADAM's predecessor program was able to achieve in zones with illicit crops in Colombia. The difference is big enough to be significant, even if one accepts the contention that the zones in Colombia are more difficult to work in than those in Peru. See "The Poverty Reduction and Alleviation (PRA) Program," p. 75; and USAID/Colombia, "Toward a Licit Economy: Colombia Alternative Development Program Final Report," Bogota, Colombia, 2006.

[185] Email to author from Bruce Brower, May 23, 2007.

[186] See George F. Will, "Cabs and Cupidity: Luis Paucar Tackles a Twisted Sense of Entitlement," *Washington Post,* May 27, 2007, p. B7.

[187] Drawing a clear line between relief and development is a major development challenge. In post-war situations, massive relief is often in order, but that very relief can inculcate a penchant toward dependency inimical to self-reliant market activity. Safety nets are essential, but, in practice, it is hard to say exactly when they start turning into what the British economist Ralph Harris used to refer to as "hammocks." See "Obituary: Ralph Harris," *Economist,* November 4, 2006, p. 96.

[188] High tariff protection can also contribute to economic isolation, sheltering domestic businesses from international competition and discouraging innovative investment. Although normally one may not identify protectionism with entitlement, the connection can be very real.

[189] James T. Riordan, "Bolivia Rural Competitiveness Program (ARCo) — Entrepreneurship Workshops: Reflections and Recommendations," Chemonics International Inc., La Paz, Bolivia, 2007.

Chapter 12
Making Language Mirror Thinking

[190] Friedman, op cit, pp. 341-42.

[191] The juxtaposition of the Asian Development Bank's advertisements is especially interesting. It is as if poverty reduction and private sector development have nothing to do with each other—a tendency foreshadowed in Part I.

[192] Thomas S. Kuhn, *The Structure of Scientific Revolutions,* 3rd ed. (Chicago: University of Chicago Press, 1996), p. 151.

Appendix to Part II
Fleshing Out a Strategy—What Not To Do

[193] See USAID/Madagascar, "Madagascar Economic Growth Strategic Objective: Statement of Work for Market and Trade Development Program," Request for Quotations No. 687-04-027, Antananarivo, Madagascar, 2004, pp. 8-24.

[194] For a comparably lengthy string of management and reporting requirements, see USAID/Nicaragua, "Request for Proposal (RFP) No. 524-05-004: More Competitive, Market Oriented Private Enterprises, and Improved Environmental Management in Nicaragua," Managua, Nicaragua, 2005, pp. C-1-C-12.

[195] At a competitiveness conference in Cairo in 2004, the author heard much the same kind of thinking. As one participant put it, "The government can't do it all. The private sector has to contribute." That is true of course, but it is the private sector, not the government, one must look to in the first place.

[196] The Market and Trade Development program in Madagascar above is one such instance. Another is USAID's SME Growth and Employment program in Brazil. See USAID/Brazil, "Scope of Work—SME Growth and Employment," Brasilia, Brazil, 2004.

[197] See Easterly, *The Elusive Quest for Growth,* for an emphatic exposition of this point.

[198] Synergy can also result in too many cooks spoiling the broth—a perfect setup for one organization to blame another when things go wrong, diluting accountability.

[199] Bill Gates, "How to Fix Capitalism," *Time,* August 11, 2008, pp. 42-43.

[200] For a discussion of how procurement incentive systems have hampered legal reform in post-Communist countries, see Channell, op cit, p. 5.

[201] Development contractors are not the only ones that try to divorce pay from performance. For an interesting example from academe, see Charles Diamond, "Economics: An Honest Wage for Honest Work," *Business Monthly,* American Chamber of Commerce in Egypt, March, 1998, p. 20. On the other side of the ledger, it is interesting that advertising agencies, which have traditionally charged for the time they have put in, are now moving to payment for results. See "Advertising's new model: Clock-watchers no more," *Economist,* May 16, 2009, p.72.

[202] For a theoretical treatment of issues in aligning incentives between "principals" and their "agents," see Kathleen M. Eisenhardt, "Agency Theory: An Assessment and Review," *Academy of Management Review,* XIV (No. 1, 1989), 57-74.

[203] See "USAID History," http://www.usaid.gov/about_usaid/usaidhist.html.

Chapter 13
Getting Started

[204] Easterly, *The White Man's Burden*, p. 179.

[205] And, operationally, made it less of a plan than an incentive structure.

[206] Like "capacity building," for example.

[207] Lenny T. Mendonca and Matt Miller, "Crafting a **message that sticks:** An Interview with Chip Heath," *McKinsey Quarterly*, November, 2007, pp. 3-4.

[208] It will, however, guard against non-performance by program implementers by building in escape clauses.

[209] In fact, one would have to make extreme assumptions about the relationship between sales and value added and the time distribution of costs and benefits for that not to be case.

[210] The non-coincidence of economic corridors with states, departments, counties, provinces, districts, etc., can have a salutary side-effect programmatically. If a buyer-led program does not "belong" to any one local government, it is difficult for any one local government to dictate its priorities, which gives the program a certain degree of independence from local political pressures and concerns. Again, the point is not that local government has nothing to do with creating a climate conducive to economic activity. It is simply to stress once again the important distinction between private goods and public goods, and that buyer-led programs have to do with the former, not the latter. By choosing to organize their work in economic corridors, buyer-led programs can protect themselves—a bit, anyway—from local governments predisposed to overreach.

[211] "The Peru Poverty Reduction and Alleviation (PRA) Program," p. 73.

[212] With few exceptions, PRA staffed its Economic Service Centers with generalists. The most notable exception was Pucallpa, where, given the corridor's propensity for forestry, the program consciously hired a forester as a business advisor. At the time, however, a concession law was in flux, and PRA was unable to find clients ready to develop and implement sustainable management plans, a precondition it had established for its assistance. For two years, therefore, the forester worked entirely outside his own field—and, to his great credit, was the business advisor who helped shepherd the Shipibo-Conibo ceramics operation through to completion.

[213] At one point a mid-sized gold jewelry manufacturer in Puno, Peru,

solicited assistance from PRA in identifying new buyers in the United States. As it developed a Client Growth Plan with the company, PRA learned that it obtained much of its gold from young children who scavenged local streams. PRA's initial reaction was not to support the company, but later the program came up with a more constructive strategy: conditioning its support on the client complying with International Labour Organization child labor standards, a demand to which the company agreed.

[214] For more on businesspeople looking at environment positively rather than negatively, see Avrom Bendavid-Val and Christopher Perine, "Environmental Competitiveness: Completing the Competitiveness Paradigm," Chemonics International Inc., Washington, D.C., 2003.

Chapter 14
Setting Up Business Promotion Offices

[215] There is always an exception to prove the rule. The ABAD program in Azerbaijan conducted a procurement to subcontract the operation of its Guba Marketing Center to a local organization. Not one bidder proved satisfactory, and the program wound up hiring individuals directly, who worked out just fine.

[216] The need for a heavy technical hand also explains why the relationship between the central program office and the operator of the Business Promotion Office is a subcontract, not a grant.

[217] At the conclusion of the MEDI program in Armenia, the business advisors in MEDI North commented on the tension occasioned by that relationship, saying that sometimes they felt they were reporting to two masters, placing them in an awkward position. That said, they also recognized the wisdom in MEDI's central program office acting in such a heavy-handed manner.

[218] The author is indebted to Juan Robles of USAID/Peru for this write-up.

[219] Management textbooks do not lack for organizational devices for identifying constraints. In the end, though, zooming in on clients' most binding problems calls for hard thought, which no management tools can replace. For that reason, this book does not single out any one management tool over another. That said, the Goldratt Institute's "5 Steps of the Theory of Constraints" lays out a compelling logic for guiding the problem-solving process:
1. Identify the constraint
2. Decide how to exploit the constraint
3. Subordinate and synchronize everything else to the above decisions
4. Elevate the performance of the constraint

5.   If, in any of the above steps the constraint has shifted, go back to Step 1 (see http://www.goldratt.com/toctpwp8.htm).

Chapter 15
Selecting and Working with Clients

[220] "Bolivia: A Major New Project," An Informative Bulletin for Friends and Patrons of Strategies for International Development, Washington, D.C., Spring 2007, p.1.

[221] They can also miss promising opportunities as they do so. A number of years ago, a program in Bolivia undertook a time-consuming assessment of numerous products grown in the Chapare. None of the assessments touched on the product, camu-camu, which turned out to be a real winner.

[222] James W. Butcher, personal communication with the author, 2005.

[223] Somewhat ironically, therefore, Business Development Offices do most of their work **outside** the office. Over the years, it has been common for development programs to operate through "incubators," "training centers," or "trade points," which see their mandate more as attracting clients **to** their offices.

[224] Gregory Kruse, "The Role of Business Advisors in the PRA Project in Peru," draft, Chemonics International Inc., Washington, D.C., 2004, pp. 4-7.

[225] James T. Riordan, "Reflections and Recommendations: Consultant Report, December 2007," USAID/Paraguay, Asunción, Paraguay, 2007, pp. 4-5. For a discussion of the multiplicity of factors that affect a program's ability to engage end-market buyers, see Ted Barber, "Engaging End-Market Buyers in Value Chain Development," USAID Briefing Paper, Accelerated Microenterprise Advancement Project, Washington, DC, n.d.

[226] A colleague of the author who has worked extensively in Eastern and Southern Africa says he continues to be amazed at how farm households claim they do not have the money to invest in technology adoption but nevertheless find a way to spend lavishly on weddings and funerals.

[227] The author is indebted to Gregory Kruse for this checklist.

[228] A classic reference is Everett M. Rogers, *Diffusion of Innovations*, 4th ed. (New York: Free Press, 1995). See also Chemonics International Inc., "Chemonics' Competitiveness Interventions: Review of Worldwide Experiences," Contract No. PCE-I-00-98-00015-00, Task Order No. 04, USAID, Washington, DC, 2001.

[229] R. Glenn Hubbard and William Duggan, *The Aid Trap: Hard Truths About Ending Poverty*, pp. 81-82. See, also, "From 10 Years of Projects to 10 Months of Business," "Rural Competitiveness Activity: Creating Opportunities," USAID/Bolivia, La Paz, Bolivia, 2008, p. 4.

[230] See Red Bolivia Emprendedora, "Primer Encuentro Internacional de Cultura Emprendedora," La Paz, 2007, p. 21.

[231] Danilo Cruz-DePaula, personal communication with the author, 2007.

[232] In a personal communication to the author, colleague Eric Howell made the point this way:

> McKinsey consultants are always saying things like, "We're not being very 80/20 about this." By which they mean, "We're wasting a lot of time on things that aren't going to produce results. We've already produced 80% of what we're going to ever achieve on this project. Let's not go crazy and spend a lot of time trying to get that last 20%; better to move on to something else more productive."

Chapter 16
Tracking and Sharing Progress

[233] In some development circles, the more generic term, "performance monitoring," has replaced and subsumed "monitoring and evaluation" under its purview. For the author, much performance monitoring has fallen into the trap of over-formalization, piling layer upon layer of results that development professionals have to worry about. To keep the focus squarely on sales and jobs, therefore, the discussion here uses the more circumscribed and pedestrian term, "monitoring and evaluation."

[234] Profitability is of course a criterion for whether a buyer-led program supports a client in the first place. Afterwards, however, it is not a concern for data collection or reporting purposes.

[235] The interim and final evaluations of PRA looked at the issue of conducting monitoring and evaluation in house vs. contracting it out. Both concluded that the benefits of doing it in house outweigh the presumed advantage of entrusting it to others.

[236] For example, if one client purchases the output of a second client as an input into its business, the value of the sales of the first client includes the value of the sales of the second client. The program can take credit only for the sales of the first client. If it took credit for both, there would be double counting.

[237] Some funding agencies—USAID, for example—like to know how much the incomes of small farmers rise as a consequence of their program support. Since the number of small farmers affected by a program can run into the thousands, applying survey methodology is appropriate in such case. Although the resultant estimates have a margin of error, they can provide a good ballpark approximation of the magnitude of program impact. The APEP program in Uganda and the MARKETS program in

Nigeria are examples of programs that have applied this approach effectively.

[238] Part II argues strongly that it makes little programmatic sense to delimit the products or sectors a buyer-led program will support. Ironically, though, a program that picks its product or sectoral winners beforehand has a much more circumscribed task of developing employment coefficients to apply the methodology discussed here.

[239] Whether to attribute causality often requires judgment. Sometimes a client says it has "plans" to make improvements to sell more, but for one reason or another never quite gets around to it. What about attribution of causality, then, if a buyer-led program comes along and prompts the client to move forward? At one level, the improvements—and corresponding results—were presumably going to take place anyway. At another level, it is highly unlikely that they would have taken place at any time close to when in fact they did. In such case, if the buyer-led program can honestly say it broke the ice and accelerated actions that otherwise would have taken place only in some undefined future, it is reasonable to attribute causality to the program. At the other extreme, if the program did nothing more than board a train that was going to pull out of the station anyway— see Example 3 below—attribution is out of the question. In practice, the truth can lie somewhere between the two extremes, and whether to assign attribution is a judgment call.

[240] "El Salvadorian Farmers Become Entrepreneurs," case study, USAID, Washington, D.C., n.d.

[241] See USAID/Paraguay, "Paraguay Poverty Reduction Program: Paraguay Vende Project Final Report," Asunción, 2007.

Exhibits, Photos, and Tables

Exhibits

Photos

Tables

Bibliography

Abadie, Alberto. "Poverty, Political Freedom, and the Roots of Terrorism." *American Economic Review*, XCVI (No. 2, May, 2006), 50-56.

"Advertising's new model: Clock-watchers no more." *Economist*, May 16, 2009.

Allen, Robert C. *The British Industrial Revolution in Global Perspective*. New York: Cambridge University Press, 2009.

Avraham Y. Goldratt Institute. "The Theory of Constraints and its Thinking Processes: A Brief Introduction to TOC." http://www.goldratt.com/toctpwp8.htm.

Baker, III, James A., Lee H. Hamilton, et al. "The Iraq Study Group Report." Washington, D.C., 2006.

Banerjee, Abhijit Vinayak. "Making Aid Work." *Boston Review*, July/August, 2006.

Banerjee, Abhijit Vinayak, Roland Bénabou, and Dilip Mookherjee (eds.). *Understanding Poverty*. New York: Oxford University Press, 2006.

Banerjee, Abhijit, Esther Duflo, Rachel Glennester, and Cynthia Kinnan. "The miracle of microfinance? Evidence from a randomized evaluation." Unpublished paper, Abdul Latif Jameel Poverty Action Lab, Department of Economics, Massachusetts Institute of Technology. Cambridge, MA, 2009.

Barber, Ted. "Engaging End-Market Buyers in Value Chain Development." USAID Briefing Paper, Accelerated Microenterprise Advancement Project. Washington, D.C., n.d.

Barbone, Luca. "Foreword." In *Employment and Shared Growth: Rethinking the Role of Labor Mobility for Development*, ed. by Pierella Paci and Pieter Serneels. Washington, D.C: World Bank, 2007.

Bauer, Peter T., and Basil S. Yamey. *The Economics of Under-Developed Countries*. Chicago: University of Chicago Press, 1957.

Bendavid-Val, Avrom. "Rural-Urban Linkages: Farming and Farm Households in Regional and Town Economies." *Review of Urban and Regional Development Studies*, No. 2, 1989.

Bendavid-Val, Avrom, and Christopher Perine. "Environmental Competitiveness: Completing the Competitiveness Paradigm." Unpublished paper, Chemonics International Inc. Washington, D.C., 2003.

Birger, Jon. "The 30 Best Stocks." *Money*, Fall, 2002.

Bureau of Economic Analysis. "Benchmark Input-Output Accounts of the United States, 1992." http://www.bea.gov/bea/an/io1992/maintext.htm.

Burnham, James. "Why Ireland Boomed." *Independent Review*, VII (No. 4, Spring, 2003), 537-56.

Butcher, James W. "Business Development Services: Setting Up and Operating a BDS Center." Presentation, Business Development Services Conference 2005: Shaping Jordan's Industry with International Best Practices, USAID/Jordan. Amman, 2005.

Center for Global Development. "When Will We Ever Learn? Improving Lives Through Impact Evaluation." Evaluation Gap Working Group. Washington, D.C., 2006. http://www.cgdev.org/content/publications/detail/7973.

Channell, Wade. "Lessons not Learned: Problems with Western Aid for Law Reform in Postcommunist Countries." Rule of Law Series, Number 57, Carnegie Endowment for International Peace. Washington, D.C., 2005.

Chaquilla, Oscar. "Evaluación de impacto del holantao en Ayacucho." Lima, Peru, 2005.

Chemonics International Inc., "Chemonics' Competitiveness Interventions: Review of Worldwide Experiences." USAID, report under Contract No. PCE-I-00-98-00015-00, Task Order No. 04. Washington, D.C., 2001.

Comin, Diego. "Total Factor Productivity." In *The New Palgrave Dictionary of Economics*, 2nd ed., Steven N. Durlauf and Lawrence E. Blume (eds.). Palgrave Macmillan, 2008; *The New Palgrave Dictionary of Economics Online*. Palgrave Macmillan. http://www.dictionaryofeconomics.com/article?id=pde2008_T000081> doi:10.1057/9780230226203.1719.

Commike, Laura, Allison Coppel, Rory Eakin, Mar Higuera, Bhavika Vyas, and Steve Walsh. "Small and Medium Size Enterprises: *What will drive future growth?*" Unpublished paper, Graduate School of Business, Stanford University. Palo Alto, California, 2005.

Coppel, Allison, and Kirsten Olsen. "Community Engagement Models for the Extractives Industry in Developing Countries." Unpublished paper, external version, Graduate School of Business, Stanford University. Palo Alto, California, 2006.

Crook, Clive. "Capitalism: The Movie: Why Americans don't value markets enough—and why that matters." *Atlantic Monthly*, March, 2006.

Dercon, Stefan. "Review of Gary S. Fields and Guy Pfeffermann (eds.), *Pathways Out of Poverty: Private Firms and Economic Mobility in Developing Countries* (Washington, D.C.: International Finance Corporation, 2003)." *Journal of Economic Literature*, XLIII (June, 2005), 508.

De Soto, Hernando. *The Mystery of Capital: Why Capitalism Triumphs in the West and Fails Everywhere Else*. New York: Basic Books, 2000.

Diamond, Charles. "Economics: An Honest Wage for Honest Work." *Business Monthly*, American Chamber of Commerce in Egypt, March, 1998.

Do, Quy-Toan, and Lakshmi Iyer. "Poverty, Social Divisions and Conflict in Nepal." Working Paper 07-065, World Bank. Washington, D.C., 2007.

Easterly, William. "4 Ways to Spend $60 Billion Wisely." *Washington Post*, July 2, 2006.

____. "The Big Push Déjà Vu: A Review of Jeffrey Sachs's *The End of Poverty: Economic Possibilities for Our Time*." *Journal of Economic Literature*, XLIV (March, 2006), 95-105.

____. *The Elusive Quest for Growth: Economists' Adventures and Misadventures in the Tropics*. Cambridge, MA: MIT Press, 2001.

____. *The White Man's Burden: Why the West's Efforts to Aid the Rest Have Done So Much Ill and So Little Good*. New York: Penguin Press, 2006.

Easterly, William, and Ross Levine. "Tropics, Germs, and Crops: How Endowments Influence Economic Development." National Bureau for Economic Research Working Paper No. 9106. Cambridge, MA, 2002.

"Economics focus: Secret sauce: China's rapid growth is due not just to heavy investment, but also to the world's fastest productivity gains." *Economist*, November 14, 2009.

Edwardsen, Matthew, and Mark Wood. "Hybrid Sunflowers: Dramatically Increasing Ugandan Farmers' Income." *Africa Journal*, Summer, 2007.

Eisenhardt, Kathleen M. "Agency Theory: An Assessment and Review." *Academy of Management Review*, XIV (No. 1, 1989), 57-74.

Ellis, Frank, and Nigel Harris. "New Thinking About Urban and Rural Development." Keynote Paper for DFID Sustainable Development Retreat, University of Surrey. Guildford, UK, 2004.

Evaluation Gap Working Group. "When Will We Ever Learn? Improving Lives Through Impact Evaluation." Center for Global Development. Washington, D.C., 2006. http://www.cgdev.org/content/publications/detail/7973.

Feenstra, R.C. "Integration of Trade and Disintegration of Production in the Global Economy." *Journal of Economic Perspectives*, XII (No. 4, 1998), 31-50.

Fintrac Inc. "Jump-Starting BDS Markets in Honduras: When Direct Provision Makes Sense." Paper, VI Foro Interamericano de la Microempresa. Guatemala, Guatemala, 2003.

_____. "SDE en el Sector de Agronegocios: Optimizando Impacto." Presentation, VI Foro Interamericano de la Microempresa. Guatemala, Guatemala, 2003.

_____. "The U.S. Market for Fresh Asparagus," Market Survey #01, Farmer Training and Development Program, Millennium Challenge Account of Honduras. La Lima Nueva, Cortés, December, 2006.

Fox, James W. "The Callao Port Concession: A USAID Home Run." Presentation, USAID Economic Growth Officers Workshop. Washington, D.C., 2007.

Friedman, Thomas. *The Lexus and the Olive Tree.* New York: Anchor Books, 2000.

Gabre-Madhin, Eleni Z. "Market Institutions, Transaction Costs, and Social Capital in the Ethiopian Grain Market." Research Report 124, International Food Policy Research Institute. Washington, D.C., 2001.

Glaeser, Edward, Rafael La Porta, Florencio Lopez-de-Silanes, and Andrei Shleifer. "Do Institutions Cause Growth?" National Bureau of Economic Research Working Paper No. 10568. Cambridge, MA, 2004.

Goldratt, Eliyahu M., and Jeff Cox. *The Goal: A Process of Ongoing Improvement.* Great Barrington, MA: North River Press, 2004.

Gordon, David. "Indicators of Poverty and Hunger." Presentation, Expert Group Meeting on Youth Development Indicators, United Nations. New York, 2005.

Gravois, John. "hey, wait a minute — The De Soto Delusion: Peruvian Economist Hernando de Soto's ideas for helping the poor have made him a global celebrity. Now, if only those ideas worked...." http://slate.msn.com/id/2112792, 2005.

Harberger, Arnold C. "The View from the Trenches: Development Processes and Policies as Seen by a Working Professional." In *Frontiers of Development Economics: The Future in Perspective,* ed. by Gerald M. Meier and Joseph E. Stiglitz. New York: World Bank and Oxford University Press, 2001.

Harrington, Michael. *The Other America: Poverty in the United States.* Baltimore: Penguin Books Inc., 1962.

Harrison, Lawrence E. "Waking from the Pan American Dream." *Foreign Policy,* Winter, 1971-72.

Hausmann, Ricardo, Lant Pritchett, and Dani Rodrik. "Growth Accelerations." National Bureau of Economic Research Working Paper No. 10566. Cambridge, MA, 2004.

Henry, Eamon, and Reem Goussous. "Conduct Economic Impact Study for Tourism Sector—Phase 1 & 2: Final Report." USAID/Jordan, Achievement of Market-Friendly Initiatives and Results Program. Amman, 2004.

Hirschman, Albert O. *The Strategy of Economic Development*. New Haven: Yale University Press, 1958.

Hubbard, R. Glenn, and William Duggan. *The Aid Trap: Hard Truths About Ending Poverty*. New York: Columbia University Press, 2009.

____. "Why Africa needs a Marshall plan." *Financial Times*, FT.com, June 5, 2007.

INOTEH Consulting. "Evaluation Report for Macedonian Competitiveness Activity." Skopje, Macedonia, 2006.

Inter-American Development Bank. "The case of the Information Technology Rio Program (Río Informático) in Brazil." Paper, VI Foro Interamericano de la Microempresa. Guatemala, Guatemala, 2003.

Kamasak, Rifat. "Firm Specific versus Industry Structure Factors in Explaining Performance Variation." Presentation, Eurasia Business and Economic Society Conference. Istanbul, Turkey, 2010.

Kanbur, Ravi, and Lyn Squire. "The Evolution of Thinking About Poverty: Exploring the Interactions." In *Frontiers of Development Economics: The Future in Perspective*, ed. by Gerald M. Meier and Joseph E. Stiglitz. New York: World Bank and Oxford University Press, 2001.

Kaplinsky, Raphael, and Mike Morris. "A Handbook for Value Chain Research." International Development Research Centre. Canada, n.d.

Karnani, Aneel. "Microfinance Misses Its Mark." *Stanford Social Innovation Review*, V (Summer, 2007), 34-40.

Kluckhohn, Clyde. "Universal Categories of Culture." In *Anthropology Today*, ed. by A.L. Kroeber. Chicago: University of Chicago Press, 1953.

Kristjanson, Patricia, and Jerry Martin. "More Than Free Markets Are Needed: The Case of a Peasant Millionaire in Madagascar." *Choices*, 4th quarter, 1991.

Krugman, Paul. "Good News from Ireland: A Geographical Perspective." In *International Perspectives on the Irish Economy*, ed. by Alan W. Gray. Dublin: Indecon Economic Consultants, 1997.

Kruse, Gregory. "The Role of Business Advisors in the PRA Project in Peru." Draft, Chemonics International Inc. Washington, D.C., 2004.

Kuhn, Thomas S. *The Structure of Scientific Revolutions*. 3rd ed. Chicago: University of Chicago Press, 1996.

Kula, Olaf, Jeanne Downing, and Michael Field. "Globalization and the Small Firm: An Industry Value Chain Approach to Economic Growth and Poverty Reduction." microREPORT #42, USAID, Accelerated Microenterprise Advancement Project—Business Development Services. Washington, D.C., 2006.

Kumar, Krishna. "Generating Broad-Based Growth Through Agribusiness Promotion: Assessment of USAID Experience." USAID Program and Operations Assessment Report No. 9. Washington, D.C., 1994.

Lamb, John E., and Bruce Brower. "Agribusiness Development Centers." Report submitted to World Bank, Chemonics International Inc. Washington, D.C., 1999.

Mateu, Pedro, and Jean Vilca. *Modelo de medición de impacto sobre el bienestar objetivo y subjetivo: Un análisis de caso del Proyecto de Reducción y Alivio a la Pobreza (PRA).* Documento de Trabajo 62. Lima, Peru: Universidad del Pacífico, 2004.

McKee, Katherine W. "Context and Evolution of BDS." Presentation, Business Development Services Conference 2005: Shaping Jordan's Industry with International Best Practices, USAID/Jordan. Amman, 2005.

Meier, Gerald M. "The Old Generation of Development Economists and the New." In *Frontiers of Development Economics: The Future in Perspective,* ed. by Gerald M. Meier and Joseph E. Stiglitz. New York: World Bank and Oxford University Press, 2001.

Mendonca, Lenny T., and Matt Miller, "Crafting a **message that sticks**: An Interview with Chip Heath." *McKinsey Quarterly,* November, 2007.

Mennonite Economic Development Associates. "Behind the Veil: Access to Markets for Homebound Women Embroiderers in Pakistan—Final Report." Islamabad, Pakistan, 2008.

Mesinas, Jorge. "Informe Final de Prácticas Profesionales." Unpublished paper, Harvard University. Cambridge, MA, 2005.

Ministry of the Presidency. "Elementos para el Desarrollo de las Ciudades Intermedias en Apoyo a la Lucha Contra la Pobreza Extrema." Final draft. Lima, Peru, 1996.

Miranda, Gonzalo. "Report on Brazilian Market Access for Raspberries and Onion." Market Access and Poverty Alleviation Program, USAID/Bolivia. Cochabamba, 2003.

Moore, Vicki. "Lessons Learned on Implementation of Competitiveness Activities." USAID. Washington, D.C., 2002.

Morduch, Jonathan. "The Microfinance Promise." *Journal of Economic Literature,* XXXVII (December, 1999), 1569-1614.

Naim, Moises. "Demise of a Metaphor: Why the Marshall Plan's success is not so easy to repeat." *Book World, Washington Post,* November 4, 2007.

Nathan Associates Inc. "The Impact of USAID-Funded Private Sector Development Programs on Mozambique's Private Sector." USAID/Mozambique. Maputo, 2008.

Ortega Landa, Ramiro. "Value Chain Financing in Rural Bolivia: Introducing Purchase Order Financing." USAID/Bolivia. La Paz, n.d.

Paci, Pierella, and Pieter Serneels (eds.). *Employment and Shared Growth: Rethinking the Role of Labor Mobility for Development.* Washington, D.C: World Bank, 2007.

Paddock, William and Elizabeth. *We Don't Know How: An Independent*

Audit of What They Call Success in Foreign Assistance. Ames: Iowa State University Press, 1973.

Paniagua V., Alberto, and Héctor Nogales S. "Bolivia: Bases para una Política de Desarrollo Rural Regional." Draft, Documento de Campo 52, Proyecto MACA/PNUD/FAO, Apoyo a la Gestión Técnico-Normativa del MACA. La Paz, Bolivia, 1993.

Papanek, Gustav F. "Economic Development Theory: The Earnest Search for a Mirage." In *Essays in Economic Development and Cultural Change in Honor of Bert F. Hoselitz,* ed. by Manning Nash. *Economic Development and Cultural Change,* XXV, Supplement, 1977.

Patrick, Stewart. "U.S. Foreign Aid Reform: Will It Fix What Is Broken?" Center for Global Development. Washington, D.C., 2006.

Perreault, Jr., William, and E. Jerome McCarthy. *Essentials of Marketing.* 10th ed. New York: McGraw-Hill Irwin, 2006.

Pineau, Carol. "The Africa You Never See." *Washington Post,* April 17, 2005.,

Porter, Michael E. *The Competitive Advantage of Nations.* New York: The Free Press, 1990.

Porter, Michael E., and Mark R. Kramer. "Strategy and Society: The Link Between Competitive Advantage and Corporate Social Responsibility." *Harvard Business Review,* December, 2006. http://hbr.org/2006/12/strategy-and-society/ar/1.

Raa, Thijs ten, and José M. Rueda-Cantuche. "Output and Employment Input-Output Multipliers on the Basis of Use and Make Matrices." 45th Congress of the European Regional Science Association. Amsterdam, 2005.

Red Bolivia Emprendedora. "Primer Encuentro Internacional de Cultura Emprendedora." La Paz, Bolivia, 2007.

Rice, Susan E. "We Must Put More on the Plate to Fight Poverty." *Washington Post,* July 5, 2005.

Riely, Frank, Nancy Mock, Bruce Cogill, Laura Bailey, and Eric Kenefick. "Food Security Indicators and Indicators for Use in the Monitoring and Evaluation of Food Aid Programs." USAID, Food and Nutrition Technical Assistance Project, Academy for Educational Development. Washington, D.C., 1999.

Riordan, James T. "Are Business Approaches to International Development Cost-Effective? A Cross-Country Analysis." Presentation, Oxford Business and Economics Conference. Oxford, England, 2010.

_____. "Azerbaijan Business Assistance and Development Project: Recommendations for Strengthening Its Marketing Centers." Chemonics International Inc. Washington, D.C., 2005.

_____. "Bolivia Rural Competitiveness Program (ARCo)—Entrepreneurship

Workshops: Reflections and Recommendations." Chemonics International Inc. La Paz, Bolivia, 2007.

_____. "One Buyer at a Time." *Stanford Social Innovation Review*, V (Winter, 2007), 48-55.

_____. "Reflections and Recommendations: Consultant Report, December 2007." USAID/Paraguay. Asunción, 2007.

_____. "A Strategy to Integrate Small Farmer Initiatives and Expand Export Agriculture in Nicaragua." Report submitted to Asociación Nicaraguense de Productores y Exportadores de Productos no Tradicionales (APENN). Managua, Nicaragua, 1997.

_____. "Trade and Economic Growth." Presentation, "Aid to Trade" Conference. Alexandria, Egypt, 1999.

Riordan, James T., and J. David Flood. "Lessons Learned from USAID Support of Agricultural Policy Reform in Ecuador and How They Compare with Lessons Learned Elsewhere." Draft, USAID/Ecuador. Quito, 1996.

Riordan, James T., and Adam Noyce. "The Sustainability of Business Development Services in Developing Economies: What Do We Want to Sustain and Why?" Presentation, Eurasia Business and Economic Society Conference. Istanbul, Turkey, 2010.

Riordan, James T., and David L. Tacker. "Interim Impact Evaluation of PL-480, Title I, Section 108 Program in the Dominican Republic." Final report, LAC TECH II Agriculture and Rural Development Technical Services Project Evaluation Team. Santo Domingo, Dominican Republic, 1995.

Riordan, James T., Enrique Vásquez H., Roberta van Haeften, Fred L. Mann, and Carlos Figueroa A. *Attacking Poverty: A Market Approach.* Lima, Peru: Universidad del Pacífico, 2003.

Robison, Gregory F. "The Cultural Challenge of Supporting Enterprise." *Grassroots Development*, XVII (No. 2) and XVIII (No. 1), 1994, 23-34.

Rodrik, Dani. "Goodbye Washington Consensus, Hello Washington Confusion? A Review of The World Bank's *Economic Growth in the 1990s: Learning from a Decade of Reform.*" *Journal of Economic Literature*, XLIV (December, 2006), 973-87.

Rogers, Everett M. *Diffusion of Innovations.* 4th ed. New York: Free Press, 1995.

Ruttan, V.W. "Institutional Innovation and Agricultural Development." *World Development*, XVII (No. 9, 1989), 1375-87.

Sachs, Jeffrey. *The End of Poverty: Economic Possibilities for Our Time.* New York: Penguin Press, 2005.

Savage, Suzanne. "Short Term Sales and Marketing Technical Assistance." USAID/Albania, Small Business Credit and Assistance Project. Tirana, 2005.

Scarborough, Andrew. "Calculating the Multiplier Effect of Targeted Households' Annual Increases in Income on Bolivia's Gross Domestic Product—Stage II: Oregano, Onion, Grape and Berry Programs." USAID/Bolivia, Market Access and Poverty Alleviation Program. Cochabamba, 2005.

Schmaedick, Gerald, Michael Glover, Antonio Tacchino, Iván Mifflin, Pedro Flores, and Renso Martínez. "A Qualitative Assessment of the Poverty Reduction and Alleviation Program of USAID/Peru: January, 2003." Checchi & Co. International Consulting, Task Order #814, Evaluation IQC under Contract No. AEP-I-00-00-00022-00. Washington, D.C., 2003.

Shepherd, Andrew W. "Approaches to linking producers to markets: A review of experiences to date." Agricultural Management, Marketing and Finance Occasional Paper, Food and Agriculture Organization of the United Nations. Rome, Italy, 2007.

Sievers, Merten, and Paul Vandenberg. "Synergies through Linkages: Who Benefits from Linking Microfinance and Business Development Services?" World Development, XXXV (No. 8, 2007), 1341-58.

Slone, Reuben E. "Leading a Supply Chain Turnaround." Reprint R0410G, Harvard Business Review, October, 2004.

Smith, Adam. An Inquiry into the Nature and Causes of the Wealth of Nations, ed. by W.B. Todd. Based on 1784 Edition, Volume 2 of The Glasgow Edition of the Works and Correspondence of Adam Smith, ed. by D.D. Raphael and Andrew Skinner. Oxford: Clarendon Press.

Snodgrass, Donald, Lara Goldmark, Jenny Pan, Tsitsi Makombe, Matthew Rees, and Jennifer Sebstad. "Inventory and Analysis of Donor-Sponsored MSE Development Programs." microREPORT #15, USAID, Accelerated Microenterprise Advancement Project. Washington, D.C., 2005.

Srinivasan, T.N. "Global Competitiveness: Developing Country Perspectives." Conference presentation, Revisiting Egypt's Competitiveness: The Road Ahead for Building Leading Sectors. Cairo, Egypt, 2004.

Stewart, Matthew. "The Management Myth." Atlantic Monthly, June, 2006.

Stifel, David, Bart Minten, and Paul Dorosh. "Transactions Costs and Agricultural Productivity: Implications of Isolation for Rural Poverty in Madagascar." Markets and Structural Studies Division Discussion Paper No. 56, International Food Policy Research Institute. Washington, D.C., 2003.

Strategies for International Development. "Bolivia: A Major New Project." An Informative Bulletin for Friends and Patrons of Washington, D.C. Spring, 2007.

Streeten, Paul P. "Comment." In Frontiers of Development Economics: The

Future in Perspective, ed. by Gerald M. Meier and Joseph E. Stiglitz. New York: World Bank and Oxford University Press, 2001.

Talavera Forlin, Gonzalo. "Medición del impacto del proyecto PRA sobre el bienestar de los productores de alcachofa en el Valle del Mantaro." Universidad del Pacífico. Lima, Peru, 2004.

Tax, Sol. *Penny Capitalism: A Guatemalan Indian Economy.* Chicago: University of Chicago Press, 1963.

The Mitchell Group, Inc. "Promoting Competitiveness in Practice: An Assessment of Cluster-Based Approaches." Washington, D.C., 2003.

Tomaszewicz, Łucja. "New I-O Table and SAMs for Poland." Draft, XIII International Conference on Input-Output Techniques. Macerata, Italy, 2000.

Ukraine Local Development Program. "ULED Tool Kit." USAID/Ukraine. Kyiv, 2009.

United Nations Economic Commission for Europe. "Entrepreneurship and SME Development: Index of SME Development." http://www.unece.org/indust/sme/ece-sme.htm, 2006. (program discontinued)

University of California, Davis. "Rehabilitating Agriculture in Afghanistan: Horticultural Market Survey." International Programs Office, College of Agricultural and Environmental Sciences. Davis, California, 2003.

U.S. Agency for International Development. "Making Markets Work for the Rural Poor: An Agenda to Advance Broadly Based, Sustainable Rural Economic Growth in Latin America and the Caribbean." Bureau for Latin America and the Caribbean. Washington, D.C., 1994.

USAID. "AMAP BDS Knowledge and Practice Task Order: Lexicon." microNOTE #6. Washington, D.C., 2005.

USAID. "El Salvadorian Farmers Become Entrepreneurs." Case study. n.d.

USAID. "Enterprise Growth Initiatives: Findings of a New USAID-Funded Report by Snodgrass & Winkler." EG Technical Briefing, No. 7. Washington, D.C., 2004.

USAID. "Moldovan Company's Rise in Productivity Yields New Clients." Program E-Spotlight, Issue 12, September, 2007.

USAID. "Pro-Poor Growth: A Guide to Policies and Programs." Washington, D.C., 2005.

USAID. "Securing the Future: A Strategy for Economic Growth." Washington, D.C., 2008.

USAID. "Strategic Goal 5: Economic Prosperity and Security." Washington, D.C., 2007. http://www.usaid.gov/policy/par06/ps_so2_sg5.html.

USAID. "USAID History." http://www.usaid.gov/about_usaid/usaidhist.html.

USAID. "Value Chain Approach to Poverty Reduction: Equitable Growth in Today's Global Economy." Paper, Accelerated Microenterprise Advancement Project—Business Development Services. Washington, D.C., n.d.

USAID/Armenia. "Fostering Small Business Growth: Micro Enterprise Development Initiative Final Report." Yerevan, 2006.

USAID/Bolivia. "From 10 Years of Projects to 10 Months of Business." Bulletin, "Rural Competitiveness Activity: Creating Opportunities," Rural Competitiveness Activity (RCA/ARCo). La Paz, 2008.

____. "Request for Proposals (RFP) No. 511-04-018, USAID/Bolivia Rural Competitiveness Activity, Amendment No. 2." La Paz, 2004.

USAID/Brazil. "Scope of Work—SME Growth and Employment." Brasilia, 2004.

USAID/Caribbean. "Identification of Lead Firms—Team Final Report." Caribbean Open Trade Support (COTS) Program. Saint John's, Antigua, 2006.

USAID/Caucasus-Azerbaijan. "Program Description (Revised): Rural Azerbaijan Business Development." Baku, 2004.

USAID/Colombia. "Request for Proposal 514-05-009." Bogota, 2005.

____. "Toward a Licit Economy: Colombia Alternative Development Program Final Report." Bogota, 2006.

USAID/Europe and Eurasia. "Moldovan Fashion Maven Takes on Milan." 2007. http://www.usaid.gov/locations/europe_eurasia/press/success/2007-09-prog.html#top.

USAID/Georgia. "Georgia: Opened for Business–Georgia Business Climate Reform Final Report." Tbilisi, 2009.

USAID/Indonesia. "Growth through Investment and Trade (GIAT): Scope of Work." Jakarta, 2003.

USAID/Kazakhstan. "Request for Proposal (RFP) No. EG115-06-007—Kazakhstan Small Business Development (KSBD) Project." Almaty, 2006.

USAID/Madagascar. "Madagascar Economic Growth Strategic Objective: Statement of Work for Market and Trade Development Program." Request for Quotations No. 687-04-027. Antananarivo, 2004.

USAID/Nicaragua. "Request for Proposal (RFP) No. 524-05-004: More Competitive, Market Oriented Private Enterprises, and Improved Environmental Management in Nicaragua." Managua, 2005.

USAID/Paraguay. "Paraguay Poverty Reduction Program: Paraguay Vende Project Final Report." Asunción, 2007.

USAID/Peru. "The Peru Poverty Reduction and Alleviation (PRA) Program." Lima, 2008.

____. "Poverty Reduction and Alleviation Activity (527-0387)." Lima, 1998.

____. "Research Brief: A Pro-Poor Analysis of the Artichoke Value Chain in Peru." Greater Access to Trade Expansion Project. Lima, 2007.

USAID Regional Economic Development Services Office for East and Southern Africa. "REDSO's Portfolio, IEHA, and SAKSS." Nairobi, Kenya, n.d.

Vergara, Ricardo. "La Ciudad y el Campo: ¿Una Danza Eterna?" *Debate Agrario*, No. 13. Lima, Peru, 1992.

Will, George F. "Cabs and Cupidity: Luis Paucar Tackles a Twisted Sense of Entitlement," *Washington Post*, May 27, 2007.

Williamson, John (ed.). *Latin American Adjustment: How Much Has It Happened?* Washington, D.C.: Institute for International Economics, 1990.

World Bank. *Assessing Aid: What Works, What Doesn't, and Why*. New York: Oxford University Press, 1998.

____. *Economic Growth in the 1990s: Learning from a Decade of Reform*. Washington, D.C.: World Bank, 2005.

____. *Globalization, Growth, and Poverty: Building an Inclusive World Economy*. New York: Oxford University Press, 2002.

____. *World Development Report 2009: Reshaping Economic Geography*. Washington, D.C.: World Bank, 2009.

Yusuf, Shahid, and Joseph E. Stiglitz. "Development Issues: Settled and Open." In *Frontiers of Development Economics: The Future in Perspective*, ed. by Gerald M. Meier and Joseph E. Stiglitz. New York: World Bank and Oxford University Press, 2001.

Index